"*The Evangelism Circle* is a cotrends in evangelism. Patrick in justice, and helpfully challenges gelism. Written with practical illustrations, this book uses a presuppositional perspective to encourage Christians to be faithful in proclaiming the gospel. If you are interested in evangelism, you will benefit from this resource."

Jesse Johnson, Dean of The Master's Seminary, Washington, D.C.

"Over the last decade and a half, Probe Ministries has done two significant surveys of both born-again Christians as well as non-Christians. We have found very few Christians are engaged in evangelism because they don't know the gospel and they don't know how to communicate it. *The Evangelism Circle* provides a biblical view of pre-evangelism, evangelism, and post-evangelism, with many examples and ample Scripture references. You will learn how to define the gospel and then learn how to proclaim the gospel. The body of Christ needs this book like never before."

Kerby Anderson, President of Probe Ministries International and host of Point of View radio talk show

"Over the last 30 years, as I have equipped the saints to share the Gospel, many of them have said they would be more faithful to the Great Commission if they knew the Gospel better. *The Evangelism Circle* is a book that will do that, along with encourage and inspire its readers to communicate the Gospel with clarity and confidence. Patrick Foss has given the church a valuable resource for its primary purpose of evangelizing those who are perishing. His practical illustrations along with his passion for biblical integrity in evangelism make this a book you will want to read and refer to often!"

Mike Gendron, Director of Proclaiming the Gospel Ministry and author of *Preparing for Eternity* and *Contending for the Gospel*

"There are few Christians I've ever known who have greater zeal for the gospel of Jesus Christ or greater compassion for lost sinners than Patrick Foss. His wise guidance on evangelism is both extremely helpful and wholly biblical. Whether here in America or overseas, Patrick is a doer of the Word who lives out what he teaches. I pray that *The Evangelism Circle* will be read widely and will motivate Christians around the world to share the good news of Jesus even more boldly and effectively!"

Janet Mefferd, Christian radio host, Janet Mefferd Today

"This book highlights the biblical distinction between justification and sanctification and drives home the powerful truth of salvation by grace, through faith in Christ alone. Patrick, an experienced evangelist, empowers and enlightens us with biblical motivation on how to share the gospel. *The Evangelism Circle* fills an important need in the body of Christ."

Mark Piland, Pastor, Oak Hills Community Church, Argyle, TX

"...do the work of an evangelist..."
2 Timothy 4:5

―――――――――○―――――――――

How to Walk the Walk and Talk the Talk of an Evangelist

Patrick Foss

Copyright © 2022 Patrick Foss

All rights reserved. No part of this book may be reproduced in any form without written permission from the author.

ISBN: 978-0-9832946-8-9

First Edition

Scripture quotations are from the ESV® Bible (The Holy Bible, English Standard Version®), Copyright © 2001 by Crossway, a publishing ministry of Good News Publishers. Used by permission. All rights reserved.

DEDICATION

My wife Kimberly who has been my constant companion in the faith and whose humility has taught me more about grace than anyone outside our Savior Jesus Christ.

ACKNOWLEDGEMENTS

When I first stepped into The Evangelism Circle almost thirty years ago, I never envisioned writing a book about my experiences. Now that I have, I have many people to thank who have encouraged me and mentored me along the way. I thank Grant Boone for sharing the gospel with me, the late Hans Moetteli for never letting up in calling me to join him in evangelism, Jim Wells who modeled for me a zeal for sharing the good news, and Mike Fisher and Jerry Brown for giving me my first teaching opportunities, despite my lack of experience. I have great admiration for brothers and sisters in the Lord like Tom and Linda Brown, Dale Smith, Lauren Clark, Dave and Jan Bohyer, Mark and Debbie Piland, Stephen Bamoleke, Sandra Burns, Joyce Oreta Ogonyo and the late Pat Aipperspach, all to whom I look as an example of the Christian character for which I strive.

I owe a special debt of gratitude to Mike Gendron for reviewing my book and encouraging me to get it published. Carolyn Bivans spent countless hours carefully editing my manuscript and making important suggestions. Artists Sergio Drumond and Christopher Fowler did great work in bringing the illustrations to life. John Manning's work in formatting the book helped it all come together.

I am eternally grateful to all those who have prayerfully and financially supported my ministry efforts throughout the past several decades. Furthermore, to all the men and women who have joined me on the ground in sharing the gospel—thank you for doing the work of an evangelist.

Finally, thanks to my wife Kimberly who sacrificed time with me as I spent many days and nights working on this book. I am grateful for her keen insights in helping me to rewrite sections that needed more clarity.

CONTENTS

Foreword by Mike Gendron	9
Preface: What is The Evangelism Circle?	11
Chapter One: Set Free by the Gospel	13
Part One—Pre-Evangelism	17
Chapter Two: Mac the Barber	19
Chapter Three: What is Pre-Evangelism?	23
Chapter Four: Pre-Evangelism Lifestyle	39
Part Two—Evangelism	57
Chapter Five: Yellowstone Evangelism	59
Chapter Six: An Unchanging Message in Changing Times	63
Chapter Seven: The Gospel Defined	67
Chapter Eight: Gospel Root and its Branches	93
Chapter Nine: The Proclamation of the Gospel	109
Chapter Ten: Bold Grace	121
Chapter Eleven: Grace and Truth	143
Chapter Twelve: Grace and Truth Applied	161
Chapter Thirteen: The 11th Commandment—Thou Shalt Not Argue	173
Chapter Fourteen: Strange Fire and the Gospel	187
Chapter Fifteen: Fear, Missed Opportunities and Numbers	211

Chapter Sixteen: Do the Work of an Evangelist	221
Chapter Seventeen: Sharing the Gospel with Family Members	237
Chapter Eighteen: All Aboard	261
Part Three—Post-Evangelism	277
Chapter Nineteen: From Milk to Meat	279
Chapter Twenty: A Teachable Disciple	293
Chapter Twenty-One: Your Best Life Now versus Suffering for Christ	303
Chapter Twenty-Two: Preaching the Gospel to Ourselves	311
Chapter Twenty-Three: Finishing the Race	321
Conclusion	349

FOREWORD

When our Lord Jesus Christ began His earthly ministry, His first priority was evangelism. His plan was to use disciples to make more disciples. Jesus called His disciples to follow Him so that He can make them fishers of men (Mark 1:14-18). Instead of casting their nets in the sea, He directed them to cast them in the depths of fallen humanity. He gave His disciples a new purpose for living, a higher calling, with a much more important priority.

This new purpose for living has been given to all who have been made alive in Christ. Our new purpose for living now has the same eternal perspective—to evangelize those who are perishing, for the glory of God! It is a royal privilege and life's highest calling to be a witness and an ambassador for the Lord Jesus Christ. Our responsibility is an endeavor in which we can always be successful. That is because our mission is to bring Christ to the lost, not the lost to Christ. Remember the words of Jesus. He said, "No one can come to me unless the Father who sent me draws him" (John 6:44).

The Evangelism Circle is a much-needed book that reminds Christians of the great privilege and awesome responsibility our Lord has given His Church. Patrick Foss is well qualified to instruct us on the biblical principles of evangelism. He has spent years being a faithful witness for Christ and has shared the Gospel in different cultures throughout the world on short-term mission trips. Now he is ready to share many of his experiences in this excellent book.

You will be equipped and encouraged through the testimonies of God's grace in Patrick's many encounters with the lost. The Evangelism Circle is written with a high view of Scripture and is both Christ-exalting and Gospel-centered. You will enjoy Patrick's fresh approach to evangelism that includes sections on Pre-evangelism and apologetics, along with

Post-evangelism and a focus on preaching the Gospel to ourselves to make every man complete in Christ.

Tragically, the Gospel in the 21st century has been corrupted and compromised like never before. Many pastors are more interested in church growth, so they preach a gospel that offers the natural man what he wants: good feelings, healings, riches and success. As a result, many professing Christians have only a superficial knowledge of the Gospel. They know Jesus died for the sins of the world, but they don't know why He had to die. Patrick Foss gives clarity to the true Gospel, which gives people what they need: the forgiveness of sin, redemption, perfect righteousness, reconciliation with God and the power to live a victorious life. Throughout The Evangelism Circle, Foss uses the power of God's Word, which exhorts, encourages and sanctifies the saints.

As a fellow evangelist, it has been my joy and privilege to serve our Lord in full-time ministry for over 30 years. During my labors in the fields that are white for harvest, I have used many of the biblical principles for God-centered evangelism that Patrick Foss has set forth in his book. I highly recommend The Evangelism Circle to anyone who would like to sharpen their focus on the glorious Gospel of grace and to increase their passion for evangelism.

Evangelist Mike Gendron
Director, Proclaiming the Gospel Ministry
Author of *Preparing for Eternity* and *Contending for the Gospel*
www.ProclaimingTheGospel.org

PREFACE

What is The Evangelism Circle? As I will explain in this book, pre-evangelism, evangelism and post-evangelism make up a cyclical lifestyle that should be common to all Christians but is not always practiced. For example, when one lets their light shine before others (Matt. 5:16), or when one helps the unsaved overcome objections or questions about God (Col. 4:2-6), they are practicing pre-evangelism. Evangelism is when we pronounce the gospel verbally to others (Rom. 10:14-17). Post-evangelism involves training ourselves for godliness (1 Tim. 4:7) so we can mature in our salvation (1 Pet. 2:2) and continue in the faith, not shifting from the hope of the gospel (Col. 1:23). This training will lead us to be more effective in our pre-evangelism and evangelism.

For some believers, evangelizing the lost may seem like a daunting task, but it need not be. We can be confident that the God who calls us is faithful and He will accomplish this work in you (1 Thess. 5:24). The God who justifies us (Rom. 8:33) is the same God who sanctifies us (2 Thess. 2:13). Therefore, you can trust that God will prepare you to be His light and empower you to be ready to answer the questions and doubts that unbelievers will certainly bring forth. He will give you the bold grace to deliver the gospel message as you do the work of an evangelist. Always remember that the God who placed you on The Evangelism Circle is the same "God who works in you, both to will and to work for his good pleasure" (Philip. 2:13).

Now, if one were to ask, "Where should I be on The Evangelism Circle?", that's the wrong question. Christians should be involved in all aspects of the circle during their daily walk with the Lord. In our pre-evangelism, our light should always be shining before others (1 Pet. 2:12). In evangelism, we should be prepared at any moment to share the gospel (2 Tim. 4:2), if necessary, "from morning till evening" (Acts 28:23). Finally, in our post-evangelism, we should always be growing in the grace and knowledge of our Lord and Savior Jesus Christ (2 Pet.

3:18). While pre-evangelism, evangelism and post-evangelism are all distinct in their own way, the three cannot be separated from each other.

In this book, we will look at how Christians should conduct their lives before the world (Philip. 1:27) as a representative of God (2 Cor. 5:20). There will be an emphasis on how the Bible must be our guide for all teaching, correction, and training in righteousness (2 Tim. 3:16-17). Different apologetic approaches will be discussed. We will define what the gospel is and what it is not, while at the same time examining the critical distinction between justification and sanctification. We will discuss what the different biblical approaches are to sharing the gospel and address the unbiblical approaches. We will show how grace and truth came through Jesus Christ (John 1:17) and how His apostles looked to imitate Him (1 Cor. 11:1). We will look at our growth in the Christian faith and how to stay in and finish the race (2 Tim. 4:7).

While I'm certainly not writing anything new, my prayer is that this book will first of all bring glory to God (1 Cor. 10:31). Secondly, I pray this book will be as much a blessing to you as it has been for me to share my experiences of being on The Evangelism Circle. I am standing on the shoulders of others who came before me, as we all stand firm in the Lord (Philip. 4:1).

1) SET FREE BY THE GOSPEL

Frederick the Great, King of Prussia during the mid-1700s, once toured a Berlin prison. As he entered one large, lower dungeon of the prison, a group of prisoners fell on their knees before him. "Have mercy on us, your majesty!" they pleaded. "We are innocent! We have been falsely imprisoned!" "*All* of you are innocent?" asked the king, surprised. "Yes!" they insisted, every last man. Then King Frederick noticed a man who stood off by himself in a dark corner of the dungeon. "You there!" said the king. "Why are you in this prison?" "I was convicted of armed robbery, your majesty." "Are you guilty?" The man hung his head. "Yes, your majesty. Guilty and ashamed. I deserve to be in this place." "Guard!" King Frederick called. "Guard! See that man in the corner? Take him out of here and release him at once!" Then, pointing at the men who had claimed to be unjustly imprisoned, he said, "I will not have these fine, innocent men corrupted by one guilty wretch!"[1]

Ray Stedman, who related the story above in his book Body Life, says, "You and I are like that guilty prisoner. It is not our facade of goodness, but the honest confession of our sin that sets us free!"[2] In order to be set free by the gospel, one has to first understand the guilt all of us are under before a holy God (Psalm 16:2; Rom. 3:10). A confession of that guilt produces a repentance that leads to salvation (2 Cor. 7:10). Such a Spirit-led confession allows us to proclaim Jesus as Lord (1 Cor. 12:3), our King of kings (1 Tim. 6:15), a King who has come to release us from our captivity to sin and to set us free (Matt. 1:21; John 8:36). Conversely, any righteousness or merit one may proclaim for themselves will continue their separation from the truth of the gospel and keep them imprisoned in their own self-deception.

Set Free From Rome

Growing up in the Catholic religion, I never heard the biblical gospel as Rome's salvation plan is one of self-merit (see Catholic Catechism 2027, 1405, 1459 and 1129). Being forced to listen to the Mass in Latin in the 1960s, of course, was no help either. It wasn't until the age of 36 that I first had the biblical gospel preached to me. The Holy Spirit convicted me of my utter depravity and meritless standing before God (John 16:8). I saw how my sin separated me from a holy and righteous God (Rom. 6:23). God granted me repentance leading to a knowledge of the truth, which set me free (2 Tim. 2:25; John 8:32), and the faith to believe in His Son (Philip. 1:29).

That truth is that we are all sinners who not only have fallen short of the glory of God (Rom. 3:23) but have in fact broken all of God's laws (James 2:10). We have no righteous standing before a holy God (Philip. 3:9; Rom. 5:6). The only remedy is in the gospel itself—the sinless Son of God, who came to live the perfect life we could not (Matt. 5:17). He met all of God's righteous requirements for us (2 Cor. 5:21). He died for our sins and rose from the dead (1 Cor. 15:3-4). For we know "Christ also suffered once for sins, the righteous [Christ] for the unrighteous [all of us], that he might bring us to God" (1 Pet. 3:18). This is the gospel that must be received in repentance (Mark 1:15) by faith through grace, not by any

---

[1] As told in Ray C. Stedman's *Body Life*. Pg. 159. I have changed a few words, but the main story was kept intact.

[2] Ibid, pg. 159.

kind of self-merit (Eph. 2:8-9; Titus 3:5). We must hold fast to the gospel Paul preached; otherwise—you have "believed in vain" (1 Cor. 15:1-2).

Grounding in the Gospel

After the Lord was pleased to reveal his Son to me in 1993, I decided to follow the Apostle Paul's example and spend years preparing myself in order that I might preach the good news (Gal. 1:16-2:1). After grounding myself in scripture (2 Tim. 2:15), I attended several training seminars on evangelism. I also read many books, listened to numerous tapes and watched videos on how to be an effective witness for the gospel. I devoted myself to memorizing as many scriptures as I could (Psalm 119:11; 2 Tim. 3:15-17). Along the way, I discovered spiritual gifts that would help me in sharing the good news.

Discovering Our Gifts

Since "the body does not consist of one member but of many" (1 Cor. 12:14), "God arranged the members in the body, each one of them, as he chose" (12:18). Our "varieties of gifts" and "varieties of service" (12:4-5) are all "empowered by one and the same Spirit, who apportions to each one individually as he wills" (12:11). While we are all of the same body, we have all been gifted in different ways. God, who created us, knows our peculiarities (Eph. 4:7).

In the past twenty-eight years, I have had the joy of not only discovering my spiritual gifts (1 Cor. 12:7) but also using them (1 Pet. 4:10). I mentioned above that I spent years preparing myself in order that I might preach the good news, grounding myself in doctrine and devoting myself to scripture memorization. Along the way, I discovered that I had these gifts: teaching (Rom. 12:7; 1 Cor. 12:28; Eph. 4:11); exhortation (Rom. 12:8); mercy (Rom. 12:8); wisdom and knowledge (1 Cor. 12:8); faith (1 Cor. 12:9; cf., Luke 22:32); the ability to distinguish between spirits (1 Cor. 12:10) and evangelism (Eph. 4:11; 2 Tim. 4:5; Acts 21:8).

I have often thought about how God has allowed me to use the spiritual gifts He has given me. The last thing Jesus told His apostles before His ascension in Acts 1:8 was, "you will receive power when the Holy Spirit has come upon you, and you will be my witnesses in Jerusalem and in all Judea and Samaria, and to the end of the earth." Just like the disciples were witnesses first in Jerusalem, I started my witnessing in my hometown of Dallas. The disciples were then told to witness in Judea and Samaria. Samaria might be considered crossing beyond the social barriers of our own culture for the gospel. As I will share later, I have done that with Muslims and others different from me. I look at Judea as witnessing in my county, state or in a broader sense—my country, all of which I have done. Finally, Acts 1:8 instructs Christ's disciples to be witnesses to the end of the earth. I have been privileged to have shared the gospel in person in Africa, Myanmar, and Siberia. Christian chat lines have also given me the opportunity to discuss the good news with people in numerous countries.

Philip's ministry seemed to follow this Acts 1:8 pattern. First, he was Philip the helper of widows (Acts 6:1-5), then the Lord decided to use him in evangelizing the Samaritans (Acts 8:5-8). He preached the gospel through Judea and all the way to Caesarea (Acts 8:40). When he preached the gospel to the Ethiopian eunuch (Acts 8:26-39), the ripple effect was amazing, as tradition has it that the eunuch carried the gospel back home to Ethiopia and founded the church there, thus sending the gospel to the ends of the earth.

We see the ministry of Philip summed up by Paul when he said, "On the next day we departed and came to Caesarea, and we entered the house of Philip the evangelist, who was one of the seven, and stayed with him" (Acts 21:8). Philip started out as one of the seven appointed to help widows in Jerusalem, then he shared the gospel in Samaria and Judea and sent the good news to the end of the earth with the Ethiopian eunuch. As a result, he became known as "Philip the evangelist" (21:8). Let us begin our Acts 1:8 mission right where we are and pray that, God willing, He will extend our ministry according to His plan and purposes.

PART ONE—PRE-EVANGELISM

② MAC THE BARBER

In 2004, I started to see a new barber. His name was Mac, a middle-aged man who was originally from South America. Mac was friendly and talkative. When we got into a discussion about religion, I asked him if he believed in God. He said, "Sometimes." He then presented me with several objections including: The Da Vinci Code, the Bible being written by men, evolution and tsunamis. I addressed each issue as he ran the trimmer across my hair, but he would just come up with new objections. As I left, Mac gave me a National Geographic article on evolution and asked me to read it. The article, with which Mac agreed, was about man evolving from apes.

The next time I went to see Mac, I thought about how I might have to do a lot of pre-evangelism with him. That certainly turned out to be the case. As I sat down in the barber's chair, Mac handed me a list of 40 questions he had prepared. He told me to take it with me and think it over for next time. I carefully considered all of Mac's questions, even getting help from some people at church. Several weeks before my next haircut, I took my answers and delivered them to Mac, telling him we could discuss them during my next appointment. His questions/objections included alleged contradictions in the Bible, the Virgin Birth, and Adam and Eve and the Genesis account, as he wondered how this could be real history.

When I returned to see Mac, he and a client were the only ones in the barbershop. I thought, great! However, as I waited my turn, I would shortly find out that all my pre-evangelism efforts with Mac were about to be undermined. When Mac saw me come in, he smiled, pulled the list out of his drawer behind him and said, "Very interesting answers, Patrick." Sitting in the barber's chair was a person named Joe. Before I came in, Mac had gone over the list with him. After I entered the shop and took a seat, Joe was quick to comment on my answers, telling me he had been a Christian for 30 years (he identified as a Baptist). He told me he "does not get hung up" on things like the Virgin Birth (which he wrongly identified as the Immaculate Conception, the unbiblical Roman Catholic doctrine of Mary being born without sin) and the literal reading of Genesis. He added that, yes, he agrees with Mac that the Bible is full of contradictions. He said, "All I need is Jesus!"

I was in a very interesting situation. How should I respond? Mac seemed to enjoy Joe's response, as it just affirmed his position. I decided to confront Joe to try to win Mac back. I told Joe, graciously but firmly, that Jesus taught about Genesis as literal history—that He did not allegorize these accounts (Adam and Eve, Mark 10:3-9; Abel, Luke 11:50-51; Noah and the Flood, Matt. 24:38-39). In fact, Jesus used these accounts to teach His disciples about the reality of His death and resurrection (Matt. 12:39-41). I added that Paul built his doctrine of sin and salvation on the fact that sin and death entered the world through the literal fall of man (Rom. 5:12-19). Furthermore, if Genesis was not telling the history of the literal Adam and the literal fall, then Jesus being called the "last Adam" (1 Cor. 15:45), to bring about new righteousness (2 Cor. 5:21) and life, makes no sense.

When I asked Joe (also for Mac's benefit) if all Jesus taught about Genesis was full of contradictions, he repeated his statement that "I'm not like you who gets hung up on these things." I told him, "I'm hung up on the truth." When I mentioned to Joe that not believing such things hurts his Christian walk, he asked, "Are you saying I'm going to hell?". I told Joe I never said anything like that. All I was saying is that the opening chapters of Genesis are foundational to the rest of the Bible, that the Virgin Birth was necessary to preserve Jesus from any sin inheritance, and that the Bible tells a cohesive, non-contradictory, story of creation, the fall, redemption and restoration.

As Mac brushed off the hair clippings and used his hand-held mirror to get Joe's final approval, I said, yes, Jesus is our all-sufficient Savior. He is all we need, but what He taught and what He accomplished, in accordance with the scriptures, is quite a bit more than the Jesus with whom you are familiar. To my surprise, Joe apologized to me as he walked out of the shop. He admitted to being a bit patronizing, but I am not sure he changed his views.

I wish I could tell you it ended well with Mac. The next time I came in a few months later, I was stunned to find out that he had passed away from cancer. When I told them that Mac did not mention to me anything about his sickness, his fellow barbers just said he wanted to keep his illness private. A great sadness came over me, as I had been praying for Mac and looking forward to further conversations with him. As we will see, pre-evangelism, like I tried to do with Mac, is an important part of The Evangelism Circle.

③ WHAT IS PRE-EVANGELISM?

"Pre-Evangelism is no soft option."
Francis Schaeffer, *The God Who is There*

What is pre-evangelism? In a nutshell, pre-evangelism is doing the necessary apologetic work of helping the unsaved clear hurdles before they are ready to receive the gospel. The subjects of our pre-evangelism run the gamut from anyone belonging to a non-Christian religion to anyone who considers the tenets of the Christian faith false, such as humanists, agnostics, or atheists. Our audience will also include members of groups who claim to be Christian (e.g., Mormons, Jehovah's Witnesses) but deny or have never understood many of the essentials of the Christian faith, including the gospel itself. In other words, our pre-evangelism is directed towards an unsaved person.

Knowing the Backstory

Francis Schaeffer, one of the greatest defenders of the Christian faith in the twentieth century, wrote, "I do not believe that there is one system of apologetics that meets the need of all people, any more than I think there is any one form of evangelism that meets the need of all people. It is to be shaped on the basis of love for the person as a person."[3] Schaeffer points out a basic principle—each person to whom we speak is different (1 Cor. 9:19-23). While we speak the truth to them in love (Eph. 4:15), we do so understanding that each person, far from the Christian faith, is still an image-bearer of God and has a backstory. Their background can include struggles, drama and transformations that lead to false worldviews and misinformation. Our goal in pre-evangelism is to understand and be sympathetic to each person's backstory, while at the same time, challenging their false worldviews and the misinformation they picked up along the way.

Some of our pre-evangelism work will be done on people whose backstory has led them to question or even deny the very existence of God. In those cases, we point to God's witness in nature: "The heavens declare the glory of God, and the sky above proclaims his handiwork" (Psalm 19:1; cf., Psalm 8:1-4; Acts 14:17). In Romans chapter one we read, "For what can be known about God is plain to them, because God has shown it to them. For his invisible attributes, namely, his eternal power and divine nature, have been clearly perceived, ever since the creation of the world, in the things that have been made. So they are without excuse" (Rom. 1:19-20). God has also placed a witness to Himself in our hearts. Ecclesiastes 3:11 says God "has put eternity into man's heart." Romans 2:15 says God has placed His laws inside the conscience of each person, for "the law is written on their hearts." Our pre-evangelism points out to the unbeliever that everyone knows God because of creation and what He has placed in our hearts.

Clarifying Biblical Concepts

In pre-evangelism, we also attempt to establish or clarify key biblical concepts that are widely misunderstood or disbelieved in our culture,

---
[3] Francis Schaeffer, *The God Who is There*, pg. 177.

yet which are foundational to the gospel. These include beliefs such as the existence of our sin and unrighteousness (Rom. 3:23, 3:10), versus God's holiness (Isa. 57:15; Rev. 15:4), righteousness and justice (Psalm 89:14). This necessitates everyone's repentance (Acts 17:30). Furthermore, because God "has fixed a day on which he will judge the world in righteousness by a man whom he has appointed; and of this he has given assurance to all by raising him from the dead" (Acts 17:31), we also stress the historical reality of the life of Jesus—His sinless life (John 8:46; 1 Pet. 2:22), death, burial and resurrection (1 Cor. 15:1-4).

We also make known the nature (John 4:24) and existence of God (Rom. 1:19-20; Psalm 19:1). We proclaim God as the necessary uncreated Creator (Rom. 11:36; Eph. 3:9; Heb. 11:3; Rev. 4:11); the infinite greatness of God (Psalm 90:2; Job 36:26; Psalm 77:13, 102:27; Exodus 3:14; Isa 40:28); the foundation of God as our moral compass (Rom. 2:15); the necessary existence of God based on the universe's design (Jer. 31:35; Job 26:7; Amos 9:6); and the necessity of God to sustain the universe (Col. 1:17; Heb. 1:3). We profess the Bible as the inerrant word of God (2 Tim. 3:16; 1 Thess. 2:13; Psalm 119:160) and the exclusivity of Christ (John 14:6; Acts 4:12). Our pre-evangelism is done with the conscious purpose of persuading others of the truth of Christianity.

Pre-Evangelism in the Bible

We see many examples of apologetic pre-evangelism in the Bible. Moses confronted the mythical creation accounts of his day in the first chapters of Genesis. Elijah at Mount Carmel demonstrated the superiority of Yahweh to the followers of Baal (1 Kings 18). David spoke of the sky and the heavens above being a witness to God's existence (Psalm 19:1-6). Jesus engaged in pre-evangelism with the woman at the well (John 4). Paul also used many pre-evangelism arguments. At Lystra, he took on idolatry (Acts 14:6-20). At Mars Hill, he reasoned with the philosophers (Acts 17). Arguing for Christianity before King Agrippa, Paul said, "I am speaking true and rational words" (Acts 26:25). He also argued that God's existence has been made plain to everyone (Romans 1:18-20).

Apologetics, Lifestyle and Prayer

I will define pre-evangelism in three ways. 1) Pre-Evangelism Apologetics. 2) Pre-Evangelism lifestyle. 3) Pre-Evangelism Prayer. Alister

McGrath says pre-evangelism "stresses the reasonableness and attractiveness of the Christian faith; evangelism makes the offer of that faith."[4] Apologetics is showing the reasonableness of the Christian faith. Our attractiveness as Christians shows the love of our faith—loving our neighbor as ourselves (Mark 12:31). Our prayer is asking God to intervene in changing a person's heart towards the gospel message.

Pre-Evangelism Apologetics

Apologetics, a defense of the Christian faith, is a big part of our pre-evangelism. The apologist answers objections (1 Pet. 3:15), exposes error (Titus 1:9) and guards the truth of the gospel (Acts 20:28; 1 Tim. 6:20; 2 Tim. 1:14). In 1 Peter 3:15 we read that we should always be "prepared to make a defense to anyone who asks you for a reason for the hope that is in you." The phrase translated "to make a defense" comes from the Greek word apologia. Paul also uses apologia in his letter to the Philippians, "I am put here for the defense [apologia] of the gospel" (Philip. 1:16). There are three basic approaches for apologetics:

1. Classical Apologetics. This approach stresses rational, logical arguments for the existence of God. For example, God's existence is necessary for the foundation of reason, logic, morality, the universe's design and first cause.

2. Evidential Apologetics. This engagement focuses on factual evidence rather than rational, logical arguments for the Christian faith. For example, evidence can include archeology, miracles, biblical manuscripts, fulfilled prophecy and Christ's resurrection.

3. Presuppositional Apologetics. This method uses the Bible as the framework and the starting point through which all experience is interpreted and all truth is known. For example, the Bible itself begins with the presupposition of God's existence, "In the beginning, God" (Gen. 1:1).

While I consider myself a presuppositionalist, that does not preclude me from using rational arguments for the existence of God or factual evidences for the Christian faith. However, as a presuppositionalist, my starting point is always to ask what God's word has to say on the subject. Therefore, my apologetic always starts and ends with the Bible, because

---

[4] Alister E. McGrath, *Evangelical Apologetics*, pg. 6.

the God of scripture is my ultimate standard.[5]

Don't Quote the Bible, Bro

I have received pushback for such an approach. For example, after an online chat with one skeptic he proclaimed, "You did not help me. You simply quoted the bible." After another lengthy chat about how sin and evil entered the world (specifically using Gen. 2-3; Rom. 5:12ff; James 1:13-15), Bill[6] challenged me with this, "Can you justify or rationalize any of this without reference to the bible?" Believe it or not, those are common objections when doing pre-evangelism apologetics.

Ken Ham, founder of Answers in Genesis, has run across this objection many times. I love his analogy of a soldier going into war but being asked to lay aside his sword and armor because his opponent does not believe they should be used in battle. Here is Ham's point: just because our opponents don't believe the Bible is the word of God does not mean we should not use it as the weapon that it is. As we put on "the helmet of salvation, and the sword of the Spirit, which is the word of God" (Eph. 6:17), the Bible, which "is living and active, sharper than any two-edged sword, piercing to the division of soul and of spirit, of joints and of marrow, and discerning the thoughts and intentions of the heart" (Heb. 4:12), will do its work. While we can offer rational arguments and factual evidence for the Christian faith, our reasoning should always be firmly grounded in God's word. The one thing we should not do is to capitulate to "philosophy and empty deceit, according to human tradition, according to the elemental spirits of the world" (Colossians 2:8).

The Believer's Circle

Another objection I sometimes receive is that I am involved in circular reasoning when I proclaim the Bible as God's word based on the Bible's own claim to be the word of God. Remember previously I said the God of scripture is my ultimate standard. In an article on defendingthebible.org, this important point is made: "there's a certain degree of circular reasoning that is absolutely unavoidable! When you have an ultimate standard, you

---

[5] Dr. Jason Lisle, founder of the Biblical Science Institute, refers to presuppositional apologetics as "biblical authority apologetics." John M. Frame, well known for his work in presuppositional apologetics, asserts that the presuppositional approach is the one that is most honoring to God. Frame contends that presuppositional apologetics brings the most glory to God because it exalts God's word more than other approaches.

[6] While I have changed the first names of people with whom I have had discussions, all the quotes in this book come from real conversations.

can't use any other standard to prove it. You must use the ultimate standard to prove itself."[7]

All ultimate authorities must appeal to themselves as part of their own proof. For example, we see where God defends Himself by appealing to Himself: "For when God made a promise to Abraham, since he had no one greater by whom to swear, he swore by himself" (Heb. 6:13). God also says, "By myself I have sworn, declares the Lord" (Gen. 22:16; cf., Isa. 45:23; Jer. 49:13). God rightfully defines Himself by Himself, stating "I am who I am" (Exodus 3:14). Here we see God using true circular reasoning.

Humans appeal to a greater authority as confirmation of an oath, "For people swear by something greater than themselves, and in all their disputes an oath is final for confirmation" (Heb. 6:16). However, since God is ultimate, and by definition nothing can be greater than Him, He can only use Himself as the authority (Heb. 6:13). In the Bible, God swearing by Himself is a true circle.[8]

The same God of the Bible, who swore by Himself, testifies, "All Scripture is breathed out by God" (2 Tim. 3:16; cf., Matt. 22:31) and "men spoke from God as they were carried along by the Holy Spirit" (2 Pet. 1:21). Because "you have exalted above all things your name and your word" (Psalm 138:2), we know "Forever, O Lord, your word is firmly fixed in the heavens" (Psalm 119:89). "The grass withers, the flower fades, but the word of our God will stand forever" (Isa. 40:8). Furthermore, since "The sum of your word is truth" (Psalm 119:160), there is no standard for knowledge greater than the Bible. Therefore, God's word must justify itself—this is another true circle.[9]

---

[7] Jesus quoted the scriptures (Mark 11:17, 12:26; Matt. 22:31) to the unbelieving Jews as proof that God had spoken to them. When we proclaim verses in the Bible to unbelievers as proof that God is speaking to them, we should stand on those scriptures as the very word of God just as Jesus did. If we get charged with circular reasoning, we are in good company.

[8] I drew several of my insights in this section from an article on GospelSpam.com, Is Circular Reasoning Always Fallacious? 3 May 2014. Also see Dr. Jason Lisle's Biblical Authority Apologetics article from October 12, 2018.

[9] Dr. Jason Lisle's Biblical Authority Apologetics article from October 12, 2018, https://biblicalscienceinstitute.com/apologetics/biblical-authority-apologetics/. Note that Dr. Lisle adds in his article, "Accepting the Bible as our ultimate standard for truth does not mean that all truth is contained in the Bible. There are things that are true (E=mc2, Jupiter is larger than Mars, Antarctica is generally colder than Houston) that are not written in the Bible. Rather, the presuppositional apologist accepts the Bible as giving us the proper worldview foundation on which all other truth claims are built (Matthew 7:24-27). As the ultimate standard for truth, everything the Bible affirms must be true, and nothing that contradicts the Bible can be true."

The Atheist's Circle

John M. Frame, noted for his work in epistemology and presuppositional apologetics, argues that atheists also have an ultimate standard for truth, and, as a result, their arguments are circular as well. In an interview with Justin Taylor of The Gospel Coalition, Frame says, "If a rationalist, for example, tries to prove that human reason is the ultimate rational authority, he can do nothing else than appeal to a rational argument, using reason to prove reason. He cannot appeal to anything higher than reason, because he believes reason is the highest authority."[10]

The atheist argues from their highest authority—so do we. While both are circular, the big question is—which authority is true? The atheist's appeal to reason as their highest authority raises an obvious question: from whom/what did the capability to reason come? What would the atheist's answer be? If God does not exist, then our ability to reason has its foundation, not in a personal, unchanging God, but in a chance, accidental universe based on evolution. If we are products of such a system, then our rules of reasoning are also a part of that system that is forever evolving.

Dr. Jason Lisle, Christian astrophysicist, speaker, author, and apologist, asks, "How can the evolutionist account for absolute standards of reasoning like the laws of logic? In an accidental evolutionary universe, why would there be universal, unchanging standards?" Lisle adds, "Laws of Logic are contingent upon God's unchanging nature. And they are necessary for logical reasoning. Thus, rational reasoning would be impossible without God." Greg Bahnsen, one of the most respected presuppositionalists of the twentieth century, says an atheist cannot account for reasoning and the laws of logic. In the end, Bahnsen says the atheist has to borrow logic from the Christian worldview: "Once he tries to justify universals and the laws of logic, he steps out of his worldview and into yours."[11]

Think about all the things the atheist has to borrow from the eternal (Deut. 33:27; Isa. 40:28; Rom. 16:26; Psalm 90:2) and unchanging God (Mal. 3:6; James 1:17; Heb. 6:17). They have to borrow reason (Isa. 1:18), logic (John 1:1), wisdom (Psalm 104:24, 147:5; 1 Sam. 2:3; Jer. 10:12; Rom. 11:33; Col. 2:3; James 3:17), truth (John 14:6, 8:31-32), morality

---

[10] https://www.thegospelcoalition.org/blogs/justin-taylor/an-interview-with-john-frame-on-apologetics-to-the-glory-of-god/

[11] I credit several thoughts and quotes in this section from an article by Henry W. Middleton, PhD, and highly recommend the full article here: https://tasc-creationscience.org/article/foundation-logic-nature-god

(Rom. 2:15) and goodness (Psalm 25:8; Mark 10:18). Of course, the atheist is not really "borrowing" anything from God. God, who has created mankind in His own image (Gen. 1:26-27), has equipped all men and women, including atheists, to use reason, logic, wisdom, truth, morality and goodness in our everyday lives. The important point is that there is no way for an atheist to account for the objective certainty of all of these things without them having their origin in an eternal and unchanging God. The problem is that atheists are tapping into God's circuit breaker and then laundering and putting their own spin on His absolute standards.

The presuppositional approach essentially says to the atheist that our worldviews each argue from our own highest authority. The atheist's highest authority is reason, which they can only attribute to a cosmic egg (from where this egg came nobody knows) accidently exploding and expanding billions of years ago (somehow it was "narrowed" down to somewhere between 10 and 20 billion years). From this expansion, matter, in some unexplained way, evenly distributed throughout the universe creating stars and then planets. On our own earth, life started with a primordial soup of atoms crashing together. Somehow, through billions of years of accidents and mutations, atoms formed molecules and then cells, which evolved into fish, apes and then man. Thus, what follows from their worldview: all of our thought processes, all our reasoning, logic, wisdom, truth, morality and goodness are the result of mere accidents or are an accidental by-product of atoms colliding with one another.

In contrast, the believer's highest authority is the eternal and unchanging God of the Bible—the God who created all things (Gen. 1) in perfect order

(Gen. 1:31). "His work is perfect" (Deut. 32:4; Psalm 18:30), with no accidents, because He has total control of all things past, present and future. An omnipotent, omniscient God does not have to plod through billions of years of accidents and mutations in order to have fellowship with humans. Rather, He created us in a microsecond (Gen. 2:7; Zechariah 12:1). God made man in His image, and we reflect that image in our ability to use His laws of reason, logic, wisdom, truth, morality and goodness. Unlike the atheist, who has no coherent foundation for such laws, we know these laws are not standards outside of God, or standards which He created, but instead are a reflection of His eternal, unchanging nature.

In the end, believers say to the atheist, "We will not allow your circle, dominated by a fallen nature (Rom. 1:18-23; 1 Cor. 1:18-21, 2:14), to judge God's circle, the ultimate standard for truth (Proverbs 1:7, 21:30; John 14:6; Col. 2:2-3; 2 Tim. 3:16), because you are the one on trial, not God." The NET Bible translates Isaiah 46:10 as God "who announces the end from the beginning and reveals beforehand what has not yet occurred." Dr. Jason Lisle writes, "God's reasoning is necessarily circular. God is all-knowing. So, whenever God draws a conclusion from premises, the conclusion is something that God already knows."[12]

God's Word Does Not Return Empty

Don't ever hesitate to quote the Bible to show the Bible's veracity. The Bible is the ultimate standard for truth because it is founded on the highest authority possible—the eternal, unchanging and sovereign God. Whenever a person challenges you with, "Can you justify or rationalize God's existence without reference to the Bible?", don't let them suppress the truth in their unrighteousness. The truth is that "what can be known about God is plain to them, because God has shown it to them. For his invisible attributes, namely, his eternal power and divine nature, have been clearly perceived, ever since the creation of the world, in the things that have been made. So they are without excuse" (Rom. 1:18-20).

Remember that God always has a purpose in giving His word to people. The Prophet Isaiah said of the Lord, "My word ... goes out from my mouth; it shall not return to me empty, but it shall accomplish that which I purpose, and shall succeed in the thing for which I sent it" (Isa. 55:11). When we use the Bible as our primary source in witnessing, God's purpose will always be accomplished. We can trust that the word of God will succeed in the very thing for which He sent it. Scripture, which allows us

---
[12] Dr. Jason Lisle, https://thecreationclub.com/vicious-circular-reasoning-or-virtuous/

to tell "the good news about Jesus" (Acts 8:35), succeeds in the conversion of unbelievers (Rom. 10:14-15; Acts 6:7, 13:5-12, 13:48, 17:11-12, 18:10-11; 1 Pet. 1:23), and the justification (Gal. 3:8; Rom. 4:3), sanctification (John 17:17; 1 Pet. 1:16; Matt. 13:23) and glorification of believers (1 Cor. 15:54-55; 2 Thess. 2:14). All this is accomplished because the word of truth, the gospel of our salvation, convicts sinners (John 16:8) and seals believers with the promised Holy Spirit (Eph. 1:13).

Those who rightly handle the word are approved by God (2 Tim. 2:15). The God-breathed scriptures are profitable for teaching, for reproof, for correction, and for training in righteousness (2 Tim. 3:16). They provide boldness (Acts 4:31; 2 Tim. 2:9), strength (1 John 2:14), blessing (Luke 11:28), comfort (2 Cor. 1:3-7; John 7:38) and assurance to the saints (1 John 5:13; Gal. 3:13-14). God's word is at work in believers (1 Thess. 2:13), living and active in our hearts (Heb. 4:12), bearing fruit (Col. 1:4-6) and instructing us to imitate the faith of our church leaders who teach us the word of God (Heb. 13:7; 1 Tim. 4:13). The word allows us to fulfill the royal law to love our neighbors as ourselves (James 2:8) and empowers believers to stand against the schemes of the devil (Eph. 6:11; 1 John 2:14).

God also accomplishes other things with His scriptures. He uses His word to reveal the heart. For some, His word (Luke 8:11), when heard but not understood, is taken away by the devil "so that they may not believe and be saved" (Luke 8:12; Matt. 13:19). For others, who at first receive the word with joy, God knows they have no root in themselves. They believe for a while, but tribulation and persecution arise on account of the word and they fall away (Matt. 13:20-21; Luke 8:13). God also knows that there are some who hear His word who will produce no fruit because the cares of the world and the deceitfulness of riches choke the word out of their lives (Matt. 13:22). However, His elect, "sown on good soil" (Matt. 13:23), who hear the word and understand it, are "born again, not of perishable seed but of imperishable, through the living and abiding word of God" (1 Pet. 1:23). Of these, God says, "He indeed bears fruit and yields, in one case a hundredfold, in another sixty, and in another thirty" (Matt. 13:23).

Other times, God's word succeeds in the thing for which He sent it by judging the unrepentant. This occurs in the condemnation of the self-righteous (Luke 18:9-14; Matthew 23; John 9:40-41; Rom. 3:10, 10:3; Gal. 3:10), the judgment of unbelievers who thrust the word of God aside (Acts 13:46) and the rebuke of those who turn away from the truth (2 Tim. 4:2-4). Jesus said a rejection of God's word is a rejection of Him (John 5:46-47). Jesus also used God's word to rebuke those for not knowing it or misinterpreting it (Matt. 12:2-4; Mark 12:24), for abusing it (Matt. 12:7), for denying its power (Matt. 22:29), and in the end, because they have "not read what was said to you by God" (Matt. 22:31).

When we use the Bible as our foundation in witnessing, some will try to mock us (Acts 17:32), while others will attempt to contradict the word of the Lord (Acts 13:44-45). Many will be willing to void the word of God for the sake of their unbiblical traditions (Matt. 15:6). There are also people, looking to have their ears tickled, who will reject the truth and instead find teachers to suit their own passions and thus wander off into myths (2 Tim. 4:2-4). Some will try to turn people away from the faith (Acts 13:5-12) or agitate and stir up the crowds when the word is preached (Acts 17:13). Some will be convinced, others will disbelieve (Acts 28:24), while others will say, "We will hear you again about this" (Acts 17:32). Always remember, God's word never fails to accomplish its purpose. Open your Bible and let God's word go out from His mouth, trusting that He will succeed in the very thing for which He sent it, whether that be in the conversion of unbelievers, the sanctification and perseverance of the saints, or the condemnation, judgment and rebuke of the enemies of God.

Nancy's Curiosity

In the early 1990s, I met Nancy at a social gathering. It turns out she was a financial analyst and she asked me some tough questions about my personal finances. Nancy didn't like the answers I gave, so she invited me to her office. Nancy not only became my financial advisor, but also a great friend. Nancy was a grandmother, a widow, a fiercely independent woman and an atheist. I would describe Nancy as a well-read person who always loved to discuss things with me, even religion. When I shared the gospel with her, she listened respectfully, but perfectly in line with Nancy's character, she asked tough questions. Looking back, I was not as prepared to answer Nancy's questions as I am today. However, as we will see, that's part of being on The Evangelism Circle.

When I bought Nancy a Bible and left it on her doorstep late one night, she genuinely thanked me. What happened next, I will never forget. She asked me to go through the background and format of the Bible. As we spent many hours going through the different genres of the Bible, I explained to Nancy the divisions of Law, History, Wisdom, Poetry,

Gospel, Epistles and Apocalyptic Literature. She listened carefully with pen in hand, marking up her new Bible.

As the years went by, Nancy gave me updates on her Bible reading. She wasn't hesitant to point out what she thought were contradictions, but she always told me she was open to hearing my answer. Here's what I find most interesting: Nancy was very transparent about her motive for reading through the Bible. She told me she prided herself on her vast array of knowledge, but humbly admitted that she needed to study the one book she had neglected. In her words, "I know the Bible has been read more than any other book in history and a person would be a fool not to at least be acquainted with it." In the end, Nancy's motivation seemed to be to put on her "Life Resume" that she had read the Bible.

When Nancy died in 2006, I received a voice mail from her family in Iowa thanking me for being Nancy's friend and for giving her a Bible (I had put my name and phone number in the presentation page with several verses). When I challenge people to read the Bible and get a response of disinterest, I often think of Nancy. When facing such disinterest, I often think to myself, "what makes you so intellectually above the Nancy's of this world?" I also wonder what Nancy's private thoughts were, as she was reading through the Bible. What purpose did God's word accomplish with my dear friend? As far as I know, she never accepted the gospel message, but I cannot be certain. However, I'm sure of this: when she read through the Bible, God's word accomplished His purpose with Nancy and succeeded in the thing for which He sent it to her (Isa. 55:11).

Pre-Evangelism and Other "Scriptures"

Do other religious texts present an ultimate authority, or a self-validating God like the God of the Bible? While this is a legitimate inquiry, the focus of this book does not allow us to go into detail to fully answer this question. However, in our pre-evangelism apologetics, we can point out that very few "scriptures" even claim to have a spoken word from God. For example, religions like Hinduism, Buddhism, Sikhism, Taoism, and New Age all present an impersonal Oneness. An impersonal Oneness, by definition, is not personal. Non-personal entities don't speak! Thus, any scriptures these world religions bring forth are mere human speculation. Most of the "scriptures" of world religions claim no supernatural inspiration or authority. In the end, they are not a word from a personal God, but just a human construct of moral rules and religious traditions.

Only the Bible and those religions that claim to be rooted in the Old Testament declare to have scriptures that are actual revelation from God. For example, the holy books of the major monotheistic religions all have claims to have words from God within their scriptures. This is true of Judaism (Exodus 24:4; Jer. 36:1-2), Christianity (2 Tim. 3:16-17; 2 Pet. 1:21; 1 Cor. 14:37), and Islam (Quran, Surah 10:37-38). In the case of Judaism, the Old Testament is the only revelation that is accepted. Christians, however, testify that the God of the Old Testament is the same God that has revealed Himself in the New Testament. Paul, in testifying before Roman Governor Felix and the Jews said, "I confess to you, that according to the Way, which they [the Jews] call a sect, I worship the God of our fathers [the Jews], believing everything laid down by the Law and written in the Prophets" (Acts 24:14).

That leaves us with Islam's Quran. While this "scripture" claims to be the words of Allah, the Quran denies almost all the essentials of the Christian faith. The Quran denies all of these things: that Jesus is the Son of God (Surah 19:88-92), that Jesus is God (5:17), that God is a Trinity (5:73), that Jesus died on the cross and rose from the dead (4:157-158), that we are saved by grace alone through faith alone (Surah 21:47, 23:102-103; cf., 7:8-9), in Christ alone (3:85, 4:112, 17:13-15, 33:17, 35:18, 40:21).

Obviously, one has to choose between the Bible and the Quran because they contradict each other. However, here is where I see a simple tie breaker. The Quran claims the Bible to be the word of God (Surah 2:136, 2:75, 5:46, 5:67-71). The Quran also states that all of God's words cannot be altered: "none can change His Words" (6:115); "there is none that can alter the Words (and Decrees) of Allah" (6:34); "No change there can be in the words of Allah" (10:64). If the Quran is speaking the truth in this area and the Old and New Testaments are inspired (2:136) and can't be changed (10:64), then those who believe the Quran is a revelation from God must take the Bible as being unaltered and inspired, and the words of Jesus as God's word.

If that's the case, then the Bible's testimony that Jesus is the Son of God (John 10:36, 3:16; Matt. 26:63-64), that Jesus is God (John 1:1,14; Titus 2:13; Heb. 1:8; Rev. 1:8), that God is a Trinity (Galatians 1:1; John 1:1,14; Acts 5:3-4; Matt. 28:19; 2 Cor. 13:14), that Jesus died on the cross and rose from the dead (Acts 2:23, 2:32; Mark 8:31; Matt. 16:21; Luke 9:22; John 10:11; 1 Cor. 15:3-4), and that we are saved by grace alone through faith alone (Eph. 2:8-9), in Christ alone (John 14:6; Acts 4:12), must all be accepted by Islam. Yet, the Quran denies all that biblical testimony. This puts those holding to the Quran as being a revelation from God in an untenable position. All of the above scriptures that the Quran says are the word of God (Surah 2:136, 2:75, 5:46, 5:67-71) and can never be altered (10:64), are at the same time all denied in the Quran itself! This simply nullifies the Quran as being a word from God, for the true God is not schizophrenic, nor does He contradict Himself (Numbers 23:19).

Seekers of Truth, or of *The Truth*?

I would like to mention one more important point. All of the major founders of religion, with the exception of Jesus Christ, are reported in their respective scriptures as having passed through a preliminary period of uncertainty, or of searching for religious light. For example, Muhammad, the founder of Islam, spent years praying in a cave on Mount Hira for religious truth. Siddhartha Gautama, the founder of Buddhism, said, "I am a teacher in search of truth." Confucius, the founder of Confucianism, said he was not able to attain "Jen", which allegedly is the true nature that resides within each person. The founders of Taoism and Zoroastrianism claimed to only be prophets in search of truth. Other religious founders said they either went through a period to attain truth or grew into their "divine" status.

When it comes to the claims of Christ, however, there is a major difference. Jesus never had periods of uncertainty, nor did He ever search for truth or religious light. Instead of pointing the way to the truth, Jesus identified Himself as "the way, and the truth" (John 14:6). Rather than showing people where to find religious light, He simply declared, "I am the light of the world" (John 9:5) and said that "whoever does what is true comes to the light" (John 3:21). Jesus said He came into the world "to bear witness to the truth. Everyone who is of the truth listens to my voice" (John 18:37). The end of our search for God is found in Christ, for "in these last days he [God] has spoken to us by his Son" (Heb. 1:2). Jesus said to see the Father is to see the Son: "Whoever has seen me has seen the Father" (John 14:9). Jesus also told His followers to "Believe in God; believe also in me" (John 14:1). Therefore, trusting in one is equal to trusting in the other.

Finally, when asking the question "Is Jesus the only way to God?", there's really only one question to answer—is Jesus God? If the answer to that question is yes (and of course the Bible testifies to this), then the question of whether Jesus is the only way to God answers itself.

Recap

As you delve into the apologetic side of pre-evangelism, keep in mind these points:

- Our pre-evangelism is directed toward an unsaved person.

- There is not one system of apologetics that meets the needs of all people. While there may be certain arguments, objections or questions that come up more than others, be prepared to adapt your answers based on the person to whom you are talking.

- Be sympathetic to each person's backstory. At the same time, our goal is to get the non-Christian to challenge their own assumptions and worldview.

- Most people have not thought deeply about their non-Christian beliefs. Francis Schaeffer wrote that every non-Christian to whom we speak "has a set of presuppositions, whether he or she has analyzed them or not.... No matter what a man may believe, he cannot change the reality of what is. As Christianity is the truth of what is there, to deny this, on the basis of another system, is to stray from the real world."[13]

- Be sure to ask an unbeliever if they consider themselves an atheist or agnostic. Have them explain what they mean by those titles and how they came to that position. Maybe they don't want to be referred to as either one of those. If so, have them explain and define what their worldview or presupposition is. Remember, Francis Schaeffer tells us that everyone has one.

- Be ready to establish or clarify key biblical concepts about sin in contrast to God's holiness and righteousness.

- Ask what a person believes about sin in general as well as their own sin. How does their god or religion look upon and deal with sin? If speaking to an atheist, ask if sin is real. If they say no, ask them a question such as this: if someone stole their identity, how would they describe that if not sin? If they say yes, ask them by what objective standard do they determine what is and isn't sin?

- Be prepared to explain the necessity of God's existence as a first cause and for the universe's design, as well as for the foundation of reason, logic and morality.

---

[13] Francis Schaeffer, *The God Who is There*, page 132.

- Point out to the unbeliever that everyone knows God because of creation and what He has placed in our hearts, and they are just suppressing knowledge of that (Rom. 1:18-20).

- If an unbeliever challenges you not to use the Bible in discussions with them, ask if a soldier going into war should lay aside their sword and armor because his opponent, who has his own sword and armor (worldview), doesn't believe they should be used in battle. Ask them if they are also willing to lay down their armor.

- Be prepared to challenge people's biblical illiteracy. While people today lack the foundation for belief that past generations had, this will not stop them from confidently trotting out passages to try and prove the Bible is full of contradictions and errors. Challenge them to sit down with you to look at the context (which many of them may not have done) and how other scriptures that speak clearly on the issue at hand can clear up their misunderstanding.

- Always remember that it is God's word that convicts and converts sinners and sanctifies the saints, while at the same time condemning, judging and rebuking unbelievers.

- Constantly be mindful that God's word never fails to accomplish its purpose. Always be ready to open your Bible when holding discussions with unbelievers. Remember, it is God who knows the hearts of all men (1 Kings 8:39; John 2:25; Rev. 2:23), and we can trust that His word will always succeed in piercing men's hearts, souls and spirits to either change or bring to light their true intentions (Heb. 4:12).

- If you are talking to a person of another religion, give them an opportunity to explain what their faith teaches. For example, how did creation come about? How would they define God and man's relationship now and into eternity? Is their religious text a word from a personal God? Do your best to learn more about that religion so you will be better equipped when it comes time to share the gospel. Being familiar with another person's faith may also make that person more open to listening to you.

4) PRE-EVANGELISM LIFESTYLE

"Ask yourself, am I making anyone around me thirsty for Christ? Am I shining my light in the darkness? Or am I contributing to the darkness through my complacency?" – Tony Evans[14]

When I first became a Christian in 1993, this followed a period of many people living out their Christian faith in front of me. One of God's ironies in my life was that He allowed me to be hired as a news announcer at a Christian radio network in Dallas at a time when I was not yet a Christian. In case you are wondering, the question of whether I was a Christian never came up in my brief job interview.

In my early years at the network, it became obvious to most I was not of the faith. Despite that, my co-workers, who were all Christians as

---

[14] Tony Evans, Senior pastor of Oak Cliff Bible Fellowship in Dallas, Shine Your Light in the Darkness, https://tonyevans.org/shine-your-light-in-the-darkness/

far as I knew, all treated me with respect. They just went about living out their Christian faith, which did not escape my notice. One day at work, I was in a discussion with a few single men and women. We were exchanging notes about our dating lives. Jim, who was one of the engineers at the network, happened to overhear me and took offense to some of my colorful language. He confronted me by saying, "Are you having fun Patrick?" After we exchanged a few words, Jim walked away angry. About ten minutes later, he walked up to my desk and humbly apologized to me. He said he overstepped his bounds and should not have called me out. The interesting thing was that I knew Jim was right in confronting me, so his apology had a huge impact on me.

Fast forward some 15 years. I was working at another Christian radio network (this time as a Christian maturing fast in the faith) and was surprised to run into Jim in the elevator as I arrived at work one night. He was there doing some consultant work and happened to have his 8-year-old son with him. I invited Jim and his son into my studio saying there was something I wanted to tell him. As we talked about how Christ had drawn me to Himself years ago, his face beamed with excitement. I then reminded him of our confrontation. I told him he was not only right to oppose my behavior, but his follow-up apology was a great example of a Christian witness, one that profoundly humbled me, and a response I had never forgotten. Jim gave me a big hug and I told his son that he was blessed to have him as a father. I was also blessed to have Jim as a co-worker; I know the Holy Spirit used him to convict me of my sin and unrighteousness (John 16:8).

When I speak of pre-evangelism lifestyle, I can think of many people who affected my eventual openness to hearing the gospel. I thank God for the Jim's in my life—Christians who not only talk the talk, but also walk the walk.

Pre-Evangelism and the Gospel

> *"Is caring for others 'the gospel'? Is that evangelism? No, not without the spoken message of the gospel of Jesus."* - J. Mack Stiles[15]

I define pre-evangelism lifestyle as a Christian who strives to live a sanctified holy life, in the power of the Holy Spirit, before God and men. When we do this, we bring glory to God (1 Cor. 10:31; 1 Pet. 2:12), while at the same time praying to capture the interest of unbelievers for an opportunity to share the gospel (Col. 4:3; cf., 2 Thess. 3:1). These two

---

[15] J. Mack Stiles, *Marks of the Messenger*, p. 68.

points I think reflect the two greatest commandments Christ gave us, "You shall love the Lord your God with all your heart and with all your soul and with all your mind. This is the great and first commandment. And a second is like it: You shall love your neighbor as yourself" (Matt. 22:37-39). If we love the Lord with all our heart, soul and mind, we will always bring glory to God. Moreover, if our life, filled with the Holy Spirit (Eph. 5:18; Gal. 5:16, 22-23), leads to an opportunity to witness the gospel with our mouth (Rom. 10:14), we will be loving our neighbor as ourselves.

Just so there is no misunderstanding, let me say up front that pre-evangelism lifestyle, as implied by the prefix "pre," comes before actual evangelism. How we live our lives before an unbelieving world is not evangelism. At best, it will open doors[16] to sharing the gospel, which we are specifically told to do verbally (Rom. 10:14-17; cf., James 1:18; 1 Pet. 1:23). Though we are to preach the gospel verbally, the context of our preaching should be a sanctified and holy life. While Peter tells us to always be prepared to share the gospel, he prefaces that by saying, "sanctify Christ as Lord in your hearts" (1 Pet. 3:15, NASB). We must never separate preaching the gospel from sanctifying Christ as Lord in our hearts—the two go hand in hand (Philip. 1:27). While our pre-evangelism lifestyle, accompanied by a sanctified and holy life, can open doors for verbally sharing the gospel, a lack of holiness in our lives can be a roadblock to people hearing the gospel.

Let Your Light Shine

Jesus said in Matthew 5:14-16 that Christians should live their lives as a witness to God. "You are the light of the world. A city set on a hill cannot be hidden. Nor do people light a lamp and put it under a basket, but on a stand, and it gives light to all in the house. In the same way, let your light shine before others, so that they may see your good works and give glory to your Father who is in heaven." In John 8:12, Jesus said He is the source of this light: "I am the light of the world. Whoever follows me will not walk in darkness, but will have the light of life." Jesus told His apostles to "become sons of light" (John 12:36). He told us not to hide our light, but instead to let others "see the light" (Luke 8:16). Tabitha,

---

[16] Paul's usage of the phrase "open doors" were God-given opportunities for service—most specifically in preaching the gospel. Paul's intended meaning of open doors thus does not mean, like so many Christians today are taught, that God is opening a door for Christians to pursue careers, a spouse, a home purchase, etc. I am indebted to Garry Friesen for this insight from his important book *Decision Making and the Will of God*, p. 221.

one of Christ's disciples, was full of this light as she "was full of good works and acts of charity" (Acts 9:36).

Paul told the Ephesian church to "Walk as children of light" (Eph. 5:8; cf., 1 Thess. 5:5). He told the saints at Philippi to "be blameless and innocent, children of God without blemish in the midst of a crooked and twisted generation, among whom you shine as lights in the world" (Philip. 2:15). Paul told Titus, "Show yourself in all respects to be a model of good works, and in your teaching show integrity, dignity, and sound speech that cannot be condemned, so that an opponent may be put to shame, having nothing evil to say about us" (Titus 2:7-8; cf., 3:8). Peter advised, "Keep your conduct among the Gentiles honorable, so that when they speak against you as evildoers, they may see your good deeds and glorify God on the day of visitation." (1 Pet. 2:12).

Notice that this light is connected with the sharing of the gospel. After the unbelieving Jews rejected his message, Paul said, "For so the Lord has commanded us, saying, I have made you a light for the Gentiles, that you may bring salvation to the ends of the earth" (Acts 13:47). Paul said the reason he openly proclaimed the gospel was because of the light God brought to his heart, "For God, who said, 'Let light shine out of darkness,' has shone in our hearts to give the light of the knowledge of the glory of God in the face of Jesus Christ" (2 Cor. 4:6; cf., 2 Tim 1:10). Peter said that God's people are to "proclaim the excellencies of him who called you out of darkness into his marvelous light" (1 Pet. 2:9).

When you let your light shine before others in your pre-evangelism lifestyle, your end goal should always be to bring salvation to the ends of the earth, to bring forth the knowledge of the glory of God in the face of Jesus Christ and to proclaim the excellencies of the One who called you into his marvelous light. The way we conduct our lives before unbelievers should be worthy of the gospel. As Paul told the Philippians, who shared a "partnership in the gospel" (Philip. 1:5) with him, "let your manner of life be worthy of the gospel of Christ" (1:27; cf., Eph. 4:1).

Sharing and Serving Go Together

We see in the New Testament several examples where Jesus and His disciples both shared the good news and served the people. For example, we read where Jesus "went on through cities and villages, proclaiming and bringing the good news of the kingdom of God" (Luke 8:1; cf., Luke 4:43; Mark 1:15; Matt. 4:23). Jesus also combined His sharing with serving. "God anointed Jesus of Nazareth with the Holy Spirit and with power. He went about doing good" (Acts 10:38; cf., John 13:1-17; Mark 6:34-44). Philip, full of the Holy Spirit, was one of the disciples chosen to help needy widows (Acts 6:1-5). Then the Lord decided to use him in evangelizing the Samaritans (Acts 8:5-8), and later, the Ethiopian eunuch (Acts 8:26-40). Ultimately, he became known as "Philip the evangelist" (Acts 21:8). In Galatians 2, James, Cephas (Peter) and John, pillars of the Jerusalem church, said they would share the gospel with the circumcised (Jews) and Paul and Barnabas with the Gentiles. Paul agreed and added this request from the leaders in Jerusalem, "Only, they asked us to remember the poor, the very thing I was eager to do." When Peter said we must "proclaim the excellencies of him" (1 Pet. 2:9), he also talked about making sure that unbelievers "see your good deeds and glorify God" (2:12).

Once while attending a retirement dinner for an executive for whom my wife worked, a lady sitting next to me asked me about my travels to Africa. When I told her that I went with a Christian ministry, she said, "Oh, you went there to dig wells?" I said no, I was part of a group that taught Christian pastors biblical doctrines so they can be better prepared to defend and share the gospel. She got a puzzled look on her face having no idea how to respond. Her understanding of Christian service in developing countries was limited to taking care of people's physical needs. Again, while such service is important, so is taking care of people's spiritual needs. The twelve apostles understood this in the early church when they selected seven men to make sure the widows' physical needs were met (Acts 6:1-6). The apostles did this in order to make sure they did not "give up preaching the word of God" (Acts 6:2). While making sure the widows were not neglected, they said, "we will devote ourselves to prayer and to the ministry of the word" (6:4).

While ministries with which I have gone to Africa have taken care of physical needs (supporting orphanages, building churches, delivering hospital supplies and general financial support), all this was done with a goal of helping these church leaders take care of their communities' spiritual needs, which includes sharing the gospel.

Pre-Evangelism Service

The following are some examples of how Christians serve, with a goal towards opening a door for a hearing of the gospel:

- Christian disaster relief ministries

- Christian charities (food banks, clothing, medical supplies, etc.)
- Establishing and supporting orphanages
- Building churches
- Building wells in developing countries
- Ministries to fight diseases (malaria, HIV/AIDS)
- Christian medical and dental ministries
- Building and fixing up homes for the needy
- Feeding and caring for the homeless
- Pro-life crisis pregnancy centers
- Christian adoption agencies
- Christian foreign exchange student programs
- Teaching English as a second language
- Hospice care

While many more ministries could be added to this list, while you are serving, always be prepared to share the gospel verbally should an opening occur. In some instances, that opening may come later for you or for those who follow you. Also keep in mind the motives for our service. Don't practice "your righteousness before other people in order to be seen by them" (Matt. 6:1a). This is why the celebrities always make sure the cameras capture their "charity" work, or why the CEO of a company, spending someone else's money, is always the one holding up the three by six-foot donation check for all to see and record.

Let us keep our service in perspective. We as Christians, of course, are not forbidden to practice righteousness before others (Matt. 5:16; 1 Pet. 2:12), but we must check the motives and manners of our actions when we do. Are we looking for praise from men? If so, "then you will have no reward from your Father who is in heaven" (Matt. 6:1b), because you have already received your praise from the world. However, if you "do not let your left hand know what your right hand is doing" (Matt. 6:3), that is, don't dwell on it, even in our own thoughts, in order to prevent spiritual pride, "your Father who sees in secret will reward you" (Matt. 6:4).

Pre-Evangelism Prayer

"The best pre-evangelistic work is prayer."

Ruth Rosen, daughter of Jews for Jesus founder Moishe Rosen

Pre-evangelism involves us praying for the Lord to open a person's heart to respond to the gospel message. This is what Paul did in Colossians 4:3-4, "pray also for us, that God may open to us a door for the word, to declare the mystery of Christ, on account of which I am in prison—that I may make it clear, which is how I ought to speak." Paul told the Thessalonians, "pray for us, that the word of the Lord may speed ahead and be honored, as happened among you" (2 Thess. 3:1).

Lydia, from the city of Thyatira, may very well have been the recipient of such prayers. When Paul came upon a group of women praying, he preached the gospel to them. We read where "The Lord opened her [Lydia's] heart to pay attention to what was said by Paul" (Acts 16:14). After that we read where Lydia "was baptized, and her household as well" (16:15).

Prayers for Boldness and Humility

We should all pray for boldness to share the gospel. Paul asked fellow believers to pray "also for me, that words may be given to me in opening my mouth boldly to proclaim the mystery of the gospel, for which I am an ambassador in chains, that I may declare it boldly, as I ought to speak" (Eph. 6:19-20). When Peter and John reported to their fellow disciples that they refused to obey the command of the chief priests to stop preaching the gospel, the disciples all lifted their voices together towards God praying "Lord, look upon their threats and grant to your servants to continue to speak your word with all boldness" (Acts 4:29; cf., 2 Cor. 3:12; 1 Thess. 2:2).

We should also pray for humility in sharing the gospel. Apollos spoke boldly in the synagogue about Christ but was humble enough to allow others to explain "to him the way of God more accurately" (Acts 18:24-28). Paul said he was "serving the Lord with all humility" (Acts 20:19) when he testified "of repentance toward God and of faith in our Lord Jesus Christ" (20:21). He also instructed those who have "participation in the Spirit" (Philip. 2:1), "Do nothing from selfish ambition or conceit, but in humility count others more significant than yourselves. Let each of you look not only to his own interests, but also to the interests of others" (Philip. 2:3-4).

George E. Sweazey, a 20th century Presbyterian minister, mentions a third thing to remember: "we are God's fellow workers" (1 Cor. 3:9). He says, "The keeping of this sense of the divine partnership—of the humble dependence on a Greater power—is the clearest essential for evangelism." Sweazey adds, "There is a special danger which comes to those who have done well in evangelism. They are likely to grow less dependent on the sort of anxious prayer which comes from fear and the knowledge of inadequacy. The members begin to feel, 'I am getting good at this; I have mastered the techniques.'…The Lord rewards only the humble. When evangelism becomes merely a matter of well-polished methods, it is finished. Prayer is the basic evangelistic method, upon which all other methods depend."[17]

Prayers for Unbelievers

When I pray for unbelievers, I pray for five specific things.

1) I pray that the Father will draw the unbeliever to the Son.

Jesus said in John 6:44, "No one can come to me unless the Father who sent me draws him." The fact is that "no one seeks for God" (Rom. 3:11), because unregenerate people are spiritually dead in their sin (Eph. 2:1; Col. 2:13). They are enemies of God (Rom. 5:10), hostile to the Lord (Rom. 8:7) and thus alienated from their Creator (Col. 1:21). Being by nature children of wrath (Eph. 2:3; Rom. 7:5) their fallen nature in Adam (Rom. 5:12-21) must be changed. God chooses us by drawing us, regenerating us and giving us a new nature (2 Cor. 5:17). We then are empowered by His amazing grace to choose Him, for all God initially chooses (elects) will come to Him (John 6:37).

2) I pray that God will grant the unbeliever the gifts of faith and repentance.

Since the Bible says faith (Eph. 2:8-9; Philip. 1:29) and repentance (2 Tim. 2:25; Acts 5:31, 11:18) are gifts from God, this, too, is something God has to initiate. Without faith being a gift from God, one would have to somehow muster up something in their fallen nature to seek after Him, something the Bible says is impossible (Rom. 3:11). When I consider the state of unbelievers (of whom, of course, I used to be), I ask myself, why was I given faith and others not? Is it because I was somehow more spiritual or smarter? I promise you, that's not the case. I was

---

[17] George E. Sweazey, *Effective Evangelism*, p. 53.

just as dead in my sin and alienated from God as everyone else is, or was, at some point. God presents faith as a gift to prevent boasting, "For by grace you have been saved through faith. And this is not your own doing; it is the gift of God, not a result of works, so that no one may boast" (Eph. 2:8-9; cf., Gal. 6:14). We understand that the same Jesus who has granted us the faith to "believe in him" (Philip. 1:29), is "the author and finisher of our faith" (Heb. 12:2, KJV).

Just like faith is a gift from God, so is repentance. As an unbeliever, any repentance I was ever able to produce was directed towards the world. That's not good news because "worldly grief produces death" (2 Cor. 7:10b). However, when "God has granted repentance that leads to life" (Acts 11:18), our repentance is no longer directed at the world but towards God, "For godly grief produces a repentance that leads to salvation without regret" (2 Cor. 7:10a). Therefore, I pray that "God may perhaps grant them repentance leading to a knowledge of the truth" (2 Tim. 2:25). Remember that it was God who exalted Jesus as "Savior, to give repentance to Israel and forgiveness of sins" (Acts 5:31; cf., Luke 24:47).

3) I pray that the Holy Spirit will convict a person concerning sin, righteousness and judgment.

Jesus said when the Holy Spirit comes, "He will convict the world concerning sin and righteousness and judgment: concerning sin, because they do not believe in me; concerning righteousness, because I go to the Father, and you will see me no longer; concerning judgment, because the ruler of this world is judged." (John 16:8-11). The world's predominant sin is an unbelief in the Savior—God's Messiah. The Holy Spirit not only points people to Jesus (John 15:26), He reveals Christ as God's righteous Servant (Acts 3:14-15; Isa. 53:11). He will also show that Satan, the prince of this world, has been judged because Jesus' death and resurrection were a condemnation of the devil (John 12:31, 14:30; Col. 2:15; Heb. 2:14). Opening a person's eyes to all these things is the Spirit's role in conversion.

I will never forget the November night in 1993, when I was alone in my room, and God brought salvation to my life. I made a simple prayer, "God, if your Son is real, I want to know Him." Looking back, I could clearly see God drawing me to the Son in the months and years preceding that prayer. He did so by using many circumstances and faithful Christians in my life. I will be eternally grateful to Grant Boone who patiently took the time to explain the gospel to me. He started, at one of our many lunches, to tell me about how Jesus fulfilled all the Old Testament sacrifices with His once for all sacrifice on the cross. When Grant later explained to me that Christ's life, death and resurrection and belief in this finished work (John 19:30) were what leads to eternal life, I wondered what it would be like to get off my works/righteous treadmill and place my trust in God alone. I could see God growing faith in me.

Also looking back, prior to my conversion, I remembered how God had been convicting me of my sin and unbelief. Concerning sin, it was almost as if a video tape of all my sins kept playing back in my mind. I could see God growing repentance in me. Concerning my unbelief, I had to admit to myself that I had readily put up with a Jesus, a spirit and a gospel that was of my own making. This was exactly what Paul warned us against, "For if someone comes and proclaims another Jesus than the one we proclaimed, or if you receive a different spirit from the one you received, or if you accept a different gospel from the one you accepted, you put up with it readily enough" (2 Cor. 11:4). I was done putting up with the false idols in my life and was ready to trust in the real Jesus, the real Holy Spirit and the real gospel.

4) I pray that God will grant the unbeliever a new heart, and a new spirit.

In Ezekiel 36:26, we read, "And I will give you a new heart, and a new spirit I will put within you. And I will remove the heart of stone from your flesh and give you a heart of flesh." Charles Spurgeon, in delivering a sermon on this passage, said, "The heart, when renewed by grace, is the best part of manhood; unrenewed, it is the very worst."[18] When God changes our heart of stone into a heart of flesh, we transition from being spiritually dead in our sins (Eph. 2:1) to being alive together with Christ (Eph. 2:5), from having a heart hardened that makes one a slave to sin (John 8:34) to a heart submissive to the will of God and a slave to righteousness (Rom. 6:15-19).

5) I end my prayer by acknowledging that our sovereign God's will be done with the person for whom I am praying.

This is how Jesus taught us how to pray: "Your kingdom come, your will be done, on earth as it is in heaven" (Matt. 6:10; cf., Psalm 115:3). Do you pray for God's will to be done, whatever that is? When we pray for our unbelieving friends and family, we want them to discover that

---

[18] Charles Haddon Spurgeon, The Heart of Flesh. https://www.spurgeon.org/resource-library/sermons/the-heart-of-flesh#flipbook/

"There is therefore now no condemnation for those who are in Christ Jesus" (Rom. 8:1). However, there is a flipside to our prayers that some may have not considered. Have you ever asked yourself this question: if you are praying for God's will to be done with a person, would that include judgment and condemnation to come on them if they were to reject Christ in the end? Jesus told us most people would end up on the wide road that leads to destruction (Matt. 7:13). That means there will be many people for whom we pray and to whom we witness who will reject Christ to the end, resulting in them not seeing life and remaining under God's wrath (John 3:36).

For those of us who have experienced a new heart and a new spirit, I can only say our attitude in answering such a question should be the same as Paul. When he spoke of his unsaved Jewish kinsmen, he made this amazing statement, "I have great sorrow and unceasing anguish in my heart. For I could wish that I myself were accursed and cut off from Christ for the sake of my brothers, my kinsmen according to the flesh" (Rom. 9:2-3; cf., 10:1; Exodus 32:32). Can you imagine, like Paul, asking God to swap your soul for the unbeliever for whom you are praying?

I have always found Paul's statement in Romans 9:3 to be curious. He knew he could not actually be cut off from Christ, for he just said at the end of Romans 8 that nothing "will be able to separate us from the love of God in Christ Jesus our Lord" (Rom. 8:39). The fact is that only Christ could do what Paul wished, becoming a curse for others (Gal. 3:13). When Paul said, "For I could wish", he meant if such a thing were allowable, possible, or proper. He knew such a "wish" was not possible, for he wrote that we "were bought with a price" (1 Cor. 6:20, 7:23), "with his [Christ's] own blood" (Acts 20:28). Yet, I don't doubt that Paul was sincere, and if it were allowable, he would have made such a swap.

Despite Jesus telling us that most people would end up on the wide road that leads to destruction, we should not stop praying for all to be led to the narrow road that leads to life (Matt. 7:14). In our prayers, we can trust that "The Lord knows those who are his" (2 Tim. 2:19). As for the rest, "Shall not the Judge of all the earth do what is just?" (Gen. 18:25; cf., Deut. 32:4; Psalm 89:14; Rom. 9:22; 1 Pet. 2:8). In the end, we simply must acknowledge and trust in God's sovereignty in salvation saying, "your will be done."

Prayers for God's Sovereignty

J.I. Packer, in one of the most widely read books on evangelism, Evangelism and the Sovereignty of God, challenges those who might deny God's divine sovereignty in salvation. Packer writes that two facts show that all Christians believe God is sovereign in our salvation. From the first chapter of his book, we read:

1) **Our own conversion.**

- You give God thanks for your conversion.

- Your thanksgiving is itself an acknowledgment that your conversion was not your own, but his work.

- You did not attribute your repenting and believing to your own wisdom, or prudence, or sound judgment, or good sense. In fact, you thank him no less sincerely for the gift of faith and repentance than for the gift of a Christ to trust and to turn to.

- You would never dream of dividing the credit for your salvation between God and yourself.

- You have never for one moment supposed that the decisive contribution to your salvation was yours and not God's.

- You give God all the glory for all that your salvation involved.

2) **Our prayers for the conversion of others.**

- Do you limit yourself to asking that God will bring them to a point where they can save themselves, independently of him? I do not think you do.

- Instead, you pray quite specifically for God to work in them everything necessary for their salvation; to open their eyes; to soften their hard hearts; renew their natures and move their wills to receive the Savior.

- When you pray for unconverted people, you do so on the assumption that it is in God's power to bring them to faith.

- You know that what makes men turn to God is God's own gracious work of drawing them to himself; and the content of your prayers is determined by this knowledge.

Packer concedes that there has been a long-standing controversy in the church about the roles of God and man in salvation, but he concludes by saying, "On our feet we may have arguments about it, but on our knees we are all agreed."[19]

I would like to add one more point on prayer. Sometimes when I pray for someone over a lengthy period of time, especially a family member, I reach the end of myself and do not know how else to pray. At that point, I ask the Holy Spirit to intercede to convey my soul's true desire to the throne of God. Indeed, this is what scripture tells us to do: "The Spirit helps us in our weakness. For we do not know what to pray for as we ought, but the Spirit himself intercedes for us with groanings too deep for words. And he who searches hearts knows what is the mind of the Spirit, because the Spirit intercedes for the saints according to the will of God" (Rom. 8:26-27).

As Many as Were Appointed to Eternal Life Believed (Acts 13:48)

"Lord, hasten to bring in all Thine elect—and then elect some more."
Charles Spurgeon[20]

While we as believers don't know who the elect are, God does (2 Tim. 2:19; Acts 13:48, 18:10; Eph. 1:4-11; 1 Pet. 1:1). While we also don't know who the Father might be drawing (John 6:44), or the Holy Spirit might be convicting of their sin and unbelief (John 16:8), we have to treat each unbeliever as if this drawing and convicting process could be possible in their lives, either presently or in the future. Having said that, I think it is important to add that no amount of persuasion on our part, be it apologetic arguments, reasoning, or challenging people's assumptions and worldviews that we bring forth in pre-evangelism or evangelism, will be fruitful unless God first gives the growth (1 Cor. 3:7) by drawing (John 6:44), changing the heart (Ez. 36:26) and placing someone "on the good soil" (Mark 4:20). As Augustine once said of God, "You have put salt in our mouths that we may thirst for you."

Jason called a gospel phone line I was manning at 12:30 am, hours after July 4th, 2019. Fireworks sparked right away when this young man started with, "I don't believe in God. I hate Christians and the Christian religion." He went on to tell me that he found religion "limiting." Af-

---

[19] J.I. Packer, *Evangelism and the Sovereignty of God*, chapter one, Divine Sovereignty.
[20] Charles Haddon Spurgeon, A Biography, W. Y. Fullerton, Ch. 8.

ter discussing with him our universal sin (Rom. 3:23) and law breaking (James 2:10), we went back and forth on several of his objections. Jason then said, "The main reason I called was to see if you could change my mind. How can you make me believe and become a Christian?" I told Jason that I could not change his mind and I can't "make" him believe because that is the prerogative of God alone, as—"Salvation belongs to the LORD!" (Jonah 2:9). I mentioned to Jason that I would pray that God would draw him, grant him the gifts of faith and repentance and change his heart from the inside out.

Jason paused for several seconds and then said that he has dared many followers of Christ to try and change his mind about Christianity, almost like it was a gotcha challenge. He then said he had never had someone tell him that it is not Christians who convert, but God. I don't know what happened to Jason, but I know my own conversion, and anyone's for that matter, "depends not on human will or exertion, but on God, who has mercy" (Rom. 9:16; cf., John 1:13), for "It is God who justifies" (Rom. 8:33).

My Life is Not the Gospel

> *"The person who says naively, 'I don't preach; I just let my life speak,' is insufferably self-righteous. None of us is good enough to witness by our life alone."*
> David Elton Trueblood[21]

For those who believe their life alone is a witness to the gospel, this is quite an arrogant and self-righteous approach. Why? Because the Christian spends time making themselves known—not Christ. It also assumes that your life is so righteous that people would be drawn just to you. However, the unsaved are going to look for you to sin in a failed attempt to justify their own unbelief (Luke 10:29, 16:15). Because of this, a Christian should make known that they are the worst of all sinners (1 Tim. 1:15), the least of all the saints (Eph. 3:8) and point people to the only sinless One—Christ (1 Pet. 2:22; 1 Corinthians 2:2), not to themselves.

In the end, the most important thing is not so much what lost people see in you (at best that can only be considered pre-evangelism), but the message they hear from the beautiful feet of those who preach the good news (Romans 10:14-17). Every biblical example of conversion is a

---

[21] Elton Trueblood, former chaplain to Harvard and Stanford universities, *The Company of the Committed*, p. 53.

result of preaching the word of God, not living the word of God. Of the dozens of conversion experiences given in the book of Acts, in each case their conversion was the result of someone preaching the gospel. The Apostles were not martyred because of their lifestyle; they were martyred for verbally proclaiming the gospel. We must remember, "What we proclaim is not ourselves, but Jesus Christ as Lord, with ourselves as your servants for Jesus' sake" (2 Cor. 4:5). Paul summarized the purpose of his whole ministry this way, "Christ in you, the hope of glory. Him we proclaim" (Col. 1:27-28).

Pollster George Barna has done helpful work in the area of surveys surrounding the Christian faith. He has also given us many key insights into evangelism. However, I think he misses the mark in this parallel he draws between our verbal evangelism and our evangelism lifestyle, "Although a verbal explanation of faith is helpful toward facilitating a non-believer's decision to follow Christ, a verbal proclamation without a lifestyle that supports that is powerless" (George Barna).[22]

While I previously mentioned how critical it is to let our light shine and to combine sharing and serving before unbelievers, even if some neglect to do that, would their verbal proclamation of the gospel really be "powerless"? Of course not! The power of the gospel does not rest on, or even partly on, our fallen and sometimes inconsistent lifestyle. It rests solely on itself (Romans 1:16; 1 Cor. 1:18, 1:23-24, 2:1-5). If conversions depended on our lifestyle matching up with our verbal proclamation of the gospel, that would be a powerless gospel, because no one's lifestyle matches up with the finished work of Christ—His perfect life on our behalf, death on the cross for our sins and resurrection from the dead. Our verbal proclamation of the gospel needs to point away from ourselves and solely to Christ. As John MacArthur says, "God's power comes through the message, not the messenger."[23]

Pre-Evangelism is Not the Gospel

When we see biblical examples of conversion, it is a result of preaching the word of God—bringing sinners to repentance and pointing them to Jesus' finished work. As Paul said, "how are they to believe in him… without someone preaching?" (Rom. 10:14). Scripture is clear that salvation is always connected to the preaching of the word. James says of the Father, "Of his own will he brought us forth by the word of truth" (James

---

[22] George Barna, *The Complete Evangelism Handbook*, p. 50.

[23] John MacArthur, *Evangelism*, p. 1.

1:18). Peter says we are, "born again…through the living and abiding word of God" (1 Pet. 1:23). In the Parable of the Sower, Jesus taught the impossibility of growth apart from sowing the imperishable seed of God's word (Mark 4:1-20).

Whenever anyone tells you that you must earn the "right" to preach the gospel to someone, please understand that right already belongs to you as a believer. The fact is that most of the time you share the gospel, it will be with strangers where you will have no opportunity, outside of a friendly greeting, to earn such a right. In the case where you have had a chance to build a relationship, your right to share the gospel with them was the same before the relationship started as it is after. While our pre-evangelism lifestyle can make people more open to us, preaching the gospel is not a right one earns, but a command God has given believers (Matt. 28:19-20; Acts 1:8; 1 Pet. 3:15). While it is up to God to make people open to the gospel message (Acts 16:14), our right to share the gospel is always there no matter how familiar or unfamiliar we are with a person. In the end, it is up to each of us to be wise as to when and how to present the gospel.

George E. Sweazey, Professor of Homiletics at Princeton Theological Seminary, said when people say, "'A good Christian life is the best evangelism.' No—it is pre-evangelism, but is not evangelism." He went on to say about people who think their life is the gospel, "It is the honest bewilderment of the person who has never found out what evangelism really is. It is the rationalization of the church member whose faith is too unclear to seem worth sharing. It is the plea of the minister who has never learned to talk with people about their faith, and of the Church college which has forgotten why it was founded." Sweazey concluded that pre-evangelism lifestyle may make people receptive to hearing the gospel, but unless "an evangelistic approach is made…the most beautiful Christian life in the community will bring no one to an experience with Christ."[24]

Recap

Here are some points to keep in mind about our pre-evangelism lifestyle:

- Pre-evangelism lifestyle is a Christian striving, through the power of the Holy Spirit, to live a sanctified holy life before God and men. When we do this, we bring glory to God (1 Cor. 10:31; 1 Pet. 2:12).

---

[24] George E. Sweazey, Ibid, p. 21.

- All our pre-evangelism efforts should lead to a hope of capturing the interest of unbelievers for an opportunity to share the gospel (Col. 4:3; cf., 2 Thess. 3:1).

- Check your motives when serving. Are you doing it for the approval of men, or for the approval of God (Matt. 6:1-4)?

- Pre-evangelism lifestyle is not evangelism. At best, it will open doors to sharing the gospel, which we are specifically told to do verbally (Rom. 10:14-17; cf., James 1:18; 1 Pet. 1:23).

- Always "sanctify Christ as Lord in your hearts" (1 Pet. 3:15, NASB). When we do this, "Christ…through us spreads the fragrance of the knowledge of him everywhere. For we are the aroma of Christ to God among those who are being saved and among those who are perishing" (2 Cor. 2:14-15).

- A lack of this sanctification in our lives can be a roadblock to people hearing the gospel. While deeds done with sinful motives can ruin our chances for a gospel hearing, even deeds done with the best motives cannot, by themselves, be our gospel witness.

- Since Jesus is the light of the world (John 8:12), we should "Walk as children of light" (Eph. 5:8). However, we can't turn our pre-evangelism lifestyle on and off like a light switch.

- Our light is connected with sharing the gospel (Acts 13:47; 2 Cor. 4:6; cf., 2 Tim 1:10; 1 Pet. 2:9).

- Pre-evangelism involves us praying for the Lord to open a person's heart to respond to the gospel message (Col. 4:3-4; 2 Thess. 3:1; Acts 16:14) and praying that they will humble themselves to receive this message (1 Pet. 5:5).

- In our prayers for unbelievers, pray that the Father will draw them to the Son, grant them the gifts of faith and repentance, giving them a new heart and a new spirit; that the Holy Spirit will convict them of their sin and unbelief; and that God's will be done with each person.

- Let us have a heart like Paul who warned of those trying to establish their own righteousness before God, "Brothers, my heart's desire and prayer to God for them is that they may be saved. For I bear them witness that they have a zeal for God, but not according to knowledge. For, being ignorant of the righteousness of God, and seeking to establish their own, they did not submit to God's righteousness. For Christ is the end of the law for righteousness to everyone who believes" (Rom. 10:1-4).

- When we know not what to pray, let us call on the Holy Spirit's intervention (Rom. 8:26-27).

- Living our life is not the gospel; preaching the good news is (Romans 10:14-17).

- When we walk the walk in our pre-evangelism lifestyle, we should always be prepared to talk the talk of the gospel when an open door arrives.

While our pre-evangelism efforts help the unsaved to clear hurdles, to understand key biblical doctrines and to see our light shine, all of this is just a precursor to actual evangelism. Many get stuck in pre-evangelism and rarely reach the evangelizing phase, or they confuse pre-evangelism with actual evangelism. Our pre-evangelism cannot be simply an excuse for no evangelism. Our goal must always be to move a person we are witnessing to from pre-evangelism to evangelism as we walk along The Evangelism Circle.

PART TWO—EVANGELISM

5 YELLOWSTONE EVANGELISM

In the summer of 2008, my wife and I vacationed in Yellowstone. Our visit included a drive through the Shoshone National Forest. As we rode by a sign that said "Trail Rides", my wife Kim pointed at the sign asking, "Should we do it?" I said it was up to her. She hesitated and then said no, so we kept driving. Kim then changed her mind and as we turned around, a divine appointment was about to happen.

As we pulled into the trail ride parking area, we noticed the sign read 35 dollars each for a one-hour ride. The scenery was too beautiful to pass up. George, in his mid-30s, wearing a cowboy hat, jeans and boots, greeted us. As he saddled up a horse named Pepper for me and one named Paco for Kim, he told us in a deep southern drawl that he would be our guide. When we started our trail ride, George remarked that he was from Kentucky and was spending the summer in Wyoming. He told us "I'm reflecting on my life and searching" after he and his dad parted over an argument. As we continued our trail ride, enjoying God's amazing creation, George mentioned that he could see that Kim and I were grounded people. I told him we were grounded in Jesus Christ. He asked me, "Do you have a strong faith?" I said yes.

As we continued our ride, George changed the subject to Grizzly bears. However, as soon as I had an opportunity, I changed the subject back to faith. I asked him, "If you died tonight, do you know where you would go?" He said no, then turned around on his horse and asked, "Do you?". I said, yes, I do. He turned to Kim and said, "Do you?". Kim said yes. I then started to explain God's law to him and how we have all broken it. After he admitted he was guilty of this, he said, "I deserve hell."

Riding through a beautiful flowing creek, I thought about Jesus' words, "If anyone thirsts, let him come to me and drink. Whoever believes in me, as the Scripture has said, 'Out of his heart will flow rivers of living water'" (John 7:37-38). As I continued to explain to George how the law drives us to Christ and the cross (Gal. 3:24), I silently prayed that God would bring the living water of faith into his heart. Since the same passage in John's gospel identified this living water as the Holy Spirit, "Now this he said about the Spirit, whom those who believed in him were to receive" (7:39), I knew that only this living water from above would satisfy George's need for God.

Seizing the moment, I told George, "You look like a man who is being convicted by the Holy Spirit." He had the humblest and yet most serious look on his face. He grabbed the reins with his left hand, reached out his right hand, and asked me, "What does a person have to do be saved and to receive eternal life?" I said, repent and believe in the gospel. George bowed his head and asked if I would pray for him. After I finished my prayer, he looked at me with tears in his eyes and said, "God sent me a messenger."

When we finished our trail ride, Kim remembered we had a brand-new Bible in the back of our car. In the presentation page, I wrote my name and e-mail along with several scriptures for George to remember. We told him we would be praying for his next step of finding a church and growing in Christ. Kim and I exchanged hugs with our host and said our goodbyes. As we drove away, we watched as George sat on the stairs of the trail ride office reading his new Bible. This is my favorite witnessing story and a good way to start our section on evangelism.

6. AN UNCHANGING MESSAGE IN CHANGING TIMES

"The grass withers, the flower fades, but the word of our God will stand forever"
Isaiah 40:8

The gospel is an unchanging message "that was once for all delivered to the saints" (Jude 3). While many Christians have faithfully delivered this unchanging message down through the centuries, consider some of these current book titles on evangelism: Reviving Evangelism, Transforming Evangelism, Reimagining Evangelism, Questioning Evangelism, Evangelism Outside the Box, Evangelism for Non-Evangelists, and The Mystic Way of Evangelism.

Of course, the gospel message is never out of date; it is relevant to all cultures and never needs to be revived, transformed or reimagined. However, it is fair to consider different *methods* of sharing the gospel message. George E. Sweazey writes, "There has been no really new discovery in evangelism in the past nineteen hundred years. Every revival has been a recovery of what Christians already knew. But what is changeless [the gospel] must be fitted into a perpetually changing scene. It must be directed to new situations, new moods, new points of view."[25]

There definitely have been changing scenes and new situations throughout history. A popular evangelistic method in the 19th and 20th centuries was tent revivals, which later made way for radio and television evangelists. Busing ministries were popular in the 60s and 70s to transport people to churches to hear the good news. Today we see churches sending out teachers to hold Bible studies at senior citizen living centers and homeless shelters. The Internet has also become an incredible tool for sharing the gospel. Evangelism approaches can include us using *the* Book (i.e. the Bible) to Facebook, YouTube to GodTube, a megaphone blast to a podcast, or a shortwave transmitter to Twitter. While the gospel message will always be changeless, the times in which the good news is delivered is not.

The Gospel and Culture

Today there are many new points of view we have to confront in our culture. For example, there are a growing number of people calling themselves "spiritual but not religious," then there are those who are post-modern versus modern, post-truth as opposed to believing in objective truth, post-Christian instead of Christian, or emergent versus traditional. How do we fit the gospel message into these new points of view? If we ignore these cultural shifts, we will turn a blind eye to "everyone doing whatever is right in his own eyes" (Deut. 12:8). If we give in to culture, we will bend the knee to those who celebrate their many sins, openly flaunting them in front of God. By bowing down to these transgressions, we can end up inadvertently participating in them and giving "approval to those who practice them" (Rom. 1:32; cf., Psalm 50:18). Instead, we should be like the men of Issachar, "men who had understanding of the times, to know what Israel ought to do" (1 Chron. 12:32; cf. Esther 1:13; Eph. 5:17).

---

[25] George E. Sweazey, *Effective Evangelism*, p. 23.

The men of Issachar had supported King Saul but then switched their allegiance to David. They had witnessed how Saul disobeyed God by giving in to the culture, fearing the people's demands more than God (1 Sam. 15:1-28). By taking stock of the situation, they understood the times and knew what to do. Likewise, it's time for us to take stock of our own times and not ignore the cultural shifts taking place right before our eyes. We must never capitulate to culture by going along with sins God has already condemned in His word. We need to be anchored to the Bible, but at the same time remain aware of the times and culture in which we live. If we have God as our foundation, we will have an understanding of the times and know what to do. Part of that understanding is learning how to proclaim the gospel's unchanging message in changing times.

We should consider that God allows different methods to be used in order to reach different culture groups. In 1 Corinthians 9:22, Paul said, "I have become all things to all people, that by all means I might save some." Paul did not mean that we act one way with one group of people and another way with another group—for his gospel message never changed. Paul simply meant that he would use each group's own beliefs and ways to show them the truth. Therefore, to a religious Jew, who was under the law, he would use the law to speak to them. Paul, who said he was not himself under the law, became as a Jew so he could show them how the law could never save anyone. In the first 8 chapters of Romans, Paul argued for freedom from a law that could never save us, "For we hold that one is justified by faith apart from works of the law" (Rom. 3:28; cf., Gal. 2:16).

To a Gentile, Paul adapted his teaching to their specific cultural thoughts in order to reach them. In Acts 17:16-34, he spoke with Epicurean and Stoic philosophers who were worshiping "an unknown god" (17:23). He used their worship of this unknown god to point them to the biblical God. He even quoted from a Hymn to Zeus, written by the Greek pagan poet Aratus (17:28) to make his case. In all this, Paul never altered the *message* of the gospel to reflect the perspective of his audience. Instead, he adapted his *method*, leveraging his audience's culture to bring them to an understanding of the gospel.

Finally, it is worth noting that there are several published books with titles like Evangelism Made Easy and Witnessing Made Easy. However, evangelism is *not* easy. It takes training, discipline, obedience, boldness, grace, truth and Christian maturity (Heb. 5:14; 1 Tim. 4:7-8; 2 Tim. 2:15, 3:16-17; Acts 4:31; Eph. 4:15). It also takes much discernment, especially to learn how to proclaim the unchanging message in changing times and cultures. How we define the unchanging message of the gospel is the subject of our next chapter.

○ ○ ○

THE GOSPEL DEFINED

"One of the reasons people are not effective in evangelism is because they are not sure about the content of the gospel."
John MacArthur[26]

To be on The Evangelism Circle, we should be able to define not only the meaning of the word gospel, but also what the gospel is. As far as the meaning is concerned, the Greek word euangelion was translated literally into Old English as godspell and eventually became gospel. The prefix in euangelion, eu, refers to something good or pleasant, which is the same as the word "god" in Old English. The word angelion is the word for message, which in Old English is the

---

[26] John MacArthur, *Evangelism*, p. 78.

word "spell" (news). So, those who share the gospel are sharing the good message, or good news, of Jesus and how God brings us into a saving relationship with Himself.

Defining what the gospel is depends on whether we are talking about the root of the gospel or the fruit of the gospel (more on this in chapter eight). The root of the gospel is the good news of salvation through the life, death and resurrection of Jesus Christ (1 Cor. 15:1-8; 2 Tim. 1:10). The fruit of the gospel is its sanctifying work in changing our lives (Col. 1:5, 23; 1 Thess. 1:5; Eph. 6:15; 1 Thess. 5:23; 2 Tim. 1:8-9) and positively changing the lives of others (2 Cor. 9:13; Phil. 1:27; 1 Thess. 2:8, 3:2; 2 Thess. 2:13-14).[27]

Having said that, this chapter will focus on the root of the gospel. There is no place where the root of the gospel is more clearly defined than in 1 Corinthians 15:1-8:

> *"Now I would remind you, brothers, of the gospel I preached to you, which you received, in which you stand, and by which you are being saved, if you hold fast to the word I preached to you—unless you believed in vain. For I delivered to you as of first importance what I also received: that Christ died for our sins in accordance with the Scriptures, that he was buried, that he was raised on the third day in accordance with the Scriptures, and that he appeared to Cephas, then to the twelve. Then he appeared to more than five hundred brothers at one time, most of whom are still alive, though some have fallen asleep. Then he appeared to James, then to all the apostles. Last of all, as to one untimely born, he appeared also to me."*

Let's pause for a moment and remember this definition:

Christ died for our sins in accordance with the Scriptures, that he was buried, that he was raised on the third day in accordance with the Scriptures.

This is the gospel, Paul says, on which we must stand and to which we should hold fast, otherwise we have believed in vain. Note that Paul not only explicitly states that he's talking about "the gospel" (15:1), but also explains what the good news is—Christ's death, burial and resurrection. This passage outlines the basics of the gospel: Man is a sinner, Christ died for our sins, He was buried and rose from the dead on the

---

[27] For a broader discussion on defining what the gospel is, read Greg Gilbert, What Is the Gospel? https://www.9marks.org/article/what-is-the-gospel/, or What Is the Gospel?, W. Robert Godfrey, https://www.ligonier.org/blog/what-gospel/.

third day. If your gospel presentation does not have these foundational points, you are not delivering the gospel. Since this is "of first importance" (15:3), we must get it right.

Many scholars believe this passage to be the first creed (a formal belief statement) of Christendom. Since it has been argued that this creed dates within 3-8 years of Christ's crucifixion, many conclude Paul received this confession from the eyewitnesses to the life, death and resurrection of Christ.[28] I agree that Paul certainly received this confession, but Paul also told the Galatians, "For I would have you know, brothers, that the gospel that was preached by me is not man's gospel. For I did not receive it from any man, nor was I taught it, but I received it through a revelation of Jesus Christ" (Gal. 1:11-12; cf., 1 Cor. 11:23). Just as the Father gave a revelation to Peter who Christ was (Matt. 16:15-17), Paul received the gospel through a revelation of Jesus Christ. The confession Paul received in 1 Corinthians 15 and the gospel revelation he received from the risen Christ were one and the same. As New Testament historian Gary Habermas writes, Paul's "testimony concerning the facts of the gospel agreed with that of the apostolic eyewitnesses."[29]

Finally, Paul says this gospel is "in accordance with the Scriptures" (15:3-4). While the Old Testament scriptures are certainly in mind here (Isa. 53:5-6, 12; Daniel 9:24-26; Psalm 22; Zechariah 12:10), the nuances of the gospel are more fully explained in the New Testament scriptures, since "All Scripture is breathed out by God" (2 Tim. 3:16). Remember that Paul said he received the gospel through a revelation of Jesus Christ" (Gal. 1:11-12; cf., 1 Cor. 11:23). Paul knew he was writing under divine inspiration, for he said, "Christ is speaking in me" (2 Cor. 13:3; cf., 1 Cor. 14:37). Peter also called all of Paul's epistles "Scripture" (2 Pet. 3:15-16).

Therefore, since Paul's epistles are scripture, we can go to other places in his writings, or to other examples from his preaching, to further explain and confirm the foundational facts of the gospel in 1 Corinthians 15. With that in mind, let's look at how Paul more fully explains the gospel he preached:

---

[28] Gary Habermas, *The Historical Jesus*, pp. 152-160.

[29] Gary Habermas, Ibid, p. 156.

Man is a Sinner	Christ Died for our Sins	Christ Rose from the Dead
"As one trespass [in the Garden] led to condemnation for all men" (Rom 5:18a).	"So one act of righteousness [Christ's death] leads to justification and life for all men" (Rom 5:18b)	"Those who receive the abundance of grace and the free gift of righteousness reign in life through the one man Jesus Christ" (Rom 5:17).
"For as by the one man's [Adam's] disobedience the many were made sinners" (Rom 5:19a).	"So by the one man's [Christ] obedience the many will be made righteous" (Rom. 5:19b).	"Now he commands all people everywhere to repent, because he has fixed a day on which he will judge the world in righteousness by a man whom he has appointed; and of this he has given assurance to all by raising him from the dead" (Acts 17:30-31).
"For as in Adam all die" (1 Cor. 15:22a).	"The last Adam" (1 Cor. 15:45), Christ, has made "peace by the blood of his cross" (Col. 1:20).	"In Christ shall all be made alive" (1 Cor. 15:22b). "The last Adam became a life-giving spirit" (1 Cor. 15:45).
We "were by nature children of wrath, like the rest of mankind" (Eph. 2:3).	"Since, therefore, we have now been justified by his blood, much more shall we be saved by him from the wrath of God" (Rom. 5:9; cf., 1 Thess. 5:9).	"His Son from heaven, whom he raised from the dead, Jesus who delivers us from the wrath to come" (1 Thess. 1:10).
"You, who were dead in your trespasses and the uncircumcision of your flesh" (Col. 2:13).	"God made alive together with him, having forgiven us all our trespasses, by canceling the record of debt that stood against us with its legal demands. This he set aside, nailing it to the cross" (Col. 2:13-14).	"Likewise, my brothers, you also have died to the law through the body of Christ, so that you may belong to another, to him who has been raised from the dead, in order that we may bear fruit for God" (Rom. 7:4).
We once were in "the domain of darkness" (Col. 1:13).	But our faith in the cross has "transferred us to the kingdom of his beloved Son, in whom we have redemption, the forgiveness of sins" (Col. 1:13-14).	Christ is "the firstborn from the dead, that in everything he might be preeminent" (Col. 1:18).

Man is a Sinner	Christ Died for our Sins	Christ Rose from the Dead
"All have sinned and fall short of the glory of God" (Rom. 3:23).	But we "are justified by his grace as a gift, through the redemption that is in Christ Jesus, whom God put forward as a propitiation by his blood, to be received by faith" (Rom. 3:24-25).	Jesus, "who was delivered up for our trespasses and raised for our justification" (Rom 4:24-25).
"The wages of sin is death" (Rom. 6:23a).	"but the free gift of God is eternal life in Christ Jesus our Lord" (Rom. 6:23b).	"Our Savior Christ Jesus, who abolished death and brought life and immortality to light through the gospel" (2 Tim. 1:10).
"Christ Jesus came into the world to save sinners, of whom I am the foremost" (1 Tim. 1:15).	"Christ died for the ungodly" (Rom. 5:6). When "the mortal puts on immortality, then shall come to pass the saying that is written: 'Death is swallowed up in victory'" (1 Cor. 15:54).	"He who raised Christ Jesus from the dead will also give life to your mortal bodies through his Spirit who dwells in you" (Rom. 8:11).
"Through the law comes knowledge of sin" (Rom. 3:20). "For all who rely on works of the law are under a curse; for it is written, "Cursed be everyone who does not abide by all things written in the Book of the Law, and do them" (Gal. 3:10).	"Christ redeemed us from the curse of the law by becoming a curse for us—for it is written, 'Cursed is everyone who is hanged on a tree'" (Gal. 3:13). "So then, the law was our guardian until Christ came, in order that we might be justified by faith" (Gal. 3:24).	"Christ is the end of the law for righteousness to everyone who believes...because, if you confess with your mouth that Jesus is Lord and believe in your heart that God raised him from the dead, you will be saved" (Rom. 10:4, 9).

Man is a Sinner	Christ Died for our Sins	Christ Rose from the Dead
"None is righteous, no, not one" (Rom. 3:10). But "If our unrighteousness serves to show the righteousness of God, what shall we say?" (Rom. 3:5).	"For our sake he made him to be sin who knew no sin, so that in him we might become the righteousness of God" (2 Cor. 5:21). The one who "believes in him who justifies the ungodly, his faith is counted as righteousness" (Rom. 4:5).	Abraham's "faith was counted to him as righteousness. But the words 'it was counted to him' were not written for his sake alone, but for ours also. It will be counted to us who believe in him who raised from the dead Jesus our Lord" (Rom. 4:22-24).
"God shows his love for us in that while we were still sinners" (Rom. 5:8).	"Christ died for us. Since, therefore, we have now been justified by his blood, much more shall we be saved by him from the wrath of God" (Rom. 5:8-9; cf., 1 Thess. 5:9).	"Who is to condemn? Christ Jesus is the one who died—more than that, who was raised—who is at the right hand of God, who indeed is interceding for us" (Rom. 8:34).

When sinners receive the gospel by repentance and faith, something amazing happens—we are united together with Christ:

We Die with Christ	We are Buried with Christ	We are Raised with Christ
"Now if we have died with Christ, we believe that we will also live with him" (Rom. 6:8; cf., 2 Tim. 2:11).	"We were buried therefore with him by baptism into death" (Rom. 6:4a).	"in order that, just as Christ was raised from the dead by the glory of the Father, we too might walk in newness of life" (Rom. 6:4b).
"For you have died, and your life is hidden with Christ in God" (Col. 3:3).	"Having been buried with him in baptism" (Col. 2:12a),	"You were also raised with him through faith in the powerful working of God, who raised him from the dead" (Col. 2:12b).
"I have been crucified with Christ. It is no longer I who live, but Christ who lives in me. And the life I now live in the flesh I live by faith in the Son of God, who loved me and gave himself for me" (Gal. 2:20).	"Truly, truly, I say to you, unless a grain of wheat falls into the earth and dies, it remains alone; but if it dies, it bears much fruit" (John 12:24).	"Christ died and lived again, that he might be Lord both of the dead and of the living" (Rom. 14:9). "My aim is to know him, to experience the power of his resurrection" (Philip. 3:10, NET Bible).

If we define the root of the gospel correctly, we will see this perfect unity:

Paul summed it up perfectly:

"For if we have been united with him in a death like his, we shall certainly be united with him in a resurrection like his" (Rom. 6:5).

Gospel Harmony

Some skeptics try to pit Paul's teaching on the gospel as being contradictory with other New Testament teachings. Their favorite targets are to set Paul against Jesus, Paul against Peter, or Paul against James. Let's look first at the Paul against Jesus conjecture. In Acts chapter 9, we see the conversion of Saul (also known as Paul). Jesus called Saul "a chosen instrument of mine to carry my name before the Gentiles and kings and the children of Israel" (Acts 9:15). If Paul and Jesus were not in agreement, then why would Jesus call him "a chosen instrument of mine"?

In Acts 26, recounting his Damascus Road conversion, Paul said Jesus appeared to him for the purpose of appointing him as a servant and witness to open people's eyes, so that they may turn from the power of Satan to God and receive forgiveness of sins (26:16-18). Why would Jesus choose, appoint and send Paul to be His witness to open the eyes of people captured by Satan if Paul was not in agreement with Jesus on how one receives forgiveness of sins? Also remember that Paul told the Galatians that the gospel he preached was received through a revelation of Jesus Christ (Gal. 1:11-12). He also said, "Christ is speaking in me" (2 Cor. 13:3) and "the truth of Christ is in me" (2 Cor. 11:10). Considering all of Paul's statements, it seems quite absurd to claim any contradictions between Paul and Jesus.

What about the claims that Paul and Peter had different messages? Many claims of contradiction don't take into account the fact that Paul had been entrusted with the gospel to the Gentiles and Peter to the Jews (Gal. 2:7). These two audiences required a special approach by Paul and Peter, in many cases a distinct approach, but not a contradictory one. Paul was filled with the Holy Spirit (Acts 9:17) and led by the Spirit (16:6-20) just as Peter (Acts 10) and the other apostles were (John 14:26). The "Spirit of truth" (John 16:13) does not give contradictory guidance.

The same skeptics who try to pit one apostle against another do so by twisting various scriptures out of context. By claiming this contradiction, they also implicitly or explicitly deny the inerrancy of the Bible (2 Tim. 3:16-17). I'll let the Apostle Peter have the final word on whether his fellow Apostle Paul taught a contradictory gospel. When Peter wrote about Christians waiting for the Lord to return and the salvation He will bring, he wrote, "Just as our beloved brother Paul also wrote to you according to the wisdom given him, as he does in all his letters when he speaks in them of these matters. There are some things in them that are hard to understand, which the ignorant and unstable twist to their own destruction, as they do the other Scriptures" (2 Pet. 3:15-16). Peter acknowledges that Paul is a beloved brother and that all his letters are "Scripture." He adds that ignorant and unstable people twist Paul's letters, even to the point of claiming that Paul and Peter had different messages.

What about James and Paul? James says, "You see that a person is justified by works and not by faith alone" (James 2:24). Paul taught, "For we hold that one is justified by faith apart from works of the law." Most people just line these verses up side-by-side and claim "contradiction!" However, a serious student of the Bible, who looks into the deeper context of these teachings, will find that Paul and James were preaching the same gospel.

James and Paul both quote Genesis 15:6 to make their point, "And he [Abram] believed the LORD, and he counted it to him as righteousness." Notice that Paul states this is the point where Abraham was justified before God, "For if Abraham was justified by works, he has something to boast about, but not before God. For what does the Scripture say? 'Abraham believed God, and it was counted to him as righteousness'" (Rom 4:2-3). Paul points to Genesis 15:6 as the point Abraham was justified by belief and not by works. To further make his point, he adds, "David also speaks of the blessing of the one to whom God counts righteousness apart from works" (Rom 4:6).

In the same section where James states a person is justified by works and not by faith alone, he starts by quoting Genesis 22, when Abraham went to sacrifice Isaac (James 2:21). This event happened 25 years *after* Abraham was declared righteous by God in Genesis 15:6. James then proceeds to quote Genesis 15:6, "and the Scripture was fulfilled that says, 'Abraham believed God, and it was counted to him as righteousness'" (James 2:23). James is saying that the offering up of Isaac was a result of what happened 25 years earlier. In other words, after Abraham was declared righteous in Genesis 15:6, Abraham's works of offering up Isaac was a fulfillment, or a continuation, of works that flowed from him being declared righteous (justified) by God 25 years earlier. From that point on "he was called a friend of God" (James 2:23).

Therefore, it is clear that the works referenced in James 2:23 flowed from an already justified man. However, while only God justifies a person for salvation, for "It is God who justifies" (Rom. 8:33), our works, done *from* our justification, can and do justify us *before others*. Jesus told His disciples, "let your light shine before others, so that they may see your good works and give glory to your Father who is in heaven" (Matt. 5:16). Paul said our good works will mean that others will have "nothing evil to say about us" (Titus 2:7-8). James said when we make peace with others, we show them our "righteousness" (James 3:18). In commenting on James 2:21, Ron Rhodes writes, "Abraham was 'shown to be righteous' *before men* by his works. It was in this sense that James says Abraham was 'justified by works' when he offered his son Isaac upon the altar."[30]

James wrote his epistle to Christians, "my brothers" (James 1:2), who already knew that works flowed from a saving relationship with God (James 1:20-22, 27; 2:8, 14-18, 20, 24, 26; 3:13, 17-18; 4:7, 15; 5:14-16). Paul taught the exact same thing about believers (Eph. 2:10; 2 Cor. 9:8; Gal. 6:9-10; Col. 1:10, 2:6; 1 Thess. 2:12, 5:15; 2 Thess. 2:16-17, 3:13; 1 Tim. 6:18; 2 Tim. 2:21; Titus 2:14, 3:8, 14). Thus, James and Paul both taught that an already justified person's works proceed from a right standing, or from a saving, justified relationship with God. This was true of Abraham and it is true of us. When God justifies us (Rom. 8:33, 5:1), our good works can then justify us before men (James 3:13, 18), but not before God (Rom. 4:2).

One final point: both James and Paul were present at the Jerusalem Council in Acts 15. Keep in mind that the subject of that Council was the gospel of justification by faith (Acts 15:7, 11). There were those who had entered into the Christian faith that insisted that Gentiles must be circumcised (15:1) and keep the law (15:5) to be saved. James and Paul, who both spoke at the Council (15:12-13, 19), rejected this. The Council's final decision was that the Gentiles, just like Jewish believers in Jesus (15:11), "should hear the word of the gospel and believe" (Acts 15:7) and be saved having "cleansed their hearts by faith" (15:9), "through the grace of the Lord Jesus" (15:11). James, who presided over the Jerusalem Council (15:13, 19), was in complete agreement with Paul on this gospel matter. The fact is that while Paul stressed the root of justification when he said, "For we hold that one is justified by faith apart from works of the law", James stressed the fruit of justification in saying, "You see that a person is justified by works and not by faith alone" (James 2:24).

Same Gospel

The same confession Paul passed on in 1 Corinthians 15:1-8 is in perfect harmony with the rest of the New Testament teachings on the gospel. For example, when it comes to the statement that Christ died for our sins, Jesus and the apostles agree. Jesus said in Luke 5:32 "I have not come to call the righteous but sinners to repentance." That's because there is no one righteous to be called—only sinners. Matthew called us sinners (Matt. 1:21), as did Mark (Mark 1:4), Luke (Luke 1:77), John

---

[30] Ron Rhodes, Reasoning from the Scriptures with Catholics, pp. 148-149. Note that Roman Catholic apologists will claim there was no one there to witness Abraham's sacrifice. But there was! His name was Isaac.

(John 16:8; 1 John 1:8-10), Peter (1 Pet. 2:24; Acts 2:38, 5:31) and James (James 1:15; 2:10; 4:8; 5:16, 20).

We also see harmony in Christ's death for our sins and resurrection from the dead. Matthew writes, "From that time Jesus began to show his disciples that he must go to Jerusalem and suffer many things from the elders and chief priests and scribes, and be killed, and on the third day be raised" (Matt. 16:21). Jesus repeated this prophecy of His death and resurrection many times to His apostles (Matt. 17:9, 22-23; 20:19, 26:31-32; Mark 8:31, 9:31, 10:33, 14:27-28; Luke 9:22, 13:33; John 2:19-22). After rising from the dead, Jesus pointed to His death and resurrection, which allowed Him to enter into His glory, as things Moses and all the Prophets testified to (Luke 24:13-27). Thus, Paul confirms the essential elements of Jesus' gospel!

All the apostles were bold in preaching Christ's death and resurrection. Peter confirmed Paul's confession in 1 Corinthians 15:1-8 (1 Pet. 1:18-21; Acts 2:23-24, 32; 3:13-15, 26; 4:10-12; 5:30-32; 10:36-43), as did Matthew (Matt. 16:21; Matt. 17:9, 22-23; 20:19, 26:31-32), Mark (Mark 8:31, 9:31, 10:33, 14:27-28), Luke (Luke 9:22, 13:33), John (John 12:32-33) and the rest of Jesus' disciples (John 2:19-22; Acts 8:12).

Gospel Stages

Some still object, however, because Jesus taught and performed many things while mentioning "the gospel" *before* He died for the sins of His people or had been raised from the dead. Indeed, even before the cross and resurrection, Jesus said, "repent and believe in the gospel" (Mark 1:15). Why would Jesus command people to believe in the gospel when the foundational elements of the gospel (His death and resurrection) had not yet happened? The answer lies in the fact that Jesus, in His Person, *is* the gospel; however, the gospel, which involves Christ's life, death and resurrection, unfolded in stages. For example, the Old Testament prophesied the gospel and the coming Messiah. The gospel was lived out by Christ and then eventually was fully proclaimed by Jesus' disciples.

Stage One—The Gospel Prophesied

Paul spoke of the Old Testament prophesying the gospel. He wrote that "my gospel and the preaching of Jesus Christ" (Rom. 16:25) was spoken of in "the prophetic writings" (16:26). Paul added that he was a servant of Christ "set apart for the gospel of God, which he promised beforehand through his prophets in the holy Scriptures, concerning his Son" (Rom.

1:1-3; cf., 3:21; Gal. 3:8; Acts 10:43, 13:27, 26:22, 28:23). When Paul explained that New Covenant believers are no longer under a penalty for breaking the Old Covenant law, or obliged to keep dietary laws, festivals, new moons or the Sabbath, he wrote "These are a shadow of the things to come, but the substance belongs to Christ" (Col. 2:17). Peter, in saying we were "born again to a living hope through the resurrection of Jesus Christ from the dead" (1 Pet. 1:3), said, "Concerning this salvation, the prophets who prophesied about the grace that was to be yours searched and inquired carefully, inquiring what person or time the Spirit of Christ in them was indicating when he predicted the sufferings of Christ and the subsequent glories" (1:10-11). Peter said these Old Testament prophecies were all part of "the gospel" (1:12, NASB) which would be preached later.

Jesus pointed to the Old Testament as prophesying His gospel ministry. He quoted Isaiah saying, "this Scripture must be fulfilled in me: 'And he was numbered with the transgressors.' For what is written about me has its fulfillment" (Luke 22:37; cf., Acts 8:35). This is a quote from Isaiah 53:12, the same chapter that describes the Messiah being pierced for our sins (53:5) and having the iniquity of us all laid on Him by the Lord (53:6). As was His custom, Jesus went to the synagogue in Nazareth. He stood up and read from the scroll of the prophet Isaiah that was given to Him, "The Spirit of the Lord is upon me, because he has anointed me to proclaim good news to the poor." (Luke 4:18). Jesus had just quoted a messianic passage from Isaiah 61:1-2 and was about to apply it to Himself. As all eyes were fixed on Him, Jesus proclaimed, "Today this Scripture has been fulfilled in your hearing" (Luke 4:21). The implication was clear—I am the Messiah standing in front of you. This is a fulfillment the Jews rejected (4:28-29).

Prophesying His death and resurrection, Jesus said to His apostles, "See, we are going up to Jerusalem, and everything that is written about the Son of Man by the prophets will be accomplished" (Luke 18:31). Speaking to the Jews who were trying to kill Him, Jesus said, "You search the Scriptures because you think that in them you have eternal life; and it is they that bear witness about me" (John 5:39). He added, "For if you believed Moses, you would believe me; for he wrote of me" (5:46). On the last day of the feast of Tabernacles, speaking before the Jewish priests, Jesus proclaimed, "If anyone thirsts, let him come to me and drink. Whoever believes in me, as the Scripture has said, 'Out of his heart will flow rivers of living water'" (John 7:37-38). At His arrest, Jesus said, "all this has taken place that the Scriptures of the prophets might be fulfilled" (Matt. 26:56).

On the Road to Emmaus, two of Jesus' followers were discussing among themselves what the crucifixion and eye-witness accounts of the resurrection of their Lord really meant. The resurrected Christ then met them on the road and said, "'O foolish ones, and slow of heart to believe all that the prophets have spoken! Was it not necessary that the Christ should suffer these things and enter into his glory?' And beginning with Moses and all the Prophets, he interpreted to them in all the Scriptures the things concerning himself" (Luke 24:25-27). He added, "everything written about me in the Law of Moses and the Prophets and the Psalms must be fulfilled" (24:44; cf., Matt. 13:17; John 1:45, 8:56, 12:41).

Stage Two—the Gospel Lived Out

From His birth, obedience to the Father's will, sinless life, miracles, healings, teachings, death, resurrection and ascension, Jesus Christ was the embodiment of the gospel. Jesus lived out the gospel as a work the Father sent Him to do, "My food is to do the will of him who sent me and to accomplish his work" (John 4:34). What was that work? To live out and finish the gospel mission: "For this is the will of my Father, that everyone who looks on the Son and believes in him should have eternal life, and I will raise him up on the last day" (John 6:40). This work was ongoing, "My Father is working until now, and I am working" (John 5:17). In His High Priestly Prayer, right before He went to the cross, Jesus told the Father, "I glorified you on earth, having accomplished the work that you gave me to do" (John 17:4). His last words on the cross were "It is finished" (John 19:30).

From His youth, Jesus knew what His gospel mission was, for "I must be about my Father's business" (Luke 2:49, NKJV). Doing the Father's business meant "the Son can do nothing of his own accord, but only what he sees the Father doing" (John 5:19; cf., 8:28, 12:49, 14:31). Jesus' biggest delight was to keep His Father's commandments (John 15:10, 17:4). In saying "I keep his word" (John 8:55), Jesus knew He was sent to fulfill the law of God as a gospel requirement: "Do not think that I have come to abolish the Law or the Prophets; I have not come to abolish them but to fulfill them" (Matt. 5:17). By fulfilling the law, Jesus was "canceling the record of debt that stood against us with its legal demands. This he set aside, nailing it to the cross" (Col. 2:14). The law was not abolished but fulfilled by our Savior's perfect walk to the cross: "For

Christ is the end of the law for righteousness to everyone who believes" (Rom. 10:4).

Our righteous law-keeper was "a lamb without blemish or spot" (1 Pet. 1:19; cf., 1 Cor. 5:7; Eph. 5:2) who was able to "offer himself unblemished to God" (Heb. 9:14). Jesus lived out God's righteous requirements of eternal life on our behalf. Therefore, He became our righteousness before God (2 Cor. 5:21). Jesus so personified all of His Father's commandments that He could say, "Which one of you convicts me of sin?" (John 8:46) for "I have kept my Father's commandments and abide in his love" (John 15:10). From His incarnation to His glorification, Jesus lived out the gospel by accomplishing the work His Father sent Him to do.

During His earthly ministry, Jesus unveiled His gospel ministry by announcing at different times who He was. He proclaimed to be the Father's revelation to man (John 5:19, 8:26-28, 14:9; Matthew 11:27). He revealed, through the Father, that He was God's Son (Matt. 16:15-17; John 10:36), the Messiah (John 4:25-26; Luke 4:14-21), God's Prophet (Matt. 13:57), King (Matt. 21:1-5, 27:11; John 18:37) and by interceding and having the authority to forgive sins (Matt. 9:6; Luke 7:48)— God's "great high priest" (Heb. 4:14; cf., 5:5, 7:26, 10:21). Jesus proclaimed that the only way to the Father was through Him (John 14:6). He said He would be the judge of all men (John 5:22) and the One who gives eternal life (John 4:14, 5:21, 10:28) by raising up on the last day all that the Father has given Him (John 6:40).

The Living Gospel Offered to the Jews

While Christ was living out the gospel and "preaching the gospel" (Luke 20:1), He also sent the twelve disciples out to preach: "He sent them out to proclaim the kingdom of God" (Luke 9:2). They "went through the villages, preaching the gospel" (9:6). He also instructed them that whenever they enter a town "say to them, 'The kingdom of God has come upon you!'" (Luke 10:9, NET Bible). When Jesus talked about the kingdom of God being upon them, He was referring to Himself—"God with us" (Matt. 1:23). God, in the Person of Jesus Christ, had joined Himself to His creation in the incarnation. When Jesus said, "The kingdom of God has come upon you!", it was because God was literally, physically among them! He was the King! Four of Jesus' disciples, Andrew, Peter, Philip and Nathanael, all understood early in Christ's ministry that He was the Jews' promised Messiah who had come (John 1:40-51). In fact,

Nathanael confessed, "Rabbi, you are the Son of God! You are the King of Israel!" (1:49).

Nathanael wasn't the only one identifying Jesus as the King of Israel. When the wise men from the east came to Jerusalem, they asked, "Where is he who has been born king of the Jews?" (Matthew 2:2). The masses who had been fed by Jesus had intentions to take Him "by force to make him king" (John 6:15). The multitude of His disciples said, "Blessed is he who comes in the name of the Lord, even the King of Israel!" (John 12:13; cf., Luke 19:37-38). When Pilate asked, "Are you the King of the Jews?" (Matt. 27:11), Jesus replied, "For this purpose I was born and for this purpose I have come into the world" (John 18:37). Even those who mocked Him ironically identified Jesus as, "the Christ, the King of Israel" (Mark 15:32). The disciples who met the resurrected Christ on the road to Emmaus "had hoped that he was the one to redeem Israel" (Luke 24:21). Right before His ascension, Christ's disciples, still looking for an earthly kingdom, asked, "Lord, will you at this time restore the kingdom to Israel?" (Acts 1:6).

When Jesus instructed His disciples to "proclaim the kingdom of God" (Luke 9:2), or to go about "preaching the gospel" (Luke 9:6), this offer was "spoken first" (Acts 13:46) to the Jews. For the One who was "born king of the Jews" (Matt. 2:2) said, "I was sent only to the lost sheep of the house of Israel" (Matt. 15:24). When He sent out His twelve apostles, He instructed them to "Go nowhere among the Gentiles and enter no town of the Samaritans, but go rather to the lost sheep of the house of Israel. And proclaim as you go, saying, 'The kingdom of heaven is at hand'" (Matt. 10:5-7). While it is true that the unbelieving Jews rejected Jesus as the Messiah (Luke 4:21, 28-29) and failed to understand the scriptures that Jesus prophesied of His upcoming death and resurrection (John 2:18-21), their rejection of who Jesus was and a lack of understanding of His mission did not mean they were not given the gospel offer. Many people reject the gospel simply because of unbelief (Mark 6:2-6; Acts 19:8-9) or because, due to having hardened minds, "a veil lies over their hearts" (2 Cor. 3:14-16) to the Messiah's true identity. The gospel offer included the fact that Jesus was the Messiah and that the kingdom of God was in their midst (Luke 10:9). The kingdom that was offered to them included a Messiah that the scriptures prophesied would be sinless (Isa. 53:9; cf., John 8:46); a Messiah who "poured out his soul to death" and "bore the sin of many" (53:12); and a Messiah who would be raised on the third day (Matt. 12:40; Jonah 1:17, 2:10).

It is interesting to note that other Jews who heard this kingdom/gospel message believed. Joseph of Arimathea, a respected member of the Sanhedrin, who was "himself looking for the kingdom of God" (Mark 15:43) "was a disciple of Jesus" (John 19:38). Jesus preached "the kingdom of God" (John 3:3, 5) to Nicodemus and told him about being "born again" (3:3, 7). He also spoke to this "teacher of Israel" (3:10) of His upcoming death which would bring eternal life for all those who believe (3:14-16). Later, Nicodemus appeared to become a disciple of Jesus (John 19:39). John the Baptist had publicly introduced Jesus' ministry by stating "Behold, the Lamb of God, who takes away the sin of the world!" (John 1:29) and had been preaching for people to "Repent, for the kingdom of heaven is at hand" (Matt. 3:2). When Jesus came to Jews who had been listening to John, they became convinced that "everything that John said about this man [Jesus] was true. And many believed in him there" (John 10:41-42). After Jesus rose Lazarus from the dead, "Many of the Jews therefore, who had come with Mary and had seen what he did, believed in him" (John 11:45). The opposition of the Jewish leaders to Jesus was not unanimous, as "many even of the authorities believed in him" (John 12:42).

From Jews to Gentiles

Notice that Jesus warned His apostles that many would reject the offer of this new kingdom. "If anyone will not receive you or listen to your words, shake off the dust from your feet when you leave that house or town" (Matt. 10:14-15). Right after this, He told His disciples of things to come: "Beware of men, for they will deliver you over to courts and flog you in their synagogues, and you will be dragged before governors and kings for my sake, to bear witness before them and the Gentiles" (10:17-18). This kingdom/gospel offer, which came first to the Jews, would soon branch out due to Israel's unbelief (Rom. 11). Since "He came to his own, and his own people did not receive him" (John 1:11), Jesus prophesied that the gospel would not long be confined to the house of Israel, but soon be opened up to the Gentiles.

Of course, God knew the Jews would repudiate His Son (Matt. 21:33-43), for "this was the Lord's doing" (Matt. 21:42); it was all part of His gospel plan (1 Pet. 1:18-21; Rev. 13:8, NKJV). The Messiah the house of Israel rejected was not only the "king of the Jews" (Matt. 2:2), He was also the "King of the nations!" (Rev. 15:3). Because of this rejection, Jesus said, "Therefore I tell you, the kingdom of God will be taken away from you and given to a people producing its fruits" (Matt. 21:43; cf., Acts 28:28).

Stage Three—the Mystery of the Gospel Disclosed

While stage one prophesied the gospel, stage two saw the gospel come alive in the unfolding life, death and resurrection of Jesus Christ. Now, stage three fully unveils the gospel which Paul called a mystery which has been disclosed: "Now to him who is able to strengthen you according to my gospel and the preaching of Jesus Christ, according to the revelation of the mystery that was kept secret for long ages but has now been disclosed and through the prophetic writings has been made known to all nations, according to the command of the eternal God" (Rom. 16:25-26; cf., Eph. 1:9, 3:9, 6:19; Col. 2:2, 4:3). Elsewhere Paul wrote, "I became a minister according to the stewardship from God that was given to me for you, to make the word of God fully known, the mystery hidden for ages and generations but now revealed to his saints" (Col. 1:25-26).

What is this mystery now revealed? That both Jew and Gentile were to be joined together in one body, fellow heirs united in the only hope for both—Jesus Christ. Paul wrote, "This mystery is that the Gentiles are fellow heirs, members of the same body, and partakers of the promise in Christ Jesus through the gospel" (Eph. 3:6). For "God chose to make known how great among the Gentiles are the riches of the glory of this mystery, which is Christ in you, the hope of glory" (Col. 1:27). The mystery is not that the Gentiles would be saved, for Isaiah prophesied that Israel would be "a light to the Gentiles" for "salvation unto the end of the earth" (Isa. 49:6, KJV; cf. Matt. 12:15-21; Rom. 15:12). Even Simeon, who was waiting for Israel's Messiah, took baby Jesus up in his arms and blessed God saying, "for my eyes have seen your salvation that you have prepared in the presence of all peoples, a light for revelation to the Gentiles, and for glory to your people Israel" (Luke 2:25-32; cf. Acts 26:23). The mystery was that Jews and Gentiles, who were both trusting in the gospel, would be joined together. This was a revolutionary concept for these former enemies.[31]

After His resurrection, Jesus instructed His disciples to "Go into all the world and proclaim the gospel to the whole creation" (Mark 16:15). He added, "Go therefore and make disciples of all nations, baptizing them in the name of the Father and of the Son and of the Holy Spirit" (Matt. 28:19). Peter, the apostle to the Jews (Gal. 2:7), was later in-

---

[31] Some Jewish men prayed, "I thank God that you have not made me a Gentile, a slave, or a woman."

structed to witness the gospel to the Gentiles (Acts 10, 11). Paul was commissioned as Jesus' "chosen instrument of mine to carry my name before the Gentiles" (Acts 9:15; cf., Gal. 1:16). Paul and Barnabas told the house of Israel, "It was necessary that the word of God be spoken first to you. Since you thrust it aside and judge yourselves unworthy of eternal life, behold, we are turning to the Gentiles" (Acts 13:46). Things were officially settled by the church at the Jerusalem Council, "the Gentiles should hear the word of the gospel and believe" (Acts 15:7).

Gospel Illumination Through the Spirit

Jesus taught His disciples about many things pertaining to the gospel, including repentance (Matt. 4:17; Mark 1:15), faith (Matt. 17:20; Mark 11:22; Luke 7:50), being born again (John 3:1-8), justification (Luke 18:9-14), sanctification (Mark 8:34-35; John 17:17) and glorification (John 6:44), all while prophesying His own death and resurrection (Luke 9:22). Yet, He said the Spirit still had to come to "guide you into all the truth" (John 16:13). The fact is that Jesus' disciples did not fully comprehend the gospel in all its glory until after He was raised from the dead. For example, as Jesus fulfilled Old Testament prophecies about Himself, "His disciples did not understand these things at first, but when Jesus was glorified, then they remembered that these things had been written about him and had been done to him" (John 12:16; cf., 2:22; Luke 18:31-34, 24:25-27). What changed? The illumination of the Holy Spirt was now upon them.

In speaking about Christ crucified, Paul said the message of the cross could not be understood outside of a "demonstration of the Spirit and of power, so that your faith might not rest in the wisdom of men but in the power of God" (1 Cor. 2:4-5). He said the rulers of this age lacked the Spirit and thus did not understand the "secret and hidden wisdom of God, which God decreed before the ages for our glory. None of the rulers of this age understood this, for if they had, they would not have crucified the Lord of glory" (2:7-8). Paul then said of this secret and hidden wisdom, "these things God has revealed to us through the Spirit. For the Spirit searches everything, even the depths of God" (1 Cor. 2:10). In commenting on this passage, the ESV Study Bible says, "Mere intellectual persuasion does not save people. Saving faith is produced by the heart-changing power of the Holy Spirit as the gospel is proclaimed."[32]

---

[32] ESV Study Bible, Crossway Bibles, Wheaton, Illinois, p. 2194.

Jesus knew that His disciples had tunnel vision as they were focusing on the Messiah bringing an immediate earthly kingdom. Right before Christ's ascension, the disciples had come together, asking him, "Lord, will you at this time restore the kingdom to Israel?" (Acts 1:6). He told them not to be concerned with times and dates the Father had fixed, but instead to prepare for new empowerment from above to spread the good news of the gospel: "But you will receive power when the Holy Spirit has come upon you, and you will be my witnesses in Jerusalem and in all Judea and Samaria, and to the end of the earth" (1:8). Earlier, Jesus told them that when He ascended to the Father, the Holy Spirit would be sent to them (John 14:16-17, 15:26, 16:7, 7:39). He added, "I still have many things to say to you, but you cannot bear them now. When the Spirit of truth comes, he will guide you into all the truth, for he will not speak on his own authority, but whatever he hears he will speak, and he will declare to you the things that are to come" (John 16:12-13).

One thing the Spirit guided the disciples into was a fuller understanding of the revelation Jesus had already given them: "the Holy Spirit, whom the Father will send in my name, he will teach you all things and bring to your remembrance all that I have said to you" (John 14:26). Secondly, since the Spirit only speaks "whatever he hears" (John 16:13), we know the guidance He would give the disciples would be in complete conformity with the teachings Jesus received from the Father (John 5:19; cf., 8:28; 12:49; 14:10, 31; 17:7-8) and had already shared with His disciples (John 15:15). Thirdly, the Spirit would disclose to them a better understanding into the nuances of the gospel, "the mystery that was kept secret for long ages but has now been disclosed" (Rom. 16:25-26). Here we can see where one of the Spirit's roles was to clear up their thinking about what had already been revealed.

Before His ascension, Jesus had already "given commands through the Holy Spirit to the apostles whom he had chosen" (Acts 1:2). Any further things Jesus had to say to them would be shown to them through the "Spirit of Christ" (Rom. 8:9-11), who would permanently dwell in them. We know that the disciples "were all filled with the Holy Spirit" (Acts 2:4) at the day of Pentecost. Saul was "filled with the Holy Spirit" (Acts 9:17) following his Damascus Road conversion. As a result, among those disciples who penned scripture, their writings were not "by the will of man, but men spoke from God as they were carried along by the Holy Spirit" (2 Pet. 1:21). The Holy Spirit would give the church written instructions through these men on all matters pertaining to teaching, reproof, correction, and for training in righteousness, to equip Christians for every good work (2 Tim 3:16-17).

As we survey the Holy Spirit's work that Jesus promised, the early evangelists were to receive power from the Spirit to be the Lord's witnesses "to the end of the earth" (Acts 1:8). Jesus also said of the Holy Spirit, "When he comes, he will convict the world concerning sin and righteousness and judgment" (John 16:8). This new power from upon high, combined with the Holy Spirit convicting people of their sin and unbelief, allowed the disciples to witness with a new confidence. The disciples "were all filled with the Holy Spirit and continued to speak the word of God with boldness" (Acts 4:31). Through the Spirit's power, they were obedient to sharing the gospel despite the authorities call for them to stop (Acts 5:28-32). Philip the evangelist (Acts 21:8) was instructed by the Spirit to convert the Ethiopian eunuch: "the Spirit said to Philip, 'Go over and join this chariot'" (Acts 8:29). Paul's gospel message was a "demonstration of the Spirit and of power" (1 Cor. 2:4; cf., 1 Thess. 1:5).

The Holy Spirit became the church's guiding force in its evangelizing effort. The Spirit sent Peter to share the good news with Cornelius (Acts 10:19-24). As Peter shared the gospel, "the Holy Spirit fell on all who heard the word" (Acts 10:44). Cornelius and his household were the first Gentiles to be taken into the church. Jesus, in warning His disciples of future persecution, said, "when they bring you before the synagogues and the rulers and the authorities, do not be anxious about how you should defend yourself or what you should say, for the Holy Spirit will teach you in that very hour what you ought to say" (Luke 12:11-12). Barnabas and Saul were "Set apart" (Acts 13:2) and "sent out by the Holy Spirit" (13:4). Paul talked about how the Holy Spirit told him where to go and where not to go as he was "forbidden by the Holy Spirit to speak the word in Asia" (Acts 16:6; cf., 21:4). We also see where "signs and wonders, by the power of the Spirit of God" (Rom. 15:19) accompanied Paul's gospel proclamation.

When church leaders at the Jerusalem Council decided that the Gentiles should hear the word of the gospel and believe and be saved by faith through the grace of the Lord Jesus (Acts 15:7, 9, 11), just as the Jewish believers were, we read where that decision "seemed good to the Holy Spirit and to us" (15:28). Jewish and Gentile believers in Christ "are being built together into a dwelling place for God by the Spirit" (Eph. 2:22). This mystery of the gospel has been revealed "by the Spirit" (Eph. 3:4-6). When Paul talked about how Jewish and Gentile believers would together "be strengthened with power through his Spirit" (Eph. 3:16), he said this union "in the church and in Christ Jesus" will be "throughout all generations, forever and ever. Amen" (Eph. 3:21).

We see where the Holy Spirit comes to build and comfort the church: "the church…was being built up. And walking in the fear of the Lord and in the comfort of the Holy Spirit, it multiplied" (Acts 9:31). For "God's Spirit dwells in" the church (1 Cor. 3:16) and in its church members, as "Your body is a temple of the Holy Spirit within you" (1 Cor. 6:19). The Spirit converts people into the body: "For in one Spirit we were all baptized into one body" (1 Cor. 12:13). God sent the Spirit to give us confidence in our faith as He has "put his seal on us and given us his Spirit in our hearts as a guarantee" (2 Cor. 1:22; cf., 5:5; Eph. 1:13, 4:30). "The Spirit himself bears witness with our spirit that we are children of God" (Rom. 8:16). God assures us that our salvation by faith "Having begun by the Spirit" (Gal. 3:3) will also be finished by the Spirit.

Paul, who said he was "taught by the Spirit" (1 Cor. 2:13; cf., 2 Pet. 1:21), gave foundational understandings and instructions to the church about many important things. He wrote about the church as the body of Christ (Rom. 12:5; 1 Cor. 12:27; Eph. 4:12, 15-16) with Jesus as its head (Eph. 1:22-23, 5:23; Col. 1:24). Through the Spirit, Paul gave instructions for church leadership. This included qualifications for elders and deacons (1 Tim. 3; Titus 1:5-10; 1 Tim. 2:12, 5:17; cf., 1 Pet. 5:1-5; Heb. 13:17). Paul told the Ephesian elders to "Pay careful attention to yourselves and to all the flock, in which the Holy Spirit has made you overseers, to care for the church of God" (Acts 20:28). When Paul talked about being "eager to maintain the unity of the Spirit" (Eph. 4:5), he said Jesus has gifted the church with evangelists, pastors and teachers "to equip the saints for the work of ministry, for building up the body of Christ" (Eph. 4:11-12).

The Holy Spirit came to give us "varieties of gifts" (1 Cor. 12:4). Each believer is given their own gift(s). This a "manifestation of the Spirit" (12:7), the "Spirit, who apportions to each one individually as he wills" (12:11; cf. Heb. 2:4). These gifts of the Spirit are for "building up the church" (1 Cor. 14:12) and for unity so "there may be no division in the body" (1 Cor. 12:25). One of the gifts "given through the Spirit" (1 Cor. 12:8) is "the ability to distinguish between spirits" (1 Cor. 12:10). Those to whom the Spirit has given the gift of distinguishing between spirits are important to the church because many can deceive Christians with false gospels and teachings from other spirits. For we read, "the Spirit expressly says that in later times some will depart from the faith by devoting themselves to deceitful spirits and teachings of demons" (1 Tim. 4:1; cf., 1 John 4:2, 6; Jude 1:19). Therefore, "By the Holy Spirit who dwells within us, guard the good deposit entrusted to you" (2 Tim. 1:14). We do warfare against evil spirits with "the sword of the Spirit, which is the word of God" (Eph. 6:17).

Paul writes, "Now we have received not the spirit of the world, but the Spirit who is from God, that we might understand the things freely given us by God" (1 Cor. 2:12). "By the Holy Spirit who dwells within us" (2 Tim. 1:14) we know that we are "justified in the name of the Lord Jesus Christ and by the Spirit of our God" (1 Cor. 6:11; cf., Titus 3:4-7). We are sanctified by the Spirit: "God chose you as the firstfruits to be saved, through sanctification by the Spirit and belief in the truth" (2 Thess. 2:13; cf., 1 Pet. 1:2). Furthermore, we will be glorified by the Spirit: "If the Spirit of him who raised Jesus from the dead dwells in you, he who raised Christ Jesus from the dead will also give life to your mortal bodies through his Spirit who dwells in you" (Rom. 8:11).

Of the many reasons for which God sent "the Helper" (John 15:26), I think the biggest one was because "no one can say, 'Jesus is Lord,' except by the Holy Spirit" (1 Cor. 12:3, NASB). Without the Spirit's conviction of sin, righteousness and judgment (John 16:8) in a person's heart, no one will ever confess Jesus as Lord. Let us be like the disciples who "were all filled with the Holy Spirit and continued to speak the word of God with boldness" (Acts 4:31). Let us not forget our calling to share the hope that is within us as we ask "that the God of our Lord Jesus Christ, the Father of glory, may give you the Spirit of wisdom and of revelation in the knowledge of him, having the eyes of your hearts enlightened, that you may know what is the hope to which he has called you" (Eph. 1:17-18). This wisdom, knowledge, enlightenment and hope should lead us to devote our lives to telling others about the gospel. Our lives should have a "participation in the Spirit" (Philip. 2:1).

The Proper Time

We have seen where the Old Testament prophesied the coming of the Messiah. Jesus fulfilled His messianic roles by living out the gospel, and after His ascension, the Holy Spirit came to guide the disciples into all truth, allowing them to fully proclaim the mystery of the gospel. In writing to Titus, a Gentile convert, Paul described himself as "a servant of God and an apostle of Jesus Christ, for the sake of the faith of God's elect and their knowledge of the truth, which accords with godliness, in hope of eternal life, which God, who never lies, promised before the ages began and *at the proper time* manifested in his word through the preaching with which I have been entrusted by the command of God our Savior" (Titus 1:1-3). Paul said God entrusted him with the preaching of this good news of eternal life "at the proper time" (1 Tim. 2:5-7). When God brought Jews and Gentiles together in a common faith and gave the Holy Spirit to guide the disciples into all truth, it then became the proper time for the mystery of the gospel to be fully known (Eph. 3:6; Col. 1:27).

The Gospel Fully Preached

As King Solomon wrote, "There is an appointed time for everything" (Ecc. 3:1, NASB). The Apostle Paul reported when he met the risen Christ on the road to Damascus, "the Lord said to me, 'Rise, and go into Damascus, and there you will be told all that is appointed for you to do'" (Acts 22:10). Jesus also told Paul, "'I have appeared to you for this purpose, to appoint you as a servant and witness to the things in which you have seen me and to those in which I will appear to you, delivering you from your people and from the Gentiles—to whom I am sending you to open their eyes, so that they may turn from darkness to light and from the power of Satan to God, that they may receive forgiveness of sins and a place among those who are sanctified by faith in me'" (Acts 26:16-18; cf., 9:15).

Paul was appointed at the proper time to make fully known the "gospel and the preaching of Jesus Christ, according to the revelation of the mystery that was kept secret for long ages" (Rom. 16:25), "the mystery hidden for ages and generations but now revealed to his saints" (Col. 1:26). All preceding ages were appointed for this proper time. This was the time God intended to reveal Christ, and His time is always the perfect time. This is why Paul said, "I have fully preached the gospel of Christ" (Rom. 15:19, NASB). After he told Timothy to "do the work of an evangelist" (2 Tim. 4:5), he said, "the Lord stood by me and strengthened me, so that through me the message might be fully proclaimed and all the Gentiles might hear it" (2 Tim. 4:17). Paul added, "God chose to make known how great among the Gentiles are the riches of the glory of this mystery, which is Christ in you, the hope of glory" (Col. 1:27). His hope was that all would have "full assurance of understanding and the knowledge of God's mystery, which is Christ"

(Col. 2:2; cf., 4:3). Speaking of "the hope of the gospel" (Col. 1:23), he said he has made "the word of God fully known" (1:25). When Paul told the Ephesian elders "I may finish my course and the ministry that I received from the Lord Jesus, to testify to the gospel of the grace of God" (Acts 20:24), he said, "I did not shrink from declaring to you the whole counsel of God" (20:27).

Paul's gospel message, that he fully preached, fully proclaimed and fully made know, can be reduced to this: "I decided to know nothing among you except Jesus Christ and him crucified" (1 Cor. 2:2; cf., Gal. 6:14). For Paul, knowing nothing except Jesus Christ and Him crucified, also meant knowing the resurrection, for he taught that the crucifixion and the resurrection are two parts of the same saving event. Paul reminded us that the cross without a risen Christ is of no effect, for "if Christ has not been raised, your faith is futile and you are still in your sins" (1 Cor. 15:17). Paul taught that Jesus' death and resurrection are linked together in an indissoluble bond, a link that is applied to our new life as well: "For if we have been united with him in a death like his, we shall certainly be united with him in a resurrection like his" (Rom. 6:5; cf., Gal. 2:20; Eph. 2:5-6; Col. 2:12-14, 3:1-4, 2 Tim. 2:11). Paul said he set aside all things to gain Christ and be found in Him "that I may know him and the power of his resurrection, and may share his sufferings, becoming like him in his death" (Philip. 3:10).

Concerning this gospel, all the prophets testified to it, Jesus fulfilled it, the Holy Spirit guided the disciples into all the truth of it, and Paul and his fellow disciples fully proclaimed it and made it the center of their lives and witness.

The Gospel of the Kingdom

The four gospels are about Jesus, who in His incarnate person was and is the gospel. Everything He did, everything He taught, in one way or another, pointed to the root of the gospel that would bring about His kingdom. Jesus preached the good news of the coming of the kingdom of God (Luke 4:43) and told His disciples to do the same (Luke 9:2). The gospel of the kingdom of God (Matt. 4:23, 9:35, 24:14) is the good news that God will establish His kingdom on earth through the two advents of the Lord Jesus Christ. The First Advent brought us the root of the gospel. The Second Advent will culminate in a kingdom of a people "who are enrolled in heaven" (Heb. 12:23) and "in Christ Jesus with eternal glory" (2 Tim. 2:10), carrying out the fruit of the gospel by worshiping Him (Rev. 22:3) and reigning with Him (Rev. 22:5).

Paul, Jesus and all the apostles are in harmony on the root of the gospel. To define the gospel correctly is the first step in being an effective evangelist. Let there be no ambiguity about what the root of the gospel is:

Christ died for our sins in accordance with the Scriptures, that he was buried, that he was raised on the third day in accordance with the Scriptures.

Those of us on The Evangelism Circle should know the distinction between the root of the gospel and the fruit of the gospel. We will discuss that in our next chapter.

8) GOSPEL ROOT AND ITS BRANCHES

"*I, Jesus…am the root and the descendant of David*" (Revelation 22:16). "*In that day the root of Jesse, who shall stand as a signal for the peoples—of him shall the nations inquire, and his resting place shall be glorious*" (Isaiah 11:10; cf., Rom. 15:12).

We have seen that the root of the gospel consists of the foundational teaching that man is a sinner and that Christ died for our sins and rose from the dead. However, just like branches spring up from a root, Paul's teaching branches out from the root of the gospel. Paul had a lot to say about the gospel beyond the foundational statement he shared in 1 Corinthians 15:1-8, even though everything he said in scripture about the gospel flowed from that foundational creed. Next, we will look at how Paul gives us more insight into the gospel he received and delivered, and how it is in perfect harmony with the rest of the New Testament.

The Apostle Paul	Jesus	Disciples of Christ
"The Scripture, foreseeing that God would justify the Gentiles by faith, preached the gospel beforehand to Abraham" (Gal. 3:8).	"Your father Abraham rejoiced that he would see my day. He saw it and was glad" (John 8:56).	Peter told the men of Israel, "The God of Abraham...glorified his servant Jesus, whom you delivered over...you killed the Author of life, whom God raised from the dead" (Acts 3:13-15; cf., Acts 8:30, 35).
"By him [Jesus] everyone who believes is freed from everything from which you could not be freed by the law of Moses" (Acts 13:39).	"Do not think that I have come to abolish the Law or the Prophets; I have not come to abolish them but to fulfill them" (Matt. 5:17).	"For the law made nothing perfect; but on the other hand, a better hope is introduced, through which we draw near to God" (Heb. 7:19), "a Son who has been made perfect forever" (7:28).
"You who boast in the law dishonor God by breaking the law" (Rom. 2:23).	"Has not Moses given you the law? Yet none of you keeps the law" (John 7:19).	"You who received the law as delivered by angels and did not keep it" (Acts 7:53).
"For we hold that one is justified by faith apart from works of the law" (Rom. 3:28). "We know that a person is not justified by works of the law but through faith in Jesus Christ" (Gal. 2:16).	"For I tell you, unless your righteousness exceeds that of the scribes and Pharisees, you will never enter the kingdom of heaven" (Matt. 5:20). "Woe to you, scribes and Pharisees, hypocrites!...you also outwardly appear righteous to others, but within you are full of hypocrisy and lawlessness" (Matt. 23:27-28).	"Some believers who belonged to the party of the Pharisees rose up and said, 'It is necessary to circumcise them and to order them to keep the law of Moses.'.... Peter stood up and said...'why are you putting God to the test by placing a yoke on the neck of the disciples that neither our fathers nor we have been able to bear? But we believe that we will be saved through the grace of the Lord Jesus'" (Acts 15:5-11).
"The Spirit gives life" (2 Cor. 3:6). We "worship by the Spirit of God and glory in Christ Jesus and put no confidence in the flesh" (Philip 3:3).	"It is the Spirit who gives life; the flesh is no help at all" (John 6:63).	"How much more will the blood of Christ, who through the eternal Spirit offered himself without blemish to God, purify our conscience from dead works to serve the living God" (Heb. 9:14).

The Apostle Paul	Jesus	Disciples of Christ
"Our Savior Christ Jesus, who abolished death and brought life and immortality to light through the gospel" (2 Tim. 1:10).	"I am the resurrection and the life. Whoever believes in me, though he die, yet shall he live, and everyone who lives and believes in me shall never die" (John 11:25-26). "The Son gives life to whom he will" (John 5:21).	"And this is the testimony, that God gave us eternal life, and this life is in his Son. Whoever has the Son has life; whoever does not have the Son of God does not have life" (1 John 5:11-12).
"None is righteous, no, not one" (Rom. 3:10).	"No one is good except God alone" (Mark 10:18).	"For Christ also suffered once for sins, the righteous for the unrighteous" (1 Pet. 3:18).
"For our sake he made him to be sin who knew no sin, so that in him we might become the righteousness of God" (2 Cor. 5:21)	"Which one of you convicts me of sin?" (John 8:46). "Jesus said He came "to fulfill all righteousness" (Matt 3:15).	"To those who have obtained a faith of equal standing with ours by the righteousness of our God and Savior Jesus Christ" (2 Pet. 1:1). "You know that he appeared in order to take away sins, and in him there is no sin" (1 John 3:5).
"He saved us, not because of works done by us in righteousness, but according to his own mercy" (Titus 3:5).	"It is done! I am the Alpha and the Omega, the beginning and the end. To the thirsty I will give from the spring of the water of life without payment" (Rev. 21:6).	"God opposes the proud but gives grace to the humble" (James 4:6).
"Therefore, since we have been justified by faith, we have peace with God through our Lord Jesus Christ" (Rom. 5:1).	"Your sins are forgiven.... Your faith has saved you; go in peace" (Luke 7:48, 50).	"To those who are called, beloved in God the Father and kept for Jesus Christ: May mercy, peace, and love be multiplied to you" (Jude 1:1-2).

Fruit Harmony

Part of Paul's gospel is that once sinners place their faith and trust in Christ's death and resurrection, a righteousness from God which is apart from ourselves (2 Peter 1:1; Philip. 3:9) is credited to us (2 Cor. 5:21; Rom. 4:1-5) and takes over our lives (Rom. 6:19). Those who have been "justified by his grace as a gift, through the redemption that is in Christ Jesus" (Rom. 3:24) are then transformed into the character of His Son (Rom. 8:29) as we are "sanctified by the Holy Spirit" (Rom. 15:16) living in us (1 Cor. 6:19). Only Christians, who have already been justified/saved by God's grace alone (as documented in the charts above), can enter into this sanctification.

In our sanctification process, we do the works that God prepared in advance for us to do (Eph. 2:10). We are obedient to God (John 14:21), but as discussed in chapter 7, these works and obedience are not something we do to get to heaven. We do them because we love the God who has already justified us "by his grace as a gift, through the redemption that is in Christ Jesus" (Rom. 3:24). The following chart defines this sanctification stage, what we call the fruit of the gospel. Again, we see how Paul's teaching on sanctification is in perfect harmony with the rest of the New Testament.

The Apostle Paul	Jesus	Disciples of Christ
"He has delivered us from the domain of darkness and transferred us to the kingdom of his beloved Son" (Col. 1:13). "At one time you were darkness, but now you are light in the Lord. Walk as children of light (for the fruit of light is found in all that is good and right and true)" (Eph. 5:8-9).	"I am the light of the world. Whoever follows me will not walk in darkness, but will have the light of life" (John 8:12; cf., 12:46). "Let your light shine before others, so that they may see your good works and give glory to your Father who is in heaven" (Matt. 5:16; cf., John 13:1-17).	He "called you out of darkness into his marvelous light" (1 Pet. 2:9). "Walk in the light, as he is in the light" (1 John 1:7). "Through him then let us continually offer up a sacrifice of praise to God, that is, the fruit of lips that acknowledge his name. Do not neglect to do good" (Heb. 13:15-16).
"For we are his workmanship, created in Christ Jesus for good works, which God prepared beforehand, that we should walk in them" (Eph. 2:10).	"As for what was sown on good soil, this is the one who hears the word and understands it. He indeed bears fruit and yields, in one case a hundredfold, in another sixty, and in another thirty" (Matt. 13:23).	"And let us consider how to stir up one another to love and good works" (Heb. 10:24). "By his good conduct let him show his works" (James 3:13).
"Those who have believed in God may be careful to devote themselves to good works. These things are excellent and profitable for people" (Titus 3:8).	"I am the vine; you are the branches. Whoever abides in me and I in him, he it is that bears much fruit, for apart from me you can do nothing" (John 15:5).	"Be doers of the word, and not hearers only" (James 1:22). "As he who called you is holy, you also be holy in all your conduct" (1 Pet. 1:14-15).

The Apostle Paul	Jesus	Disciples of Christ
"Now we know that the law is good, if one uses it lawfully" (1 Tim. 1:8). "So the law is holy" (Rom. 7:12). "I delight in the law of God" (Rom. 7:22). "Bear one another's burdens, and so fulfill the law of Christ" (Gal. 6:2).	"Whoever has my commandments and keeps them, he it is who loves me" (John 14:21). "When you have done all that you were commanded, say, 'We are unworthy servants; we have only done what was our duty'" (Luke 17:10).	"For this is the love of God, that we keep his commandments. And his commandments are not burdensome" (1 John 5:3). "And by this we know that we have come to know him, if we keep his commandments" (1 John 2:3).
"Our great God and Savior Jesus Christ, who gave himself for us to redeem us from all lawlessness and to purify for himself a people for his own possession who are zealous for good works" (Titus 2:13-14).	"I am the good shepherd. I know my own and my own know me" (John 10:14). "My sheep hear my voice, and I know them, and they follow me" (10:27). Jesus gives His kingdom "to a people producing its fruits" (Matt. 21:43).	"But you are a chosen race, a royal priesthood, a holy nation, a people for his own possession, that you may proclaim the excellencies of him" (1 Pet. 2:9).
We are "a vessel for honorable use, set apart as holy, useful to the master of the house, ready for every good work" (2 Tim. 2:21).	"If anyone serves me, the Father will honor him" (John 12:26). "My Father is glorified, that you bear much fruit and so prove to be my disciples" (John 15:8).	"What sort of people ought you to be in lives of holiness and godliness, waiting for and hastening the coming of the day of God" (2 Pet. 3:11-12).
"Let your manner of life be worthy of the gospel of Christ" (Philip. 1:27).	"Whoever does not take his cross and follow me is not worthy of me" (Mat. 10:38).	"For God is not unjust so as to overlook your work and the love that you have shown for his name" (Heb. 6:10).
"Continue in the faith, stable and steadfast, not shifting from the hope of the gospel that you heard" (Col. 1:23).	"Jesus said to the twelve, 'Do you want to go away as well?' Simon Peter answered him, 'Lord, to whom shall we go? You have the words of eternal life'" (John 6:67-68).	"The apostles said to the Lord, 'Increase our faith!'" (Luke 17:5). We are "looking to Jesus, the founder and perfecter of our faith" (Heb. 12:2).

The Apostle Paul	Jesus	Disciples of Christ
"When you heard the word of truth, the gospel of your salvation, and believed in him, were sealed with the promised Holy Spirit, who is the guarantee of our inheritance" (Eph. 1:13-14).	"Whoever believes in me, as the Scripture has said, 'Out of his heart will flow rivers of living water.' Now this he said about the Spirit, whom those who believed in him were to receive" (John 7:38-39).	"Whoever keeps his commandments abides in God, and God in him. And by this we know that he abides in us, by the Spirit whom he has given us" (1 John 3:24).
"Christ Jesus is the one who died—more than that, who was raised—who is at the right hand of God, who indeed is interceding for us" (Rom. 8:34). "If then you have been raised with Christ, seek the things that are above, where Christ is, seated at the right hand of God" (Col. 3:1).	"From now on the Son of Man shall be seated at the right hand of the power of God" (Luke 22:69). "You heard me say to you, 'I am going away, and I will come to you.' If you loved me, you would have rejoiced, because I am going to the Father" (John 14:28).	"He is able to save to the uttermost those who draw near to God through him, since he always lives to make intercession for them" (Heb. 7:25). "If anyone does sin, we have an advocate with the Father, Jesus Christ the righteous" (1 John 2:1).
"He called you through our gospel, so that you may obtain the glory of our Lord Jesus Christ" (2 Thess. 2:14). "When Christ who is your life appears, then you also will appear with him in glory" (Col. 3:4).	"The glory that you have given me I have given to them, that they may be one even as we are one, I in them and you in me, that they may become perfectly one, so that the world may know that you sent me and loved them even as you loved me" (John 17:22-23).	Jesus is "bringing many sons to glory" (Heb. 2:10). "The Spirit of glory and of God rests upon you" (1 Pet. 4:14). "And when the chief Shepherd appears, you will receive the unfading crown of glory" (1 Pet. 5:4).

Root and Fruit Distinction

It is important that we make a distinction between the root of the gospel and the fruit of the gospel, as the following illustration shows.

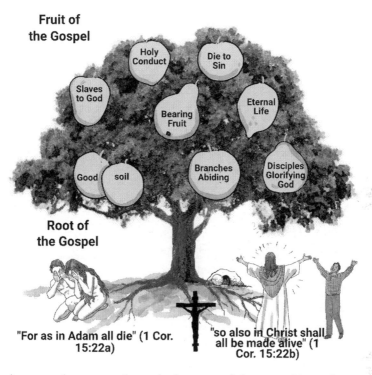

A person has to go through the root of the gospel in order to produce the fruit of the gospel.

Root of the Gospel	Fruit of the Gospel
"Christ died for our sins in accordance with the scriptures, that he was buried, that he was raised on the third day in accordance with the Scriptures." (1 Cor. 15:3-4).	"Now that you have been set free from sin and have become slaves of God, the fruit you get leads to sanctification and its end, eternal life" (Rom. 6:22).
"Because of one man's trespass, death reigned through that one man, much more will those who receive the abundance of grace and the free gift of righteousness reign in life through the one man Jesus Christ" (Rom. 5:17).	Jesus told His disciples, "I am the vine; you are the branches. Whoever abides in me and I in him, he it is that bears much fruit, for apart from me you can do nothing" (John 15:5).

Root of the Gospel	Fruit of the Gospel
"My brothers, you also have died to the law through the body of Christ, so that you may belong to another, to him who has been raised from the dead,	in order that we may bear fruit for God" (Rom. 7:4).
"Our Savior Christ Jesus, who abolished death and brought life and immortality to light through the gospel" (2 Tim. 1:10).	"The gospel, which has come to you, as indeed in the whole world it is bearing fruit and increasing—as it also does among you, since the day you heard it and understood the grace of God in truth" (Col. 1:5-6).
"He has delivered us from the domain of darkness and transferred us to the kingdom of his beloved Son" (Col. 1:13).	"Those that were sown on the good soil are the ones who hear the word and accept it and bear fruit" (Mark 4:20).
Jesus said to the Father, "I glorified you on earth, having accomplished the work that you gave me to do" (John 17:4).	"My Father is glorified, that you bear much fruit and so prove to be my disciples" (John 15:8).
"For Christ also suffered once for sins, the righteous for the unrighteous" (1 Pet. 3:18).	"He himself bore our sins in his body on the tree, that we might die to sin and live to righteousness" (1 Pet. 2:24).
"He saved us, not because of works done by us in righteousness, but according to his own mercy" (Titus 3:5).	"Let your manner of life be worthy of the gospel of Christ" (Philip. 1:27).
"For while we were still weak, at the right time Christ died for the ungodly" (Rom. 5:6). "And to the one who does not work but believes in him who justifies the ungodly, his faith is counted as righteousness" (Rom. 4:5).	"For the grace of God has appeared, bringing salvation for all people, training us to renounce ungodliness and worldly passions, and to live self-controlled, upright, and godly lives in the present age" (Titus 2:11-12).
"We know that a person is not justified by works of the law but through faith in Jesus Christ" (Gal. 2:16).	"Our great God and Savior Jesus Christ, who gave himself for us to redeem us from all lawlessness and to purify for himself a people for his own possession who are zealous for good works" (Titus 2:13-14).
"The gospel of God, which he promised beforehand through his prophets in the holy Scriptures, concerning his Son, who was descended from David according to the flesh and was declared to be the Son of God in power according to the Spirit of holiness by his resurrection from the dead, Jesus Christ our Lord" (Rom. 1:1-4).	"The gospel by the power of God, who saved us and called us to a holy calling, not because of our works but because of his own purpose and grace" (2 Tim. 1:8-9).

While the root of the gospel is our justification, the fruit of the gospel is our sanctification.

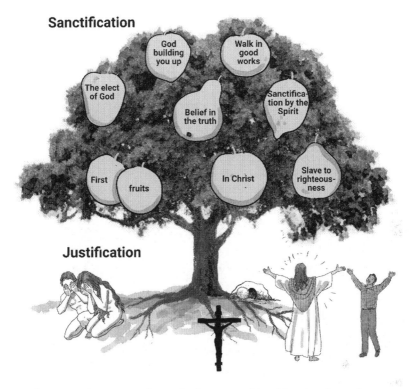

A person has to go through the root of justification in order to produce the fruit of sanctification.

Justification	Sanctification
"As one trespass led to condemnation for all men, so one act of righteousness leads to justification and life for all men " (Rom. 5:18).	"For by a single offering he has perfected for all time those who are being sanctified"(Heb. 10:14).
"We have now been justified by his blood" (Rom. 5:9).	"To those who are elect... according to the foreknowledge of God the Father, in the sanctification of the Spirit, for obedience to Jesus Christ and for sprinkling with his blood" (1 Pet. 1:1-2).

Justification	Sanctification
"Jesus our Lord, who was delivered up for our trespasses and raised for our justification" (Rom. 4:24-25).	"You are in Christ Jesus, who became to us wisdom from God, righteousness and sanctification and redemption" (1 Cor. 1:30).
"All have sinned and fall short of the glory of God, and are justified by his grace as a gift, through the redemption that is in Christ Jesus, whom God put forward as a propitiation by his blood, to be received by faith" (Rom. 3:23-25).	"I commend you to God and to the word of his grace, which is able to build you up and to give you the inheritance among all those who are sanctified" (Acts 20:32).
"The law was our guardian until Christ came, in order that we might be justified by faith" (Gal. 3:24).	"So now present your members as slaves to righteousness leading to sanctification" (Rom. 6:19).
"For we hold that one is justified by faith apart from works of the law" (Rom. 3:28).	"For we are his workmanship, created in Christ Jesus for good works, which God prepared beforehand, that we should walk in them" (Eph. 2:10).
"Since we have been justified by faith, we have peace with God through our Lord Jesus Christ" (Rom. 5:1).	"Now may the God of peace himself sanctify you completely" (1 Thess. 5:23).
"I am the way, and the truth, and the life. No one comes to the Father except through me" (John 14:6).	"God chose you as the firstfruits to be saved, through sanctification by the Spirit and belief in the truth" (2 Thess. 2:13).
"You were justified in the name of the Lord Jesus Christ and by the Spirit of our God" (1 Cor. 6:11).	"For this is the will of God, your sanctification" (1 Thess. 4:3).

As we can see by these two illustrations, God first justifies us by bringing us from death to life, "as in Adam all die, so also in Christ shall all be made alive" (1 Cor. 15:22). No one can enter the sanctification stage, or produce sanctified fruit, until they have been brought from death to life through justification. Justification always precedes sanctification. The biggest problem is that many try to reverse this order, putting sanctification before justification. In other words, they claim you must go through the sanctification stage before you are justified before God.

The following illustration shows that a person without the root of justification is still unregenerate in the first Adam, without the Holy Spirit, and thus is incapable of producing godly fruit. The unregenerate only have dead works that produce bad fruit that falls from the tree.

Those alive in Christ produce good fruit. Those dead in Adam can only produce dead fruit.

Good Fruit	Bad Fruit
"Present your members as slaves to righteousness" (Rom. 6:19).	Those still in Adam are "slaves to various passions and pleasures" (Titus 3:3).
"I am the vine; you are the branches. Whoever abides in me and I in him, he it is that bears much fruit" (John 15:5).	"A branch cannot bear fruit by itself" (John 15:4).
"My brothers, you also have died to the law through the body of Christ, so that you may belong to another, to him who has been raised from the dead, in order that we may bear fruit for God" (Rom. 7:4).	"For while we were living in the flesh, our sinful passions, aroused by the law, were at work in our members to bear fruit for death" (Rom. 7:5).

Good Fruit	Bad Fruit
"Be holy in all your conduct" (1 Pet. 1:15).	Unholy vessels will self-destruct (Rom. 9:22), "as they were destined to do" (1 Pet. 2:8).
Good fruit will: "die to sin and live to righteousness" (1 Pet. 2:24).	Bad fruit rejects being called out of their sin and unrighteousness (Luke 5:32) and are dead in sin (Eph. 2:1; Col. 2:13).
The gospel "bears fruit" (Matt. 13:23).	"The diseased tree bears bad fruit" (Matt. 7:17).
"Those that were sown on the good soil are the ones who hear the word and accept it and bear fruit, thirtyfold and sixtyfold and a hundredfold" (Mark 4:20).	The "ones sown on rocky ground...have no root in themselves" and "they fall away" (Mark 4:16-17).
"God chose you as the firstfruits to be saved, through sanctification by the Spirit" (2 Thess. 2:13).	Those not chosen are "fruitless trees in late autumn, twice dead, uprooted" (Jude 1:12).
"The eye is the lamp of the body. So, if your eye is healthy, your whole body will be full of light," (Matt. 6:22).	"but if your eye is bad, your whole body will be full of darkness" (Matt. 6:23).
"Sanctify them in the truth; your word is truth" (John 17:17).	"The natural person does not accept the things of the Spirit of God, for they are folly to him, and he is not able to understand them" (1 Cor. 2:14).
We "walk not according to the flesh but according to the Spirit" (Rom. 8:4). "Put on the Lord Jesus Christ, and make no provision for the flesh, to gratify its desires" (Rom. 13:14).	"For the mind that is set on the flesh is hostile to God, for it does not submit to God's law; indeed, it cannot. Those who are in the flesh cannot please God" (Rom. 8:7-8).
Good fruit looks "not only to his own interests, but also to the interests of others" (Philip. 2:4).	For bad fruit, "They all seek their own interests, not those of Jesus Christ" (Philip. 2:21).
Good fruit produces "good works, which God prepared beforehand, that we should walk in them" (Eph. 2:10).	"The body apart from the spirit is dead" (James 2:26).

If a person has not been justified in Christ, the "last Adam" (1 Cor. 15:45), they are still in the first Adam, which means they are under "condemnation" (Rom. 5:18). It also means they are dead in their sins (Eph. 2:1; Col. 2:13). Since "they have no root in themselves" (Mark 4:17), they are a branch by itself that cannot bear sanctified fruit (John 15:1-6). This condition results in branches sprouting up from diseased roots, which can only bear bad fruit (Luke 6:43). Only a tree that has the root of the gospel can bear good fruit for life. If there is no root in you (Matt. 13:21), you can only "bear fruit for death" (Rom. 7:5). Therefore, rootless people "cannot please God" (Rom. 8:8).

God Alone is Good

Am I saying the unregenerate cannot do "good" to their fellow man? The answer is in how we define "good" and the foundation of goodness. In Mark 10:18, Jesus said, "No one is good except God alone." Thus, any goodness that we have or do comes from God. When a believer is justified in Christ, we become a "vessel for honorable use" (Rom. 9:21; cf., 2 Tim. 2:20), "set apart as holy" (2 Tim. 2:21; cf., 1 Pet. 1:16), and are a reflection of God's light (Mat. 5:14; Eph. 5:8). Therefore, God has given believers access to His goodness through His Spirit (Gal. 5:22). This goodness produces godly works (Eph. 2:10; Matt. 5:16; Mark 4:8; 2 Cor. 9:8; Gal. 6:9-10; Col. 1:10; 1 Thess. 5:15; 2 Thess. 2:16-17; 2 Tim. 2:21; Titus 2:14, 3:8, 14; Heb. 13:21; James 3:17; 1 Pet. 2:12, 15, 4:19).

While the "good" works of believers and unbelievers can look the same in outward appearance, inwardly they are different. The inward source for a Christian's good works is God (James 1:17-18; John 15:5; Gal. 5:22-23; Philip. 2:13). For believers in Christ, we know the Lord is our "Master" (Col. 4:1; Jude 1:4). In contrast to the unregenerate, we are aware that any good we do is first "to the Lord and not to man" (Eph. 6:7; Col. 3:23; cf., Matt. 25:40). When we consider the scriptural command, "whatever you do, do all to the glory of God" (1 Cor. 10:31), whether we please men or not *is* important (Matt. 5:16), but it becomes a secondary consideration to pleasing our Master. Is that true for the unregenerate, who because of their unbelief and rebellion towards God give credit to themselves for the good work and not God (Philip. 2:21)? Even if the unbeliever engages in self-effacing behavior, the credit is still not directed towards God.[33]

While the good works unbelievers do may be pleasing to man and positively affect both saved and unsaved alike, they are not satisfying to God. They have no righteous value, nor any salvific merit attached to them. Chapter 16 of the Westminster Confession of Faith says of good

---

[33] In an effort to show humility, an unbeliever might say something like, "I can't take any or all the credit for this good work. The credit goes to the many men and women who supported and made this work possible." The source of this goodness remains men—not God.

works, "Works done by unregenerate men, although for the matter of them they may be things which God commands; and of good use both to themselves and others: yet, because they proceed not from an heart purified by faith; nor are done in a right manner, according to the Word; nor to a right end, the glory of God, they are therefore sinful, and cannot please God, or make a man meet to receive grace from God: and yet, their neglect of them is more sinful and displeasing unto God."[34]

Everything that comes out of an unbelieving heart is not purified by faith, nor is it purified by the very Lord who sanctifies believers by faith (Acts 26:18). Therefore, it is not done for the glory of the one true God. Since "whatever does not proceed from faith is sin" (Rom. 14:23), for "without faith it is impossible to please him" (Heb. 11:6), the "good" efforts of a faithless person cannot please God. Only those who have been justified by the root of the gospel are capable of doing deeds God considers good and pleasing. The fruit we produce is the result of an internal relationship we now have with God, a relationship that can only come by first going through the root of the gospel.

Fruit-Only Gospel

So, why do so many continue to define the gospel as the fruit we produce? I believe it is because they are ignorant of the critical root/fruit-distinction and what comes first. I repeat, unless you first preach the root of the gospel (*Christ died for our sins in accordance with the Scriptures, that he was buried, that he was raised on the third day in accordance with the Scriptures*) and explain that our justification in Christ must come first, presenting the "gospel" solely as the fruit one produces will lead to a dead sanctification that is sure to produce false converts.

When a person has been presented with a fruit-only gospel, including any claims that works will allow one to receive justification before God, all it can produce is diseased, bad and dead fruit that will result in Jesus saying, "I never knew you" (Matt. 7:23). Why? Because only those who have the root of justification can then produce the fruit of sanctification that is pleasing to God. If we get the root/fruit distinction and order right, we will always preach the gospel correctly. One must first come through the root to be justified and freed from their sin in order to produce true, sanctified fruit. Paul sums it up this way, "You have been set free from sin and have become slaves of God, the fruit you get leads to sanctification and its end, eternal life" (Rom. 6:22).

---

[34] WCF XVI.7

Jesus the Root

Jesus said He was the ancestor of David (Matt. 22:41-45) as well as His descendant: "I am the root and the descendant of David" (Rev. 22:16). David sprang from Jesus, who is the Creator of all things (John 1:3; Col 1:16), but Christ's human nature sprang from David. Because Jesus is "the root" as well as the offspring of David (Isa. 11:1, 10; Rom. 15:12), as the Divine Messiah, He fulfills all the prophecies concerning King David's family. He is both David's Lord and David's Son, possessing David's throne (Acts 2:30; Luke 1:32). Therefore, He is the root of the gospel, the resurrected, sinless, righteous son of David (Acts 2:31) and "God has made him both Lord and Christ" (Acts 2:36).

When people struggle to define the gospel, I believe it is because they don't understand that Jesus Himself is the gospel. Christians, who believe that we are saved by Christ alone, intuitively know that it is not our works (Eph. 2:8-9; 2 Tim. 1:9; Rom. 9:31-32), not our obedience (Rom. 3:28), nor our righteousness (Titus 3:5; Philip. 3:9) that saves us. It is Christ alone who justifies us before the Father (Rom. 5:1, 9). It is His works (Matt. 5:17; John 4:34, 8:46, 8:55, 17:4, 19:30), His obedience (Rom. 5:19; Heb. 12:2) and His righteousness (2 Cor. 5:21; Philip. 3:9; 1 Pet. 3:18) alone that saves us. If we were to define the gospel as Christ coming to perfectly "fulfill all righteousness" (Matt. 3:15; cf., Rom. 10:4; Acts 13:39) and "becoming obedient to the point of death, even death on a cross" (Philip. 2:8; cf., Matt. 26:39; Heb. 5:8), as He "condemned sin in the flesh" (Rom. 8:1-3) and "abolished death and brought life and immortality to light through the gospel" (2 Tim. 1:10; cf., Heb. 2:14; Rom. 6:3-5) with His resurrection from the dead (Rom. 4:25), then the gospel is not about what we do, but about what Christ has already done (John 19:30). This is what Christ alone means. Thus, if the gospel is what Christ alone did, then we can see how Christ Himself is the gospel.

How Do we Obey the Gospel?

The phrase "obey the gospel" is used on three separate occasions by New Testament writers (Rom. 10:16; 2 Thess. 1:8; 1 Pet. 4:17). In all three contexts, this is speaking in particular of those Jews who rejected the good news of Jesus' kingship and who coupled that rejection with a persecution of Christians. Those Jews failed to act on the truth regarding who Jesus was and what He came to do. Paul talked about how those self-righteous Jews "do not obey the truth" (Rom. 2:8). He also scolded the Galatians for submitting to the Judaizers, who insisted on adding circumcision to the gospel: "You were running well. Who hindered you from obeying the truth?" (Gal. 5:7). Not obeying the truth is disobeying the gospel.

Many do not obey the gospel because they act "ignorantly in unbelief" (1 Tim. 1:13; cf., Acts 3:17, 13:27), lacking the "wisdom of God" (1 Cor. 2:6-8; 2 Cor. 3:14-16). For others, "the cross is folly" (1 Cor. 1:18). Still others close their eyes and ears to the truth as their "heart has grown dull" (Matt. 13:15; John 8:43). Some ignore the gospel by choosing to "enjoy the fleeting pleasures of sin" (Heb. 11:25; cf. 2 Pet. 2:14; Jude 1:16), having no fear in their hearts of the eternal consequences of their evil deeds (Ecc. 8:11). Some disobey the gospel because of fear that they would "be put out of the synagogue; for they loved the glory that comes from man more than the glory that comes from God" (John 12:42-43). Others are simply on the wrong soil (Mark 4:13-20). Let us also not forget that Satan "has blinded the minds of the unbelievers, to keep them from seeing the light of the gospel of the glory of Christ" (2 Cor. 4:4).

We have seen the case of those who fail to obey the gospel. What about those who obey the gospel? In the latter case, I think the most important point to make is that obedience is a result of one receiving and trusting in the gospel. In other words, if we believe in the root of the gospel, our fruit-producing obedience to the gospel will follow. Paul told the saints at Philippi, because of their partnership in the gospel, "that he who began a good work in you will bring it to completion at the day of Jesus Christ" (Philip. 1:6). He said his prayer was that they would "be pure and blameless for the day of Christ, filled with the fruit of righteousness that comes through Jesus Christ, to the glory and praise of God" (1:10-11). He added, "let your manner of life be worthy of the gospel of Christ" as you continue "striving side by side for the faith of the gospel" (1:27; cf., Mark 8:35). One of the main fruits of "obeying the gospel" is sharing the gospel.

Australian evangelical Anglican theologian Graeme Goldsworthy points out, "Christians cannot 'live the gospel', as they are often exhorted to do. They can only believe it, proclaim it and seek to live consistently with it. Only Jesus lived (and died) the gospel. It is a once-for-all finished and perfect event done for us by another."[35]

---

[35] Graeme Goldsworthy, Confusing the Gospel with the Fruit of the Gospel, https://www.monergism.com/blog/confusing-gospel-fruit-gospel.

⑨ THE PROCLAMATION OF THE GOSPEL

"If you knew how to be saved, you know how to tell somebody else how."
John MacArthur[36]

The death, burial and resurrection of Jesus was at the heart of the earliest Christian faith, confession and proclamation. The root of the gospel message was of first importance then and also throughout the past two thousand years, and it must be the priority of the Christian faith, confession and proclamation today.

Having said that, evangelists preach the gospel in different ways. While the root of the gospel always remains the same, what strategy an evangelist uses to deliver the gospel can change depending on the situation

---

[36] John MacArthur, Attitudes of Effective Evangelism sermon, www.gty.org/library/sermons-library/42-134/attitudes-of-effective-evangelism.

or the evangelist's preferred method. The following is not an exhaustive list of evangelism methods but is meant to highlight some of the more well-known approaches to sharing the gospel.

Law and Gospel

> *"We cannot come to Christ to be justified until we have first been to Moses to be condemned."*
> John Stott[37]

How many times has someone mentioned they have something important to tell you and then asked, "Do you want the bad news or the good news first?" Not knowing what the bad or good news is, most of us just arbitrarily pick one or the other. At the same time, we must be wondering if the good news will outweigh the bad or vice versa. What if the same person delivering this important information knew that you could not fully appreciate the good news unless you heard the bad news first. Would they give you the option of what to hear first? Would they go ahead and deliver the good news first, knowing that it wouldn't be fully understood without the context of the bad news?

What if the previous scenario happened in your doctor's office for a follow up on some routine blood tests you have done every year. Without first revealing the results of those tests, what if your doctor just handed you a pill and declared, "Good news, take this pill and you will be cured." What would your response be? Most likely one of confusion as most would certainly ask, "Cured of what?"

On the other hand, let's say your doctor first told you that the blood tests revealed that you have a disease that will kill you in six months and that your death would be slow and painful. He then hands you a pill and says, "Good news, take this pill and you will be cured." Your whole perspective is changed by not only receiving the diagnosis (bad news), but by having it delivered *before* the cure (good news). The diagnosis put the cure in proper context. You are now convinced that taking the pill is an appropriate and beneficial thing to do.

Many people try to do evangelism by offering the cure—the good news of Jesus' life, death and resurrection—without first making their hearer aware of their uncleanliness—their law breaking against a holy God. God presented the law before He presented the gospel for a reason. The law teaches us that we could never meet its demands, and therefore

---

[37] John Stott, *The Message of Galatians*, p. 102.

it is the tutor that brings us unto Christ, that we might be justified by faith (Gal. 3:24).

The Law and Gospel approach will include these points:

1. The law must be presented first, "since through the law comes knowledge of sin" (Rom. 3:20). "If it had not been for the law, I would not have known sin" (Rom. 7:7). In fact, "sin is lawlessness" (1 John 3:4). In our failure to keep the law, "every mouth may be stopped, and the whole world may be held accountable to God" (Rom. 3:19).

2. No one can keep the law of God (Gal. 3:10-11, 2:16; James 2:10), except the One who came to fulfill the law (Matt. 5:17) in our place (2 Cor. 5:21). "So then, the law was our guardian until Christ came, in order that we might be justified by faith" (Gal. 3:24).

3. "Christ redeemed us from the curse of the law by becoming a curse for us—for it is written, "Cursed is everyone who is hanged on a tree" (Gal. 3:13). We know that "Christ is the end of the law for righteousness to everyone who believes" (Rom. 10:4).

4. "God opposes the proud [those who place themselves under the law to receive righteousness before God] but gives grace [the gospel] to the humble" (1 Pet. 5:5). We see Jesus always giving the law to the proud (Luke 10:25-28, 18:18-25) and grace to the humble (John 3:1-16, 1:43-51).

5. God is calling us to repent of any thought that following the law (Gal. 2:16) or establishing our own righteousness (Rom. 10:3; Titus 3:5) could merit entrance into heaven.

6. Instead of trying to exalt ourselves (Luke 18:9-12) through a law that was never meant to save (Rom. 3:20), we should humble ourselves and be justified and exalted by faith in Christ (Luke 18:13-14; Rom. 3:21-26, 4:25). In the end, "The law of the LORD is perfect, converting the soul" (Psalm 19:7, NKJV).

7. Therefore, "if you confess with your mouth that Jesus is Lord and believe in your heart that God raised him from the dead, you will be saved" (Rom. 10:9).

The purpose of the law is to break down our self-righteousness and to humble us to receive the gospel of grace. Those who use this approach believe that giving the good news (Christ died for our sins and rose from the dead for our justification) without first giving the bad news (our law-breaking, which reveals our sin) makes no sense. A person must first be humbled by the problem of their sin before they are ready to receive the cure. Will Metzger laments, "Our object has become merely to convince people to take the cure. They do not need to know the problem—just the answer."[38]

Most Christians, even though they may not be aware of it, already have a basic understanding of the law and gospel principle: "You are a sinner (law) and you need Christ as your Savior (gospel)." When you tell people the bad news that they are a sinner, you have already implicitly told them they have broken God's law, because "sin is lawlessness" (1 John 3:4). When you tell them the good news of Jesus dying and rising from the dead to be our Savior, you are pointing them to the gospel redemption in Christ for which the law was put in place (Gal. 3:24; Acts 13:39).

Whether we know it or not, every time we mention a person's sin and the necessity of repenting of that sin and believing in Christ's redemptive work on our behalf, we are giving law and gospel. Since that is the case, shouldn't we strive to get the details and the order right? When we get out our law and gospel spreader, let us sow the law seed first and then the gospel seed second. That way we can rest in God's sovereignty that those "on the good soil are the ones who hear the word and accept it and bear fruit" (Mark 4:20).

Good Person Test

When asked to comment on the popular book by Rabbi Harold Kushner, "When Bad Things Happen to Good People", R.C. Sproul simply said, "There are no good people." The "Good Person Test" is similar to the Law and Gospel approach in that it shows us:

1. No one can be good by keeping the law (Gal. 2:16, 3:10).

2. One can prove this by taking an unsaved person through the Ten Commandments (Exodus 20:1-17). For example, have you ever lied (9th commandment)? Stolen anything (8th commandment)? Used God's name in vain (3rd commandment)? Disobeyed your parents (5th commandment)? Not put God first (1st commandment)? Pursued money more than God (2nd commandment)? Jealously desired something that did not belong to you (10th commandment)? Be-

---

[38] Will Metzger, *Tell The Truth*, p. 86.

come angry at someone in your heart (6th commandment; cf., Matt. 5:21-22; 1 John 3:15)? Looked lustfully at another (7th commandment; cf., Matt. 5:28)? Failed to set aside time to thank or worship God (4th commandment)? If God judges you by the Ten Commandments on the Day of Judgment, will you be innocent or guilty? After taking this test, do you still think you are a good person?

3. Since James 2:10 says, "For whoever keeps the whole law but fails in one point has become guilty of all of it", we are all guilty. There are no guiltless people: "None is righteous, no, not one" (Rom. 3:10; cf., Psalm 14:3, 143:2).

4. If being a good person is what it takes to get to heaven and have a relationship with God, why did Jesus have to die (Gal. 2:21)?

5. We must repent of the belief that obedience to the law (Gal. 2:16) or works done by us in righteousness (Titus 3:5; Philip. 3:9; Proverbs 20:9) can justify anyone before God.

6. The only true good person who ever walked among us was Jesus Christ (Mark 10:18; cf., Matt. 5:17). Jesus, the sinless Savior (John 8:46), became our righteousness before God (2 Cor. 5:21; Rom. 4:22-25). Come to God by faith alone, through grace alone, in Christ alone knowing that "he has now reconciled in his body of flesh by his death, in order to present you holy and blameless and above reproach before him" (Col. 1:22).[39]

Instead of asking someone if they are a good person, many Christians will ask them if they think they are a sinner. Most, realizing they are far from perfect, will readily admit to this, while at the same time believing they are still a good person. They redefine sin as a lack of perfection. They may even go further by putting sin into categories of big and small, like Catholics do with so-called mortal and venial sins. Since they believe their good outweighs their bad, they have convinced themselves that they don't deserve hell.

At her place of employment in a Fortune 500 company, my wife once overheard a high-ranking executive say, "My bad is better than most people's good." For some people, so steeped in their own self-righteousness, there's no convincing them they are not a good person. However, as Jesus told the rich young ruler, "No one is good except God alone" (Luke 18:19). So, either someone who insists they are a good person is lying or

---

[39] Both the Law and Gospel and Good Person Test utilize the Ten Commandments.

Jesus is lying. Lying, of course, is impossible for the sinless Son of God (John 8:46; 1 Pet. 2:22; 1 John 3:5).

I sometimes tell people that while their friends and family may judge them to be a good person, my question is not whether they are good before man, but whether they are a good person before God. In the latter and more important case, you are not a good person, you are just like the rest of us. We have all sinned and fall short of the glory of God (Rom. 3:23) and we all deserve death and hell.

Jesus said, "I have not come to call the righteous but sinners to repentance" (Luke 5:32). That's because there is no one who is righteous (Rom. 3:10) to be called—only sinners. You see, "Christ died for the ungodly" (5:6) and God only "justifies the ungodly" (4:5). If you think you are a good person, you need to repent of your sin, repent of any goodness you think you may have before a holy God, and put your faith and trust in Christ alone to save you. Your alleged goodness cannot save you, but His perfect goodness and righteousness will (2 Cor. 5:21; 1 Pet. 3:18).

Anyone who wants to pass the Good Person Test needs to be saved by Christ's life, not their own, as "God shows his love for us in that while we were still sinners, Christ died for us. Since, therefore, we have now been justified by his blood, much more shall we be saved by him from the wrath of God. For if while we were enemies we were reconciled to God by the death of his Son, much more, now that we are reconciled, shall we be *saved by his life*" (Rom. 5:8-10).

Creation, Fall, Redemption, Restoration

The "Creation, Fall, Redemption, Restoration" approach instructs us that:

1. Creation: God created the world and said, "it was very good" (Gen. 1:31).

2. Fall: Humanity through Adam fell into sin and decay, separating us from a holy God (Gen. 3; Isa. 59:2; Rom. 5:12ff).

3. Redemption: God has acted through Christ's sinless life, death and resurrection to bring redemption to a fallen world. Out of His love (John 3:16; 1 John 3:16) and righteousness (Rom. 3:25-26), God sent His Son to redeem His people (Matt. 1:21; Rom. 3:24; 1 Cor. 1:30; Gal. 4:5; Eph. 1:7; Col. 1:14; Titus 2:14; Heb. 9:12), making those who believe into a new creation in Christ (2 Cor. 5:17), producing "a repentance that leads to salvation without regret" (2 Cor. 7:10a).

4. Restoration: Eventually the whole world will be renewed and restored. Death, decay, injustice, and suffering will be all removed (Rev. 21:1-7). God will purge this world of evil once and for all (21:8, 27a). "Only those who are written in the Lamb's book of life" (21:27b) will take part in this restoration.

By including these four storylines in our concept of the gospel, we provide the context needed to understand God's purpose and actions in history. In creation and the fall, we see how God worked in the past. In redemption, we see how, through a fallen world, He is working in the present. In restoration, we see how He will work in the future. We also see a clear division between an old order, where sin is still twisting things, and a new order where sin and evil will pass away. Eden will not only be restored, but it will also be fulfilled. Redeemed humanity will come to live in final peace and fullness in God's presence.

God, Man, Christ, Response

John Calvin opened his famed Institutes of the Christian Religion with the words, "nearly all the wisdom we possess, that is to say, true and sound wisdom, consists of two parts: The knowledge of God and of ourselves."[40] In the "God, Man, Christ, Response" approach, the first two points show the critical distinction between God and man—God is holy, man is not. The next two points show us the solution to this problem. Mark Dever, the president of 9Marks, makes these points when discussing the "God, Man, Christ, Response":

1. God: God is perfectly holy and will punish sin (1 John 1:5; Rom. 2:5-8).

2. Man: Through Adam's fall we all inherited a sin nature (Rom. 5:12-21) that makes us all subject to the wrath of God (Eph. 2:1-3).

3. Christ: Jesus Christ, who is fully God and fully man, lived a sinless life to fulfill all of God's holy, righteous standards in our place (Matt. 5:17; 1 Pet. 3:18; 2 Cor. 5:21). His death on the cross bears God's wrath for all who would believe in Him (Rom. 3:21-26; 1 Thess. 5:9). His resurrection from the grave brings God's elect to a new resurrection life (Rom. 6:3-4, 4:25; 1 Cor. 15:20-22).

4. Response: God calls everyone everywhere to repent of their sins (Acts 17:30, 20:21; Mark 1:15) and trust in Christ in order to be saved (Mark 1:15, Acts 20:21; Rom. 10:9-10).

---

[40] John Calvin, Calvin, Institutes, I.i.1.

This approach focuses on why God's holiness requires His wrath against man's sin, why Christ's finished work is necessary to appease that wrath, and why our response should be to receive God's salvation through Christ.[41]

The Romans Road

When the Roman Empire was at the height of its glory, a common saying was, "All roads lead to Rome." However, in the book of Romans, Paul gave us a road that has never led to Rome but rather to saving faith in Christ. Many evangelical missionaries, evangelists and lay people memorize and use the Romans Road when sharing the good news.

Rom. 3:10— "As it is written, 'None is righteous, no, not one.'"

Rom. 3:23— "For all have sinned and fall short of the glory of God."

Rom. 5:12— "Therefore, just as sin came into the world through one man, and death through sin, and so death spread to all men because all sinned."

Rom. 5:18-19— "Therefore, as one trespass led to condemnation for all men, so one act of righteousness leads to justification and life for all men. For as by the one man's disobedience the many were made sinners, so by the one man's obedience the many will be made righteous."

Rom. 6:23— "For the wages of sin is death, but the free gift of God is eternal life in Christ Jesus our Lord."

Rom. 5:8— "God shows his love for us in that while we were still sinners, Christ died for us."

Rom. 10:9-10— "If you confess with your mouth that Jesus is Lord and believe in your heart that God raised him from the dead, you will be saved. For with the heart one believes and is justified, and with the mouth one confesses and is saved."

Rom. 10:13— "Everyone who calls on the name of the Lord will be saved."

Since the time the original Romans Road plan was presented a half a century ago, variations have arisen. However, the basic message remains—our human condition, sin's penalty, God's provision and solu-

---

[41] This is the basic outline of Mark Dever's God, Man, Christ, Response approach. I have added a few scriptures.

tion, and our necessary response.[42]

Did you notice a similar theme running through all the above approaches? Every approach contains God's holy requirements (law), and Christ fulfilling those requirements through His perfect life, death and resurrection (gospel).

May I Ask You a Question?

A less formal way to get to the proclamation of the gospel is to simply start your witnessing conversation with questions. The only limit to how many questions you can ask is your own creativity. Let me offer the following questions to help you get started when talking to unbelievers:

- If you were wrong about eternal matters, would you want to know?
- What will happen to you when you die? Is this life all there is?
- Do you believe in God and heaven?
- If you were God, how would you best reveal yourself to mankind?
- If someone asked you how one gets to heaven to be with God, what would you tell them?
- What are God's requirements to get to heaven? Is it to follow His law? How are you doing with that?
- Are you a good person? Do only good people get to heaven?
- If you died tonight and God asked why He should let you into heaven, what would you say?
- Do you know what the Bible has to say about eternal life? Would you like to know?
- As a Christian, God has called me to share the gospel of Jesus Christ. Do you know it?

Some are critical of several of the previous questions, complaining you won't find such inquiries being made in the Bible. I understand that, but as I mentioned, these are *informal* questions to determine whether a person believes in God, an afterlife, or is trusting in their own righteousness to get to heaven. These questions are simply conversation starters

---

[42] The original Romans Road method is said to have been preached by Baptist Pastor Jack Hyles in a June 1970 sermon.

that we can use to transition into a *formal* presentation of the gospel.

What if you are talking to a person who claims to be a Christian? Here are some questions you might ask:

- Are you willing to examine yourself to see whether you are truly in the faith? Did you know that Paul exhorted Christians to do just that (2 Cor. 13:5)?

- Are your beliefs and convictions as a Christian based on your own understanding and study, or have they been handed down to you by your family or church? Have you tested those beliefs by the Bible?

- Can you tell me what you experienced when you were saved? Since the Bible tells us we go from death to life (John 5:24) and have been delivered from darkness into light (Col. 1:12-14), what was that transformation like for you?

- Since you testify to being a Christian, if you shared the gospel with someone you wanted to come to salvation, what would you tell them?

- Is Jesus the only way to salvation? If yes, why? If no, what do you do with John 14:6?

These questions can give people a chance to contemplate their own thinking on eternal matters and for you to challenge their thinking. Through it all, remember, our ultimate goal is to present the gospel.

Pulpit Evangelism

"Preach the gospel from the pulpit. We pastors shouldn't feel guilty that our primary way of evangelism is preaching. We need to present the gospel in every sermon. Visitors need to hear it."
Mark Dever[43]

The pulpit is probably the most important venue to share the gospel. Paul talked about unbelievers being present in church gatherings (1 Cor. 14:23-25). He said of the gospel, "How are they to hear without someone preaching?" (Rom. 10:14), and "Woe to me if I do not preach the gospel!" (1 Cor. 9:16). Peter said Jesus "commanded us to preach to the people and to testify that he is the one appointed by God to be judge of the living and the dead" (Acts 10:42). Jesus said, "Repentance and remission of sins should be preached in his name among all nations" (Luke 24:47, KJV).

---

[43] Mark Dever, The Pastor and Evangelism, Desiring God 2009 Conference for Pastors.

Am I saying that *every* sermon from a church pulpit should be exclusively about the gospel? No! However, I am advocating for the gospel to at least be woven into each sermon. The main theme of some sermons will certainly be the gospel. Other messages may have the gospel as a shadow (Col. 2:17; Heb. 8:5, 10:1). Still others, at some point, will directly connect the gospel with the rest of their message, and, at the end of their sermon, announce a call to repent and believe. Unfortunately, many pulpits are filled with self-help sermons that have more to do with the culture than the Bible. Other times, congregants may be directed to the huge overhead projection screen to watch something that more closely resembles "America's Funniest Home Videos" than any gospel message.

While many pastors are focused on entertaining the goats (non-converted) rather than feeding the sheep (converted), too often, neither the goats nor the sheep in the pews are fed the gospel. For the goats, hearing a verbal gospel presentation is their road to salvation and a regenerated life. For the sheep, being constantly fed the gospel makes sure we "continue in the faith, stable and steadfast, not shifting from the hope of the gospel that you heard" (Col. 1:23). Gospel preaching also reminds us of "the hope laid up for you in heaven" (Col. 1:5).

Gospel preaching shows us "our Savior Christ Jesus, who abolished death and brought life and immortality to light through the gospel" (2 Tim. 1:10-11). It takes the sheep back to "when you heard the word of truth, the gospel of your salvation, and believed in him," and "were sealed with the promised Holy Spirit" (Eph. 1:13). Pulpit evangelism teaches us that we should preserve "the truth of the gospel" (Gal. 2:5), be a "minister" of the gospel (Eph. 3:7) and be in "partnership in the gospel" (Philp. 1:5). When our pastor tells us that we have been "entrusted with the gospel" (1 Thess. 2:4), we should be about defending and confirming the gospel (Philp. 1:7, 1:16), so we can "advance the gospel" (Philp. 1:12, 2:22, 4:3), which will include "suffering for the gospel by the power of God" (2 Tim. 1:8).

Rick Holland, Executive Pastor at Grace Community Church, writes, "Preachers need to come to terms with the fact that the sermon is not an end. It is a means to a few ends, such as strengthening faith, encouraging the saints, and confronting sins. But certainly one of the main ends is the salvation of souls. Pastors should embrace the fact that Sunday is not just an opportunity to deliver a sermon, but more important, to see souls converted."[44]

---

[44] Rick Holland, John MacArthur, *Evangelism*, p. 113.

Gospel Ambassadors

> *"Therefore, we are ambassadors for Christ, God making his appeal through us"* (2 Cor. 5:20).

There are countless loyal ambassadors for Christ who proclaim the gospel in many other different ways:

- Revival services, also known as Crusades
- Street preaching
- Prison ministries
- High school and college evangelism clubs
- Apologetic ministries
- Ministries sharing the gospel with cults
- Television evangelism
- Radio evangelism
- Internet evangelism
- Billboard evangelism
- Tract evangelism
- Letter evangelism (writing to a lost friend or family member)
- One-on-one evangelism
- Vacation Bible School
- Sunday School evangelism
- Child evangelism programs
- Home Bible study
- Books on evangelism

    I will end this chapter by saying I am aware that some may criticize the approaches and methods I have given in this book so far. To those that do, I simply offer words I once read from the great nineteenth century American evangelist Dwight L. Moody, "It is clear you don't like my way of doing evangelism. You raise some good points. Frankly, I sometimes do not like my way of doing evangelism. But I like my way of doing it better than your way of not doing it."

⑩ BOLD GRACE

"They shook off the dust from their feet against them" (Acts 13:51)

"Some people are just waiting for a contagious Christian who won't beat around the bush, but who'll clarify the truth of Christ and challenge them to do something about it. Could that Christian be you?"
Mark Mittelberg[45]

Confrontational Evangelism (hereafter referred to as CE) is often highly criticized by Christians and non-Christians alike. Critics of this approach have caricatured CE as a "street preacher" standing on a soapbox and shouting at the top of his lungs at the passersby that they are all going to hell, or as "evangelists" waving signs that mock unbelievers. I'm not saying those things don't happen—they do. I am saying that they are not examples of biblical CE.

---

[45] Mark Mittelberg, *Becoming a Contagious Christian*, p. 127.

Other critics are more charitable and define CE as those who confront unbelievers with the law and how their sin (law-breaking) separates them from God. They are correct that CE involves using the Ten Commandments to show how no one is good but God. Yet, while the critics dislike this approach, they almost always leave off the fact that this bad news approach is always followed by the good news of the gospel. One (law) is never used in isolation of the other (grace). CE is bold grace.

Properly understood, CE involves confronting the unbeliever with their failure to keep the law and showing them their unrighteous standing before a holy and righteous God, in order to bring them to repentance and belief in the root of the gospel. As Charles Spurgeon once said, "God never clothes men until He has first stripped them, nor does He quicken them by the gospel till first they are slain by the law."[46]

Type A-B Disciples

CE, boldly confronting someone's sin with an aim to bring them to a proper understanding of God's grace, is something many evangelists do all the time. This not a split personality but a complimentary approach. Typically, Type A personalities are defined as people who are more aggressive; Type B people are more laid-back. I would define a Type A Christian as bold, direct, confrontational and decisive. They lift up truth and rebuke falsehood. They expose unrighteousness, showing the way to repentance. They have a sense of urgency not only to share the gospel with a lost world, but also to contend for the faith.

The Type B Christian is generally restrained and sometimes can experience thoughts of fear when it comes to sharing the gospel. Despite their inhibitions, they know that God will supply them the grace needed to deliver the good news. They are self-effacing, pointing to their own sin while at the same time pointing to the Savior. Their obedience to the truth of the gospel means no compromise, but also showing mercy, peace and love towards those who doubt.

The disciples we read about in the New Testament fully employed CE, using both Type A and Type B approaches. As we will see, they debated, refuted, destroyed arguments and exposed people for their unbelief and hostility towards God. They referred to people as stiff-necked, fruitless trees, puffed up and conceited, loud-mouthed boasters, children of the devil and followers of Satan. They said such people are enemies of Christ, deceivers, part of a wicked and crooked generation, under God's

---
[46] Charles Spurgeon, *The Soul Winner*, p. 10.

wrath and headed for damnation. They had their spirit within them provoked and shook the dust off their feet and withdrew in the face of unbelief.

Yet, we also see how they showed meekness and the gentleness of Christ. They had a gracious approach, demonstrating the love of Christ by calling people to repentance and gently reproving those who opposed them. Their conduct was always honorable. They spoke with great wisdom as they served the Lord with humility and tears, always striving to know how to answer everyone. They gave law to the proud and grace to the humble, knowing that God's gospel would go forward as He promised them.

The bold grace of CE may sound contradictory to some, but as we will see, it was not to the original disciples of Christ. Paul asked the Ephesians to pray "that words may be given to me in opening my mouth boldly to proclaim the mystery of the gospel, for which I am an ambassador in chains, that I may declare it boldly, as I ought to speak" (Eph. 6:19-20). He also acknowledged the role of grace in his life, "By the grace of God I am what I am" (1 Cor. 15:10). J. Mack Stiles writes, "If anything is needed in Christian witness today, it is boldness…wise boldness, gracious boldness, mixed with love, but boldness nonetheless."[47]

Type A Paul

Paul "confounded the Jews who lived in Damascus by proving that Jesus was the Christ" (Acts 9:22). "He reasoned with them from the Scriptures, explaining and proving that it was necessary for the Christ to suffer and to rise from the dead" (Acts 17:2-3, 17; cf., 18:4-5, 19; 19:8-9). He "had no small dissension and debate" (Acts 15:2) with the Judaizers who said one must be circumcised to be saved. "He spoke and disputed against the Hellenists" (Acts 9:29) who were seeking to kill him. He even withdrew in the face of unbelief from those calling his message about the kingdom of God "evil" (Acts 19:8-9).

Paul said while God had overlooked men's ignorance in the past, "now he commands all people everywhere to repent" (Acts 17:30; cf., 3:17). When the disbelieving Jews walked out on Paul after he was "testifying to the kingdom of God and trying to convince them about Jesus both from the Law of Moses and from the Prophets", he quoted Isaiah in telling them that they can "hear but never understand…see but never perceive", because their "hearts have grown dull" and "their eyes they have closed" (Acts 28:23-27).

---

[47] J. Mack Stiles, *Marks of the Messenger*, p. 92.

Paul also followed Jesus' example to shake the dust off his feet when a town rejected his gospel message (Luke 10:10-11). In a synagogue in Antioch, Paul spoke of the crucifixion of Jesus and forgiveness of sins proclaimed in His name. He warned them of the judgment that awaited those who rejected this message. When he and Barnabas returned the next week, the whole city came out to hear them, but when "the Jews saw the crowds, they were filled with jealousy and began to contradict what was spoken by Paul, reviling him" (Acts 13:45). Therefore, Paul and Barnabas spoke out boldly, saying, "It was necessary that the word of God be spoken first to you. Since you thrust it aside and judge yourselves unworthy of eternal life, behold, we are turning to the Gentiles" (13:46). Thus "they shook off the dust from their feet against them and went to Iconium" (13:51). Paul was even more direct at the synagogue at Corinth. After his gospel message was delivered, "they opposed and reviled him" (Acts 18:6a). Paul then dismissed them as he "shook out his garments and said to them, 'Your blood be on your own heads!'" (18:6b).

Paul was blunt about his theology. He spoke of "the wrath of God" 18 times in his epistles. He said ungodly men who "suppress the truth" about God (Rom 1:18) deserve His wrath, because, "Claiming to be wise, they became fools" (1:22). Paul warned the self-righteous and unrepentant Jews they were "storing up wrath" (Rom. 2:5) and "fury" (2:8) for themselves before God.

Paul talked about those before salvation being "dead in the trespasses and sins" (Eph. 2:1; cf., Col. 2:13; Titus 3:3) and "sons of disobedience" (Eph. 2:2), for we "were by nature children of wrath, like the rest of mankind" (2:3; cf., Rom. 7:5). He said such people are "darkened in their understanding, alienated from the life of God because of the ignorance that is in them" (Eph. 4:18; cf., Col 1:21; 1 Peter 2:9-10).

Not leaving anyone out, Paul said all people "are under sin" (Rom. 3:9) and do not have a righteous standing before God. In fact, he added, "None is righteous, no, not one" (3:10). He said believers live "in the midst of a crooked and twisted generation" (Philip. 2:15). Paul said many "walk as enemies of the cross of Christ. Their end is destruction, their god is their belly, and they glory in their shame" (Philip. 3:18-19).

Paul did not mince words concerning those who rejected the gospel by insisting one must be circumcised to be right with God: "Look out for the dogs, look out for the evildoers, look out for those who mutilate the flesh" (Philip. 3:2). Pointing out the "deceivers, especially those of the circumcision party" (Titus 1:10), he said, "They must be silenced" (Titus 1:11). Paul even called out Peter, his "fellow elder" (1 Pet. 5:1), for trying to appease the heretical circumcision party: "I opposed him to his face" for not being "in step with the truth of the gospel" (Gal. 2:11-21).

Paul rebuked the Galatians by saying, "I am astonished that you… are turning to a different gospel" (Gal. 1:6). Because some Galatians were placing their hopes for salvation on Jewish ceremonies like circumcision, and not on Christ alone, Paul said, "I am afraid I may have labored over you in vain" (Gal. 4:11). Seeing that some still sided with the Judaizers, Paul asked, "Have I then become your enemy by telling you the truth?" (4:16). In the end, Paul said, "I am perplexed about you" (4:20).

Paul confronted the issue of people mocking Jesus' resurrection (Acts 17:32). He knew that the resurrection was so critical to the gospel (Rom. 4:25) that if those who denied Christ had risen from the dead were right, "then our preaching is in vain and your faith is in vain" (1 Cor. 15:14). He said if there is no risen Christ, that would mean we would "be misrepresenting God" (15:15). He added, "if Christ has not been raised, your faith is futile and you are still in your sins…we are of all people most to be pitied" (15:17-19).

Paul addressed those being influenced by false teachers and false doctrines. He called out some in Corinth for easily being duped into accepting from false teachers "another Jesus…a different spirit…or…a different gospel" (2 Cor. 11:4) than the one he proclaimed. He called such teachers, "false apostles, deceitful workmen, disguising themselves as apostles of Christ" (2 Cor. 11:13; cf., Eph. 4:14). He equated these teachers as being the devil in disguise, "And no wonder, for even Satan disguises himself as an angel of light. So, it is no surprise if his [the devil's] servants, also, disguise themselves as servants of righteousness. Their end will correspond to their deeds" (11:15). Paul also had to deal with a person in the Corinthian church who was caught up in sexual immorality: "deliver this man to Satan for the destruction of the flesh, so that his spirit may be saved in the day of the Lord" (1 Cor. 5:5). In Cyprus, Paul rebuked a Jewish sorcerer and false prophet named Bar-Jesus by saying, "You son of the devil, you enemy of all righteousness, full of all deceit and villainy" (Acts 13:10).

Paul said the gospel is founded on our "belief in the truth" (2 Thess. 2:13; cf., Eph. 1:13; Col. 1:5-6; 1 Tim. 2:4). Yet, he remarked that some "will turn away from listening to the truth and wander off into myths" (2 Tim. 4:4). He cautioned believers to make sure about "the firmness of your faith in Christ" so "that no one will delude you with plausible arguments" (Col. 2:4-5). He warned that "no one takes you captive by philosophy and empty deceit, according to human tradition, according to the elemental spirits of the world, and not according to Christ" (Col. 2:8). Believers should stay away from "human precepts and teachings" (Col. 2:22) that have "an appearance of wisdom in promoting self-made religion" (Col. 2:23). Therefore, we should "destroy arguments and every lofty opinion raised against the knowledge of God" (2 Cor. 10:5).

Paul had much to say about doctrine and divisions. He told the "brothers, to watch out for those who cause divisions and create obstacles contrary to the doctrine that you have been taught; avoid them" (Rom. 16:17; cf., Eph. 4:14; 1 Tim. 1:3, 1:10, 4:1-6, 6:20-21; 2 Tim. 2:14, 16, 23, 4:3-4; Titus 3:9-11). He said these same people are "desiring to be teachers of the law, without understanding either what they are saying or the things about which they make confident assertions" (1 Tim. 1:7). In addition, "If anyone teaches a different doctrine and does not agree with the sound words of our Lord Jesus Christ and the teaching that accords with godliness, he is puffed up with conceit and understands nothing" (1 Tim. 6:3-4). Elders are thus told to "give instruction in sound doctrine and also to rebuke those who contradict it" (Titus 1:9; cf., 2:15). In fact, if needed, they should "rebuke them sharply" (Titus 1:13). Paul reminded those same elders, "But as for you, teach what accords with sound doctrine" (Titus 2:1, 7-8, 10; 1:9).

Ironically, Paul did not believe all divisions were bad. Believers in Corinth were divided on many issues. There were divisions over which apostle to follow (1 Cor. 1), Christian maturity (Ch. 3), sexual immorality (Ch. 5, 6), lawsuits against believers (Ch. 6), marriage and divorce (Ch. 7), food offered to idols (Ch. 8, 10), roles of husbands and wives (Ch. 11), the Lord's Supper (Ch. 11), spiritual gifts (Ch. 12-14), Christ's resurrection (Ch. 15) and the believer's resurrection (Ch. 15). Therefore, it was not surprising when Paul said, "when you come together as a church, I hear that there are divisions among you. And I believe it in part, for there must be factions among you in order that those who are genuine among you may be recognized" (1 Cor. 11:18-19).

While in context of verse 19, Paul seems to be referring to divisions in approaching the Lord's Supper (11:20-22), verse 18 could certainly be referring back to all the divisions he wrote about in his first letter to the church at Corinth. Regardless, we know the Corinthians were divided on the Lord's Supper and many other issues. Paul explained the reason that God allows factions (faction comes from the Greek word for heresy) in the church is to test integrity of believers, so that over time those who truly belong to God will be made clear. People who are sound in doctrine and truth will abide by Paul's earlier admonition to the church at Corinth that "you may learn by us not to go beyond what is written" (1 Cor. 4:6). The ones who let God's word be the final authority will be those who are recognized as genuine.

Paul also named names of those who were teaching falsely or causing trouble in the church. For example, he noted that "some have made shipwreck of their faith, among whom are Hymenaeus and Alexander, whom I have handed over to Satan that they may learn not to blaspheme" (1 Tim. 1:19-20). Paul also said, "their talk will spread like gangrene. Among them are Hymenaeus and Philetus, who have swerved from the truth, saying that the resurrection has already happened. They are upsetting the faith of some" (2 Tim. 2:17-18). Paul went on: "Alexander the coppersmith did me great harm; the Lord will repay him according to his deeds. Beware of him yourself, for he strongly opposed our message" (2 Tim. 4:14-15; cf., 2 Tim. 3:7-8). Paul remarked that "Phygelus and Hermogenes" abandoned him while he was in Asia (2 Tim. 1:15). Paul even reported that former companion "Demas, in love with this present world, has deserted me" (2 Tim. 4:10; cf., 3 John 1:9-10).

Paul strongly stressed the importance of correct teaching in the church. He told the church at Corinth if they failed to follow his instructions on speaking in tongues, if "outsiders or unbelievers enter, will they not say that you are out of your minds?" (1 Cor. 14:23). Responding to some Corinthians who were unsure of the logistics of the resurrection from the dead, he said that they were foolish for not comprehending it (1 Cor. 15:36). About the Judaizers, who were adding circumcision to the gospel, Paul said, "I wish those agitators would go so far as to castrate themselves!" (Gal. 5:12, NET Bible). Most importantly, if someone preached a false gospel, Paul said, "let him be accursed" (Gal. 1:8).

Finally, Paul addressed those who outright rejected the gospel. He called the unbelieving Jews in Thessalonica part of a group "who killed both the Lord Jesus and the prophets, and drove us out" (1 Thess. 2:15). Not only that, this group who rejected the gospel drew Paul's ire for "hindering us from speaking to the Gentiles that they might be saved" (2:16). For all their rebellion, Paul said they had filled "up the measure of their sins" (2:16). As a result, Paul concluded, "wrath has come upon them at last!" (2:16). When men reject the Savior and oppose the preaching of Him to others, they incur God's wrath. Paul had to be tough when circumstances warranted it, even blunt. However, Paul noted he did not want to "have to be severe in my use of the authority that the Lord has given me" (2 Cor. 13:10).

Type B Paul

Paul, who risked his life to spread the gospel (Acts 15:26), "spoke in such a way that a great number of both Jews and Greeks believed" (Acts 14:1). This was accomplished because he was "serving the Lord with all humility and with tears and with trials that happened to me through the plots of the Jews" (Acts 20:19). Paul ran the race for the gospel: "If only I may finish my course and the ministry that I received from the Lord Jesus, to testify to the gospel of the grace of God" (Acts 20:24). He wanted believers to understand that "the love of Christ controls us" (2 Cor. 5:14, 6:6; cf., 1 Cor. 14:1, 16:14; Eph. 3:17, 5:2; Col. 3:14; Titus 3:2) and we should "speak the truth in love" (Eph. 4:15). He encouraged the saints, "Let your speech always be gracious, seasoned with salt, so that you may know how to answer everyone" (Col. 4:6). Additionally, we must gently reprove those who oppose us in the hope that "God may perhaps grant them repentance leading to a knowledge of the truth" (2 Tim. 2:25; cf., Gal. 6:1).

When Paul preached the gospel of "Jesus Christ and him crucified", he said he did so "in weakness and in fear and much trembling" (1 Cor. 2:2-3). He said, "If I must boast, I will boast of the things that show my weakness" (2 Cor. 11:30). "Therefore I will boast all the more gladly of my weaknesses, so that the power of Christ may rest upon me. For the sake of Christ, then, I am content with weaknesses, insults, hardships, persecutions, and calamities. For when I am weak, then I am strong" (2 Cor. 12:9-10). Paul said Christ "was crucified in weakness, but lives by the power of God. For we also are weak in him" (2 Cor. 13:4).

Paul proclaimed "that Christ Jesus came into the world to save sinners, of whom I am the foremost" (1 Tim. 1:15). He said he considered all his days in Judaism as a Pharisee a "loss because of the surpassing worth of knowing Christ Jesus my Lord. For his sake I have suffered the loss of all things and count them as rubbish, in order that I may gain Christ and be found in him" (Philip. 3:8-9). He called himself "the least of the apostles" (1 Cor. 15:9). He also said, "I am nothing" (2 Cor. 12:11). Yet, though Paul said he was "the very least of all the saints, this grace was given, to preach to the Gentiles the unsearchable riches of Christ" (Eph. 3:8).

Speaking about the hope of the resurrection, Paul told Governor Felix, "I myself always strive to have a conscience without offense toward God and men" (Acts 24:16, NKJV). He said when talking to Jews or Greeks, "Give no offense" (1 Cor. 10:32) so "that they may be saved" (10:33). When speaking of his unsaved Jewish kinsmen, Paul lamented, "I have great sorrow and unceasing anguish in my heart. For I could wish that I myself were accursed and cut off from Christ for the sake of my brothers, my kinsmen according to the flesh" (Rom. 9:2-3).

As we have seen, Paul displayed both Type A and Type B approaches. Furthermore, he was not hesitant to show both at the same time. Addressing the pride and division in the church at Corinth, Paul said he loved the Corinthians like a father: "For I became your father in Christ Jesus through the gospel" (1 Cor. 4:15). However, he also told them that because there were "arrogant people" (4:18-19) among them, a loving father does not shy away from discipline. He asked, "Shall I come to you with a rod, or with love in a spirit of gentleness?" (1 Cor. 4:21).

Type A Peter

Peter took Christ aside "to rebuke him" (Matt. 16:22). He also cut off the ear of one of the men who wanted to arrest Jesus (John 18:3-11). Peter, not understanding the significance of Jesus showing His servanthood to His disciples, told Him, "You shall never wash my feet" (John 13:8). While Peter was rebuked by Christ for being in the wrong in those previous situations, God still placed him in positions that required directness and boldness. On the day of Pentecost, it was Peter who became the spokesman for a group of believers, right in Jerusalem where Jesus had been crucified just weeks earlier.

In speaking to the "Men of Israel" of the crucifixion and resurrection, Peter directly charged them of taking part in killing Jesus: "this Jesus, delivered up according to the definite plan and foreknowledge of God, you crucified and killed by the hands of lawless men" (Acts 2:23). He concluded by telling them, "Save yourselves from this crooked generation" (2:40). He also told other Jews that they "killed the Author of life, whom God raised from the dead" (Acts 3:15). He said that God raised Jesus "to bless you by turning every one of you from your wickedness" (Acts 3:26).

When Peter shared the gospel with the rulers, elders, scribes and the high-priestly family, he was "filled with the Holy Spirit" (Acts 4:8). He reminded them of "Jesus Christ of Nazareth, whom you crucified, whom God raised from the dead" (Acts 4:10). After Peter and John were released from prison for preaching the gospel, Peter prayed, "Now, Lord, look upon their threats and grant to your servants to continue to speak your word with all boldness" (Acts 4:29). God answered their prayer: "And they were all filled with the Holy Spirit and continued to speak the word of God with boldness" (4:31).

When Peter was taken before the council of these Jewish religious leaders, and the high priest told him to stop preaching the gospel, "Peter and the apostles answered, 'We must obey God rather than men. The God of our fathers raised Jesus, whom you killed by hanging him on a tree. God exalted him at his right hand as Leader and Savior, to give repentance to Israel and forgiveness of sins'" (Acts 5:29-31). Despite the fact that the council "wanted to kill them" (5:33) because of their message, "every day, in the temple and from house to house, they did not cease teaching and preaching that the Christ is Jesus" (5:42), for they could not stop speaking about what they had "seen and heard" (Acts 4:20).

Peter, like Paul, rebuked the Judaizers for claiming the Gentile disciples needed to be circumcised and to keep the law of Moses to be saved (Acts 15:1, 5). Peter said that God had decided the "Gentiles should hear the word of the gospel and believe. And God, who knows the heart, bore witness to them, by giving them the Holy Spirit just as he did to us" (15:7-8). Peter then said, "why are you putting God to the test by placing a yoke on the neck of the disciples that neither our fathers nor we have been able to bear?" (Acts 15:10). Peter said, when it came to Jews and Gentiles, God "made no distinction between us and them, having cleansed their hearts by faith" (Acts 15:9).

Peter also despised those who sought God's power for their own use. After Simon the Magician saw Peter and John bestow the gift of the Holy Spirit among those who believed in Samaria, he offered them money to do the same to him. Peter said to him, "May your silver perish with you, because you thought you could obtain the gift of God with money! You have neither part nor lot in this matter, for your heart is not right before God. Repent, therefore, of this wickedness of yours, and pray to the Lord that, if possible, the intent of your heart may be forgiven you. For I see that you are in the gall of bitterness and in the bond of iniquity" (Acts 8:20-23).

Finally, Peter sternly warned fellow Christians that "there will be false teachers among you, who will secretly bring in destructive heresies" (2 Pet. 2:1). He said these teachers would face condemnation (2:3). He even compared them to "irrational animals, creatures of instinct, born to be caught and destroyed, blaspheming about matters of which they are ignorant" (2:12). He noted they were "reveling in their deceptions, while they feast with you. They have eyes full of adultery, insatiable for sin. They entice unsteady souls. They have hearts trained in greed" (2:13-14). His conclusion for these heretics: "For them the gloom of utter darkness has been reserved" (2:17; cf., 3:7). Peter knew their destructive teachings brought them into a deeper damnation (2:20-21). "What the true proverb says has happened to them: 'The dog returns to its own vomit, and the sow, after washing herself, returns to wallow in the mire'" (2:22).

Type B Peter

Peter said that we should show "gentleness and respect" (1 Pet. 3:15) when giving an answer for the hope we have in Christ. He encouraged believers to "Keep your conduct among the Gentiles honorable, so that when they speak against you as evildoers, they may see your good deeds and glorify God" (1 Pet. 2:12). He said we must be holy so that we "may proclaim the excellencies of him" (1 Pet. 2:9). Peter said because of our obedience to the truth of the gospel, we should have "a sincere brotherly love" and "love one another earnestly from a pure heart" (1 Pet. 1:22).

When Jesus called His first disciples, He stepped into Peter's boat. Despite Peter toiling all night and catching no fish, Jesus instructed him to put out into the deep and let down his nets for a catch. Peter obeyed immediately, "at your word I will let down the nets" (Luke 5:5). As a result, the number of fish they caught caused the nets to start breaking. Another boat came to help and as the two boats were overfilled, they started to sink. At this, Simon Peter was overcome with an awe of God and a sense of his own sinfulness. After witnessing this miracle of Jesus, Peter "fell down at Jesus' knees, saying, 'Depart from me, for I am a sinful man, O Lord'" (Luke 5:8). Peter had seen a presentation of Christ's glory and humbled himself like Isaiah did: "Isaiah said these things because he saw Christ's glory, and spoke about him" (John 12:41, NET Bible). Peter knew, like Isaiah, that he was "a man of unclean lips... for my eyes have seen the King, the Lord of hosts!" (Isa. 6:5).

Peter described himself as "a servant and apostle of Jesus Christ" (2 Pet. 1:1). Peter never saw himself as a "Pope" of the church as the Roman

Catholic religion would have us believe. Knowing there is no such office of a papacy in the entire New Testament, he was unpretentious in calling himself "a fellow elder" (1 Pet. 5:1). Peter also humbled himself before fellow believers, saying we all possess "a royal priesthood" (1 Pet. 2:9) as we "offer spiritual sacrifices acceptable to God through Jesus Christ" (1 Pet. 2:5). He never spoke of a sacramental priesthood that mediates between God and man. Peter knew we have only one High Priest who mediates—the One he said Paul spoke about in his "Scriptures" (2 Pet. 3:16), the "one mediator between God and men, the man Christ Jesus" (1 Tim. 2:5).

Popes in the Roman Catholic religion frequently allow and encourage people to bow down before them, but Peter, whom Rome calls the first "Pope" of the church, knew nothing of this. When Peter was sent to deliver the gospel to Cornelius, "Cornelius met him and fell down at his feet and worshiped him. But Peter lifted him up, saying, 'Stand up; I too am a man'" (Acts 10:25-26). Peter, an apostle to the Jews (Gal. 2:8), was humbled by God in a vision (Acts 10:9-23) and instructed to deliver the gospel to Gentiles like Cornelius. Unlike Roman Catholic Popes who offer their hand to be kissed, Peter simply offered Cornelius the gospel message, which brought Cornelius and his household the Holy Spirit and salvation (11:14-15).

Peter, like Paul, had both Type A and Type B reactions. After Jesus was arrested, several people asked Peter whether he knew Jesus. Despite telling the Lord he would never deny Him, we get a glimpse of Peter's temper in this reaction to one of his accusers: "Then he began to invoke a curse on himself and to swear, 'I do not know the man'" (Matt. 26:74). Yet, after Peter realized how he had indeed denied the Lord three times, "He went out and wept bitterly" (26:75). We also get a glimpse of Peter's love for his Lord in his reaction to the resurrection. When several women told the disciples they had seen the empty tomb and had been told Christ had risen from the dead, "these words seemed to them an idle tale, and they did not believe them. But Peter rose and ran to the tomb; stooping and looking in, he saw the linen cloths by themselves; and he went home marveling at what had happened" (Luke 24:11-12).

Type A John

John's three epistles showed that he possessed a fervor of spirit. John's denunciation of sins and sinners is very forceful, including describing people who lie (1 John 1:6, 10; 2:4, 22; 4:20; 5:10) as an "antichrist" (1

John 2:22, 4:1-3; 2 John 1:7), a "deceiver" (2 John 1:7) and "children of the devil" (1 John 3:8-10). He not only warned about those who deny that Jesus Christ came in the flesh but added that "whoever greets him takes part in his wicked works" (2 John 1:7-11).

John called out people who departed from the faith as proof that they were "not of us" (1 John 2:19). He said we have to "test the spirits to see whether they are from God" (1 John 4:1), because there are many false prophets. John said if we hold to the apostle's teaching, we can distinguish between "the Spirit of truth and the spirit of error" (1 John 4:6). He declared, "Everyone who hates his brother is a murderer, and you know that no murderer has eternal life abiding in him" (1 John 3:15).

John even warned about divisive leaders in the church, who are so prideful of their position that they won't acknowledge the leadership of other godly people: "I have written something to the church, but Diotrephes, who likes to put himself first, does not acknowledge our authority" (3 John 1:9). John called this "wicked nonsense against us" and stated that Diotrephes also "refuses to welcome the brothers" and "puts them out of the church" (1:10). John said this was evil behavior and thus remarked, "Beloved, do not imitate evil" (1:11).

John and his brother James were given the names "Sons of Thunder" by Jesus (Mark 3:17). We can see how they might have earned this name. In Luke chapter 9, Jesus sent messengers ahead of Him to a village of the Samaritans to make preparations for Him. However, the Samaritans, who were prejudiced towards Jews, did not receive Jesus simply because His destination was Jerusalem. Then we read, "When the disciples James and John saw this, they asked, 'Lord, do you want us to call fire down from heaven to destroy them?'" (Luke 9:54). Like Peter above, James and John were told to stand down by Jesus.

There was another time John and his brother's thunder had to be calmed down by Jesus after they approached the Lord saying, "Teacher, we want you to do for us whatever we ask of you" (Mark 10:35). After they said, "Grant us to sit, one at your right hand and one at your left, in your glory" (10:37), Jesus said to them, "You do not know what you are asking" (10:38). When the other ten apostles heard this request "they began to be indignant at James and John" (10:41).

In Mark 9, John approached Jesus and said to him, "Teacher, we saw someone casting out demons in your name, and we tried to stop him, because he was not following us" (9:38). Jesus had to rein in John's thunder yet again. He said, just because he was not one of the twelve, do not stop him, "For the one who is not against us is for us" (Mark 9:40).

John's "Thunder" nickname may also have been the result of his zeal and power in preaching the gospel. John was standing with Peter as he preached the Pentecost sermon (Acts 2:14). When the Jerusalem crowd heard the gospel, they asked "the apostles, 'Brothers, what shall we do?'" (Acts 2:37). "Three thousand souls" (2:41) were saved that day due to the bold stance of Peter, John and the rest of the apostles.

John was with Peter at the gates of the temple when they were both thrown in jail for the preaching of the gospel (Acts 3:11-4:3). God used their boldness for, "many of those who had heard the word believed, and the number of the men came to about five thousand" (Acts 4:4). When the rulers, elders and scribes commanded them to stop preaching the gospel, "Peter and John answered them, 'Whether it is right in the sight of God to listen to you rather than to God, you must judge, for we cannot but speak of what we have seen and heard'" (4:19-20). After Peter and John reported this harassment to the church, they all prayed, "Lord, look upon their threats and grant to your servants to continue to speak your word with all boldness" (4:29). God granted their request: "And they were all filled with the Holy Spirit and continued to speak the word of God with boldness" (4:31).

John's courage and boldness caused Paul to call him one of the "pillars" of the church along with James and Peter (Galatians 2:9). The fact that Paul appealed to John as one of those who had the most authority in the church says a lot about his leadership. He played an important role in supporting, building up, and maintaining the early church. Later, you can see more of John's thunder come out in the Book of Revelation.

Type B John

John was loyal and subservient to Jesus from the start. When Jesus first called John to be His disciple, John immediately put down his fishing net and left his "father Zebedee in the boat with the hired servants and followed him" (Mark 1:20). John, the "disciple whom Jesus loved" (John 21:7; cf., 13:23, 19:26, 20:2, 21:20), learned "grace and truth" (1:14) through his Lord (John 13:25). John said of believers in Christ, "we have all received, grace upon grace" (John 1:16). John submitted himself to the grace Christ provided, knowing that believers receive a daily supply of grace for the accomplishment of His work (John 15:5, 15; 17:22).

Thirty-one times in his three epistles, John mentions the importance of love. "Beloved, let us love one another, for love is from God" (1 John 4:7). Indeed, "We love because he first loved us" (1 John 4:19). He said, "Whoever loves his brother abides in the light" (1 John 2:10). This love is a self-sacrificial love: "By this we know love, that he laid down his life for us, and we ought to lay down our lives for the brothers" (1 John 3:16). Encouraging us to look forward to the Second Coming of Christ, John reminds us, "everyone who thus hopes in him purifies himself as he is pure" (1 John 3:3).

John was the only one of the twelve apostles present at the crucifixion. He obeyed Jesus's orders from the cross by taking a grieving Mary into his home (John 19:26-27). His obedience in taking in and caring for the widow Mary shows his devotion to a "pure religion", for we read, "Religion that is pure and undefiled before God the Father is this: to visit orphans and widows in their affliction" (James 1:27).

As a disciple, the quick-tempered but tender John was known as the Son of Thunder (Mark 3:17) as well as the apostle of love (John 13:23, 21:20; 1 John 4:7-21). It is very interesting to remember that the same John, who earlier called down fire on the Samarians to consume them (Luke 9:51-56), later came down to Samaria with Peter, to confer the gift of the Holy Spirit on the Samaritan believers (Acts 8:14-17). John was part of evangelism teams in the early church, for "they proclaimed the word of God in the synagogues of the Jews. And they had John to assist them" (Acts 13:5).

Type A Stephen

When Stephen was brought before the Sanhedrin, he was accused of preaching "blasphemous words against Moses and God" (Acts 6:11). When the high priest asked: "Are these things so?" (Acts 7:1), Stephen then proceeded to call the Jews "stiff-necked people, uncircumcised in heart and ears, you always resist the Holy Spirit" (7:51). As the Jewish leaders were getting angrier and angrier, Stephen preached on—rebuking them because they "killed those who announced beforehand the coming of the Righteous One [Jesus Christ], whom you have now betrayed and murdered" (7:52).

After saying all this, Stephen then admonished them for not keeping the law God had given them: "you who received the law as delivered by angels and did not keep it" (7:53). Their reaction? "They were enraged, and they ground their teeth at him" (7:54). They then stoned him to death (7:58) and began a persecution of the church.

Type B Stephen

Stephen was "full of grace" (Acts 6:8). He spoke with "wisdom and the Spirit" (Acts 6:10). When he spoke before the Sanhedrin, "his face was like the face of an angel" (Acts 6:15). Despite being stoned for his speech, "he cried out with a loud voice, 'Lord, do not hold this sin against them'" (Acts 7:60).

Once again, we see a disciple of Christ who was full of grace and the Spirit of truth. Stephen admonished unbelievers for violating God's law and rejecting God's Righteous One. Do you see a pattern here of employing both grace and truth?

Type A John the Baptist

John was an Old Testament prophet (Matt. 11:13), "The voice of one crying in the wilderness" (Matt. 3:3) who prepared the way for Jesus, "to give knowledge of salvation to his people in the forgiveness of their sins" (Luke 1:77). John, like Elijah (2 Kings 1:8), "wore a garment of camel's hair and a leather belt around his waist" (Matt. 3:4a). His diet consisted of "locusts and wild honey" (Matt. 3:4b). Locusts were eaten by the poor (Lev. 11:21-22). Louis A. Barbieri Jr., Chair of the Department of Theology at the Moody Bible Institute, writes, "Like Elijah he was a rough outdoorsman with a forthright message."[48]

If John the Baptist was known for one thing, it was a call to repentance: "Repent, for the kingdom of heaven is at hand" (Matt. 3:2). He rebuked the Pharisees and Sadducees as a "brood of vipers" for their lack of true repentance at his baptism (Matt. 3:7). He said they would experience "the wrath to come" (3:7) adding that they would be "thrown into the fire" (3:10). He called them "chaff" whom Jesus "will burn with unquenchable fire" (3:12) for having "rejected the purpose of God for themselves" (Luke 7:30).

John did no miraculous signs as the apostles did; however, the multitudes reported, "everything that John said about this man [Christ] was true" (John 10:41). His message about repentance and faith in Jesus was transparent in itself. When John called King Herod out for his sinful and unlawful behavior of taking his brother's wife (Mark 6:18), Herod put John in prison (Mark 6:17) and later beheaded him (6:27).

---

[48] Louis A. Barbieri Jr., *The Bible Knowledge Commentary*, p. 24.

Type B John the Baptist

Even though John the Baptist was chronologically older than the incarnate Jesus, he declared that Christ "was before me" (John 1:15, 30). John always pointed to Jesus and away from himself: "Behold, the Lamb of God, who takes away the sin of the world!" (John 1:29). When people confused him with the Messiah, John said, "You yourselves bear me witness, that I said, 'I am not the Christ, but I have been sent before him'" (John 3:28). He called Jesus mightier than himself and one "whose sandals I am not worthy to untie" (Luke 3:16). When Jesus came to be baptized, John said, "I need to be baptized by you, and do you come to me?" (Matt. 3:14). John willingly gave up the spotlight to Jesus, saying, "He must increase, but I must decrease" (John 3:30).

Typical of a Type A personality, John said whatever was on his mind. While in prison, he sent disciples to Jesus to ask Him, "Are you the one who is to come, or shall we look for another?" (Matt. 11:2-3). John may have been wondering why he was in prison. Wasn't the Messiah supposed to overcome wickedness and sin like that of Herod? Wasn't the Messiah "at this time [going to] restore the kingdom to Israel?" (Acts 1:6). However, in his heart, the same John who humbled himself in the presence of Jesus (Luke 3:16; Matt. 3:14; John 3:30), knew his Lord's First Advent was for Christ to be the sin bearer for the world (John 1:29).

Type A Jude

Jude focused on exposing the false teachers that had secretly snuck in among the church: "For certain people have crept in unnoticed who long ago were designated for this condemnation, ungodly people, who pervert the grace of our God into sensuality and deny our only Master and Lord, Jesus Christ" (Jude 1:4). He challenged Christians to "contend for the faith" (1:3) and fight for the truth against these apostate, ungodly people who were blaspheming God's name.

Jude then mentioned apostasies of past history as a way of warning against present and ongoing apostasy. He wrote about how God judged the Israelites who had come out of Egypt and were destroyed in the wilderness because they "did not believe" (1:5). He wrote that the people of Sodom and Gomorrah, who "indulged in sexual immorality and pursued unnatural desire", are "undergoing a punishment of eternal fire" (1:7).

Jude says those who "defile the flesh, reject authority, and blaspheme" (1:8) are "like unreasoning animals" (1:10). He pronounced woe to them, because they sin "without fear" (1:11-12). He said they are "shepherds feeding themselves; waterless clouds, swept along by winds; fruitless trees" (1:12), people of "shame" destined for "the gloom of utter darkness" (1:13). Jude says Enoch prophesied about such people's deeds "that they have committed in such an ungodly way" (1:14-15). He declared that they "are grumblers, malcontents, following their own sinful desires; they are loud-mouthed boasters, showing favoritism to gain advantage" (1:16).

Type B Jude

Jude, the half-brother of Jesus (Matt. 13:55; Mark 6:3; 1 Cor. 9:5; Jude 1:1), identified himself as "a servant of Jesus Christ" (Jude 1:1). In his epistle, he said, "those who are called, beloved in God the Father and kept for Jesus Christ: May mercy, peace, and love be multiplied to you" (1:1-2). In our daily walk, we should reciprocate with the same by offering mercy, peace and love towards others. He also said believers should go about "building yourselves up in your most holy faith and praying in the Holy Spirit, keep yourselves in the love of God, waiting for the mercy of our Lord Jesus Christ that leads to eternal life" (1:20-21).

At the end of his short letter, Jude tells the "beloved" (1:20) to "have mercy on those who doubt; save others by snatching them out of the fire; to others show mercy with fear, hating even the garment stained by the flesh" (1:22-23). This last admonishment is important. When encountering such "scoffers...who cause divisions, worldly people, devoid of the Spirit" (1:18-19), we are told to have mercy while trying to rescue them from eternal punishment. Notice that Jude warns us that our mercy must be accompanied by fear and hatred for their sin. While we go about our attempts of "snatching them out of the fire", we must be aware that such people are stained by sin. Thus, we must keep our separation and purity during our rescue attempts.

Again, we see a servant of Christ telling us to show mercy, peace, and love, while at the same time contending for the faith against ungodly people who pervert the grace of God and deny the Lordship of Jesus Christ. We should keep ourselves in the love of God while also warning those who indulge in sexual immorality, pursue unnatural desires and defile the flesh. We are told to have mercy while exposing fruitless trees, ungodly deeds and loud-mouthed boasters. To actually show mercy with fear, we must hate the sin so much that we make sure we ourselves are not stained by it.

Note that Jude wrote to all believers, not just the elders and deacons. In verse 1, he began his letter with the greeting: "To those who are called, beloved in God the Father and kept for Jesus Christ." Since Jude addressed the whole congregation, this means every believer should contend for the faith. Chuck Swindoll, in his overview of Jude, writes, "Jude reminds us that there is a time and a place for the aggressive protection of the truth from those who would seek to tear it down. How can you participate in defending the truth from error?"[49]

Type A or Type B?

If you are stuck in an exclusive Type A or Type B approach in your gospel witness, consider the disciples' examples. They shared the truth in love, yet they were bold and straightforward in calling sinners to repentance and faith. Let us not set up a false dichotomy between Type A and Type B gospel preaching or create a bifurcation between truth and love. The fact is, as we have documented from the disciples, their use of Confrontational Evangelism, combining Type A and Type B approaches together in perfect synergy, was how they delivered the gospel.

We see this synergy exemplified in Acts chapter 4. Peter and John were "teaching the people and proclaiming in Jesus the resurrection from the dead" (Acts 4:2). They told the rulers and elders and scribes gathered together in Jerusalem that they were guilty of rejecting and crucifying Jesus. While the rulers were astonished at Peter and John's boldness (4:13), they were also greatly annoyed at their message. Despite this, many believed and the church continued in the Spirit with boldness (4:31). Finally, notice this: "And with great power the apostles were giving their testimony to the resurrection of the Lord Jesus, and great grace was upon them all" (4:33). Do you see the harmony here? They were all filled with the Holy Spirit and great grace was upon them all. As a result, there was boldness *and* grace in their testimony.

While it is certainly true that Christ's disciples all spoke the truth in love and with respect, they also clearly destroyed arguments, confronted and opposed error, and debated, refuted and rebuked false teachers. At times, they had their spirit within them provoked and walked away when the situation warranted it. Speaking the truth in love and confronting error are not contradictory things. When we confront someone with their

---

[49] Chuck Swindoll, https://www.insight.org/resources/bible/the-general-epistles/jude.

law breaking, knowing that "through the law comes knowledge of sin" (Rom. 3:20), we can point out some truthful things to sinners that are hard to hear. Yet as we speak these truthful things in love, some will say, "we will hear you again about this" (Acts 17:32). How blessed we would be if we were like the early disciples, where some "people begged" (Acts 13:42) them to come back and preach the gospel to them. However, we also must be prepared for a similar rejection like Paul received while teaching the gospel at Ephesus: "some became stubborn and continued in unbelief, speaking evil of the Way" (Acts 19:9). Still others may "become your enemy" even when you tell them the truth (Gal. 4:16).

When Paul addressed all the saints at Philippi, he commended them for "their partnership in the gospel" (Philip. 1:5) and for their "defense and confirmation of the gospel" (1:7). He added, "it is my prayer that your love may abound more and more, with knowledge and all discernment" (1:9). We have to possess love along with knowledge and discernment in preaching the gospel. As Will Metzger tells us, "We must learn to become assertive without being obnoxious."[50]

Furthermore, Nathan Busenitz, Professor of Theology at The Master's Seminary, writes, "The New Testament draws a clear distinction between compassion and compromise. Though we seek to win sinners by presenting the truth to them in love, we must avoid any accommodation toward false teachers—even in an effort to be nice.... Biblical love rejoices in the truth (1 Cor. 13:6), abhors that which is evil (Rom. 12:9), and walks in the commandments of Christ (2 John 6). Thus, the Christian apologist aspires to balance a biblical compassion toward those who are lost with a righteous indignation toward those who are leading others astray."[51]

Some Christians may have a naturally contentious disposition, while other believers have it in their nature to be peacemakers. As we have seen, the disciples were both! They would "contend for the faith" (Jude 3), while at the same time putting on "the readiness given by the gospel of peace" (Eph. 6:15). This is the essence of CE. Evangelist Mike Gendron writes, "We need to ask God for courage and boldness as we rely on the power of His Word. May we all become more like the apostles who were strong, bold, fearless, dogmatic, unaccommodating of error, courageous, intolerant of sin, inflexible concerning the Gospel, controversial, willing to die for the truth."[52]

---

[50] Will Metzger, *Tell The Truth*, p. 216.
[51] Nathan Busenitz, John MacArthur, *Evangelism*, p. 54.
[52] Mike Gendron, *Contending for the Gospel*, p. 57.

The disciples' balance of making sure they shared the truth in love mirrored that of their Lord, for "grace and truth came through Jesus Christ" (John 1:17). This grace and truth paradigm is what we turn to in our next chapter.

GRACE AND TRUTH

"For the law was given through Moses; grace and truth came through Jesus Christ" (John 1:17).

For the One who is the embodiment of grace and truth, it is no surprise that "all the people were hanging on his words" (Luke 19:48), for "No one ever spoke like this man!" (John 7:46). When the Pharisees "plotted how to entangle him in his words" (Matt. 22:15) and how "to trap him in his talk" (Mark 12:13), Jesus responded to their challenges with grace and truth. Thus, His enemies ended up trapped themselves, and "marveling at his answer they became silent" (Luke 20:26).

While Christ is the fountain of grace (Acts 15:11; John 4:14), He is also the foundation of all that is true (John 14:6, 18:37). Jesus embodies the fullness of grace and truth. He is the only person who has done both perfectly. We can see a simple example of this when Jesus instructed His disciples, "If your brother sins, rebuke him, and if he repents, forgive him" (Luke 17:3). A brother sinning requires we point out the truth of their sin by rebuking them. If they repent, the second half of the truth/grace paradigm kicks in when we gracefully offer God's forgiveness to them.

Just as Christ's disciples balanced truth and love (see chapter ten), we look to follow Jesus, who came "from the Father, full of grace and truth" (John 1:14). When we display grace and truth, we reflect Jesus in our witnessing, as people see both aspects of His character. Randy Alcorn of Eternal Perspective Ministries writes, "Attempts to 'soften' the gospel by minimizing truth keep people from Jesus. Attempts to 'toughen' the gospel by minimizing grace keep people from Jesus. It's not enough for us to offer grace or truth. We must offer both. When we offend everybody, we've declared truth without grace. When we offend nobody, we've watered down truth in the name of grace. John 1:14 tells us Jesus came full of grace AND truth. Let's not choose between them, but be characterized by both."[53]

Jesus, Full of Grace

When we read that Christ was full of grace, the scriptures tell us the incarnation allowed Him to sympathize with our weaknesses so that we may receive mercy and find grace in time of need. He came as one gentle and lowly in heart. At times, He was moved with pity and wept. He said in Him we will have peace and rest for our souls. He had compassion on sinners and healed and forgave sins at the same time. Jesus washed His disciples' feet and prayed for them. He prayed for all believers, calling us His friends and brothers. He said He would love His own to the end. He was the good shepherd who laid down His life for His sheep. He humbled himself by becoming obedient to death on a cross. He promised us that He would be with us always to the end of the age. He said He would confess our names before the Father and give His faithful the crown of life.

We see the grace of Jesus when He took little children "in his arms and blessed them" (Mark 10:16). The "children were brought to him that he might lay his hands on them and pray" (Matt. 19:13). He welcomed

---

[53] Randy Alcorn, Full of Grace and Truth, Like Jesus, https://www.epm.org/blog/2018/Apr/4/grace-truth-jesus

sinners and tax collectors and ate with them (Mark 2:15). When the scribes and the Pharisees questioned why He would associate with such "sinners", Jesus responded, "I came not to call the righteous, but sinners" (Mark 2:17). Our Lord said He was "gentle and lowly in heart, and you will find rest for your souls" in Him (Matt. 11:29; cf., Rev. 2:3). He said that we "may have peace" in Him because He has "overcome the world" (John 16:33).

Right after His close friend John the Baptist was beheaded, "when Jesus heard this, he withdrew from there in a boat to a desolate place by himself" (Matt. 14:13). Despite His sorrow, when people followed Him on foot from the towns, Jesus "saw a great crowd, and he had compassion on them and healed their sick" (14:13-14). When Christ saw the crowds were hungry and far from home, "He had compassion on them, because they were like sheep without a shepherd. And he began to teach them many things" (Mark 6:34). After this, He miraculously fed "five thousand" (6:41-44).

Jesus gave a blessing to "those who hear the word of God and keep it" (Luke 11:28). He said God's word will transform us daily: "Sanctify them in the truth; your word is truth" (John 17:17). Jesus said the seed that is sown in our hearts to bring us to salvation "is the word of God" (Luke 8:11), creating new life in "those who, hearing the word, hold it fast in an honest and good heart, and bear fruit with patience" (8:15). He said, "Everyone who comes to me and hears my words" (Luke 6:47) has a foundation as solid as rock that will not be shaken. Jesus told His disciples to abide in Him and keep His commandments so that "my joy may be in you, and that your joy may be full" (John 15:11).

He healed and forgave sins at the same time (Matt. 9:1-8). Jesus healed the lepers, the lame, the blind, the deaf and raised people from the dead (Matt. 11:5, 4:24, 9:25, 15:30, 20:34, 21:14; Mark 5:41-42, 7:37, 8:25, 9:25, 10:52; Luke 7:18; John 9:1-7, 11:43-44). He even healed His enemies who came to arrest Him (Luke 22:51). He cast out demons (Matt. 12:22; Mark 1:23-25, 39, 5:15, 9:25; Luke 8:2) and showed pity by healing a woman who had been ailing for eighteen years (Luke 13:16). He allowed people who simply "touched his garment" (Mark 5:27, 6:56) to be healed. When a man asked Jesus to come to his house to heal his son who was near death, Jesus told him to go back to his home and he would find his son healed, "Go; your son will live" (John 4:46-54). Jesus did the same for a Centurion, whose slave was suffering terribly, "Go; let it be done for you as you have believed" (Matt. 8:13). Telling a man that

He could restore his lifeless daughter, Jesus said, "Do not fear, only believe" (Mark. 5:36). Despite the fact that some in the crowd "laughed at him" (5:40), Jesus proceeded to graciously raise the child from the dead.

He blessed the poor in spirit and those who mourn, "for theirs is the kingdom of heaven" (Matt. 5:3-4). Jesus told us not to be anxious about our lives, as God will provide everything we need (Matt. 6:25-33). When the disciples became fearful, He told them, "Do not be afraid" (Matt. 14:27; cf., 17:7, 28:10; Mark 6:50; John 6:20; Rev. 1:17). While promising to send the Holy Spirit, He said, "Let not your hearts be troubled, neither let them be afraid" (John 14:27). He washed His disciples' feet (John 13:5), and He prayed for His disciples, both as a group (John 17:9) and individually (Luke 22:32). He also prayed for all believers to be one (John 17:20-23). Jesus called His followers "friends" (John 15:14-15), "children" (John 21:5) and "my brother and sister" (Mark 3:35). At times, our Lord was "deeply moved" (John 11:33) and "wept" (John 11:35; cf., Matt. 14:13) with His followers when tragedy struck. At other times, He was "Moved with pity" (Mark 1:41) when people came to Him for healing.

Jesus told us to love our enemies (Matt. 5:44), forgive them (Matt. 6:14; Mark 11:25) and to pray for them (Luke 6:28). When He was asked how many times we should forgive someone for sinning against us, Jesus said, "seventy-seven times" (Matt. 18:22, in other words—no limit). He said He "loved his own who were in the world, he loved them to the end" (John 13:1). Therefore, we should "love one another" (John 15:17), remembering that "whatever you wish that others would do to you, do also to them" (Matt. 7:12). He told us to "Be merciful, even as your Father is merciful" (Luke 6:36). Jesus said He was "gentle" (Matt. 11:29; cf., 21:5) and told His disciples to be the same (Matt. 18:4, 23:12) and to "be at peace with one another" (Mark 9:50).

While Jesus, during the course of His teaching and ministry, pronounced judgments, woes and indictments against the evil and hypocritical scribes and Pharisees, He left the judgment of the suffering He endured at the hands of the lawless men, who crucified and killed Him, in the hands of God. Peter tells us, "When he was reviled, he did not revile in return; when he suffered, he did not threaten, but continued entrusting himself to him who judges justly" (1 Pet. 2:23).

Several times, Jesus commended people for their faith. At one time, "some people brought to him a paralytic, lying on a bed" (Matt 9:2). When Jesus saw their faith, He not only healed the man but told him "your sins are forgiven" (9:1-7). Jesus gave sight to two blind men who cried out for mercy—telling Jesus they believed He could heal them. Jesus told them, "According to your faith be it done to you" (Matt. 9:29; cf., Matt. 8:10). When a Canaanite woman begged Jesus to heal her demon-oppressed daughter, she knew well that she was not of the house of Israel, of whom Jesus had come. When she told Christ that she would be as a dog and settle for the crumbs that fell on the floor of that house, Jesus responded, "'O woman, great is your faith! Be it done for you as you desire.' And her daughter was healed instantly" (Matt. 15:28). When "a woman of the city, who was a sinner…brought an alabaster flask of ointment" (Luke 7:37) and anointed Jesus' head with oil and wet His feet with her tears, Jesus said to her, "Your faith has saved you" (Luke 7:50).

Jesus told His disciples, "the Son of Man came not to be served but to serve, and to give his life as a ransom for many" (Matt. 20:28). Despite this, Jesus showed real emotions when speaking of His upcoming crucifixion, "Now is my soul troubled" (John 12:27). When telling His disciples Judas would betray Him, "Jesus was troubled in his spirit" (John 13:21). At His arrest, Christ gave Pilate "no answer, not even to a single charge, so that the governor was greatly amazed" (Matt. 27:14). Yet, Jesus made a "good confession" before Pontius Pilate (1 Timothy 6:13). He called Himself the good shepherd who "lays down his life for the sheep" (John 10:11). Our Savior "humbled himself by becoming obedient to the point of death, even death on a cross" (Philip. 2:8), despite the fact that He told His disciples His enemies would "mock him and spit on him, and flog him" (Mark 10:34). When the thief on the cross, next to Jesus, simply asked for grace in spite of his guilt, "we are receiving the due reward of our deeds… Jesus, remember me when you come into your kingdom" (Luke 23:41-42), the Lord told him, "Truly, I say to you, today you will be with me in paradise" (23:43).

In an appearance to His disciples after His resurrection, the risen Christ calmed His apostles, who were behind locked doors "for fear of the Jews" (John 20:19), saying, "Peace be with you" (20:21). A few days later, Jesus put to rest the doubts of Thomas by showing him His resurrected-scarred hands, "Do not disbelieve, but believe" (20:27). Jesus then gave a future blessing for the faithful of all ages who will not see such direct evidence: "Blessed are those who have not seen and yet have believed" (20:29; cf., 1 Pet. 1:8). He reassured His followers by saying, "I am with you always, to the end of the age" (Matt. 28:20) and "Because I live, you also will live" (John 14:19). The risen Christ told Paul to "Take courage" (Acts 23:11) as he was instructed to take the gospel to Rome.

As our High Priest "who has gone into heaven and is at the right hand of God" (1 Pet. 3:22), Jesus is able to "sympathize with our weaknesses" because He had "been tempted as we are, yet without sin" (Heb. 4:14-15). As a result, we can "with confidence draw near to the throne of grace, that we may receive mercy and find grace to help in time of need" (4:16), because "He always lives to make intercession" (Heb. 7:25; cf., 9:24; 1 Tim. 2:5) for us (Rom. 8:34; cf., 1 John 2:1-2).

Jesus showed His grace to the churches He addressed in The Book of Revelation. To the church in Ephesus, He commended them for enduring evil and "bearing up for my name's sake" (Rev. 2:3). To the church in Smyrna, He said despite the persecution they suffered, "Be faithful unto death, and I will give you the crown of life" (2:10). Jesus commended the church in Pergamum because "you hold fast my name, and you did not deny my faith" (2:13). To the church in Thyatira, Jesus said, "I know your works, your love and faith and service and patient endurance, and that your latter works exceed the first" (2:19). To the church in Sardis, Jesus said of the remnant still loyal to Him, "The one who conquers will be clothed thus in white garments, and I will never blot his name out of the book of life. I will confess his name before my Father and before his angels" (3:5).

To the church in Philadelphia, Jesus encouraged them, "you have but little power, and yet you have kept my word and have not denied my name" (3:8). He advised them, "Hold fast what you have, so that no one may seize your crown" (3:11). To the church in Laodicea, Jesus made this offer: "I counsel you to buy from me gold refined by fire, so that you may be rich, and white garments so that you may clothe yourself and the shame of your nakedness may not be seen" (3:18).

Yes, Jesus came with a message full of grace, and we are reminded of that in the final verse of the Bible, "The grace of the Lord Jesus be with all. Amen" (Rev. 22:21). Let us keep in mind that a biblical message of grace is also full of truth. Grace doesn't make people disregard truth; it makes them uphold and honor truth. In the grace section above, we saw where Jesus befriended sinners; in the truth section below, we will see where He never befriended sin.

Jesus, Full of Truth

For those familiar with the Bible, they know that Jesus balanced His grace with truth. The truth He spoke, much of which was manifested from a righteous anger, is carefully considered by mature Christians who understand the context of such biblical texts. However, for those who are not biblically literate and have only heard of the sentimental Jesus, what you are about to read may shock you. Some may even deny Jesus ever said or did such things. While the truth with which Jesus confronted people may be unfamiliar to some, those of us who love the scriptures see a perfect righteousness in all Jesus said and did. What Jesus, the Holy One of God, said and did, is written in the Bible for all of us to see.

Jesus opposed the scribes and Pharisees for teaching doctrines of men that contradicted God's word. He rebuked those for misinterpreting scripture, telling them they knew neither the scriptures nor the power of God. At times, Jesus sighed deeply in his spirit and got so angry at sin that He drove people out of the temple with a whip. He referred to people as blind fools, workers of lawlessness, hypocrites, a devil, serpents, ravenous wolves, diseased trees, liars, corpses, murderers, adulterers, heathens, pigs and children of hell, who not only won't escape being sentenced to hell but also will send others there with their contaminated teachings. When some told Jesus He was offending them, He simply said "woe to you."

Jesus silenced enemies with His arguments. He marveled because of people's unbelief. He even rebuked His own disciples at times for their faithlessness and hardness of heart. He warned that the devil can have people's ears and that their father even can be the devil. We also read where Jesus displayed hate and wrath, and that unbelievers will face His wrath when in His righteousness He judges and makes war in the end times. If you don't believe what you just read, you probably are a grace-oriented Christian who needs to balance your grace with a strong dose of truth. Keep reading.

Jesus said, "I have come into the world—to bear witness to the truth. Everyone who is of the truth listens to my voice" (John 18:37). The scriptures tell us Jesus confronted people with the truth of their sin and unrighteousness (Luke 5:32). Jesus told the Jews they were slaves to sin (John 8:34). He told them the only way to have liberty from their slavery to sin was to be freed through Him. He said if you want to be my disciples, "you will know the truth, and the truth will set you free" (8:32). The truth Jesus spoke of is that God has acted in history through His Messiah, the same Messiah who came "to proclaim liberty to the captives, and the opening of the prison to those who are bound" (Isa. 61:1). Jesus read from this verse in Isaiah when speaking at the synagogue in Nazareth, proclaiming Himself to be the Messiah who brings good news, "The Spirit of the Lord is upon me, because he has anointed me to proclaim good news to the poor. He has sent me to proclaim liberty to the captives and recovering of sight to the blind" (Luke 4:18).

Despite the truth Jesus spoke, "they laughed at him" (Mark 5:40; cf., Luke 8:53), "they ridiculed him" (Luke 16:14) and they "mocked him" (Luke 23:36). He was called "A glutton and a drunkard" (Luke 7:34). Some said, "He has a demon, and is insane; why listen to him?" (John 10:20). Others said, "He is out of his mind" (Mark 3:21). They concluded, "This man is not from God" (John 9:16). While in the end, "they spit in his face and struck him. And some slapped him" (Matt. 26:67), the biggest mistake they made was to claim, "We know that this man is a sinner" (John 9:24). The very One who came to "save his people from their sins" (Matt. 1:21) was the sinless Son of God (John 8:46), "a lamb without blemish or spot" (1 Pet. 1:19; cf., 1 Cor. 5:7; Eph. 5:2) whose truth would be available for those with open ears: "He who has ears to hear, let him hear" (Luke 8:8).

Jesus condemned many of the religious leaders of His day for being liars and hypocrites. The sinless Son of God "looked around at them with anger" (Mark 3:5; cf., Eph. 4:26). He confronted the greed and corruption of the money-changers in the Temple by saying they made God's house into a "den of robbers" (Mark 11:17). He made "a whip of cords" (John 2:15) and physically drove them out of the Temple. He also "poured out the coins of the money-changers and overturned their tables" (John 2:15).

Jesus called each of the unbelieving scribes and Pharisees, as well as their proselytes, "a child of hell" (Matt. 23:15). He referred to them as "blind fools" (23:17; cf., 19, 24, 26); "hypocrites" (23:13, 15, 23, 25, 27, 29); "full of greed and self-indulgence" (23:25); "whitewashed tombs, which outwardly appear beautiful, but within are full of dead people's bones and all uncleanness" (23:27); "full of hypocrisy and lawlessness" (23:28); "sons of those who murdered the prophets" (23:31); guilty because they "kill and crucify" the prophets and wise men God sent them (23:34); and "serpents" and a "brood of vipers" who won't "escape being sentenced to hell" (23:33). He challenged them, "Has not Moses given you the law? Yet none of you keeps the law" (John 7:19).

When the Pharisees challenged Jesus for not following their legalistic traditions, He responded by saying "You fools!" (Luke 11:40). He rebuked them for thinking they were clean on the outside, but inside they were "full of greed and wickedness" (Luke 11:39-40). He pointed to the prophets in saying, "Well did Isaiah prophesy of you hypocrites" (Mark 7:6), for you are wrongly "teaching as doctrines the commandments of men" (Mark 7:7; Matt. 15:1-9). Christ said the Pharisees were so defiled by their doctrines of men that they neglected "justice and the love of God" (Luke 11:42). Their doctrines of men made them so dead to God that they contaminated others, who stumbled over their teachings: "Woe to you! For you are like unmarked graves, and people walk over them without knowing it." (Luke 11:44; cf., Numbers 19:16). When one of the lawyers told Jesus, "you insult us also" (Luke 11:45), Christ responded, "Woe to you lawyers also!" (11:46). He told them they had so misinterpreted the scriptures that refer to the Messiah and the gospel dispensation that, "you have taken away the key of knowledge" (11:52). As a result, not only would they not enter into His kingdom, but they were hindering others as well (11:52; cf., 12:56).

Jesus rhetorically asked the Pharisees, "How can you speak good, when you are evil?" (Matt. 12:34). He told them because their hearts were evil, "on the day of judgment… by your words you will be condemned" (Matt. 12:36-37). He said their lack of repentance left them open targets for Satan. As a result, their final state will be "worse than the first" (Matt. 12:43-45; cf., 2 Pet. 2:20). When Jesus' disciples told Him that the Pharisees were "offended" at His teaching, He called them "Blind guides. And if the blind lead the blind, both will fall into a pit" (Matt. 15:12-14; cf., John 9:41).

Jesus told the Jews, who professed God as their Father, that by rejecting Him as the Father's Son, they belied their own profession and ended up becoming "a liar" (John 8:55). Furthermore, Christ noted, "the one who rejects me rejects him who sent me" (Luke 10:16). As a result, "For whoever is ashamed of me and of my words in this adulterous and sinful generation, of him will the Son of Man also be ashamed when he comes in the glory of his Father with the holy angels" (Mark 8:38). Of those rejecting that He had come in His Father's name, Jesus said, "I know that you do not have the love of God within you" (John 5:42). He told them God was not with them because they were too busy patting each other on the back: "How can you believe, when you receive glory from one another and do not seek the glory that comes from the only God?" (5:44). Jesus said of those in the Jewish nation who will reject Him at His second coming, they will be before God a corpse that will be eaten by "vultures" (Matt. 24:28).

When the Pharisees accused Jesus of casting out demons by the power of Satan, rather than by the power of the Holy Spirit, for such a false charge, He told them, "blasphemy against the Spirit will not be forgiven" (Matt. 12:22-31). He called the unbelieving scribes and Pharisees "An evil and adulterous generation" for demanding a sign from Him (Matt. 12:38-39, 16:4). Jesus "sighed deeply in his spirit" (Mark 8:12) as the Pharisees tried to argue with Him and test Him (8:11-13). When the Pharisees "plotted how to entangle him in his words" (Matt. 22:15), "Jesus, aware of their malice, said, 'Why put me to the test, you hypocrites?'" (22:18).

Jesus told Pilate that those "who delivered me over to you" have "the greater sin" (John 19:11). The Lord told unrepentant cities of Chorazin, Bethsaida and Capernaum, "Woe to you" (Luke 10:13-15), because their penalties on judgment day would be more severe for their unbelief, "it will be more bearable in the judgment for Tyre and Sidon than for you" (10:14). He denounced the cities that denied His mighty works to a worse fate than Sodom (Matt. 11:20-24). He said those who rejected His miracles "do not believe because you are not among my sheep" (John 10:26). Unbelieving Jews took great offense because He called them "thieves and robbers" (John 10:8) for trying to enter the sheep gate outside of Him. Jesus told them, while "The good shepherd lays down his life for the sheep" (10:11), "The thief comes only to steal and kill and destroy" (10:10).

One man asked Jesus' help in getting his brother to divide an inheritance with him. Jesus, who came to preach salvation, replied, "Man, who made me a judge or arbitrator over you?" (Luke 12:14). He then called the man out for his "covetousness" (Luke 12:13-15) and told him to be "rich toward God" (12:21) not himself. Jesus "silenced" (Matt. 22:34) religious leaders with His arguments. When the chief priests and elders asked Jesus where He got His authority, He said He wouldn't tell them unless they answered His question about John the Baptist. Jesus asked them, "The baptism of John, from where did it come? From heaven or from man?" (Matt. 21:25). When they would not answer Him, He reminded them that the people they despised the most (tax collectors and prostitutes) believed John's baptism was from heaven. His conclusion, "Truly, I say to you, the tax collectors and the prostitutes go into the kingdom of God before you" (Matt. 21:31-32).

Jesus said the self-righteous who try to exalt and "justify yourselves before men" are "an abomination in the sight of God" (Luke 16:15; cf., Luke 10:29). He warned about those "who trusted in themselves that they were righteous, and treated others with contempt" (Luke 18:9). Such men who exalt themselves will not be justified before God and instead "will be humbled" (18:14). He said the scribes, who strutted around in long robes hoping for attention, looked for the best seats in the synagogues, and tried to extort widows, "will receive the greater condemnation" (Mark 12:38-40). Concerning the Pharisees, Jesus warned against doing "the works they do. For they preach, but do not practice" (Matt. 23:3). They also were so sanctimonious that they practiced their "righteousness before other people in order to be seen by them" (Matt. 6:1). Jesus said such people are "hypocrites" for sounding a trumpet when giving to the needy (6:2) and for praying so "that they may be seen by others" (6:5). Jesus also said, "when you fast, do not look gloomy like the hypocrites, for they disfigure their faces that their fasting may be seen by others" (6:16).

Jesus referred to teachers of Pharisaic righteousness as a "gate…that leads to destruction" (Matt. 7:13); "false prophets, who come to you in sheep's clothing but inwardly are ravenous wolves" (7:15); a "diseased tree [that] bears bad fruit" (7:17); and "workers of lawlessness" (7:23; cf., John 7:19). Jesus said those who trust in these false prophet's teachings are "like a foolish man who built his house on the sand" (7:26). In contrast, Jesus taught that those who build their foundation on Him "Enter by the narrow gate…that leads to life" (7:13-14). They are like a "healthy tree [that] bears good fruit" (7:17) and will be the "one who does the will of my Father who is in heaven" (7:21). Jesus concluded, "Everyone then who hears these words of mine and does them will be like a wise man who built his house on the rock" (7:24).

Jesus told a group of Jews who wanted to stone Him, "you do not believe because you are not among my sheep. My sheep hear my voice, and I know them, and they follow me" (John 10:26-27). Jesus knew some were spiritually deaf to His message: "you seek to kill me because my word finds no place in you" (John 8:37). Jesus said they are deaf to His teaching because the devil has their ear, "Why do you not understand what I say? It is because you cannot bear to hear my word. You are of your father the devil, and your will is to do your father's desires" (8:43-44).

He said He spoke in parables to those outside the kingdom of God (Mark 4:11) and who would not perceive nor understand His message, "lest they should turn and be forgiven" (4:12). Also, concerning salvation truths, He thanked His Father for having "hidden these things from the wise and understanding" who despised Him (Matt. 11:25a) and for having "revealed them to little children" who humbly received Him (Matt. 11:25b). He told the unbelieving Jews who were grumbling among themselves, "No one can come to me unless the Father who sent me draws him" (John 6:44). Thus, in His prayer to the Father, Jesus said, "I am not praying for the world but for those whom you have given me" (John 17:9).

Jesus told His disciples to go "into every town and place" (Luke 10:1) to spread the message that "The kingdom of God has come near to you" (10:9). At the same time, He warned, "whenever you enter a town and they do not receive you, go into its streets and say, 'Even the dust of your town that clings to our feet we wipe off against you. Nevertheless know this, that the kingdom of God has come near.' I tell you, it will be more bearable on that day for Sodom than for that town" (10:10-12). We see Jesus gave a similar message when He said, "Do not give dogs what is holy, and do not throw your pearls before pigs, lest they trample them underfoot and turn to attack you" (Matt. 7:6). The dogs and pigs refer to unclean and vicious persons who have no desire to apprehend biblical truth. Since Jesus compared pearls to "the kingdom of heaven" (Matt. 13:45), to offer pearls (claims of the gospel) indiscriminately to those who despise your message, can result in attacks upon you with people trampling down the truth.

Jesus rebuked people for misinterpreting scripture. He told the Sadducees, who denied the resurrection, "You are wrong, because you know neither the Scriptures nor the power of God" (Matt. 22:29-32; cf., 21:42, 12:7, 15:3, 19:4; Mark 12:24-27). He rebuked the Pharisees for their lack of knowledge or abuse of scripture by saying things like, "if you had known what this means" (Matt. 12:7); "have you not read in the book of Moses" (Mark 12:26; cf., Matt. 19:4, 12:3, 22:31); "For if you believed Moses, you would believe me; for he wrote of me" (John 5:46); "Is it not written" (Mark 11:17); "You are quite wrong" (Mark 12:27); "Have you never read in the Scriptures" (Matt. 21:42; cf., Mark 12:10); "Is it not written in your Law" (John 10:34); "have you not read what was said to you by God" (Matt. 22:31); "He wrote you this commandment" (Mark 10:5); and "it is written of him" (Mark 9:13; cf., Luke 24:46). He told the Jews, "You search the Scriptures because you think that in them you have eternal life; and it is they that bear witness about me, yet you refuse to come to me that you may have life" (John 5:39-40). Jesus told the Jews who wanted to kill Him that they have never heard the Father's voice because "you do not have his word abiding in you" (John 5:38).

When questioned about His teachings by the high priest after His arrest, Jesus said, "I have always taught in synagogues and in the temple, where all Jews come together. I have said nothing in secret" (John 18:20). Despite this truthful response, an officer struck Him in the face. Notice that Jesus did not turn the other cheek, but challenged the officer, "If what I said is wrong, bear witness about the wrong; but if what I said is right [and of course it was], why do you strike me?" (John 18:22-23). Additionally, at His trial, "the chief priests and the whole council were seeking false testimony against Jesus that they might put him to death, but they found none" (Matt. 26:59-60). All during this time, "Jesus remained silent" (26:63). Despite knowing that He was about to be attacked (John 18:4), He ended His silence after they insisted that He tell them whether He is the Christ, "You have said so. But I tell you, from now on you will see the Son of Man seated at the right hand of Power and coming on the clouds of heaven" (Matt. 26:64; cf., Daniel 7:13-14). This truth about His divinity caused the high priest to tear his robes and charge Him with blasphemy. After the whole council called for His death, "they spit in his face and struck him" (26:67). In both instances above, knowing that the Jewish leaders would be offended to the point of physically attacking Him, Jesus stood firm confronting His enemies with the truth of who He was.

He warned anyone not to put a stumbling block in the way of an impressionable child, for "whoever causes one of these little ones who believe in me to sin, it would be better for him to have a great millstone fastened around his neck and to be drowned in the depth of the sea" (Matt. 18:6). Jesus said, "Everyone who is angry with his brother" is akin to a murderer (Matt. 5:22; cf., 1 John 3:15, 4:20-21) and "everyone who looks at a woman with lustful intent has already committed adultery with her in his heart" (Matt. 5:28).

Jesus asked, "Why do you call me 'Lord, Lord,' and not do what I tell you?" (Luke 6:46). He said that some who call Him "Lord, Lord" would not "enter the kingdom of heaven" (Matt. 7:21). Instead, they would hear Him say, "I never knew you; depart from me, you workers of lawlessness" (7:23; cf., 25:12, 41; Luke 6:46, 13:27). He taught more about hell than about heaven (Luke 16:19-31; Mark 9:43, 48; Matt. 7:13-14, 10:28, 13:42, 25:30, 41, 46; John 5:29). He warned people to "repent and believe in the gospel" (Mark 1:15) or "perish" (Luke 13:1-5).

Jesus taught that love for Him must take precedence over every human relationship, for "Whoever loves father or mother more than me is not worthy of me, and whoever loves son or daughter more than me is not worthy of me" (Matt. 10:37). Jesus' call for an unqualified allegiance could result in Him setting "a man against his father, and a daughter against her mother, and a daughter-in-law against her mother-in-law. And a person's enemies will be those of his own household" (10:35-36). While some who follow Christ are opposed by their own family members, let us remember that some in Jesus' own family initially opposed Him as well (John 7:5).

Jesus, in comparing those who would follow Him with salt, said if the salt should ever lose its saltiness, it then becomes "of no use either for the soil or for the manure pile" (Luke 14:35). Jesus taught that failure to pursue discipleship can indicate that faith is not really present, and that Christians who lose their distinctive saltiness become worthless. That's why "Jesus told his disciples, 'If anyone would come after me, let him deny himself and take up his cross and follow me'" (Matt. 16:24). For "Whoever does not bear his own cross and come after me cannot be my disciple" (Luke 14:27).

In contrasting our yet to be redeemed flesh with the perfect righteous of the Father, Jesus referred to His disciples as "evil" (Luke 11:13; cf., Rom. 3:23; Matt. 9:13). Since Jesus taught, "No one is good except God alone" (Mark 10:18), in the pervasive nature of our remaining sin, we are all evil in comparison to God, who is absolute goodness. Therefore, "If you then, who are evil, know how to give good gifts to your children, how much more will your Father who is in heaven give good things to those who ask him!" (Matt. 7:11). Jesus said, "out of the heart of man, come evil thoughts, sexual immorality, theft, murder, adultery" (Mark 7:21). He said the world's "works are evil" (John 7:7).

Jesus said if your brother sins against you, privately point out his fault. If he doesn't listen, bring one or two others along to establish the evidence against him. If he still doesn't listen, tell it to the church. If that fails, Jesus said, treat him "like a heathen" (Matt. 18:17, NKJV). The liberal Christian mantra is that "Jesus told us not to judge." However, Jesus said, "Do not judge by appearances, but judge with right judgment" (John 7:24; cf., Luke 12:57). If we make a right judgment, Jesus will say, "You have judged rightly" (Luke 7:43).[54]

Jesus also called Judas a "thief" (John 12:6), "a devil" (John 6:70), "the son of destruction" (John 17:12) and told the betrayer to his face,

---

[54] I actually had a woman once tell me that "Thou shalt not judge" was one of the Ten Commandments.

"Woe to that man by whom the Son of Man is betrayed! It would have been better for that man if he had not been born. Judas, who would betray him, answered, 'Is it I, Rabbi?' He said to him, 'You have said so'" (Matt. 26:24-25).

Jesus did not reserve His rebukes for unbelievers alone. He called Peter "Satan" for trying to thwart His mission, telling him, "You are a hindrance to me" (Matt. 16:22-23) as He "rebuked Peter" (Mark 8:33) in front of the disciples. After the disciples failed to cast out a demon from a man, Jesus rebuked them for being a "faithless and twisted generation" (Luke 9:41). When the disciples cried out to the Lord to save them from a raging sea that was about to tip over their boat, Jesus said to them, "'Why are you afraid, O you of little faith?' Then he rose and rebuked the winds and the sea, and there was a great calm" (Matt. 8:25-27). Jesus told His disciples to "Watch and beware of the leaven of the Pharisees and Sadducees" (Matt. 16:6). However, when they mistook this statement for bread, Jesus corrected them, "O you of little faith, why are you discussing among yourselves the fact that you have no bread?" (16:8). "Then they understood that he did not tell them to beware of the leaven of bread, but of the teaching of the Pharisees and Sadducees" (16:12). Shortly before their faith would really be tested with the crucifixion and their scattering, Jesus asked them, "Do you now believe?" (John 16:31). He was asking almost in a warning sense, "Do you truly and really believe?"

Even the risen Christ had to rebuke His disciples, "Afterward he appeared to the eleven themselves as they were reclining at table, and he rebuked them for their unbelief and hardness of heart, because they had not believed those who saw him after he had risen" (Mark 16:14; cf., Matt. 6:30, 14:31, 17:20; Mark 4:40, 9:19). To the disciples He met on the Road to Emmaus who had lost hope after His death, the risen Christ said to them "O foolish ones, and slow of heart to believe all that the prophets have spoken!" (Luke 24:25). When Peter asked the risen Jesus what the future held for his fellow apostle John, Jesus replied, "what is that to you? You follow me!" (John 21:22).

In the Book of Revelation, Jesus often spoke forcefully. He commended the church in Ephesus for testing and exposing false apostles, "You cannot bear with those who are evil, but have tested those who call themselves apostles and are not, and found them to be false" (Rev. 2:2). He also warned this church that unless they repented and returned to their original devotion and love for Him, their "lampstand", or witness in Ephesus, would be extinguished (Rev. 2:5). Then Jesus commended them for standing up against a group of heretics, "Yes this you have: you hate the works of the Nicolaitans, which I also hate" (2:6).

To the church in Smyrna, Jesus told them He knew they were being persecuted and slandered by the Jews who He said, "are a synagogue of Satan" (Rev. 2:9; cf., 3:9). To the church in Pergamum, Jesus warned that some in the church were being tempted into sexual immorality and idolatry, "Therefore repent. If not, I will come to you soon and war against them with the sword of my mouth" (2:16). To the church in Thyatira, Jesus warned them against following a self-proclaimed prophetess named Jezebel. He said, "you tolerate that woman" who was "teaching and seducing my servants to practice sexual immorality and to eat food sacrificed to idols" (2:20). Jesus warned, "those who commit adultery with her I will throw into great tribulation, unless they repent of her works, and I will strike her children dead" (2:22-23).

To the church in Sardis, Jesus said, "I know your works. You have the reputation of being alive, but you are dead" (Rev. 3:1). He warned those who have "soiled their garments" (3:4) to repent. To the church in Philadelphia, Jesus again called Jews who were enemies of the faith, "the synagogue of Satan" (3:9; cf. 2:9). To the church in Laodicea, Jesus gave them the harshest rebuke, saying of their works, "because you are lukewarm, and neither hot nor cold, I will spit you out of my mouth" (3:16). He also said, "you are wretched, pitiable, poor, blind, and naked" (3:17).

Yes, the Book of Revelation gives us a new perspective of the ascended Jesus, who is sitting at the right hand of God (Acts 7:55-56; Rom. 8:34; Eph. 1:20) and on His own throne (Rev. 3:21). We see where His divine love will be transformed to divine wrath. Those who reject Him will have to face "the wrath of the Lamb" (Rev. 6:16, 11:18, 14:10, 19:15; cf., Matt. 16:27, 25:41; John 5:22). We learn that "in righteousness he judges and makes war" (Rev. 19:11) and that He will "strike down the nations" (19:15). At Christ's return, all unbelievers will be judged (2 Thess. 1:7-9), with Jesus saying that those who rejected the greatest amount of divine revelation "will receive a severe beating" (Luke 12:47). He said, "on the day when Lot went out from Sodom, fire and sulfur rained from heaven and destroyed them all—so will it be on the day when the Son of Man is revealed" (Luke 17:29-30).

At His Second Coming, Jesus says, "He will separate people one from another as a shepherd separates the sheep [believers] from the goats [unbelievers]. And he will place the sheep on his right, but the goats on the left" (Matt. 25:31-33). "Then he will say to those on his left,

'Depart from me, you cursed, into the eternal fire prepared for the devil and his angels'" (25:41). "And these [the goats] will go away into eternal punishment, but the righteous [His sheep] into eternal life" (25:46; cf. John 5:28-29).[55]

For those who may have finished reading the previous section and found yourselves rejecting these things as not agreeing with the sentimental Jesus you have embraced, Paul said you have "another Jesus than the one we proclaimed" (2 Cor. 11:4). The Jesus of the Bible was not just grace and He was not just truth, He was both, as "grace and truth came through Jesus Christ" (John 1:17).

Jesus Came Full of Grace and Truth

When Jesus went to the synagogue in Nazareth and read from the scroll of the prophet Isaiah, notice the contrast in the response He received from that reading compared with a confrontation that followed. After He said, "Today this Scripture has been fulfilled in your hearing" (Luke 4:21), we read where "all spoke well of him and marveled at the gracious words that were coming from his mouth" (4:22). However, when the synagogue crowd began to question the authority by which He could say these things, Jesus, sensing their opposition, pointed to Israel's rejection of God's prophets, resulting in God sending them elsewhere—even to Gentiles (Elijah miraculously replenishing the widow's flour and oil in 1 Kings 17:8-16 and Elisha healing Naaman from his leprosy in 2 Kings 5:1-19). The mere mention of Gentiles having God's blessings rather than the Jews flipped the crowd into a furor: "all in the synagogue were filled with wrath" (4:28). They were so upset that they tried to kill Jesus before He left them. When the Jews first heard Jesus speak, they marveled at His gracious words, but when Jesus spoke the truth to them about rejecting Him as God's prophet, we see that they could not handle the truth.

While Jesus is "gentle and lowly in heart" (Matt. 11:29), there was also a time when He "looked around at them with anger" (Mark 3:5; cf., Eph. 4:26). Speaking in His typical straightforward way, Jesus told the unbelieving Jews that the Messiah *they expected* would not come. He told them because they rejected Him as the *true* Messiah, they would face the

---

[55] For those who believe that appearances of the angel of the Lord in the Old Testament were manifestations of Jesus before His incarnation, we see where Jesus led the Israeli army against their enemies (Exodus 23:20-23). Jesus, as the angel of the Lord, also was ready to destroy Jerusalem before the Father stopped Him (2 Sam. 24:16), and this same angel struck down 185,000 Assyrians in a single night (2 Kings 19:35).

consequences of their unbelief: "unless you believe that I am he you will die in your sins" (John 8:24). While Jesus spoke of the truth of who He really was and is, His words were also full of grace, for "As he was saying these things, many believed in him" (8:30). If we want to stand mature and preach the full counsel of God, we will preach a gospel that is not just full of grace or truth, but full of grace *and* truth. That way, we will understand the grace of God in truth and preach the way Jesus did.

Christian author and blogger Tom Gilson writes, "Grace and truth can't really be separated. Grace without truth isn't fully grace, for the truth is good for us even if it's hard. And truth without grace isn't fully truth: it's ugly and unloving, unlike God Himself."[56] Randy Alcorn puts all this in perspective in his book *The Grace and Truth Paradox*: "The apparent conflict that exists between grace and truth isn't because they're incompatible, but because we lack perspective to resolve their paradox. The two are *interdependent*. We should never approach truth except in a spirit of grace, or grace except in a spirit of truth. Jesus wasn't 50 percent grace, 50 percent truth, but 100 percent grace, 100 percent truth."[57] Alcorn went on to say, "Unfortunately, many non-believers only know two kinds of Christians: those who speak the truth without grace and those who are very nice but never share the truth. What they need to see is a third type of Christian—one who, in a spirit of grace, loves them enough to tell them the truth."[58]

As we balance grace and truth in our gospel preaching, we are most reflective of Jesus, as people see both aspects of His character through us. Yet some, when challenged to imitate Christ in finding the grace and truth balance, will object—we are not Christ! However, Paul said, "Be imitators of me, as I am of Christ" (1 Cor. 11:1). When "speaking the truth in love, we are to grow up in every way into him who is the head, into Christ" (Eph. 4:15). So, what would Jesus do, as many are fond of asking? He spoke with grace and truth; so should we.

---

[56] Tom Gilson, There's No Christian Strategy Without Grace and Truth, https://stream.org/no-christian-strategy-without-grace-truth/
[57] Randy Alcorn, *The Grace and Truth Paradox*, p. 16.
[58] Ibid, p.77.

⑫ GRACE AND TRUTH APPLIED

"Be wise as serpents and innocent as doves"
(Matthew 10:16)

"The snake-intelligence and the dove-innocence are both designed to keep the sheep out of trouble." - John Piper[59]

In the last two chapters, we have seen how the disciples balanced truth and love and that Jesus came full of grace and truth. Now comes time to see how these principles are applied to The Evangelism Circle. One thing we have learned so far is that when it comes to truth and love, or grace and truth, it's not one or the other, but both! We tell the truth in love and share the truth with grace. The application is to possess the

[59] John Piper, Sheep, Wolves, Snakes, and Doves, https://www.desiringgod.org/articles/sheep-wolves-snakes-and-doves

wisdom and boldness to tell the truth and also have the innocence before our Lord to show His grace.

Sheep, Wolves, Serpents and Doves

Jesus told His disciples in Matthew 10:16, "Behold, I am sending you out as sheep in the midst of wolves, so be wise as serpents and innocent as doves." Notice that He didn't say be serpents *or* doves but be serpents *and* doves. We are called to be wise *and* innocent, not just one or the other. Before we take a closer look at this, let's examine the metaphors in this passage.

Wolves are enemies of the gospel. Paul said, "I know that after my departure fierce wolves will come in among you, not sparing the flock" (Acts 20:29). Wolves also come "in sheep's clothing" (Matt. 7:15). Followers of Christ will find themselves facing wolves in the form of false prophets and false teachers, the arrogant, the proud, the mockers and even the violent. Only Christ's sheep, who are wise as serpents and innocent as doves, can successfully encounter and maneuver "ravenous wolves" (7:15).

How can we be a wise serpent? The serpent will lay low, taking in the dangers of its surroundings: "The serpent was more crafty than any other beast of the field" (Genesis 3:1). As snakes evaluate a new situation, they identify how or when to act. When all the facts are understood, the wise and patient serpent is ready to respond. Just like a wise serpent is crafty and patient, we need to use wisdom to move carefully and slowly into a witnessing situation, "Walk in wisdom toward outsiders, making the best use of the time" (Col. 4:5). A common mistake is to respond too quickly. In fact, one misstep can cause us to lose an opportunity altogether. It is better to lay low and evaluate a new situation before we identify how or when to act, "Look carefully then how you walk, not as unwise but as wise, making the best use of the time, because the days are evil" (Eph. 5:16).

At the same time, we are to be innocent as doves. Under Mosaic law, doves were clean (Gen. 15:9; Lev. 5:7, 12:6; Luke 2:24); a harbinger of peace according to Noah (Gen. 8:8-12); mentioned as the emblem of purity (Psalm 68:13); a symbol of the Holy Spirit (Gen. 1:2; Matt. 3:16); and the creature David wished that he could be, that he might fly away from the anguish within him to be at rest (Psalm 55:6-8). Doves are excellent navigators, bearing different weather conditions to deliver messages. They have the ability to move between two worlds—sky and earth. A dove can adjust to almost every kind of environment, as they are found in most places around the world.

We are to be like doves, navigating our way through difficult situations to be messengers of the good news. We are between two worlds. While "our citizenship is in heaven" (Philip. 3:20), we deliver the gospel to a fallen earth that can have "ravenous wolves" (Matt. 7:15). To be an effective harbinger of peace, we must be clean in our behavior and be filled with the Holy Spirit. We adjust to each witnessing situation by becoming all things to all men (1 Cor. 9:22), to be Christ's witnesses to the ends of the earth (Acts 1:8).

Before Jesus sent out His apostles, He told them to "proclaim as you go, saying, 'The kingdom of heaven is at hand'" (Matt. 10:7). Then He advised His sheep to be "wise as serpents and innocent as doves" (10:16). The very next verses show that the context of this passage is suffering persecution for the sake of the gospel. He told them, "Beware of men, for they will deliver you over to courts and flog you in their synagogues, and you will be dragged before governors and kings for my sake, to bear witness before them and the Gentiles. When they deliver you over, do not be anxious how you are to speak or what you are to say, for what you are to say will be given to you in that hour. For it is not you who speak, but the Spirit of your Father speaking through you" (Matt. 10:17-20). Christ informed us that while opposition and persecution can occur while sharing the gospel, He will not leave us unequipped for such circumstances. Jesus intended for us, as sheep among wolves, to assume all the good characteristics associated with the serpent and the dove in order to share the kingdom of heaven.

The Serpent's Wisdom and Truth

As the serpent uses wisdom and patience, we must have "wisdom from God" (1 Cor. 1:30) to evaluate each witnessing situation in order to "bear fruit with patience" (Luke 8:15). A Christian's faith is also founded in a "belief in the truth" (2 Thess. 2:13). Therefore, we should be "acquainted with the sacred writings, which are able to make you wise for salvation through faith in Christ Jesus" (2 Tim. 3:15). With this knowledge, we "teach what accords with sound doctrine" (Titus 2:1), because we "know the Spirit of truth and the spirit of error" (1 John 4:6). We "contend for the faith" (Jude 1:3) as "We destroy arguments and every lofty opinion raised against the knowledge of God, and take every thought captive to obey Christ" (2 Cor. 10:5). Let us all be "wise in Christ" (1 Cor. 4:10), for "we have the mind of Christ" (1 Cor. 2:16; cf., Eph. 1:17; 1 John 5:20).

The Dove's Innocence and Grace

How can we be innocent as doves when delivering the gospel? Paul demonstrated this when speaking to Felix about the resurrection of Christ. He told the governor at his trial, "I myself always strive to have a conscience without offense toward God and men" (Acts 24:16, NKJV, cf. Acts 23:1; Rom. 9:1-3; 2 Tim. 1:3; Heb. 13:18). When people ask us about the hope we have, we give an answer with "gentleness and respect" (1 Pet. 3:15). Christians are called to "Let your speech always be gracious, seasoned with salt, so that you may know how you ought to answer each person" (Col. 4:6).

Serpents and Doves Together

Jesus' disciples were both wise and innocent. For example, we read where Stephen was "full of grace and power" (Acts 6:8). Enemies of the gospel "rose up and disputed with Stephen. But they could not withstand the wisdom and the Spirit with which he was speaking" (Acts 6:9-10). Peter reminded the saints scattered throughout Asia Minor that they were born again through "the precious blood of Christ" (1 Pet. 1:19) and that they were "believers in God, who raised him from the dead" (1:21). Because of their devotion to the truth of the gospel, Peter said, "Having purified your souls by your obedience to the truth for a sincere brotherly love, love one another earnestly from a pure heart" (1:22). James asked, "Who is wise and understanding among you? By his good conduct let him show his works in the meekness of wisdom" (James 3:13). He said to seek "wisdom that comes down from above" (3:15), because "the wisdom from above is first pure, then peaceable, gentle, open to reason, full of mercy and good fruits, impartial and sincere" (3:17).

When Paul wrote to the church at Philippi about the "defense and confirmation of the gospel" (Philip. 1:7), he told them to have "knowledge and all discernment, so that you may approve what is excellent, and so be pure and blameless for the day of Christ" (1:9-10). Later, he told the Philippians, before their testimony about Christ could be effective, to be sure to "Do all things without grumbling or disputing, that you may be blameless and innocent, children of God without blemish in the midst of a crooked and twisted generation, among whom you shine as lights in the world, holding fast to the word of life, so that in the day of Christ I may be proud that I did not run in vain or labor in vain" (Philip. 2:14-16).

The serpent without the dove can deliver a message that is so venomous that it can give truth without grace. The dove without the serpent can deliver a seemingly harmless message that actually lacks wisdom and the whole council of God, thus giving grace without truth. Their match makes them a perfect fit for our Savior, because "grace and truth came through Jesus Christ" (John 1:17).

Separating Truth and Grace

Sometimes Christians only know how to speak truth but do not show love, or they only know how to love but don't have wisdom. When Phil Robertson, the small-town Louisiana patriarch of the nationally televised A&E reality show "Duck Dynasty," spoke out several times against homosexuality, calling it evil and akin to bestiality, he was suspended from the popular show, which eventually was not renewed. Many believe the show was canceled because of Robertson's stance. While Robertson spoke the truth when he quoted the Bible to support his statement that homosexuality is sinful, he had no balance of love. It was only after receiving a lot of criticism that he said he loves gay people but did not want to see them end up in hell. However, the damage had been done.

Chip Gaines and his wife Joanna hosted the popular HGTV series "Fixer Upper." When gay activists found out that Chip and his family attended a church that held the biblical position that homosexuality is a sin, all of a sudden, he and HGTV were under attack from the politically correct police. While Chip and Joanna would often speak of their Christian faith, when pressured to make a statement on their church's stance on homosexuality, Gaines said that he and his wife had their own "personal convictions", and that they would not be "throwing stones" by questioning someone's "sexual orientation."

Gaines wrapped up his statement by saying this, "The bottom line is, I would rather be loving than be right."[60] This is a false dichotomy for a Christian, because if we are loving, we will be right. The Bible says, "Love finds no joy in unrighteousness but rejoices in the truth" (1 Cor. 13:6, HCSB). Since Paul called homosexuality unrighteous in 1 Corinthians 6:9, it is never loving to fail to speak the truth about a practice God calls unrighteous. For Chip Gaines and all other Christians that take his unbalanced approach, the bottom line should always be "speaking the truth in love" (Eph. 4:15). That way, we will always be loving *and* right and not set up a false distinction between the two.

---

[60] Chip Gaines blog, https://magnolia.com/chips-new-years-revelation/

Phil Robertson's "pulpit pounding" gave truth but not love. To Robertson's credit, he later tried to find that balance. Chip Gaines' attempt at being loving, I have no doubt, was sincere on his part. However, he failed on being either loving or truthful, because biblical love will not be silent about unrighteousness, but will speak the truth in love about what God calls sin (1 Cor. 13:6; cf., 1 Cor. 6:9; Eph. 4:15). We as Christians need to find the balance to proclaim the truth in love—because love without truth is not truly love. In contrast, truth without love is still truth, but the serpent's truth bite without the innocence of a dove can be so stinging that it can lead to ears that won't hear.

While many Christians have failed in balancing out grace and truth, or even understanding the distinction between the two, others, mature in the faith, understand this balance and make it a daily part of their walk with Christ. While I confess that I have failed many times to live out this balance in my life, I have witnessed many others who have. I continue to marvel at how they consistently live out grace and truth, and I hope one day to be as they are.

The Grace and Truth Principle in Action

Well-known pastor and author John MacArthur gave us a great example of balancing grace and truth when he appeared on the TV show Larry King Live in 2010. Pastor MacArthur was one of four guests on a show that tackled the contentious issue of so-called same-sex marriage. While then U.S. Congresswoman Marilyn Musgrave of Colorado and Pastor MacArthur were defending biblical marriage between one man and one woman, Gavin Newsom, then the mayor of San Francisco, and Chad Allen, best known for his role on the 1990's TV series Dr. Quinn: Medicine Woman, were promoting the redefinition of marriage to include homosexuals.

While Newson and Musgrave were being interviewed via a remote feed, Pastor MacArthur sat in the studio right next to Chad Allen, across from Larry King. Allen, 36-years-old at the time, was openly living with his gay boyfriend. From the very beginning, there was an incredibly interesting dynamic occurring. While Pastor MacArthur received derision and obvious disdain for his position from the liberal Democratic San Francisco mayor, Allen not only showed great respect to the pastor that night, but he also seemed to have a sincere demeanor in listening when the pastor spoke. How could that be, you might ask? After all, Allen had won several awards from the gay community for his activism in support of "LGBT" causes. Here's why—Pastor MacArthur spoke to him with an amazing balance of grace and truth. While you can watch the whole interaction on YouTube,[61] I would like to highlight some key points of this discussion:

Larry King: "Why should the State be involved in a marriage?"

John MacArthur: "It's the State's responsibility to uphold what is right, to uphold righteousness, I mean, it is in the fabric of human thinking to understand a man and a woman make a marriage and a family. God has put that in the very thinking of people, it's in the heart."

Larry King: "Who is contributing more to the moral decay of the society, the adulterous husband with the female wife, or the loving gay couple who don't do that?"

John MacArthur: "You are asking me to do something I really can't do and that is make a judgment on which sin is better or worse than the other. We suffer in this country from adultery, divorce, the abuse of children, pedophilia, you name it. I'm not going to classify those in rank—they're sins! And they destroy the family."

Larry King: "Homosexuality is a sin?"

John MacArthur: "It is a sinful choice you make."

Larry King: "Did you make the choice to be heterosexual?"

John MacArthur: "It is natural to be heterosexual."

Larry King: "What do you mean natural?"

John MacArthur: "That's the way God made us, that's the normal."

Larry King: "But if he [Chad] doesn't feel that way, what is he then? He wasn't a sinner; it wasn't his decision."

John MacArthur: "Yeah. I think it was his decision."

Chad Allen: "I would love, absolutely love the pastor to point out to me where and when in my life I made that decision, cause I have to tell you it has caused a lot of pain to my parents, a lot of pain to me. It was a very, very tough thing I had to go through.

---

[61] Larry King Live. https://www.youtube.com/watch?v=zNQLhjlnzBA

I don't remember making that decision. If I did, maybe you can point it out, but it wasn't the case with me. It's who I am. You also said that, that it is in the fabric of the human being that, that, to understand that marriage was between a man and a woman. And that's what family was. It must not be, because it is not in the fabric of who I am. That's not the way I see it. Families come in all shapes, sizes and color."

John MacArthur: [Leaning gently into Chad.] "If I could respond this way, Chad. It had to be in the fabric of humanity, or you wouldn't be here."

Chad Allen: "I believe that reproduction is, I will give you that."

John MacArthur: "Let me respond to Chad, too, just on a personal basis, Chad, by saying, um, I don't think at some point you said, 'Okay, I'm going to be a homosexual [Chad nods in agreement], I got two alternatives, you know, I'm going to go and be a homosexual.' But I do think whatever sin patterns show up in our lives, I mean, they may be different for us, we can choose to continue down those paths of sin whether it is adultery or whatever it is, uh, or we can say, 'Look, this is sin and I need to deal with this in my heart. This is the way I'm being led. It's not right. It doesn't honor God. It is not according to His word. It is not going to ultimately bring blessing on my life.' I make the choice at that point. I can't make the choice to be a sinner, okay—*I am*—we all are. But once you start down the path of sin, if you recognize that it is that, then you look to the Lord for the remedy for that."

Chad Allen: "And I respect you beyond anything for your belief on that, I really do. And let me tell you what the sin was in my life as I see it.... The sin for me is hiding who I was.... I believe that it is God who has called me to open up and start talking about this."

John MacArthur: "That kind of a union [same-sex marriage] is sinful before God."

Chad Allen: "Even if that is the case, and listen, we'll all find out at the end of the day, can't we let God decide that?"

John MacArthur: "God has already decided that! I mean, it, it is in the word of God. It is unmistakably clear in the Bible."

Chad Allen: "Then what are we so worried about? What are we so scared about? Why, why all this trouble because they prevent me from being able to accept these privileges while I'm here? If God will ultimately take care of it?"

John MacArthur: "Let me, let me answer that personally. Because the Bible says in no uncertain terms that no homosexual or adulterer will ever inherit the kingdom of God. The question is not open."

Larry King: "Supposing then, Chad doesn't want to enter the kingdom of heaven? His right."

John MacArthur: "Oh, I think he does. Don't you?"

Chad Allen: [Chad takes his left hand and gently places it over John's shoulder.] "Absolutely, and you know what, and, and if that's the case great, but however, there may be people that don't, and I don't want this country governed by the word of the Bible. I don't want it. We have to be open to people who believe in all kinds of things."

John MacArthur: "But the Bible says that no sinner, and what's the category, more than just homosexuals, will ever enter the kingdom of God. And then it says this, but such were some of you. But you have been washed. You have been sanctified through faith in Jesus Christ. This is the great message of Christianity. We are all sinners, not just this, but there is forgiveness and the kingdom of God is open to us."

During that last discussion, Chad kept his left hand on John's shoulder the whole time. Furthermore, when John MacArthur was again quoting 1 Corinthians 6:9-11, the pastor's amazing grace and truth approach was like a magnet for Chad. On the YouTube channel where this discussion can be found, there were several people who saw the grace and truth of this conversation. Rick wrote in the comments section, "Thank you John for explaining in love the truth to this young man and Larry and the world. God bless you for speaking the truth!" Casey wrote, "what i love most about this is the fact that John McArthur speaks the truth. Chad Allen responds and then John McArthur begins to speak to him in LOVE but not one bit of compromising TRUTH!! and in doing so his heart was touched because he was approached in TRUTH and LOVE operating perfectly together! and what happened next? he began to empty out and confess... wow it was just wonderful to watch that heart be touched!!! I LOVE IT!!! :)" Happy added, "Man, I love how pastor MacArthur decided to change the perspective of how he was speaking to look at Chad sincerely and be clear on the bible. He looked at Chad what he meant, he leveled with him that he also was sinful by nature, then he explained the truth of the bible."

Another important point about this discussion: while the dialogue between Pastor MacArthur and Chad Allen was a constant display of John MacArthur being a serpent and a dove, things went differently when Gavin Newsom and the pastor interacted. There comes a time when facing a ravenous wolf like Newsom, who had, at that time, broken existing state and city laws by allowing officials to issue marriage licenses to homosexuals in San Francisco, that the focus needs to be on truth, as they will surely "turn to attack you" (Matt. 7:6).

> Gavin Newsom: "With respect, uh, to, uh, the pastor. I, I, just, you know, I'm a practicing Catholic. I got married in the church. Two plus years. Uh, I don't see what we are doing in terms of advancing the bond of love and monogamy and extending that to families, families of same-sex, in any way shape or form takes away anything from the church or the sanctity of the union that my wife and I have."
>
> John MacArthur: "I would just like to ask the mayor, as a practicing Catholic, do you believe the Bible is the word of God?"
>
> Gavin Newsom: "Look pastor, I'm not going to get into a theological debate with you."
>
> John MacArthur: "No, that's not a theological debate. That's just a straight question. Do you believe the Bible is the authoritative word of God?"
>
> Gavin Newsom: [With a smirk on his face.] "Yeah, I, I, uh, uh, with respect, I guess I do."
>
> John MacArthur: "The Bible says when God created man, He said one man, one woman, cleave together for life, that's a family. Jesus in the New Testament reaffirms that. All the writers of the Old and the New Testaments affirm it."
>
> John MacArthur: "The point at this juncture is, well he's representing the State, he's coming back and saying I'm a Catholic and

I'm a Catholic and somehow this fits into my Catholicism, and I'm saying what's your authority then?"

Gavin Newsom: "I'm proud to represent a city that has diverse points of view, open points of view that doesn't believe in discrimination. And has evolved from the old, uh, constructs that I think have frankly held back society and many that are inconsistent, yes, with your faith."

John MacArthur: "If it's going to be done [legalizing same-sex marriage], it's going to be done through the law, through the process that's in place [the legislative process, not the courts]. The mayor has just literally violated the law, determined what the interpretation of the constitution should be for him and acted on it. He knew what the law says, because in California there is a law defining marriage and he went in direct opposition against that law. It's already been defined in this state."

Pastor MacArthur spoke boldly to Gavin Newsom with a heavy dose of truth. He acted wise as a serpent in asking the law-breaking mayor if the Bible is the authoritative word of God. When Newsom insincerely said "I guess" it is, MacArthur then showed him what the Bible teaches. That interaction revealed Newsom's true authority. The real authority for the leftist Democratic mayor was himself—King Newsom, as he had placed himself upon a throne, unilaterally determining what his own interpretation of the state constitution was and acted on it. When Pastor MacArthur demonstrated that Newsom in actuality despised the Bible because it speaks against everything on which he had ruled, the mayor called God's word an outdated construct that is holding back society. Therefore, Newsom contradicted his earlier feigned affirmation that the Bible is the authoritative word of God. Thanks to the wisdom of Pastor MacArthur, we saw grace (1 Cor. 6:11) unveiled that evening, as well as evil (Eph. 5:11), hypocrisy and lawlessness (Matt. 23:28).

When unbelievers like Chad Allen hear truth spoken gracefully, their conflicting thoughts can accuse them as their conscience bears witness to God's law, which is written on their hearts (Rom. 2:15). On the other hand, when we confront people like Gavin Newsom, who "reject authority, and blaspheme" (Jude 1:8), they will be offended by the truth—just as others were offended when Jesus spoke truth (Matt. 15:12).

A Sanctifying Truth

The last three chapters have shown that speaking the truth in love, being full of grace and truth, and being wise as serpents and innocent as doves, takes great discernment. This knowledge is not something that is acquired overnight but comes to those who are being sanctified. It takes prayer, study, patience, maturity, practice and a reliance on "God who gives the growth" (1 Cor. 3:7). That is why being on The Evangelism Circle is so important, because God will sanctify us all along the way (Acts 20:32; 1 Cor. 1:2; Rom. 15:16; 1 Thess. 5:23; 2 Tim. 2:21; Philip. 2:13).

(13) THE 11ᵀᴴ COMMANDMENT: THOU SHALT NOT ARGUE

"Arguing is a virtue because it helps us hold to what is true and discard what is false." - Greg Koukl[62]

We have already seen in chapter ten where the disciples taught us that our speech should always be gracious (Col. 4:6), with no offense (Acts 24:16; 1 Cor. 10:32), and our conduct should be honorable (1 Pet. 2:12). For many Christians, this settles the issue. Their 11th commandment is, thou shalt not argue. The irony is that they themselves argue about this very point. They *argue* that Christians should not argue, dispute, refute, rebuke, or cause dissension and debate.

---
[62] Greg Koukl, *Tactics*, Updated and Expanded, p. 41.

However, we have also seen in chapter ten where the disciples did all of those things and more. Let's review.

- "Paul *argued* in his defense" (Acts 25:8).
- Paul "*disputed* against the Hellenists" (Acts 9:29).
- Apollos "powerfully *refuted* the Jews in public" (Acts 18:28).
- Paul said about false teachers, "*rebuke* them sharply" (Titus 1:13).
- "Paul and Barnabas had no small *dissension and debate* with them" (Acts 15:2).

Notice that all of the above were in the context of sharing or defending the gospel. The fact is that the disciples argued and debated their case when it came to the truth of the gospel (see chapter ten).

No Quarrelling

For those who promote the 11th commandment—thou shalt not argue, they usually point to certain passages where Paul instructs Christians not to quarrel. It is true he did say that, but a closer look at the context of such passages reveals something interesting. When Paul told Timothy, "not to quarrel about words, which does no good, but only ruins the hearers" (2 Tim. 2:14), the words he was referring to were "foolish, ignorant controversies" (2:23). We know that Paul talked about these controversies elsewhere. The false teachers of Crete were using the law of Moses to attempt to force circumcision on Titus and his fellow Christians (Titus 1:10). Paul later instructed Titus to "avoid foolish controversies, genealogies, dissensions, and quarrels about the law" (Titus 3:9).

At the same time Paul was telling Titus to avoid quarreling about controversies of the law with the Judaizers, he also told him to "rebuke them sharply, that they may be sound in the faith, not devoting themselves to Jewish myths" (Titus 1:13-14). Likewise, in the very same passage where Paul told Timothy not to quarrel about words (2 Tim. 2:14), he said we need to be about "rightly handling the word of truth" (2:15) and "correcting his [the Lord's] opponents" (2:25). Paul instructed Timothy to teach "the words of the faith and of the good doctrine that you have followed" (1 Tim. 4:6). He added, "for by so doing you will save both yourself and your hearers" (4:16).

When Paul told Titus and Timothy not to quarrel, he wasn't giving a blanket command for all Christians never to argue. The context above shows there is a distinction between quarrelling and giving an argument for sound doctrine. Paul told Titus and Timothy, instead of quarrelling, or getting into a heated blowup about controversies of the law with false teachers, take a different approach. Call them aside and rebuke them sharply to bring them back into the faith. Paul told Titus and Timothy to be sure to correct their opponents with an argument from the sound doctrine they had been taught. That way, they would save their hearers.

Let us not have a contentious spirit when we take on false teachings that creep into the church. While we certainly rebuke these disruptive teachers, we do so with a gracious demeanor and sound arguments from the Bible. The contrasts of truth in love and grace and truth that we documented in chapters 10-12 are found throughout the New Testament. Furthermore, while it is true the disciples argued, disputed, refuted, rebuked and debated when the truth of the gospel was at stake, they did it by speaking the truth in love and by demonstrating grace and truth. We need to find this balance as well.

Plausible Arguments

When Paul spoke "To the saints and faithful brothers in Christ at Colossae" (Col. 1:2), he wanted them to have "full assurance of understanding and the knowledge of God's mystery, which is Christ, in whom are hidden all the treasures of wisdom and knowledge" (Col. 2:2-3). Paul then adds, "I say this in order that no one may delude you with plausible arguments" (2:4). Arguments from false teachers can persuade some. The Gnostic teachers (against whom Paul argued in Colossians chapters one and two) argued that the Colossians could find secret wisdom and knowledge through them. This secret knowledge denied the all-sufficiency and pre-eminence of Christ (1:15-20, 2:8) and even His incarnation as the God-man (1:19, 2:9). Why do you think so many intelligent people are caught up in cults like Mormonism, Jehovah's Witnesses and Unitarian churches, which argue against the sufficiency, pre-eminence, and deity of Christ and the Trinity? Why do the liberal mainline denominations, which offer rationalizations for abortion, homosexuality and transgenderism, take people captive? The answer is that they have bought into plausible arguments from the world that go against the wisdom and knowledge of Christ.

How do we strengthen Christians against these plausible arguments? We have to have an argument of our own, an argument that will prevent people from being taken "captive by philosophy and empty deceit, according to human tradition, according to the elemental spirits of the world, and not according to Christ" (Col. 2:8). Paul said we should "destroy arguments and every lofty opinion raised against the knowledge of God, and take every thought captive to obey Christ" (2 Cor. 10:5). Plausible arguments that are from the world or from deceitful spirits must be destroyed with biblical arguments. We do this by arguing against those who "depart from the faith by devoting themselves to deceitful spirits and teachings of demons" (1 Tim. 4:1). We argue against "destructive heresies" (2 Pet. 2:1); "false brothers secretly brought in" (Gal. 2:4); "ungodly people, who pervert the grace of our God" (Jude 1:4); those who speak "false words" (2 Peter 2:3); "what is falsely called 'knowledge'" (1 Tim. 6:20); "deceivers" (2 John 1:7) who "teach any different doctrine" (1 Tim. 1:3); and "men speaking twisted things" (Acts 20:30) who "distort the gospel of Christ" (Gal. 1:7).

In 2 Corinthians 11, Paul argued against another Jesus, a different spirit and a different gospel from the one he taught (2 Cor. 11:4). He also argued that there were "false apostles, deceitful workmen, disguising themselves as apostles of Christ" (11:13). Why was this happening? It occurred because some in the Corinthian Church fell for plausible arguments and were deceived into leaving their "sincere and pure devotion to Christ" (11:3). As Paul lamented, "you put up with it readily enough" (11:4).

The surest defense against falling for plausible arguments of a different Jesus, a different spirit and a different gospel requires two actions. First, we need to learn from Christ's disciples and destroy these deceitful arguments that rise up against the knowledge of God with biblical arguments to refute and correct them. Second, we should take every thought captive to obey the biblical Christ. We accomplish this by maintaining our sincere and pure devotion to Christ so that we can have a "full assurance of understanding and the knowledge of God's mystery, which is Christ" (Col. 2:2). Don't fall for plausible arguments that at best can only be reasonable or probable in the world's eyes; instead, follow the disciple's arguments in order to devote yourself to the One "in whom are hidden all the treasures of wisdom and knowledge" (Col. 2:3).

Arguing People into the Kingdom

In the late 1990s, I was attending a Bible study at church when the pastor said, "You can't argue anyone into the kingdom." He actually was directing his comment towards me after I had said I was able to argue with evidences for the proof of Christianity while witnessing. At the time, I did not have a response, but I instinctively felt there was something wrong with what he had said.

Several years later, when I had come to see God's sovereignty in salvation, it occurred to me that when God draws someone, He can and does use even our arguments to accomplish that drawing. Let me explain. In John 6:65, Jesus said, "no one can come to me unless it is granted him by the Father." Here we see that man does not have the ability to come to Jesus in and of himself—the Father must first grant this coming. When the Father grants someone to come to Christ, He will infallibly draw them to the Son. How do we know this? It is because Jesus said, "All that the Father gives me will come to me" (6:37).

In the end, we can't persuade anyone to come to God unless it is His elective will to first intercede in their life. Unless the Father has already granted and drawn a person to come Christ, nothing we say will bring them into the kingdom. However, if the Father has already granted and drawn a person to come to His Son, He will use many things we say to bring them into the kingdom. If the table has been set by the Father, why would arguments for the evidence of Christianity fail to work? Greg Koukl states in his popular book Tactics, "The fact is, you can argue someone into the kingdom. It happens all the time. But when arguments are effective, they are not working in a vacuum."[63] As Koukl explained, our arguments can certainly be effective if the person we are witnessing to is presently being drawn by the Father to the Son.[64]

That same pastor from the Bible study also stated that we *must always* use God's love, not arguments, to bring people into the kingdom. However, Koukl writes, "When people say you can't argue anyone into the kingdom, they usually have an alternative approach in mind. They

---
[63] Ibid. p. 44.
[64] Koukl cites this example: "My close friend and bestselling author (Cold-Case Christianity et al.) J. Warner Wallace is a noteworthy case in point. And he is just one of many." The late Nabeel Qureshi, a former Muslim who interacted with the apologist David Wood in college, tells his conversion to Christianity in his book "Seeking Allah, Finding Jesus." Christian philosopher J. P. Moreland is quoted as having said, "You can argue someone into the Christian faith, I've done it."

might be thinking that a genuine expression of love, kindness, and acceptance coupled with a simple presentation of the gospel is a more biblical approach. If you are tempted to think this way, let me say something that may shock you: you cannot love someone into the kingdom. It can't be done. Neither is the simple gospel itself adequate to do that job. How do I know? Because many people who were treated with sacrificial love and kindness by Christians never surrendered to the Savior. Many who have heard a clear explanation of God's gift in Christ never put their trust in him. In each case, something was missing that, when present, always results in conversion. What's missing is that special work of the Father that Jesus referred to—drawing a lost soul into his arms."[65]

If the Father has set the table by granting a person to come Christ, we *can* sit down at that table and allow God to use many things to bring a person sitting across from us into the kingdom. Our approach will always include combining grace and truth and sharing the truth in love, not excluding one or the other. Koukl adds, "Why do you think God is just as pleased to use a good argument as a warm expression of love? Because both love and reason are consistent with God's character. The same God who is the essence of love (1 John 4:8) also gave the invitation, 'Come now, and let us reason together' (Isa. 1:18). Therefore both approaches honor him."[66]

A Spirited Argument

When the Father grants someone to come to the Son, this drawing includes the Holy Spirit convicting them of their sin and showing them the truth of who Jesus is—God's righteous Servant (John 16:8-11). The Holy Spirit not only convinces men of their guilt but also turns them to a saving belief in the substitutionary work of Christ. Unless the Holy Spirit does this work in the sinner's heart, no argument, no expression of love, no biblical explanation of the gospel will bring someone into the kingdom. However, as we mentioned above, when the Holy Spirit completes His role, many things work, including arguments for the faith accompanied by the graceful "feet of those who preach the good news" (Rom. 10:15). In all of this, the Spirit uses His weapon, "the sword of the Spirit, which is the word of God" (Eph. 6:17), to bring about conversions.

Since the Holy Spirit lives in us (1 Cor. 6:19), gives us power to

---

[65] Ibid. p. 44.

[66] Ibid. p. 45.

witness (Acts 1:8), and is our Helper (John 14:16), we are led by, live by, and keep in step with the Spirit (Gal. 5:18, 25). Therefore, our arguments are a part of His work. When the Holy Spirit is working ahead of us in regeneration (John 16:8-11), our "spirited" arguments will always have a place at the table.

An unregenerate person with a heart of stone cannot be argued into the kingdom, but neither can they be loved into the kingdom, or convinced by any clear biblical presentation of the gospel. The fact is that their heart of stone (a hardened heart of unbelief) will reject any and all methods of persuasion. However, Ezekiel 36 shows us what happens when God intervenes: "I will give you a new heart, and a new spirit I will put within you. And I will remove the heart of stone from your flesh and give you a heart of flesh. And I will put my Spirit within you" (Ezek. 36:26-27). Such radical surgery means a new heart of flesh, a heart that is now open to many approaches.

When God does open heart surgery, like He did on Lydia when "The Lord opened her heart to pay attention to what was said by Paul" (Acts 16:14), our hearers will pay attention to what we say, even Spirited arguments. Greg Koukl summarizes, "Here's the key principle: without God's work, nothing else works; but with God's work, many things work. Under the influence of the Holy Spirit, love persuades. With Jesus' help, arguments convince. By the power of God, the gospel transforms through each of these methods."[67]

Meeting One Argument with Another

Let's face it, people argue against the Christian faith all the time. When skeptics try to disprove the Bible, do we stay silent? What is our response when they call our message evil? When a person argues, with no fear in their heart, that there is no God, isn't this a case where it is a time to give a counter-argument, "lest he be wise in his own eyes" (Proverbs 26:5)? In the latter case, we can point out the internal inconsistency of their worldview by arguing for God as the necessary uncreated Creator. We can explain the foundation of God as our moral compass, the necessary existence of God based on the universe's design, and the necessity of God to sustain the universe.[68] If we fail to make an attempt to counter unbeliever's arguments, we may appear emotionally and intellectually distant from the gospel we preach.

---

[67] Ibid. p. 45

[68] As we have seen in chapter three, we also argue for these things in pre-evangelism. Here is a case where we see paths crossing on *The Evangelism Circle*.

When the Judaizers argued one must be circumcised to be saved, Paul "had no small dissension and debate with them" (Acts 15:2). Of such people, he warned, "They must be silenced" (Titus 1:11). Peter, in encountering these same Judaizers, argued, "why are you putting God to the test by placing a yoke on the neck of the disciples that neither our fathers nor we have been able to bear?" (Acts 15:10). When the Sanhedrin argued that Stephen was preaching "blasphemous words against Moses and God" (Acts 6:11), he countered that they had "received the law as delivered by angels and did not keep it" (7:53). Jude challenged Christians to "contend for the faith" (Jude 1:3) against those "who pervert the grace of our God" (Jude 1:4).

Both Peter and James tell us, "God opposes the proud but gives grace to the humble" (1 Pet. 5:5; James 4:6). Why does God oppose the proud? Because the proud oppose God. They are so preoccupied with their self-proclaimed goodness and alleged law keeping that they never realize their true rebellion and desperate need for a Savior from their sin. What if we were to argue against their alleged goodness and their law breaking with a law and gospel approach, or a good person test (see chapter 9)? Wouldn't we be doing the same thing Jesus and the disciples did? Jesus showed the rich young ruler that he was not keeping the law like he thought he was (Mark 10:19-22). He said, "No one is good except God alone" (10:18). Jesus also argued against the self-righteousness of the Jews, "Has not Moses given you the law? Yet none of you keeps the law" (John 7:19).

When we challenge the proud to show them that they are not keeping the law (James 2:10) and that they have no righteousness in and of themselves (Rom. 3:10; Philip. 3:9), we are arguing against any righteous standing they may think they have before God. This approach can cause a person to harden themselves in their self-proclaimed goodness or strip away their pride so we can then give grace to the humble. The pattern should be this: we argue against a person's self-righteous pride (just like Jesus and His disciples did) with hopes that God will humble them in order to receive His grace. "For everyone who exalts himself will be humbled, but the one who humbles himself will be exalted" (Luke 18:14).

The New Testament is not short of instructions for the need to give an argument. While telling us not to be quarrelsome (Titus 3:2; 2 Tim. 2:14), it instructs us on how to "persuade others" (2 Cor. 5:11) to "be reconciled to God" (5:20). We see time and again where this persuasion comes in the form of an argument (Acts 25:8), dispute (Acts 9:29), debate (Acts 15:2) rebuke (Titus 1:13), defense (1 Pet. 3:15), or a call to contend for the faith (Jude 1:3). Again, all of these things can be accomplished by "speaking the truth in love" (Eph. 4:15). The same Paul who spoke of love, patience, kindness, gentleness and self-control as fruit of the Spirit in Galatians chapter five, opposed Peter to his face in Galatians chapter two for conduct that was not in step with the truth of the gospel.

Rethinking the 11th Commandment

Instead of "Thou shalt not argue", I would like to offer a more balanced way to think about this: "Thou shalt not quarrel or be argumentative. Instead, thou shalt argue for the gospel and against those who oppose it." Christian apologist and teacher J. Steve Lee writes, "Don't confuse the word 'argument' with 'argumentative.' We are not to be argumentative as in to bicker or quarrel. The later portion of 1 Peter 3:15 says to give a reason with gentleness and respect. That is not quarreling or fighting. We are to give a justification for the truth claims of Christianity."[69] Lee adds, "Why can't good reasons, arguments, evidence, and a clear justification of Christianity lead someone to the Kingdom of God? Is your God too small and unable to use evidence and arguments? Why put God in a box. If he wants to use arguments, evidence, and reason (which he commands us to do in 1 Peter) then that is God's prerogative."

As we have seen, it is biblical to argue, dispute, debate, rebuke, answer objections and to contend for the faith over matters as a way to get to the truth; however, quarrelling is prohibited. Arguing for the faith uses a systematic approach employing scripture, reason, logic and facts to teach and defend sound doctrine. While respectful give and take should always occur during an argument, quarrelling often devolves into emotions where one is not listening or both are just talking over one another. While we want to win the argument, we don't want to lose the person behind the argument. While our hope is to win people with scripture, reason, logic and facts to teach and defend sound doctrine, we can just as easily lose their hearing by departing from all those things.

To present arguments over issues of salvation means that I am willing to argue for the truth that Jesus alone is sufficient to save (John 14:6; Acts 4:12). I am willing to argue that God "saved us, not because

---

[69] J. Steve Lee, The "You Can't Argue Someone Into the Kingdom of God" Myth, https://ischristianitytrue.wordpress.com/2015/08/25/the-you-cant-argue-someone-into-the-kingdom-of-god-myth/

of works done by us in righteousness, but according to his own mercy" (Titus 3:5). I am willing to argue against a gospel contrary to the one the Bible preaches (Gal. 1:8). I'm willing to argue that the truth of God's word always trumps the traditions of men (Matt. 15:6; Col. 2:8). Here's the key: don't have a quarrelsome demeanor, yet, always be prepared to argue for the gospel and against those who oppose it, just like Jesus and His disciples did. Mark Dever suggests, "Lower their defensiveness toward you, but not toward your message."[70]

Contend for the Turf

"Offense sells tickets. Defense wins championships." - Alabama football coach Paul "Bear" Bryant

There are times when we are contending for the faith that we have to be prepared to take different approaches. To carry a football analogy into evangelism, an evangelist can gain ground by going on the offense. On first down, we take advantage of a wide-open hole, telling those on the other side of the line that "Jesus came into the world to save sinners" (1 Tim. 1:15), because "all have sinned and fall short of the glory of God"

---

[70] Mark Dever, *The Gospel and Personal Evangelism*, p. 66.

(Rom. 3:23). On second down, our pre-snap read allows us to tell them they are "dead in the trespasses and sins" (Eph. 2:1; Col. 2:13), with "iniquities [that] have made a separation between you and your God" (Isa. 59:2). On third down, we run a trap play, blocking out any notion that we can be right with God in and of ourselves by proclaiming "None is righteous, no, not one" (Rom. 3:10).

After our initial first down, we look to keep the drive alive by showing them our safety valve—Christ's perfect righteousness in place of their unrighteousness, "For our sake he made him to be sin who knew no sin, so that in him we might become the righteousness of God" (2 Cor. 5:21; cf., 1 Pet. 3:18). On second and short, we pull out the jumbo package, nailing home the point that "God shows his love for us in that while we were still sinners, Christ died for us" (Rom. 5:8) and that Jesus "was delivered up for our trespasses and raised for our justification" (Rom. 4:25).

Finally, after we move the chains again and are close to seeing them take a knee, we go man-to-man with them, explaining that "repentance toward God and of faith in our Lord Jesus Christ" (Acts 20:21) is necessary for salvation. However, sometimes as we are moving toward a conversion, the drive stalls. Suddenly, we find ourselves on defense. Are we equipped to play both ways?

As our opponent goes on offense, we shift into a prevent defense. As bombs, in the form of questions and objections, are sure to be tossed our way, we are ready since we are all called to "always be prepared to make a defense to anyone who asks" (1 Pet. 3:15). We snap on our chinstraps and get ready for a "defense and confirmation of the gospel" (Philip. 1:7). Knowing this is probably not going to be a three-and-out, we brace ourselves to be ready for a weak-side or strong-side attack.

On first down, our opponent calls a screen, asking us why other religions cannot be a valid way to God. Our strong-side linebacker sniffs out the play for no gain. On second down, they do a hard count, trying to draw us offside by claiming the Trinity makes no sense, but they end up fumbling the exchange and losing yardage. On third and long, they go into the spread formation and shotgun a dozen different objections at us. Finding everything covered, the quarterback throws the ball away to avoid a sack. Running out of options, they try a fake punt on fourth down, hoping to catch us off guard by claiming the Bible is full of contradictions. However, because our scout team prepared us for this move, we were able to answer their trick play and regain the ball on downs.

In the end, by the Lord's mercy, we had many gospel zone opportunities that God allowed us to turn into conversions where people ran to daylight. After every conversion, there were no self-congratulatory end zone dances, only a humble sharing in the "joy before the angels of God over one sinner who repents" (Luke 15:10). In each of our extra points, we emphasized "sanctification by the Spirit and belief in the truth" (2 Thess. 2:13) so that they will "be worthy of the gospel of Christ" (Philip. 1:27). However, if the game clock expires without a salvation, we shake our unconverted opponent's hands. If they say to us, "In a short time would you persuade me to be a Christian?" (Acts 26:28), we respond, "Whether short or long, I would to God that not only you but also all who hear me this day might become such as I am" (26:29).

As we have seen, the effective evangelist needs to be prepared to move deftly between offense and defense. Another thing to consider: some evangelists spend most of their time on one side of the ball planting seeds (1 Cor. 3:6a). However, while one person on offense sows the gospel in the heart of their hearer (Mark 4:1-9), what they planted may start to wither as their opponent's questions and objections go unanswered. That's where your offense should welcome and appreciate a good defense—a defense that can water what you planted (1 Cor. 3:6b). When the defense starts to answer questions and objections, it gives water to the seed you sowed, and it starts to grow again. A loyal evangelist knows the balance and foundation of their calling. As Paul wrote, "I planted, Apollos watered, but God gave the growth. So neither he who plants nor he who waters is anything, but only God who gives the growth. He who plants and he who waters are one, and each will receive his wages according to his labor. For we are God's fellow workers. You are God's field, God's building" (1 Cor. 3:6-9).

Like a winning football team, the offensive players should support the defensive players and vice-versa, because we "are one." So, the next time you want to criticize a defensive player when they may be watering what you planted, or you want to criticize an offensive player for doing the opposite, remember that we are "God's fellow workers." Finally, through all this, the most important point we should keep in mind—it is "only God who gives the growth."

Paul told us to make sure we are "standing firm in one spirit, with one mind striving side by side for the faith of the gospel, and not frightened in anything by your opponents" (Philip. 1:27-28). Robert P. Lightner, in his commentary on The Book of Philippians, writes that striving side by side for the faith of the gospel, "suggests a joint effort, like that of an athletic team."[71] In paraphrasing Bear Bryant's famous quote, "Offense offers tickets to heaven, defense contends for the turf, but only God converts souls."

How about those who don't even want to get into the game? Mike Gendron says, for many Christians, "They will gather in holy huddles on Sunday morning, but when the play is called, they go sit on the bench to watch others run the offense. They say they are too busy or not equipped or fearful."[72] Get off the bench. Go and get yourself equipped for the work of ministry (Eph. 4:12), because "knowing the fear of the Lord, we persuade others" (2 Cor. 5:11).

---

[71] Robert P. Lightner, *The Bible Knowledge Commentary*, p. 652.

[72] Mike Gendron, *Contending for the Gospel*, p. 246.

⑭ STRANGE FIRE AND THE GOSPEL

"And Nadab and Abihu, the sons of Aaron, took either of them his censer, and put fire therein, and put incense thereon, and offered strange fire before the Lord, which he commanded them not. And there went out fire from the Lord, and devoured them, and they died before the Lord."
(Leviticus 10:1-2, KJV).

After Nadab and Abihu came with an unauthorized offering (strange fire), they were consumed by fire from the Lord and died. Serving as priests before the Lord, Aaron's sons brought incense and fire of their own into the sanctuary, an act which God had not commanded. Here we see where God's wrath is poured out on people who try to deal with Him in a manner He has not authorized. If we bring strange fire before Him, there will be a price to be paid.

When it comes to the gospel, we see a lot of strange fire out there. People are making up their own ideas of who God is and how to have a relationship with Him. These are ideas and beliefs which the true God of the Bible has not commanded, fire which has not been kindled by a coal from His altar. While it is true that all believers are "a holy priesthood, to offer spiritual sacrifices acceptable to God through Jesus Christ" (1 Peter 2:5), this does not mean that everyone who calls themselves a Christian is qualified to preach the gospel. While all Christians *should* be prepared to share the good news, many, still in the infant stage, possess only a superficial knowledge of the truth. Therefore, they can distort the gospel and delude, confuse, or even give a false confidence to those whose ears they gain.

The Sanitized Gospel

Sanitize: to make more acceptable by removing unpleasant or undesired features (Merriam-Webster.com).

Unfortunately, many present a sanitized gospel in their attempt to evangelize. There are various reasons why this happens. I think the most common reason is quite simply that many are not well-versed in the root of the gospel (see chapters seven and eight). As a result, we often hear things like, "God loves you and has a wonderful plan for your life." While it is true that God does have a purpose for a believer's life, His intention involves rescuing us from being dead in sin (Eph. 2:1). The gospel allows us to pass from death to life (John 5:24) and will deliver us from the wrath to come (1 Thess. 1:10, 5:9). God accomplishes all this by bringing us to repentance and belief (Mark 1:15; 2 Tim. 2:25), which makes us alive with Christ (Eph. 2:5) and raised with Him (Col. 3:1).

With only a superficial knowledge of the truth, many make God's love the exclusive part of their witnessing, with no mention of sin or repentance. However, this message will not cause an unbeliever to tremble like Peter, who said to Jesus, "Depart from me, for I am a sinful man, O Lord" (Luke 5:8). They will not be "cut to the heart" (Acts 2:37). They will not receive "godly grief [that] produces a repentance that leads to salvation without regret" (2 Cor. 7:10). As Mike Gendron writes, "The call to repentance is the critical truth that is most often left out of Gospel preaching and evangelism."[73]

It often has been pointed out that The Book of Acts, our main example of evangelism, never mentions the word love. Instead, the disciples

---

[73] Mike Gendron, *Contending for the Gospel*, p. 34.

confront their hearers as enemies of God. For example, in calling for repentance, the disciples said, "Save yourselves from this crooked generation" (Acts 2:40). They warned people to turn "every one of you from your wickedness" (Acts 3:26), because in "times of ignorance God overlooked, but now he commands all people everywhere to repent" (Acts 17:30; cf., 3:17). To others they said, "You stiff-necked people, uncircumcised in heart and ears, you always resist the Holy Spirit" (Acts 7:51) and "this people's heart has grown dull" (Acts 28:27). To idol worshippers they warned, "turn from these vain things to a living God" (Acts 14:15).

Half-Baked Gospel

Those who preach an exclusive gospel of God's love without the mention of sin and repentance are like cooks who make a pancake that is not turned. If you present a half-baked pancake, the cooked part may be pleasing to the eye, but the undone side makes the whole cake unfit for anything. Likewise, a half-baked gospel is dished out by many. At first, the done side is so pleasing to the recipient's eyes, they won't even notice the undone gooey side when they consume it. However, the more they try to digest this half-baked gospel and share it with others, eventually they will become frustrated at the heartburn and reflux that continually accompanies it. A half-baked gospel will never convict people that their sin separates them from God. It will never bring to life a hunger for repentance and obedience, and in the end, it is unfit for anything and is distasteful to God.

In order to avoid a half-baked gospel, we must flip the pancake to make sure the sin and repentance side is done as well. That way, we will present a fully baked gospel of God's love on one side and an awareness of our unrighteousness and need for repentance on the other. This will make the fully baked gospel fit for consumption and bring about a lifelong gratitude for God's grace and a hunger for repentance and obedience that will be tasteful to us and to God.

Something else to consider: Richard Owen Roberts, who has preached extensively on the biblical theme of repentance, writes that while God's love is critical to our gospel presentation, "The first word of the gospel is not 'love.' It is not even 'grace.' The first word of the gospel is 'repent.' From Matthew through the Revelation, repentance is an urgent and indispensable theme that is kept at the very forefront of the gospel message."[74] The pancake has to be done on both sides, but when we serve it, the sin and repentance side should be face up.

---

[74] Richard Owen Roberts, *Repentance: The First Word of the Gospel*, p. 23.

Faith without Repentance is Dead

It often has been said that faith and repentance are two sides of the same coin. We can tell the difference between them, but we can't separate them. When it comes to the gospel, at times we are told to believe (Acts 16:30-31; John 3:16; Rom. 10:9). Other times, we are told to repent (Luke 24:45-47; Acts 2:38, 3:19; 2 Cor 7:10). Still, other times, both are explicitly mentioned. Christ's first command was to "repent and believe the Gospel" (Mark 1:15; cf., Matt. 4:17). His last command to His apostles was "that repentance for the forgiveness of sins should be proclaimed in his name to all nations" (Luke 24:47). Paul testified to both to Jews and to Greeks "of repentance toward God and of faith in our Lord Jesus Christ" (Acts 20:21). Sinclair Ferguson writes, "Repentance implies faith and faith implies repentance. One cannot exist without the other."[75] God's justification of sinners is complete when the gifts of repentance and faith are joined together in a fully baked gospel.

Repentance as a Gift

Many make two errors when it comes to repentance. First, they treat repentance as a necessary work, a part of a works/righteousness system that makes satisfaction for sin.[76] Second, some view repentance in another distorted way, saying it is a work and thus must be rejected as part of coming to Christ by grace alone.[77] Both sides fail to realize a critical point—there is only one source of repentance, it is a gift granted by God. For example, we read, "God may perhaps grant them repentance leading to a knowledge of the truth" (2 Tim. 2:25). "God exalted him at his right hand as Leader and Savior, to give repentance to Israel and forgiveness of sins" (Acts 5:31). "When they heard these things they fell silent. And they glorified God, saying, 'Then to the Gentiles also God has granted repentance that leads to life'" (Acts 11:18). As Richard Owen Roberts points out, "Repentance is not self-generated; it is a gift granted by God."[78]

---

[75] Sinclair Ferguson, "Faith and Repentance." Ligonier Ministries, https://www.ligonier.org/learn/articles/faith-and-repentance/.
[76] For example, the Catholic Catechism states, "The sinner must make satisfaction for or expiate his sins" (Catechism 1459).
[77] Independent Fundamentalist Baptists are one group that holds to this.
[78] Richard Owen Roberts, *Repentance: The First Word of the Gospel*, p. 108.

The biblical fact is that when God draws us to come to His Son (John 6:44), He grants us repentance in the coming. Repentance is not a "work" any more than faith is (Eph. 2:8-9). Repentance and faith are the result of God's drawing—not the cause of it. The Westminster Confession of Faith states, "Although repentance is not to be rested in, as any satisfaction for sin, or any cause of the pardon thereof, which is the act of God's free grace in Christ, yet it is of such necessity to all sinners, that none may expect pardon without it."[79]

19th century Presbyterian preacher James Henley Thornwell takes on the legalists, who claim repentance makes satisfaction for sin, and the Antinomians, who claim there are no moral laws God expects Christians to obey. Thornwell writes, "The Gospel, like its blessed Master, is always crucified between two thieves—legalists of all sorts on the one hand and Antinomians on the other; the former robbing the Savior of the glory of his work for us, and the other robbing him of the glory of his work within us."[80]

If we realized that the Bible says repentance is a gift God gives us, we would not consider it a work that saves us. Rather, it is a gift that God bestows upon all He draws to Himself to change our heart for repentance towards Him.

All You Need is Love

The Beatles, arguably one of the most popular rock bands of all time, had one of their biggest hits in 1967 with "All You Need is Love." Apparently, they didn't really believe these lyrics, as two years later the band broke up! For those who share an exclusive gospel of God's love, what do they do when they find out many to whom they witnessed later "break up" with God? Despite these failures, they continue to serve unturned pancakes. The other side of the pancake, displaying the law, sin and the wrath of God, can't possibly be served alongside God's love they say, insisting "that God's kindness is meant to lead you to repentance" (Rom. 2:4). However, in context, this verse is in the middle of a lengthy argument by Paul "that all, both Jews and Greeks, are under sin" (3:9). God's kindness can and does show us how bad we are through the law, sin and the wrath of God. All three are mentioned prominently in this section (Law is mentioned 24 times in chapters 2-5. Sin is mentioned 22 times

---

[79] WCF, Section Three, Of Repentance Unto Life.
[80] J.H. Thornwell, "Antinomianism" in The Collected Writings of James Henley Thornwell (Richmond: Presbyterian Committee of Publication, 1871) p. 386 https://www.monergism.com/blog/legalism-and-antinomianism-two-gospel-thieves-pastor-nick-batzig-guest-post.

in this section and wrath at least a half a dozen times: 1:18, 2:5, 2:8, 3:5, 4:15, 5:9). Jonathan Rourke, in a chapter for John MacArthur's book on evangelism, reminds us, "Love and wrath coexist in God, and this is part of His glory."[81]

Still, some will object, saying we should never condemn unbelievers. Yet, the Bible tells us they are already condemned: "Whoever believes in him is not condemned, but whoever does not believe is condemned already, because he has not believed in the name of the only Son of God" (John 3:18). While God's love is certainly a central part of the gospel (John 3:16), so is God's law that reveals our sin (Rom. 3:20, 7:7) and leads us to Christ (Gal. 2:16, 3:24), who then saves us from God's wrath (Rom. 5:9; 1 Thess. 5:9). Tony Evans, senior pastor at Oak Cliff Bible Fellowship in Dallas, Texas, reminds us that to have a balanced view of God, Romans 11:22 must be considered, "Note then the kindness and the severity of God." Instead of a message that emphasizes God's love and kindness, while downplaying or not mentioning the law, sin and the wrath of God, we need to incorporate both in our gospel message so there can be a true "repentance that leads to salvation without regret" (2 Cor. 7:10).

Flip the pancake, so you don't have an undone (unspoken) side in your gospel presentation. When people make pancakes for the first time, they will be wise to read the directions on the box. The directions for Betty Crocker's Classic Pancakes read, "Cook 2 to 3 minutes or until bubbly on top and dry around edges. Turn; cook other side until golden brown." If those venturing into evangelism would first read God's directions in the Bible, they would be sure to have a fully baked gospel. However, as Will Metzger writes, "People are loyal to a certain approach and not the Scriptures."[82]

Strange Gospels

Paul warned us of the strange fire of different gospels than the one he preached, "I am astonished that you are so quickly deserting him who called you in the grace of Christ and are turning to a different gospel— not that there is another one, but there are some who trouble you and want to distort the gospel of Christ. But even if we or an angel from heaven should preach to you a gospel contrary to the one we preached to you, let him be accursed. As we have said before, so now I say again: If anyone is preaching to you a gospel contrary to the one you received, let him be accursed" (Gal. 1:6-9).

---

[81] Jonathan Rourke, John MacArthur, *Evangelism*, p. 37.
[82] Will Metzger, *Tell The Truth*, p. 81.

Paul was warning against the Judaizers, "false brothers" (Gal. 2:4; cf., Acts 20:30) who required that the Galatians accept circumcision (Gal. 2:3-5, 5:2-6, 6:12-13) and submit to the Old Testament law (Gal. 2:16, 21, 3:2-25) to be part of the people of God. This "different gospel" was grace plus circumcision and the Old Testament law. The Judaizers' gospel takes us away from "our freedom that we have in Christ Jesus, so that they [the false brothers] might bring us into slavery" (Gal. 2:4). If we dare put ourselves under this slavery, we are "under a curse" (Gal. 3:10), "obligated to keep the whole law" (Gal. 5:3). In that case, "Christ will be of no advantage to you" (Gal. 5:2); in fact, "You are severed from Christ, you who would be justified by the law; you have fallen away from grace" (Gal. 5:4; cf., 2:16).

The Judaizers were undermining the doctrine of justification by faith alone by adding the necessity of circumcision and adherence to the Old Testament law to the gospel. Unfortunately, such additions to the gospel are the fatal flaws that have been repeated over and over again by many groups over the past two thousand years.

Different Gospels of Today

There are so many different gospels today that sever people from Christ that it requires those on The Evangelism Circle to have great discernment. As we have seen, while it is critical for us to know what the gospel is, we must also know what it is not. The following is not an exhaustive list of different gospels, but some of the more popular ones.

Synergism Gospel (Mixing Jesus and good works to attain salvation)

This gospel presentation can include the basic facts of the gospel outlined previously, but while Christ's death on the cross for our sins and His burial and resurrection are deemed necessary for salvation—they are not sufficient. Christ did His part, now you have to do yours. Yet, the Bible specifically addresses anyone who would dare add their own righteousness to Christ's finished work, "I do not nullify the grace of God, for if righteousness were through the law, then Christ died for no purpose" (Gal. 2:21). If one chooses to mix law and grace, or works and grace, for their justification, they have alienated themselves from Christ and have fallen away from grace (Gal. 5:4). For if there were any other way, outside God's free grace, whereby men and women could be justified before God, then Jesus was a fool to die. However, the truth is: "God counts righteousness apart from works" (Rom. 4:6).

Inclusive Gospel (The cross covers "good people" from other religions)

Inclusivism is the belief that even though the work of Christ is the only means of salvation, there exists an "exception clause" to the gospel. This "exception" claims that God, due to His love and mercy, will extend Christ's redemptive work to many who have an imperfect or even no knowledge of Him. All those who have lived a "God-centered" life will have an opportunity to be saved. However, those outside of being born again through faith in Jesus Christ are dead in their sins (Eph. 2:1-5; Titus 3:3) and cannot live a "God-centered" life (Rom. 8:7; Col. 1:21, 2:13; Eph. 4:18). God's elect will always be directed towards His appointed Savior, as Jesus said, "All that the Father gives me will come to me" (John 6:37). The elect, who come to Christ, will not have an imperfect or no knowledge of Him, because God "predestined [them] to be conformed to the likeness of his Son" (Rom. 8:29).

Will Metzger comments on the Inclusive Gospel, "This apparently inclusive approach is really quite exclusive. It says, 'The good people can find God, and the bad people do not.' What does this mean for those of us with moral failures? We are excluded?"[83]

Self-Esteem Gospel (Finding "good" in ourselves)

This gospel approach preaches that our big problem is sins (plural) and not our sin nature (singular). Instead of focusing on our sins, we are told we need to seek out the "good" in all of us. Finding worth in self is the message of this false gospel. The Bible presents sin as a state of being (Eph. 2:1-3; Rom. 5:12), not just a series of stumbles. Scripture says, "None is righteous, no, not one" (Rom. 3:10) and in all of us is a desperate sickness (Jer. 17:9). The call of the biblical gospel is away from self and unto Jesus, because self is the problem and Jesus is the solution. We need to turn away from ourselves and discover our life and identity in Jesus. The title of Lutheran pastor Don Matzat's popular book says it all, "Christ Esteem, Where the Search For Self-Esteem Ends."

Universalist Gospel (All will be saved)

God does not have "just one" way of salvation. Instead, He makes sure that no human being will be lost. He saves *every* person. It is said an omnibenevolent (all-loving) God would never allow any of His creatures to perish or suffer. However, the Universalist Gospel is false because it isolates God's love without taking into account His other attributes like

---

[83] Ibid. p. 8.

holiness, righteousness, wrath and justice. The fact is that God's omnibenevolence does not transcend His holiness, but the two work hand in hand. For example, the very fact that God can satisfy His holiness and justice with His Son's death on the cross (Rom. 3:25-26) is a divine expression of His love (Rom. 5:8).

James White, of Alpha and Omega Ministries, explains three possibilities for God to show Himself: 1) God could save no one. This would be a revelation of His justice and holiness but not of His love, mercy and grace. 2) God could save everyone. This would be a revelation of His love, mercy and grace but you wouldn't see His holiness and His justice. 3) God could save some. Only when He is left to save the way He chooses to save can you see the entire range of God's attributes in the creation itself—justice, holiness, love, mercy, and grace.[84]

Prosperity and Health Gospel (Name it and Claim it)

Prosperity gospel teachers claim that God wants you to be healthy, wealthy, and prosperous in all areas of life. This alleged promise from God is always contingent on you sending these false teachers your money. The prosperity gospel is about what someone can gain in this life, not what God promises us after death. One of the most famous teachers of this false gospel, Benny Hinn, once said, "I'm sick and tired of hearing about streets of gold. I don't need gold in heaven. I gotta have it now!"[85]

I have been to Africa over a dozen times, where the prosperity teaching has unfortunately been widely received. I can tell you from firsthand knowledge, it doesn't work in Africa. In fact, it doesn't work anywhere unless you are a false teacher or one of their underlings in this pyramid scheme receiving a financial windfall from these unbiblical promises.

Jesus taught us to "be on your guard against all covetousness, for one's life does not consist in the abundance of his possessions" (Luke 12:15). He said, "For the poor you always have with you" (John 12:8). He told us to "Sell your possessions, and give to the needy" (Luke 12:33) and "Do not lay up for yourselves treasures on earth…but lay up for yourselves treasures in heaven" (Matt. 6:19-20). Paul told us, "As for the rich in this present age, charge them not to be haughty, nor to set their hopes on the uncertainty of riches, but on God" (1 Tim. 6:17). Furthermore, "if we have food and clothing, with these we will be content. But those who desire to be rich fall into temptation" (1 Tim. 6:8-9). Elsewhere we read, "Keep your life free from love of money, and be content with what you

---

[84] Dr. White has explained this many times on his Dividing Line program.
[85] Hinn made this statement on TBN, November, 8, 1990.

have" (Heb. 13:5). Finally, the word exhorts us "Give me neither poverty nor riches, but give me only my daily bread" (Proverbs 30:8, NIV).

As far as guaranteed health, due to the fall of man, "we wait eagerly for…the redemption of our bodies" (Rom. 8:23). Our hope is not in the false promise of guaranteed health now, but for our fallen flesh to be turned into glorified perfect bodies in the resurrection (1 Cor. 15; Rev. 21:4). Elisha, Jeremiah, Timothy and Paul all suffered health afflictions, and no wonder, for "It is good for me that I was afflicted, that I might learn your statutes" (Psalm 119:71). A true gospel faith trusts God in the face of financial anxieties and death, not just for earthly riches and healing.

New Age Gospel (I am God)

Man is viewed as divine, as co-creator, as the hope for future peace and harmony. If one gets it wrong in this lifetime, there's always the next. However, man is not divine (Isa. 43:10; Hosea 11:9), nor co-creator (Isa. 44:24). Jesus is the only hope for peace (Rom. 5:1; Eph. 2:13-14). The Bible teaches resurrection (Rom. 4:25), not reincarnation (Heb. 9:27).

Notice that a basic theme runs through all the false gospels above—man is the focus. Either man has to cooperate with God to be saved, or man and his potential is the focus of the gospel itself. However, the biblical gospel is all about Jesus and what He accomplished for man to meet God, not about what man accomplished to achieve self-righteousness or to win God's approval and favor.

Ashamed of the Gospel?

"Some shrink from evangelism because they don't understand it—and others because they do."- George E. Sweazey[86]

What a great quote above by George E. Sweazey, a 20th century Presbyterian pastor. How many people have you run into, who claim to be Christian, who don't have a clue as to how to share the good news of the gospel? On the flip side, how many, claiming to be Christian, do understand the message of the gospel, but, for whatever reason, refuse to share it?

Sharing God's salvific plan is a given in the Bible. In Romans 1:16, Paul said, "For I am not ashamed of the gospel, for it is the power of God for salvation to everyone who believes." Elsewhere he wrote, "Far be it from me to boast except in the cross of our Lord Jesus Christ" (Gal.

---

[86] George E. Sweazey, *Effective Evangelism*, p. 51.

6:14). He added, "For I decided to know nothing among you except Jesus Christ and him crucified" (1 Cor. 2:2) and "we preach Christ crucified" (1 Cor. 1:23). Paul told Timothy, "do not be ashamed of the testimony about our Lord, nor of me his prisoner, but share in suffering for the gospel by the power of God" (2 Tim. 1:8). David said in Psalm 40:10, "I have not hidden your deliverance within my heart; I have spoken of your faithfulness and your salvation." Psalm 96:2 instructs us to "tell of his salvation from day to day."

Why would a person who has claimed the name of Christ be ashamed to tell the greatest news ever? Let me offer some possible reasons:

1) Some are ashamed of their lack of knowledge of the gospel.

If someone is reluctant to discuss the gospel due to ignorance of what it is, it's either time to make a true profession of faith (Rom. 10:9), or to "grow up in your salvation" (1 Peter 2:2; Eph. 4:15) and become obedient to the call to share the gospel (2 Tim. 4:5; Matt. 4:19; Acts 1:8).

2) Some treat the gospel as just one of many ways to God. They will say things like, "Jesus died for me, that's my truth. I would never force my path on to you."

Jesus' death and resurrection are not just true for some, but true for everyone (John 14:6; Acts 4:12), otherwise—the gospel is not true at all (1 Cor. 15:12-19). For those claiming to be a Christ follower, they should heed the words of the One they call their Savior, as Jesus said He came "proclaiming the gospel" (Mark 1:14) and told us to do the same, "Go into all the world and proclaim the gospel to the whole creation" (Mark 16:15). God only has one path (Matt. 7:13-14); by neglecting to share that, you are facilitating people on their path towards destruction.

3) Some distance themselves from the gospel because they are afraid of persecution.

For those who avoid sharing the gospel out of fear of persecution, we must realize that "all who desire to live a godly life in Christ Jesus will be persecuted" (2 Tim. 3:12; cf., John 15:20). However, persecution comes with a blessing, "If you are insulted for the name of Christ, you are blessed, because the Spirit of glory and of God rests upon you" (1 Pet. 4:14). Instead of distancing ourselves from persecution, we are told to "Bless those who persecute you; bless and do not curse them" (Rom. 12:14).

J. Mack Stiles tells us that we should not let our mind be filled with fears and doubts, "We become people pleasers and so tell people what they want to hear. We shift blame and convince ourselves people won't listen. We tell ourselves that evangelism is too offensive. We run all the possible negative responses through our heads. The list goes on. By not dealing with our fear problem, we limit or distort evangelistic opportunities."[87]

4) Some are so desperate to win the approval of man that they are willing to change the gospel's message to accommodate the ear of their listeners.

Paul told the Galatians that anyone preaching a different gospel than what he preached was trying to seek the approval of man and not God. As a result, they "would not be a servant of Christ" (Gal. 1:10). In altering the gospel, the me-centered evangelist may congratulate himself on being able to live peaceably with all. Yet, such an approach will offer no salvific peace between God and men. To this, Andrew Rappaport, founder and president of Striving for Eternity Ministries, says, "People who water down the gospel don't do it because they love God and want people to know God. They do it because they want people to love them and we have to get over ourselves."

5) Certain groups dare not mention sin, human depravity, our unrighteousness, God's wrath, or Jesus' "gruesome" death so as not to offend anyone.

When we preach Christ crucified as the sole ground of our justification, this will offend the self-righteous among us. As a result, we will be persecuted (John 15:18-21; cf., 1 Pet. 4:12-19). Peter called Christ the cornerstone and then said for those who have "rejected" the cornerstone, Christ is "a rock of offense" (1 Pet. 2:7-8). For this group, Mark Dever comments, "A gospel that in no way offends the sinner has not been understood."[88] Mike Gendron adds, "The Gospel is inherently offensive."[89] So true, "For the word of the cross is folly to those who are perishing, but to us who are being saved it is the power of God" (1 Cor. 1:18; cf., Gal. 5:11). Dave Miller, editor of SBC Voices, reminds us, "The gospel is an offense. If you take the offense out of the gospel, you also remove the saving power of the gospel."[90]

6) Many convince themselves the gospel is for others to share.

---

[87] J. Mack Stiles, *Marks of the Messenger*, pp. 83-82.
[88] Mark Dever, *The Gospel and Personal Evangelism*, p. 19.
[89] Mike Gendron, *Contending for the Gospel*, p. 146.
[90] Dave Miller, An Inoffensive Gospel is No Gospel At All, https://sbcvoices.com/an-inoffensive-gospel-is-no-gospel-at-all/

They may do this out of a disobedient attitude and unwillingness to equip themselves to do the work of an evangelist. Others may have an overwhelming fear of not being able to deliver the message correctly. Some may have had such a traumatic experience in delivering the gospel that they have sworn off ever sharing it again. The gospel is not just for others to share, all of us are called to "do the work of an evangelist" (2 Tim. 4:5; 1 Pet. 3:15). If one can't overcome their fears of sharing the gospel, let's not forget that "knowing the fear of the Lord, we persuade others" (2 Cor. 5:11). If we are afraid of not delivering the gospel correctly, then we must prepare properly: "Do your best to present yourself to God as one approved, a worker who has no need to be ashamed, rightly handling the word of truth" (2 Tim. 2:15; cf., 1 Pet. 3:15). One bad experience in sharing the good news should not hinder any faithful Christian who knows, "I planted, Apollos watered, but God gave the growth. So neither he who plants nor he who waters is anything, but only God who gives the growth" (1 Cor. 3:6-7).

7) Some are ashamed of the gospel because they don't really believe it is true.

Since the Bible teaches that the subject of the gospel is the Messiah and His kingdom, "the gospel of Christ" (1 Cor. 9:12; 2 Cor. 2:12, 4:4, 9:13, 10:14; Gal. 1:7; Philp. 1:27; 1 Thess. 3:2; Mark 1:1; 2 Thess. 1:8; Rom. 1:9), to deny the gospel is to deny Christ. Such a denial makes that person out to be a "liar" (1 John 2:22), who will be denied by Christ Himself (Matt. 10:33; 2 Tim. 2:12). Therefore, such people are Christians in name only (Matt. 7:21; Rev. 3:15-16; Titus 1:16). Whatever it is they believe, they have "believed in vain" (1 Cor. 15:2). True Christians, who are here for "the defense and confirmation of the gospel" (Philip. 1:7), must be on guard for these "certain people [that] have crept in unnoticed" who "deny our only Master and Lord, Jesus Christ" (Jude 1:4).

Aversion to Conversion

Many today see conversion attempts as repulsive. This usually comes from people outside the Christian faith. However, Sheri Faye Rosendahl, a blogger and author who calls herself a follower of Jesus, writes, "I really like Jesus and I talk about him all the time, but not with the agenda to convert anyone.... I choose simply to try to love boldly and not live to convert."[91] Unfortunately, there are many self-proclaimed Christians today who feel the same way. Is it really possible that Christians could

---

[91] Sheri Faye Rosendahl, It's Okay To Love Your Religion Without Forcing People To Convert, https://www.huffpost.com/entry/to-love-not-convert_b_58fa5affe4b086ce58981090

"love boldly" and have this negative attitude toward evangelism? John MacArthur writes, "The New Testament presents a simple truism: those who love Jesus Christ care about evangelism."[92] Paul, who said Christians should go about "speaking the truth in love" (Eph. 4:15), also said we should be "praying at all times in the Spirit…that words may be given to me in opening my mouth boldly to proclaim the mystery of the gospel, for which I am an ambassador in chains, that I may declare it boldly, as I ought to speak" (Eph. 6:18-20; cf., 2 Cor. 3:12).

Jesus told Paul he would stand before kings, Gentiles and the children of Israel to share the gospel (Acts 9:15). In Acts 26, Paul, a prisoner in chains, told King Agrippa of his own conversion on the road to Damascus. He told the king that Jesus had sent him to open the eyes of the unconverted "so that they may turn from darkness to light and from the power of Satan to God" (26:18). Paul told King Agrippa, and many hearers at the Judgment Hall in Caesarea, that out of his love and concern for them, "that not only you but also all who hear me this day might become such as I am [a convert of Christ]—except for these chains" (26:29).

If Christians are to love boldly, the way Paul and the apostles did, conversion should never be avoided, but be the main goal of all our dealings with the non-believing world. Paul spoke with great pride when he said, "Greet my beloved Epaenetus, who was the first convert to Christ in Asia" (Rom. 16:5). Paul also joyfully reported conversions to the church leaders in Jerusalem, "So, being sent on their way by the church, they passed through both Phoenicia and Samaria, describing in detail the conversion of the Gentiles, and brought great joy to all the brothers" (Acts 15:3).

This has to make one wonder which Jesus Sheri Faye Rosendahl is following (2 Cor. 11:4). Listen to what else she warns Christians about, "When we have a goal or agenda of conversion, we put ourselves on a pedestal. We have the 'truth' and they need it from us. That's not the way of Jesus. That's the way of Manifest Destiny; it gives us a fabricated sense of power as if we are the savior. Come on now, we are a mess, we can't save the soul of anyone and god ["god" is in lower case in her article] doesn't need us to."[93]

Christian evangelists never put themselves on a pedestal, they only lift up Jesus Christ as Lord (2 Cor. 4:5). The Jesus we proclaim said He is "the way, and the truth, and the life" (John 14:6), and the unconverted

---

[92] John MacArthur, *Evangelism*, p. 93.
[93] Sheri Faye Rosendahl, cited from same article above.

desperately need this truth from us, as Jesus is the only answer (Acts 4:12). Therefore, yes, conversion is the way of Jesus and His disciples (Matt. 28:19-20; Acts 1:8, 26:16-18). No Christian ever said, "we are the savior" for that role belongs to God alone (Rom. 8:33; Isa. 43:11). Finally, the Christian evangelist does not have a fabricated sense of power, as we know conversion is the work of the Holy Spirit (John 3:8, 16:8-11).

If a person, who has claimed the name of Christ, is offended by or embarrassed at the thought of converting their family, friends or strangers, then maybe they are the one who needs converting. I once heard Pastor Tommy Nelson of Denton Bible Church in Denton, Texas say of God, "You can have a personal relationship with Me, not a private relationship."

The Gospel and Covid-19

After the Coronavirus hit, the Roman Catholic pope, Jorge Mario Begoglio, who has given himself the name Pope Francis, said the Coronavirus pandemic is one of "nature's responses" to humans ignoring the current ecological crisis.[94] Francis also told a Spanish journalist that he believes that the Coronavirus pandemic is nature "having a fit"[95] in response to environmental pollution. This should come as no surprise, as the animist believing Francis has referred to our globe as "Mother Earth"[96] and has talked about how "nature never forgives."[97] Francis has also called on Catholics to have an "ecological conversion"[98] for their sin against Mother Earth.

First of all, nature is not sentient. Nature does not respond or have a fit. Nature does not forgive nor absolve. God created nature (Gen. 1:1; Col. 1:16) and thus is in control of nature (Col. 1:17). Nothing happens without the will of God (Job 42:2; Isa. 14:27), including all that occurs under the heavens and earth (Exodus 32:35; Jer. 31:35; Psalm 89:9; Psalm 104; Matt. 8:26). Pope Francis' elevation of nature discounts God's sovereignty, control and will over His own creation.

---

[94] https://www.cnn.com/2020/04/08/europe/pope-francis-coronavirus-nature-response-intl/index.html
[95] https://www.lifesitenews.com/news/pope-francis-blames-coronavirus-on-nature-having-a-fit-over-environmental-damage
[96] https://www.vaticannews.va/en/pope/news/2019-10/pope-francis-the-christian-foundations-for-the-care-of-creation.html
[97] https://www.ecowatch.com/pope-francis-coronavirus-climate-crisis-2645677364.html?rebelltitem=2#rebelltitem2
[98] https://www.americamagazine.org/faith/2020/04/22/50th-anniversary-earth-day-pope-francis-calls-ecological-conversion

While many have speculated what purpose God may have in allowing for such a pandemic, there is a bigger virus about which we must all be concerned. It infects everyone from birth and is the deepest and darkest infection of all. This virus is called sin, a disease that is more dangerous and destructive than Covid-19 will ever be. No amount of hand washing, using disinfectant, wearing protective masks, or social distancing can halt the spread of sin, for the entire human race is already infected (Psalm 51:5; 1 Kings 8:46; Ecc. 7:20; 1 John 1:8). While this virus is sure to bring death (Rom. 6:23), the only cure is the gospel.

While some have used the Coronavirus pandemic as a time to spread strange fire, Christians should look upon it as a great time for the harvest—a time to speak of the gospel and the security we have in Christ. Spread the gospel, not Covid-19!

Social Justice and the Gospel

The Social Justice movement embodies several concepts, including Woke,[99] Critical Race Theory,[100] and Intersectionality.[101] Though the movement has morphed over the years, in its current form, it focuses on the supposed systemic oppression "white supremacists" have foisted on people of color, feminists, those of different ethnic origins, the lower class, or persons who identify as transgender or homosexual. If one could sum up this lobby in one phrase it might be—a call for "justice" against the upper class white systemic oppression.

Without even commenting on the merits of The Social Justice movement, it should be clear that this campaign is a temporal concept having to do with sociological and economic matters as opposed to spiritual affairs. With that in mind, Pastor John MacArthur says, "No temporal, political, social enterprise is a component of the saving gospel."[102] Pastor MacArthur adds that injecting a temporal concept into the gos-

---

[99] Woke means to be awake to sensitive social issues, such as racism.

[100] Critical Race Theory states that an individual is either oppressed or the oppressor based on skin color. Since CRT teaches that all institutions are designed to maintain white supremacy, whites are the oppressors and people of color the oppressed.

[101] Intersectionality posits that one's race, gender, sexuality, nationality and class all contribute to the specific type of privileges people enjoy or the systemic oppression they face. If one is a white heterosexual male from middle to upper class America, they supposedly enjoy privileges as the oppressor. If one is a person of color, female, transgender, homosexual, of an ethnicity other than descendants from Western European nations, and is from the lower class, they will be the subject of systemic oppression from the former group.

[102] John MacArthur, Bible Questions and Answers, Part 67, https://www.gty.org/library/sermons-library/70-43/bible-questions-and-answers-part-67. I credit this sermon by Pastor MacArthur in helping me form several of my comments on Social Justice.

pel is injecting something alien into the gospel. Christian author Kevin DeYoung states, "We ought to be extremely cautious about linking something as politically prescriptive as social justice with something as universally salvific as the gospel."[103]

In The Social Justice movement, nearly everyone is searching for some kind of victimhood, either from some perceived current oppression or from past generational oppression. A victim mentality is fundamental to their identity. However, throughout all of human history, every single individual and every group has been responsible for some form of injustice against others at any given time. No one escapes this charge, no matter who they are. How do I know this? Because even those who judge their oppressors can't claim any state of innocence, as all people are guilty of sinning against God and others (Rom. 3:23, 3:10). Those who think they are innocent victims are just like the hypocritical Jews Paul addressed in Romans chapter two: "Do you suppose, O man—you who judge those who practice such things and yet do them yourself—that you will escape the judgment of God?" (Rom. 2:3).[104]

While The Social Justice Movement speaks of generational sin holding them down, there is some truth to that but not in the way they think. The generational sin the Bible speaks of started in the Garden, for when "Your first father sinned" (Isa. 43:27), all generations since have inherited the sin of Adam (Rom. 5:12-21). The salvific gospel is not about what side we are on in a temporal movement having to do with sociological and economic issues, it is about what side we are on when it comes to being either in the first Adam, through whom all of us fell in the Garden, or in Christ, the "last Adam [who] became a life-giving spirit" (1 Cor. 15:45).

Every single person will be judged for their sin and their sin alone. At the final judgment, just like Eve won't be able to say she was a victim of the serpent and Adam won't be able to say he was a victim of Eve, no one will be able to claim they are the victims of somebody else's sin. Instead, the gospel of our salvation tells us to look at our own iniquity

---

[103] Kevin DeYoung, Is Social Justice a Gospel Issue? https://www.thegospelcoalition.org/blogs/kevin-deyoung/social-justice-gospel-issue/

[104] The danger of this movement is that those who feel they are oppressed become the oppressors, which becomes social revenge instead of social justice. They single out a race, gender and sexuality—white, male (and their white female co-conspirators) and heterosexual—and proclaimed the entire group guilty. These personal perceptions are often rooted in personal hatred, not because of what individuals in that group have actually done. Decades ago, we used to call this kind of thinking prejudice. If it wasn't right then, it shouldn't be acceptable now, either.

(Ezekiel 18:20), which will then point us to the Savior who "was crushed for our iniquities" (Isa. 53:5), giving us the peace and assurance that "the Lord has laid on him the iniquity of us all" (53:6; cf., Rom. 8:1-4).

We have to be on guard against those in The Social Justice movement who link their campaign with the actual, salvific gospel. As has been famously said, the gospel of our salvation is not a skin issue, it's a sin issue (Rom. 3:23). The gospel is not about race but about grace (Eph. 2:8-9). Furthermore, if I may add, the gospel is not about gender but surrender (Mark 1:15), and the gospel is not about identifying oneself with a fleshly vice but identifying with the One who bought you with a price (2 Cor. 5:17; 1 Cor. 6:18-20).[105]

Extraterrestrial Life and the Gospel

There has been much speculation about the existence of alien intelligent life beyond our earth. If such life were discovered, or made manifest to us, how would this impact the gospel?

Several points must be made. First, the idea of such life is mostly promoted in movies, TV shows, books and magazines that we call science fiction. Notice the word fiction, which refers to narratives that are imaginary, made-up and not based on history or fact. Many will object that UFO sightings are not fiction. While I grant that such sightings are common, since no proof outside of anecdotal accounts (i.e.: "I was abducted by an alien") has ever been presented to corroborate these UFOs are from alien life, objectively, we must remain skeptical.

Secondly, one has to wonder—why the fascination with discovering alien life? We may be able to look to Blaise Pascal, the 17th century philosopher, to find a partial answer to this. Pascal referred to the emptiness of fallen man, who tries in vain to fill their life with everything around them except God. He wrote that man seeks things "that are not there." He added that "none can help, since this infinite abyss can be

[105] When the Bible speaks of "the gospel of your salvation" (Eph. 1:13), it does not have the Social Justice movement in mind. Instead, the good news that saves us is only about the root of the gospel—the grace we receive from Jesus' perfect life on our behalf, His death and resurrection. However, the fruit of the gospel (sanctification) does include addressing biblical justice in the kingdom. Gospel-transformed Christians do strive for biblical justice, which is conformity to God's moral standard as revealed in the Ten Commandments. Biblical justice also embodies the two greatest commandments to love the Lord your God with all your heart and with all your soul and with all your mind and to love your neighbor as yourself (Matt. 22:37-40). In other words, the root of the gospel is exclusively about the King and His finished work. The fruit of the gospel is how the King transforms believers in His kingdom. We should never confuse the fruit with the root when it comes to justification.

filled only with an infinite and immutable object; in other words by God himself."[106] Augustine wrote in Confessions, "O Lord, and our heart is restless until it rests in you."

In an eagerness to seek out aliens, we often hear things like, "Their advanced intelligence will certainly be able to help us in areas of healing, compassion, love, ecosystems and technological advancements." What they are missing is that there is no greater healing (Isa. 53:5; 1 Pet. 2:24), compassion (Eph. 4:32, NASB20), or love (John 15:13) than in Christ giving of Himself on the cross. Read about the ecosystems of the new heavens and new earth in the Bible (Rev. 22:1-5; Isa. 11:6-9). As for technological advancements, no eye has seen, heard, nor imagined what God has prepared for those who love Him (1 Cor. 2:9; Rev. 21:1, 15-21). There is also no more advanced wisdom or intelligence than that which is hidden in Christ (Col. 2:3).

Thirdly, we have to ask the most important question—what does the Bible have to say about this topic? Most people, including many Christians, will say the Bible is silent on this issue. Is that true? Let's take a closer look. The Bible tells us that "In the beginning, God created the heavens and the earth" (Gen. 1:1), and then later, on day four of the Creation Week, He created the sun, moon, stars and other planets (1:14-16). Since God made the earth first on day one, our own planet should be our focus of understanding on this issue.

In Isaiah 45:18, we read that when God created the earth, "He did not create it empty, he formed it to be inhabited!" Psalm 115:16 likewise states, "The earth he has given to the children of man". While the Bible speaks clearly about God's plans for the earth, what is written elsewhere in the scriptures also gives us a guide for God's plans for His other planetary creations. For example, while God made man the ruler of earth (Gen. 1:28), the Bible suggests the heavens are also subject to man. While warning against making idols of the sun, moon, stars, and all the host of heaven,[107] we read where these creations in the universe are "things that the Lord your God has allotted to all the peoples under the whole heaven" (Deut. 4:19). All the peoples are obviously a reference to "all the peoples who are on the face of the earth" (7:6). The obvious question here would be—if God has allotted, or assigned, mankind dominion over all His other planetary creations, would we then have dominion

---

[106] Blaise Pascal, Pensées VII (425).
[107] When you think about it, what better way to make an idol of the sun, moon, stars, and all the host of heaven than to ascribe to them alien life about which God does not speak one word in scripture.

over any extraterrestrial life out there? How would that fit into the popular idea that intelligent and more advanced life from other planets could one day seek to have dominion over us?

We should also remember that the Bible tells us that "creation was subjected to futility" (Rom. 8:20) and "we know that the whole creation has been groaning" (8:22) since the fall of Adam. If God had created intelligent beings on other worlds, would their lives be subjected to the sin of earth's inhabitants? Yes, Romans 8:19-22 makes it clear that the curse that followed Adam's sin (Gen. 3:17-19) means that not only is our world fallen, but all other possible alien inhabited worlds would have to be fallen as well.

This leads to another question—why would God, who wrapped up Creation Week by declaring that "everything that he had made...was very good" (1:31), create alien life on another planet that was subjected to futility and under a curse? God was very specific in the details of what He created on days one through six of Creation Week and He finished His work in those six days (Gen. 2:1); therefore, we know He did not create alien life on another planet during this week. Since the fall immediately occurred in Genesis 3, that only leaves the possibility of God creating alien life on another planet *after* the fall. Since Deuteronomy 32:4 (NKJV) states of God, "He is the Rock, His work is perfect", it makes little sense that God would create alien life after Creation Week, placing them on a planet already subjected to futility and under a curse. We have already seen this is not His order of creating.

Furthermore, since aliens would then be under the same curse as the rest of creation, the only One who would be able to rescue them from that curse is Jesus, because "Christ redeemed us from the curse of the law by becoming a curse for us—for it is written, 'Cursed is everyone who is hanged on a tree'" (Gal. 3:13). This brings up other problems for the possibility of extraterrestrial life elsewhere in the solar system.

The Bible tells us that Jesus created all things and all creation is subjected to Him (Col. 1:16-17). When David wrote about God setting the heavens, moon and the stars in place (Psalm 8:3), he said of the Messiah, "You have given him dominion over the works of your hands; you have put *all* things under his feet" (8:6; cf., 1 Cor. 15:27a; Matt. 28:18; Heb. 2:6-8). We must remember that Jesus is the God-man, fully God (John 1:1; Philip. 2:6; Col. 1:19) and fully man (Heb. 2:14, 17; Rom. 1:3). As the representative of man before the Father (1 Tim. 2:5), only Jesus' shed blood can lift the curse (Heb. 9:22; Matt. 26:28; Rom. 5:9; 1 John 1:7; Rev. 1:5, 5:9).

Hebrews 2:17 speaks of this blood connection as Jesus "had to be made like his brothers in every respect, so that he might become a merciful and faithful high priest in the service of God, to make propitiation for the sins of the people." Notice that the very verse before this we read, "For surely it is not angels that he helps, but he helps the offspring of Abraham" (Heb. 2:16). We have yet another important question—who among any extraterrestrial life would be the offspring of Abraham? If any intelligent life on any other planet is not of the offspring of Abraham, or does not have human blood, then Jesus can't lift their curse. We know when Jesus came the first time, the promise was that "He will save his people from their sins" (Matt. 1:21). Since aliens on other planets are not His people, they can't be saved from their sins. Jason Lisle writes, "When we consider how the salvation plan might apply to any hypothetical extraterrestrial (but otherwise human-like) beings, we are presented with a problem. If there were Vulcans or Klingons out there, how would they be saved? They are not blood relatives of Jesus, and so Christ's shed blood cannot pay for their sin."[108]

If one to were speculate that Jesus could have visited an alien world, lived there, and died there as well, that also goes against the biblical testimony, for the Bible states that Jesus died only once in order to redeem sinners. Peter writes that Christ "suffered once for sins, the righteous for the unrighteous, that he might bring us to God" (1 Peter 3:18). Paul says of Jesus, "For the death he died he died to sin, once for all" (Rom. 6:10). The writer of Hebrews repeatedly confirms that Jesus offered Himself up as a sacrifice for sins "once for all" (Heb. 7:27, 9:11-12, 10:10) and that He won't make any other sacrifice "again and again" (Heb. 9:25, NIV), otherwise, "He would have had to suffer repeatedly since the foundation of the world" (9:26). If God did make intelligent life on other planets, then it would require them to believe in the once for all sacrifice that Christ, the God-man, made on our earth to redeem them of the curse that affects the whole of creation (Acts 4:12). As Jason Lisle points out, "Jesus is now and forever both God and man; but He is not an alien."[109]

One final point: the Bible teaches that the fate of the whole creation is linked to Christ's Second Coming on earth. One day, Jesus will return

---

[108] Jason Lisle, Are Aliens Real?, https://answersingenesis.org/astronomy/alien-life/are-aliens-real/
[109] Ibid.

to our planet, and not only will our earth be subject to a refining fire,[110] but so will all of creation, "the heavens and earth that now exist are stored up for fire, being kept until the day of judgment...then the heavens will pass away with a roar, and the heavenly bodies will be burned up and dissolved" (2 Peter 3:7, 10). Not only our earth, but *all* the stars and planets will be subject to this fate. This is to make way for a new heavens and new earth (Rev. 21:1). This leads to our final question—why would God burn up and remake all the planets outside of earth where the alleged extraterrestrial beings now inhabit? We know that when the earth goes through this, the endgame for those in Christ will be a new paradise (Rev. 2:7), but what would be the fate of any extraterrestrial life when that fulfillment occurs?

My conclusion is that while it might be argued that the Bible is silent about the existence of any alleged extraterrestrial life, it is not silent about how such alien intelligent life would relate to the gospel. In fact, I think our closer look shows that the scripture has a lot to say about this topic, both explicitly and implicitly. I don't think the question should be, "Could God choose to create intelligent life elsewhere?" I think the biblical question is, "Did He, and for what purpose?"

From a biblical perspective, alien life on other planets does not seem plausible. The search for aliens is actually an alienation from Christ, the God-man, and His gospel.

Dousing the Strange Fire

When it comes to sanitized, half-baked and different gospels, we need to keep them out of the sanctuary of the church. If we allow these false gospels to be taught from the pulpit, they can end up in the mission field. Anyone who preaches these unauthorized offerings, which God has not commanded, should be prepared to take the heat from God. Their only consolation should be that they don't live in the dispensation that Nadab and Abihu did, when a fire from God devoured them, and they died

---

[110] Instead of being completely destroyed by fire, it seems more likely that God's plan is to refine the heavens and earth and restore all things. In Acts chapter 3, we read where Jesus' return will not happen "until the time for restoring all the things" (Acts 3:21). Randy Alcorn points out, "God's agenda is not to destroy everything and start over, but to restore everything. The perfection of creation once lost will be fully regained, and then some. The same Peter who spoke these words in Acts 3 wrote the words about the earth's destruction in 2 Peter 3—apparently he saw no conflict between them" (Randy Alcorn, Heaven, pp. 147-148). The destruction will be partial, as in destroying the surface things on the earth, but the renewal will be complete. The present fallen condition will pass away and be restored to perfection.

before the Lord (Leviticus 10:1-2). However, unless those who preach and believe in these false gospels repent, another fire is sure to come later (Rev. 20:14-15).

○ ○ ○

15) FEAR, MISSED OPPORTUNITIES AND NUMBERS

"Boldness in evangelism isn't about starting a conversation, it's about turning a conversation towards the gospel." - IMB Missionary, Seba Vazquez

From the moment God brought me into His kingdom in 1993, I felt an urgency to share God's saving grace. Early on, it was mostly telling people that I had become a Christian—a follower of Jesus. Honestly, it didn't go much deeper than that. I was just starting to read the Bible for the first time. By the Lord's power, I had to learn how to present my body as a living sacrifice, holy and acceptable to God. I had to no longer be conformed to this world but allow God to transform me by the renewing of my mind (Rom. 12:1-2).

This renewal came in stages. It included grounding myself in scripture (2 Tim. 2:15), memorizing God's word (Psalm 119:11; 2 Tim. 3:15-17) and watching my life and doctrine closely (1 Tim. 4:16). I was becoming a new man, because "if anyone is in Christ, he is a new creation. The old has passed away; behold, the new has come" (2 Cor. 5:17). God had placed a new heart and a new spirit within me (Ezekiel 36:26). The more I experienced this "newness of life" (Rom. 6:4), the more I wanted to tell people about it. While all the above scriptures are true about having a new spirit within us, we are also still in the flesh (Rom. 7:22-25). The flesh of my previous life was dominated by anxiety and keeping a safe distance from people. How that would work with evangelism would be a challenge I would have to meet.

Sharing Jesus With Fear and Power

I have to admit, based on my personal experiences in evangelism, books with titles like, "Share Jesus Without Fear," "Sharing Jesus without Freaking Out," "Witnessing Without Fear," and "How To Share Your Faith Without Fear," have always puzzled me. I can't think of a time that I have witnessed to someone where fear did not play some factor.

Several years after my conversion, when I first started sharing the gospel, I was a nervous wreck. A young man named Bill and a young woman, Trina, approached me as I was watering my front lawn. They told me they were selling magazines. After looking through their catalogue, I told them I would purchase a subscription to U.S. News & World Report if they would listen to my gospel presentation. While Bill cracked a smile and took a seat on my front porch, Trina seemed hesitant. In fact, after I started to share the gospel, she walked out into the street waving her hands saying she did not want to hear anything about religion.

I don't remember much of what I said to Bill except me nervously going through my presentation. In fact, I remember pacing back and forth while talking to him. At the end, I told Bill that I would pray that one day he would come to trust in Christ. The ironic thing is, when we were finished, it was Trina who gleefully came back from the street and took my money for the subscription.

As they both walked away, I remember feeling quite convicted. While I'm not sure Bill showed true repentance or understanding of the gospel, Trina's actions really bothered me. What transpired that day was made worse after I never received a single magazine. When I later checked out the company for which they were selling, it all appeared to be a scam.

I learned many lessons that day. I learned that I needed to present the gospel without any strings attached. God doesn't need me to bargain for a gospel hearing, because "The Lord knows those who are his" (2 Tim. 2:19). I was young in the faith when this happened, so when I later read what Paul said about his own witnessing, I was convicted and comforted at the same time. To the church in Corinth, Paul said this, "And I, when I came to you, brothers, did not come proclaiming to you the testimony of God with lofty speech or wisdom. For I decided to know nothing among you except Jesus Christ and him crucified. And I was with you in weakness and in fear and much trembling, and my speech and my message were not in plausible words of wisdom, but in demonstration of the Spirit and of power, so that your faith might not rest in the wisdom of men but in the power of God" (1 Cor. 2:1-5).

I learned it is the demonstration of the Holy Spirit and of power that convicts a person of their sin and unrighteousness and leads them to Christ (John 16:8-9), not me. Most of all, I learned that God uses our fear and trembling in our witnessing encounters to show us our weakness in the midst of His sovereignty. If the same God who works in us tells us to "work out your own salvation with fear and trembling" (Philip. 2:12), why would we not expect such fear and trembling in our witnessing opportunities? Moses so feared being God's messenger that he asked the Lord to allow his brother Aaron to speak for him (Exodus 4:10-16, 6:12, 30, 7:1-2). Jeremiah thought he was too young, "Ah, Lord God! Behold, I do not know how to speak, for I am only a youth" (Jeremiah 1:6). However, the Lord said to Jeremiah, "Do not be afraid of them, for I am with you to deliver you, declares the Lord" (1:8). Jonah initially ran away instead of obeying God's call to witness to the people of Ninevah (Jonah 1-4). In our fear and trembling, God is strong, and His message is proclaimed!

When Paul spoke to the Corinthians about being ambassadors for Christ and God making His appeal through us, he said, "Therefore, knowing the fear of the Lord, we persuade others" (2 Cor. 5:11). Yet, didn't Paul also tell Timothy "God gave us a spirit not of fear but of power" (2 Tim. 1:7)? Certainly, but Paul was speaking to Timothy from prison, in jail, while being persecuted for his own witnessing (1:8; 2:8-9). Paul warned Timothy that while similar persecution would come his way (3:12), he must rely on the Spirit's power (1:14) to overcome his fear of persecution. Fear of being put in jail for sharing the gospel is what Paul was speaking to Timothy about in 2 Timothy 1:7, not a blanket statement that Christians should never fear.

Paul gave a similar reminder to the Philippians, "I want you to know, brothers, that what has happened to me has really served to advance the gospel, so that it has become known throughout the whole imperial guard and to all the rest that my imprisonment is for Christ. And most of the brothers, having become confident in the Lord by my imprisonment, are much more bold to speak the word without fear" (Philip. 1:12-14). While there certainly are Christians around the globe that have to deal with a fear of being jailed for sharing the gospel (North Korea, Iran), that doesn't apply to most of us, especially in the United States.

I understand that God at times tell us *not* to fear (Matt. 10:28; Rom. 8:15; 1 John 4:18), but He also at other times admonishes us *to* fear (Rom. 11:20; 1 Pet. 1:17, 2:17; Philip. 2:12-13; Luke 12:5; Isa. 66:2; Acts 9:31; 2 Cor. 5:11, 7:1; Proverbs 9:10; Ecc. 12:13). We also see where there are times when people turned to the gospel *with* fear (Acts 13:16, 16:29-34), and for others, "There is no fear of God before their eyes" (Rom. 3:18).

While some proclaim that they share the gospel without fear and write books and hold seminars to show others how to do likewise, I am not going to question their methods or results. I only know for myself, as one Christian friend once said to me, "a little Holy Spirit nervousness can be a good thing." I also have learned that any power, boldness or persuasion that I may have in my witnessing only comes when I have a healthy fear of the Lord. Knowing that He is in control of the situation transcends any fear I might be experiencing.

J. Mack Stiles writes, "Paul says when we fear God rather than people, we become agents of reconciliation (2 Corinthians 5:11-20). Developing the proper fear of God is a critical key to produce bold healthy evangelism."[111] Stiles adds, "Fear of the Lord results in healthy evangelism."[112]

---

[111] J. Mack Stiles, *Marks of the Messenger*, p. 87.
[112] Ibid, p. 87.

Missed Opportunities

I appreciate Pastor Mark Dever's transparency about missed opportunities in evangelism. He writes, "If you are anything like me, you're probably not quite so blunt about your failures in evangelism. You've altered your mental records. In fact, even at the time you're not witnessing, you're busy spinning, justifying, rationalizing, and explaining to your conscience why it was really wise and faithful and kind and obedient not to share the gospel with a particular person at that time and in that situation."[113]

As far as my failures in evangelism, there have been many. When I look back at my missteps, the thing that was always missing was a balance of grace and truth. I would be tipped way over to one side or the other. As a truth-oriented Christian, I have spoken truth in an ungracious way. It took me a while to learn that when people hear truth spoken graciously, it can at least make them pause and listen, even if in the end they reject what you say. On the other hand, I have failed when I avoided speaking truth into a matter so I wouldn't risk offending. As Randy Alcorn says, "We need to examine ourselves and correct ourselves. We who are truth-oriented need to go out of our way to affirm grace. We who are grace-oriented need to go out of our way to affirm truth."[114]

There have been times when I'm talking to a non-Christian when they might unintentionally give me an opening to discuss the gospel. I have to confess that a part of me says, "don't go there." Why would I tell myself that? I'm going to be honest and say I think it is a combination of me not wanting to risk a friendship, a neighborly standing, cause conflict in the work place, cause division within my family, or even to make sure a service provider does not get detoured from repairing or installing something in my house properly. If/when I am called out at the judgment seat of Christ (2 Cor. 5:10) for neglected opportunities and missteps when sharing the gospel, my reproof will be well deserved.

Numbers Game

> *"The question whether or not one is evangelizing cannot be settled simply by asking whether one has had conversions. There have been missionaries to Muslims who labored for a lifetime and saw no converts; must we conclude from this that they were not evangelizing?"* - J.I. Packer[115]

---

[113] Mark Dever, *The Gospel and Personal Evangelism*, p. 19.
[114] Randy Alcorn, *The Grace and Truth Paradox*, p. 88.
[115] J.I. Packer, *Evangelism and the Sovereignty of God*, chapter one, p. 44.

For years, I faithfully entered into a notebook what I considered conversions. I would even count them up at the end of the year and compare them with the year before. After maturing in my understanding of God's sovereignty in salvation, I set the book aside. I came to realize that that the only true converts are those "whose names are in the book of life" (Philip. 4:3), "the Lamb's book of life" (Rev. 21:27).

Nathan Busenitz, Professor of Theology at The Master's Seminary, writes, "Numbers of opponents confounded or unbelievers converted is no real measure of how well we have done. If it were, the prophet Jonah would be a runaway sensation (with the entire city of Nineveh responding to his preaching), while the prophet Jeremiah would be a dismal failure (with his ministry bearing virtually no visible fruit). Yet from God's perspective, Jeremiah's faithful obedience made his ministry the true success, while Jonah's rebellious resistance rendered him a disappointing failure."[116]

Some people declare their evangelism successful by the number of "converts" they believe they have acquired. We often hear things like, "I led five people to Christ this week." Without having the ability to do much follow-up work, or keep tabs on these new "converts", the honest evangelist has to admit they can't know how many, if any, of these people were truly born again.

The big evangelistic crusades will regularly announce what seem like some impressive convert numbers. We are often told that 5,000 or 10,000 made commitments to Christ. However, the late Billy Graham once stated that only about twenty-five percent of those who come forward at one of his events actually became Christians. Even that might be high, as recent studies have shown that only about six percent of people who make a profession of faith at an evangelistic crusade become true Christ followers.

Peter's Sermon at Pentecost

"Those who received his word were baptized, and there were added that day about three thousand souls" (Acts 2:41). How can we not share in Luke's enthusiasm that Peter's sermon at Pentecost resulted in 3,000 converts in one day? Many will point to this passage to legitimize today's large evangelist crusades. Yet, they often forget the next verse, "And they devoted themselves to the apostles' teaching and the fellowship, to the breaking of bread and the prayers" (Acts 2:42; cf., 1:14). The reason

---

[116] Nathan Busenitz, John MacArthur, *Evangelism*, p. 57.

Peter's sermon was so effective: there was follow-up. Not only were they baptized, but they devoted themselves to the apostles teaching and to fellowship in the church. Peter did not just count conversions, he and the church made disciples.[117]

When the time is right (Acts 2:37, 16:14, 30), we should call for decisions (Acts 16:31, 17:30; Mark 1:15; 2 Cor. 5:20). However, we should also, if possible, follow up with each person who makes a profession of faith. If personal follow-up is not possible (this may be the only time we see that person), we should encourage them to seek out a local church and ask about the steps to becoming a disciple of Christ. Remember that Jesus told His hearers to "count the cost" of following Him (Luke 14:25-33), which will take time and growth (Philip. 4:9; 2 Pet. 1:10). Again, Jesus said, "If you abide in my word, you are truly my disciples" (John 8:31).

Counting or Measuring?

Instead of counting heads, wouldn't it be better to measure converts? What if those who make a profession of faith were gauged by whether they are baptized (Matt. 28:19) and become a member of a Bible believing church (Heb. 10:24-25; Acts 2:42)? Whether they count the cost of following Jesus (Luke 14:27-28), are seen growing in the grace and knowledge of our Lord and Savior Jesus Christ (2 Pet. 3:18), and are able to lead others to Christ (Mark 16:15) and make disciples themselves (Matt. 28:19-20)? Of course, there is no measurement that will perfect this on this side of heaven, as that will only come when we see Jesus face-to-face (1 John 3:2-3).

If a person was drawn by the Father (John 6:44) and sealed with the promised Holy Spirit (Eph. 1:13), they are immediately part of the body of Christ (1 Cor. 12:13). While God infallibly knows those who are His (2 Tim. 2:19; Luke 10:20; Philip. 4:3), we don't (1 Sam. 16:7). However, consider this: God instructs us to make judgments to determine if someone is qualified to be a leader in a church (1 Timothy 3:1-7; Titus 1:5-9), if someone is a false prophet (Deut. 13:1-3; Matt. 7:15-16), and if one is teaching a false gospel (Gal. 1:8) or preaching another Jesus (2 Cor. 11:4). Does He also tell us how to determine a false convert? The answer is yes! "They went out from us, but they were not of us; for if they had

---

[117] In Acts 4, as Peter and John were teaching the people and proclaiming the resurrection of Jesus, we also read, "But many of those who had heard the word believed, and the number of the men came to about five thousand" (Acts 4:4).

been of us, they would have continued with us. But they went out, that it might become plain that they all are not of us" (1 John 2:19).

37-year-old Jonathan Steingard, who says he grew up in a Christian home and is a pastor's kid, was the lead vocalist and lead guitarist for the Christian pop-punk band Hawk Nelson. He stunned his fans when he announced in 2020 that he no longer believes in God. He became the latest in a number of high profile "Christians" to abandon the faith. In discussing how he had a hard time connecting up with a church, Steingard pledged his devotion for the DC Comics Avengers series when saying, "If every Sunday sermon involved an Avenger's reference, I'd be more likely to go to church."[118] This just illustrates how some people don't have a foundation in the faith they profess. Their interests are captured by worldly things and not the things of Christ. They are in the world and of it. However, as Paul said, "Set your minds on things that are above, not on things that are on earth" (Col. 3:2).

When most of these high profile "Christians" go out from us, they inevitably post a list of their "concerns." Their most common talking point is that no one wants to discuss the hard issues of Christianity. They will list things like alleged Bible contradictions, how a God of love would allow evil, or how salvation through Jesus alone is not inclusive. To that I would say—where have you been? Christians who are on The Evangelism Circle are always growing in the faith and take seriously the command to "sanctify Christ as Lord in your hearts, always being ready to make a defense to everyone who asks you to give an account for the hope that is in you" (1 Pet. 3:15, NASB). The Christian who has sanctified Christ as Lord in their hearts is continually addressing such concerns, not only for themselves, but for the sake of others who might ask about the hope that we have. Christians who are answering questions about the faith, instead of those who just keep repeating objections that have been adequately responded to many times and in many ways, should be looked at as examples of those undergoing sanctification.

When you look back on the lives of these celebrated personalities who have publicly left the faith, you will see that there was ultimately no real evidence of sanctification. However, a true convert will not go out from us, but continue with us. Furthermore, their continuing will be evidence of sanctification (Rom. 6:6, 18, 8:9-14, 29; 2 Cor. 3:18, 4:16; Gal. 3:3, 4:19, 5:16-25; Eph. 4:22-32; 1 John 1:5-10; 2 Pet. 1:2-11; Heb. 10:10) of an already justified person (Acts 13:39; Rom. 3:23-24, 4:24-25,

---

[118] Unbelievable Premier Christian Radio podcast, Saturday June 20th, 2020.

5:1, 9, 8:33; Gal. 2:16, 3:24). In other words, for those who go through the root of the gospel to be justified, the fruit of the gospel (our sanctification) will follow (see chapter 8). The sanctification that God produces through us (Philip. 2:13) will include the fruit of Him growing us in the knowledge of His Savior (2 Pet. 3:18), so that we will "have mercy on those who doubt" (Jude 1:22) by always being ready to answer their concerns.

While God knows who are His own (John 10:14), He has also instructed us to take a measurement so *we* can know who are not (1 John 2:19; Mark 4:2-19; Acts 20:29-30; 1 Cor. 11:19; 2 Cor. 11:4; Jude 1:3-4). As far as who *are* His, when Paul referred to "members of the household of God" (Eph. 2:19), he called them "saints" (Rom. 1:7; 1 Cor. 1:2; Eph. 1:1; Philip. 1:1; Col. 1:2; Philemon 1:5) and the "elect" (Rom. 8:33; 2 Tim. 2:10; Titus 1:1). In the same passages where Paul referred to the "saints" and the "elect", he measured these elect saints as "called" (Rom. 1:7); "worthy" (Rom. 16:2); "sanctified in Christ Jesus" (1 Cor. 1:2); "faithful in Christ Jesus" (Eph. 1:1); "equip[ped]... for the work of ministry" (Eph. 4:12); avoiding "sexual immorality and all impurity or covetousness" (Eph. 5:3); "servants of Christ Jesus" (Philip. 1:1); "faithful brothers in Christ" (Col. 1:2); those "who have believed, because [of] our testimony" (2 Thess. 1:10); having "a reputation for good works" (1 Tim. 5:10; cf., Gal. 6:9; 2 Thess. 2:16-17) and possessing a "knowledge of the truth, which accords with godliness" (Titus 1:1).

In the end, we will see clearly that God's elect saints were just as much His the day they repented and believed (Acts 13:48) as the day they finished the race (2 Tim. 4:7), because the race is only for those who are "predestined to be conformed to the image of his Son" (Rom. 8:29; cf., Philip. 1:6). God does not predestine His saints to be conformed to this world (Rom. 12:2), but He equips and sanctifies His elect to run the race to the end, having "run with endurance" (Heb. 12:1) because "our citizenship is in heaven" (Philip. 3:20).

Finally, since unbelievers can mask themselves as believers (Matt. 7:15) and false converts will eventually go back to acting like unbelievers (Mark 4:15-19), a "measurement" to determine true converts seems more appropriate than counting. That way, we will be able to judge "each according to the measure of faith that God has assigned" (Rom. 12:3; cf., Eph. 4:7, 13). Let us therefore measure those who have proclaimed to enter the faith, so one day we may count them.

Counting False Converts

False converts never "count the cost" (Luke 14:28). They call Jesus "Lord" but don't do what He says (Luke 6:46). Many give lip service to God, but their hearts are far from Him (Matt. 15:8). They profess to know Jesus, but they deny Him by their disobedience (Titus 1:16). When tribulation or persecution arise to challenge their false faith, they fall away (Mark 4:17). When the cares of the world, the deceitfulness of riches and the desires for other things appear, the world always wins out (4:19). Then why do we keep counting them?

Maybe some keep counting false converts because they have been taught an unbiblical approach to evangelism. Not only do they offer a candy-coated gospel that neither offends nor convicts anyone, they never mention the cost, or measurement, that comes with accepting the gospel. As John MacArthur points out, "Salvation is absolutely free. So is joining the Army."[119] Presented with a gospel that does not convict a person of their sin and unrighteousness before God, and leaves out calls for repentance and a faith that will be measured, many will happily declare, "Count me in!" Sadly, many Christians today are happy to accommodate them.

What happens when, or even if, there is a follow-up attempt at true disciple-making with a false convert? Ray Comfort writes, "'Following up' with a false convert is like putting a stillborn baby into intensive care. Neither approach solves the problem."[120] Charles Spurgeon called false converts "unhatched chickens."[121] The moral of this story—don't count your chickens before they hatch.[122]

---

[119] John MacArthur, *Evangelism*, p. 159.
[120] Ray Comfort, *Way of the Master*, p. 64.
[121] Charles Spurgeon, *The Soul Winner*, p. 4.
[122] To make sure no one misunderstands my position, I am not saying we need to measure converts through some works/righteousness scale that determines their justification. Since we know that a person truly justified by grace alone, through faith alone, in Christ alone, will move on to being sanctified by the same God who justified them, we measure them to make sure they have been justified by God and are not a false convert. For we know that all those God justifies, He will then sanctify. As John Calvin wrote, "Christ justifies no one whom He does not also sanctify. By virtue of our union with Christ, He bestows both gifts, the one never without the other." Calvin's Commentary on 1 Corinthians 1:30, Volume XX, Baker, 1993, p. 93.

16) DO THE WORK OF AN EVANGELIST

"To call a man evangelical who is not evangelistic is an utter contradiction."
G. Campbell Morgan, British evangelist, preacher, 1863-1945

In doing the work of an evangelist, I have found that the gospel hearer's heart can run the gamut from hardness, apathy, mocking, and self-righteousness, to confusion, or, God willing—a great awakening. While it is true that most of the time we don't know the final state of people's hearts with whom we share the gospel, I wanted to share some unique responses I have had while witnessing. What you are about to read are real conversations I have had over the last two and a half decades that I documented in my daily journal. I have taken extra care to detail these conversations just as they occurred.[123]

Darin told me he had accidently run over and killed a 5-year-old child seven years earlier. He teared up as he told me he did not deserve heaven. After I told him no one deserves heaven and shared the gospel with him, he gave his life to Christ. 23-year-old Adrienne, who had been raped and also lost her two-month-old son, came to an understanding of God's grace even in the midst of the world's evil. Lucas has been blind ever since being shot in the head, but God showed him the light of the gospel during our conversation. 17-year-old Karen is autistic. I guess I shouldn't have been surprised when she was able to articulate the gospel back to me with amazing clarity.

Dedra trusted in Jesus as her Savior and then asked me to stay on the phone while she shared my message in Spanish with her grandmother. Chris told me he had to make financial restitution for a criminal offense. After he mentioned to me that the courthouse clerk stamped his last payment with "Debt Paid in Full", I shared with him the story of Jesus on the cross. When I told him Jesus's last words, "it is finished" (John 19:30), translate as "tetelestai" in Greek, meaning "debt paid in full", he trusted in Christ, the author and finisher of our faith (Heb. 12:2, NKJV). When Wanda told me she wanted to pray out loud to trust in Christ, she had a classic line I have never forgotten, "You finished the business for me."

Sam told me he questioned why his Catholic religion always had Jesus on the cross. After I explained to him that an empty cross signifies Christ's finished work, as opposed to the Catholic religion which repeatedly crucifies Christ in the Mass, he said a light bulb went off in his head. Joyce called to complain about her cheating husband, but it turned out she was being unfaithful to the Lord by adding works to Christ's finished work. She repented and said she would trust in Christ alone. 33-year-old Charles told me he lost trust in Christianity after his pastor had tried to seduce him. After I told him the gospel is not about what wolves in sheep's clothing do, but what about Christ did, he broke down and placed his faith in his true Shepherd—Jesus Christ. Matthew said Jesus was "The main factor" to get to heaven and then he had to do the rest. After I explained to him that Jesus is the "only factor" (John 14:6; Acts 4:12; Gal. 2:21), he repented and made Christ his only Savior.

---

[123] These documented conversations occurred via e-mail, live chat, or phone conversations while volunteering at various gospel ministries. Other witnessing accounts were in person. Again, the first names have been changed.

As I was challenging one man with the law, I asked him, "On a scale of one to ten, how would you rank yourself on how you are doing following the Ten Commandments, with ten being the best and one the worst?" Cam asked in response, "Are there any negative rankings?" I asked Ron if he wanted to know what the Bible has to say about how we to get to heaven and he said, "No, I'm good." I told him the very point of the gospel is that no one is good (Rom. 3:10). I asked one woman if she had assurance of her salvation. She said, yes, but then asked, "What if I stood before God on judgment day and maybe he's having a bad day?"

Betsy, on the phone from Tennessee, said, "I'm unsure of my salvation. I need to get the whole thing nailed down." Another woman called and said she was a Christian. After she gave a solid gospel testimony, she threw me for quite a loop when she told me she had been diagnosed with multiple personality disorder. She told me she was worried that one of her personalities was not saved. Roger called and said he was saved in the 7th Day Adventist Church but had problems with the church's prophet Ellen DeGeneres. Robert had confused the TV personality with the actual 7th Day Adventist "Prophet" Ellen G. White.

Melissa told me, "Patrick, I am not worthy, I am a great sinner." I told her she was the tax collector in Luke 18 who Jesus said went home justified, rather than the Pharisee who had bragged about his alleged righteousness before God. When 76-year-old Marge told me she "didn't sin as much as others," I explained to her that any sin condemns us before a holy God. She told me what I said made sense, because she previously had heard a preacher speak on those things. This was a classic case of me watering where someone else had planted (1 Cor. 3:6).

Tasha, a 17-year-old Hindu girl, said she was interested in Christianity, but was confused after some Jehovah's Witnesses came to her door. She said she had been praying for someone to explain more fully salvation in Jesus to her. She trusted in the gospel after finding out about the real Jesus. Sisters Azhaar and Adeela, Muslims from India, had many questions about the Trinity and the gospel. After a two-hour chat, they both converted to Christianity.

21-year-old Devance was in the U.S. from Nepal. He told me he hated his country's caste system, but then was quick to add, since he came from a high caste, "It's good for me." I reminded him of Jesus's words in Matthew 19:30, "many who are first will be last, and the last first." Amita, an atheist from India, told me, "I don't think I have committed anything immoral, if you don't count killing a mosquito." When

I took her through the Ten Commandments, she realized she had done more than just exterminate an insect.

27-year-old Brian told me after a woman he was dating cheated on him, he fell into the arms of a gay man in college and since has been with over 100 homosexual partners. He said he knew it was wrong but tried to tell people he was born that way. He told me with humility, "Patrick, I spread the lie." He said ever since his father passed away three months earlier (a father who said he would love him no matter what, but could not be involved in his sin), he had wanted to repent. He said he wished he could tell his father he was right. I shared the gospel with him, and he said he wanted salvation.

26-year-old Mona said, "I'm a good person on the outside, but not so sure about the inside." 47-year-old Chuck told me he won't repent because, "I love money, beer, cigarettes and that stuff" more than Jesus. After I went through the commandments with Randall, he said, "I thought this call would make me happy" and then he hung up the phone. 70-year-old Arthur said he played in the NFL under Vince Lombardi and Tom Landry in the 1960s (when I Googled the full name he gave me, his claim appeared to be correct). He told me, "I have more good deeds than bad." I told him that may work on the football field, but not when it comes to receiving God's grace. 19-year-old Libby told me she would get to heaven on her good works. After I explained the gospel of grace to her, she asked, "So, you are saying I am slapping God in the face if I believe my works get me to heaven?" I said, yes! (Gal. 2:21, 5:4).

Melba, who identified as a bisexual, announced three things she knew about her "god." She told me her god does not hate, smite or judge. I told Melba what she believed was very ironic because the Bible says God does all three (Proverbs 6:16-19; Exodus 3:20, KJV; Rev. 20:11-15). I pointed this out to Melba to show her how God's attributes all work together, and how His wrath and judgment are necessary for His love and mercy (Rom. 5:8, 3:23-26).

Jake, a Mormon and BYU student, contacted me saying he was interested in learning about other people's religions. We chatted for more than three hours. After I went through the biblical gospel with him, telling him I cared about his eternal destination, he said, "That means a lot to me. This conversation has, too. It truly is generous of you." However, Jake had been so indoctrinated with the false gospel of Mormonism that, in the end, he rejected salvation by faith alone, through grace alone, in Christ alone. Doubling down on his LDS doctrine of works/righteousness salvation, Jake made this amazing statement to me, "I understand my religion so much better than I ever had. May the angels in heaven witness this day that if I have the power to do so, I void any present or future ties or faith to the tyrant God who plans to feed my loved ones who are incapable of doing good to the fires of hell to prove how just he is. If reality truly is what this man says it is, then I side with Satan and spit in the face of God."

In It for the Long Run

Sometimes God gives us an extended opportunity to evangelize a person. In 1998, I had just finished delivering one of my overnight newscasts for a national radio network for which I worked. Cal was listening in Idaho on one of our affiliates, and he called me on the phone. Cal, a Mormon, said he wanted to correct some things in a story I reported on about his church. That conversation started an e-mail discussion that has lasted to this day.

Have Cal and I argued, disputed, debated, refuted and rebuked each other? Yes we have! I have warned Cal many times that he will receive an eternal banishment from the Lord for believeing in a different God, different Jesus and different gospel than biblical Christianity. Cal has responded with his own warning. He once told me, "Patrick, one day you will stand before the judgment bar of God, and my words will testify against you. If you do not ask God about the truthfulness of this latter-day work, then condemnation falls upon you. Your friend, Cal."[124]

I consider Cal, who is ten years older than me, a good friend. One time when he was passing through DFW airport, we met and shared a hug. Over the decades, Cal and I have been forthright with each other about our theological differences. Through it all, I have developed a love for my friend and he has expressed the same for me. I pray for him on a regular basis hoping that one day God will open his eyes to the biblical gospel.

Michael the Archangel

A husband and wife Jehovah's Witness couple once visited my house. As we sat down at my living room table, I asked them if they believed Jesus was Michael the Archangel. They agreed, with the husband saying, "Yes, Jesus is an angel." I then asked him to read out loud from Hebrews 1:5

---

[124] When Cal spoke of the truthfulness of this latter-day work, he was referring to the LDS Church allegedly "restoring" the gospel that the original church supposedly lost.

in his New World Translation, which reads, "To which one of the angels did God ever say: 'You are my son.'" There was an uncomfortable long pause as the husband stared down at the verse. It was made even more uncomfortable for this couple as the wife kept staring at her husband with a panicked look on her face, waiting for him to come up with some kind of a response.

As the minutes passed by, I thought about the grace-truth scale. I had already confronted them with the truth that their doctrine of Jesus being a created being, Michael the Archangel, was false. Now they could see in their own translation that Jesus was not who they had been taught. Instead of hammering away at the point, I gave this couple some grace. I told them they may not have an answer right now, but maybe they could go to the Kingdom Hall, get some answers and come back. Despite saying they would return, they never did. Sometimes knowing where to be on the grace and truth scale can plant a seed of doubt that God will use later in a person's life.

Allah or Jesus?

I once met with the Imam of a local mosque after he accepted my request over the phone to have a conversation about Christianity and Islam. As I sat down in his office, he started into a long defense of the Quran followed by a negative critique of the Bible. His approach took me off guard, as he went on a frontal assault against Christianity. When I started to defend the preservation of the biblical texts, he waved me off saying, "We don't care about your history."

The Imam then expressed his strong denial that Jesus died on the cross, rose from the dead and is God incarnate. This was no surprise to me as the Quran clearly affirms his denial (Surah 4:157-158, 5:17). After I told him Christians do believe in Jesus' death, resurrection and deity, he then shook his head and said, "We don't believe in the same God." I then asked him how he would respond at his Mosque if asked by non-Christians or secularists whether Muslims and Christians believe in the same God. He hesitated a bit (considering what he just confessed to me) and then said, "Yes, I would tell them we believe in the same God." It seemed for public relations' sake, he was willing to be deceptive. Yet, in private, he would take off his pluralistic hat and revel in mocking the Christian God and the Bible as an invention of unbelievers and a blasphemy to Allah.

At another Mosque, I was greeted by the community outreach coordinator. She said she was raised a Baptist, but only converted to Islam two years ago. As I shared the gospel with her, it seemed by her facial expressions and questions as if she was hearing the good news for the very first time. When I mentioned that the Quran in Surah 4:157-158 claims that Jesus did not die on the cross, nor was Christ resurrected, she said Muslims believe God substituted Judas for Jesus on the cross (this is standard Islamic belief). After I explained to her that Jesus was the Father's substitute for our sin (2 Cor. 5:21; 1 Pet. 2:24, 3:18), I asked her, "Why would God substitute for the substitute?" Then an amazing thing happened—she laughed out loud! She got it. At that one precious moment she could see the foolishness of the Islamic doctrine. However, it was only for a moment, as she quickly composed herself, adjusting her hijab (a headscarf worn by Muslim women) and put back on her Muslim face.

I had an appointment with the Imam at that same Mosque the next day. Before I met with him, I gave the community outreach coordinator a copy of Lee Strobel's "The Case for Christ" along with several gospel tracts. The Imam, predictably, said the Bible was corrupted, the Trinity was false, and Jesus did not die on the cross, nor was He resurrected. He said this all this while at the same time claiming he believed in Jesus.

These Mosque visits ended up producing much fruit. At one of the Mosque's bookstores, I bought 100 paperback copies of the Quran at two dollars apiece. I handed them out to Christian pastors at a conference I was teaching at in Uganda on how to witness to Muslims. I had certain sections highlighted in each Quran to show the pastors the differences between Islam and Christianity. With Islam having a stronghold in Northern Africa and moving south, the African pastors were intensely interested in being able to know more about the Quran so they could be an effective witness to their Muslim neighbors.

During that conference, the pastors told me of their many witnessing encounters with Muslims. I'll never forget one pastor who stood up in the seminar of over 100 attendees and said several of his Muslim neighbors had claimed that Jesus could not be superior to Muhammad because He had sinned. They asked me how I would respond. My first reaction was one of surprise. I had the pastors open their Qurans to Surahs 3:42, 3:46 and 19:19 that states Allah kept Jesus from sin. I also had them turn to Surahs 40:55, 48:2, and 47:19 where the Muslim God asked Muhammad to ask forgiveness of *his* sins. Naturally, I also directed them to biblical passages that show Jesus was without sin (John 8:46; 1 Pet. 2:22; 1 John 3:5). This made the whole room burst into cheers.

Siberia Gospel

In 2010 and 2011, I had the privilege of joining Pastor Tom Watson with Bended Knee International Ministry to Tuva, a Russian Republic. After holding a seminar at an evangelical church in Tuva, we would travel for hours by car into the remote Siberian landscape to seek out schools to give a gospel presentation. During Tom's talk in the school's gymnasium, which was usually packed with up to 400 students, many would sit on the edge of their seats. At the end of his presentation, we would hand out hundreds of Russian New Testaments to the mostly Buddhist students and staff.

Afterwards, I asked a group of students, who were clutching their Russian New Testaments, how one gets to heaven. They responded, "Be clean and don't sin." Through my translator I asked them if that described any of them. They all laughed and said no! Siberia may be cold, but a universal knowledge of sin (Rom. 1:18-3:20) will never be frozen out of the human heart.

While resistance to our mesasge was amazingly minor, as the years went by, Tom's ministry received more and more pushback from the leaders in this mostly Buddhist country. In the years to come, Tom and his evangelistic team were arrested for sharing the gospel. They were later locked out of returning to this Russian Republic due to Vladimir Putin's law against evangelistic missionary activity in Russia.

State Fair Evangelism

Every year in the fall, I spend a week witnessing to visitors to the State Fair of Texas in Dallas at the Fair Gospel Booth. This includes handing out tracts. I gave several tracts to Jim from Australia while presenting the gospel to him. I asked him what he was going to do with this information. He said he would give it to his child. I said, "No, Jim, *you* must become a child of God." On several occasions we had young children run up to the booth and want to talk about Jesus, only to have their soccer mom, wearing a cross necklace, scold them and pull them away (Luke 18:16).

When one man dismissed the Bible in front of a booth volunteer, based on his evolutionary beliefs, another volunteer, who had been studying Creation science in school, stepped in to challenge him. When volunteer Angie was talking to someone who denied the deity of Christ, she caught my eye and waved me over. One woman, with two infants in a stroller, told one gospel presenter that she believed in reincarnation and wanted to come back as a cat. Eddie, one of our more zealous volunteers and never at a loss for words, stepped in and told the woman, "Your kids need a mom, not a cat."

As one man walked by our booth, I started to hand him a tract and he said, "I don't do Jesus." One woman came pointing her finger at us and asked, "Do you believe nuns sin?" I said of course, "for all have sinned and fall short of the glory of God" (Rom. 3:23). She walked away waving her hands at us in defiance saying she didn't believe that. Two lesbians stopped by the booth. They held hands and wanted us to know how happy they were with each other. After I presented the gospel to them, I asked them if they wanted to repent and believe. They just smiled and said, "No, we're fine." I quickly thanked them for visiting our booth, handed them some tracts and then moved on (Matt. 10:14-15).

Another young man came up to the booth, and I started a gospel conversation with him. He was so focused on the scriptures I was giving him that he had his right elbow planted on the booth counter in front of me, with his head resting on his hand which was constantly stroking his chin. About ten minutes into our discussion, his friend aggressively introduced himself into the conversation by getting right in my face and saying, "Do you know we are having...sex?" When I asked the young man to whom I was talking if that was true, he did not deny it, but at the same he time he turned to his friend and said in a frustrated tone, "Why are you saying that?"

Undeterred, I continued my gospel presentation, but this young man's friend continued to snicker and mock me in the background. As I left my new friend with some gospel tracts and a pocket New Testament, I silently prayed that God would deliver and redeem both of them from their sin, so one day I might say about them, "And such were some of you. But you were washed, you were sanctified, you were justified in the name of the Lord Jesus Christ and by the Spirit of our God" (1 Cor. 6:11).

Abortion Gospel

One of my most unique witnessing opportunities has come as a volunteer for many years at a Crisis Pregnancy Center. 20-year-old Dewey watched one of our videos showing how abortion clinics tear unborn babies apart. He was so shaken that he walked out of the room. I caught him and asked him what he was thinking. With his head down he said, "I'm murdering my son." We sat back down in the room, and as I started to present the law and gospel to him, Dewey responded by saying he was a good person and that "I haven't done anything bad like murder someone." I reminded him of what he had just said about murdering his unborn child, and his head sunk again. I then presented the gospel, and through repentance and faith Dewey made a commitment to trust Christ. He also made an appointment to come back to see a sonogram of his child.

Sometimes we find out the real wolves in sheep's clothing during our witnessing opportunities. A young teenage girl came into the center and told us she was pregnant by a youth minister at her church. She told us she had a previous abortion with this same guy, who amazingly was still in his position at her church. Other times we see the real sheep. 17-year-old Merle is a Christian who told us he is not abortion-minded at all. In fact, he said that abortion, "Would be playing God" with his baby's life.

Fahad was excited to see the sonogram and find out the sex of his child. Last time we talked, I gave him the gospel comparing Islam with Christianity. He told me at first he didn't like that. However, after I e-mailed him my document on Islam and Christianity, he told me he and his Christian girlfriend had started to compare the Bible and the Quran together.

33-year-old Tony told us he and his girlfriend regret aborting a previous 6-month-old unborn child. Tony said he went through a 12-step program where the secular counselor had him make out a certificate for the aborted child and then burn it. I explained to him that did not honor the life of his unborn child. I told him at our center, we take parents, who aborted their child, through a biblical program where repentance and forgiveness are the goal. When I attempted to share the gospel with Tony, he told me, "I have a Higher Power that I have made up for myself."

32-year-old Austin wants to, as he said, "terminate" their pregnancy. I asked him if he was a religious man. He said yes. He then looked at me seriously and asked, "All religions teach abortion is killing, right?" Austin agreed that abortion is murder but told me, "I'm ready to deal with the consequences." When I shared the gospel with him, he told me he was going to heaven because he was "a good person." When I explained to him that the Bible says there is no such thing as a good person (Rom. 3:10; Mark 10:18), he told me, "The Bible was written by man and is full of crap."

Neil and Emily came in because Planned Parenthood charged for a sonogram, while our services were free. Neil said he did not want the sin of convincing Emily to have an abortion to send him to hell. After I explained the gospel to him he said, "I think God is speaking to me through you."

A Homeless Gospel

In the late 90s, a good Christian friend and I had a ministry of bringing food and clothes to homeless people in downtown Dallas. Part of our ministry was handing out gospel tracts. One instance, when I got into a discussion with one man about salvation, James walked back to the car wanting to get to our next homeless destination, as we still had food to give out. About halfway through my discussion, James started impatiently beeping his horn. I broke off my witness and returned to the car.

James is one of the most mature Christian men I have ever met. He not only understands the word, he lives it. However, in this case, he was in the wrong. Back in the car, I explained to James that I had not completed my gospel message to that man. I reminded James that he had stressed that getting the gospel out was our main goal. If that is the case, I asked, then why was he undermining our "main goal?" James humbly apologized and we had many fruitful gospel encounters together in the years following. My point in telling this story is to show that sometimes even the most gospel-minded Christians can lose sight of our main purpose. The real food we have for the lost comes from the feet of those who preach the good news (Romans 10:14-17).

Planes, Trains and Automobiles

Long plane rides can literally give you a captive audience to share the gospel. God has provided me with several of these opportunities while returning from Christian mission trips abroad. On a 16-hour flight from Dubai to Dallas, I sat next to Arban. He is a Buddhist, originally from Southeast Asia, now living and working in Dallas. He was returning from his father's funeral and seemed open to discussing spiritual matters. Our main conversation revolved around how one is made righteous before God. While Arban claimed he could make himself righteous, I challenged him with the law. As I explained to him that righteous deeds could never account for our salvation (Rom. 3:10; Isa. 64:6; 2 Cor. 5:21), but are the appropriate outcome of a faith-filled life (Eph. 2:10), Arban paused just long enough to take it in before he went on to other objections.

23-year-old Bill was an anthropology student from London and was in the seat next to me. He said he was a bit disillusioned after his professors taught him that you can't really know history. If that's true, he asked rhetorically, why bother purchasing and reading the history text books they require? I liked this guy. He seemed to intuitively know that we can know things about history. After Bill told me he was raised in a nominal Catholic home, we spent the next four hours talking about the gospel. I'll never forget his response, "I've never heard this. Why hasn't someone told me this before?"

Jacob, a young man from South Africa, questioned why God allows evil in the world. I told him all of us have sinned and done evil in God's sight and we shouldn't try to compare our "less" sin with others, because all is sin to God. "So, why does God allow your sin?", I asked Jacob as I presented the gospel to him. As we departed the plane, I repeated to Jacob, "Just one sin will separate you from your God."

In 1998, while on vacation with my friend Marcus in Colorado, we rode the famous Durango and Silverton train. Marcus and I were fairly new Christians and our conversations would sometimes revolve around the Bible. During our trip, Marcus started to ask questions about Adam and Eve. He said he was having some doubts about the Garden of Eden account in the Bible. As a young Christian, I answered him as best I could at the time. The thing I remember the most is that, for me, I never doubted God's word. Though I would be better equipped to answer Marcus in the coming years, God placed in my heart, from the very beginning of my salvation, a love and unwavering devotion for His word, "And we also thank God constantly for this, that when you received the word of God, which you heard from us, you accepted it not as the word of men but as what it really is, the word of God, which is at work in you believers" (1 Thess. 2:13; cf., 2 Tim. 3:15-16; Psalm 138:2, 119:9, 119:105; Matt. 4:4; John 17:17).

In 2008, I was in Rwanda teaching African pastors. During a long taxi ride with some fellow teachers, Ayo, our Muslim driver, asked us, "Are you a born-again Christian?" As I said yes, I took the opportunity to start a gospel conversation. I asked him if he prayed five times a day as required by Islamic tradition. He said yes. I then asked him if he repeats the same rote prayer every time, also a requirement. He said yes. Finally, I asked him if he talks to his wife that way—speaking to her only five times a day and saying the exact same thing over and over. He said, no, it is different with my wife. I told Ayo that Christians can talk to God at anytime (1 Thess. 5:17), with every kind of prayer and petition (Eph. 6:18).

As we drove along the bumpy dirt roads, with Ayo deftly maneuvering the many pot holes, I asked him if his good deeds were heavy and outweighed his bad ones, because Allah only forgives if one's scales are balanced this way (Quran, Surah 21:47, 23:102-103, cf., 7:8-9). He said yes. At that point I went into the law and gospel. After being convicted by the law and realizing his scales were weighted down with many sins, my Muslim friend cried out, "How do I get born again?" At that point, I told him the good news about Jesus and how He fulfilled the law in our place (Gal. 3:24, 2:16). His scales have only unblemished deeds (2 Cor. 5:21). In fact, at the cross, we see our salvation "with the precious blood of Christ, like that of a lamb without blemish or spot" (1 Pet. 1:19).

This whole time, Deven, who was one of our conference teachers from Massachusetts, was listening intently in the back seat of the cab. I told Ayo that Pastor Deven now had something to say to him. Deven then explained repentance and belief to our Muslim friend. He asked Ayo if he wanted to be set free from the legalism and yoke that Islam has placed on him and trust in Christ alone for his salvation. Ayo said "Yes!"

In 2001, I met Chen as part of my church's Friendship Partner program. Chen was an international student from Taiwan and visiting the United States for the first time. Over the next two years, Chen and I got together on a regular basis. He came over to my house for meals, we played basketball, hiked and just had fun spending time with each other. Chen was raised in a Buddhist culture but was open to discussing Christianity. One day on a car trip to Lake Mineral Wells State Park, I got into the specifics of the gospel with my friend. Chen had commented that he was "sad" that someone had to die for him. I explained that Christ gave up His life voluntarily (John 10:17-18) to satisfy God's holy standards (Rom. 3:25) in our place (2 Cor. 5:21). While seeds were planted during that car trip, Chen later came to repent and believe the gospel.

Bicycles too!

Sometimes God literally delivers a gospel appointment right up to you when you least expect it. My wife Kim and I were walking our dogs when a man in his 40s rode his bicycle right up to us. Max said he had never ridden down by this part of the lake and commented on how pretty it was. He started to talk about how he was recently divorced, in drug rehab, and trying to get his life together. He said he just went back to church for the first time in decades. I knew right then this was an open door. Max talked about his kids and how he was trying to change his life. He jokingly asked us how much we charged per hour to listen to him. I told him we were Christians and were concerned about all peoples' souls. I jumped right into a gospel diagnosis and determined he thought getting to heaven was by good works. When I started to explain to him that it was not about us but about Christ's righteousness (2 Cor. 5:21), his eyes lit up and he proclaimed, "What you are telling me takes the pressure off me, I don't have to be perfect."

I talked with Max about our one-time justification in the finished work of Christ and how our sanctification naturally follows. He told me he needs to be set free. He took his hands off his bicycle handlebars and put them up in the air and said, "What do I do? I'm in!" I prayed as he sat on his bicycle that God would grant him repentance and belief. I pointed to our house on the corner and told him he was welcome to stop by at anytime to discuss these matters further. With his eyes tearing up, he thanked me and rode off.

Obedience to the Gospel

Christian author and speaker Elisabeth Elliot once said, "Obedience is our responsibility. The result of our obedience is up to God." While being obedient to our call to share the gospel, we never know when or if God will give the growth (1 Cor. 3:6). Sometimes we get a Philippian jailer (Acts 16:25-34) or an Ethiopian Eunuch (Acts 8:26-39), where we see a conversion before our eyes. At other times, the results of our obedience won't come to full growth until months or years down the road, and we may or may not know about it. Sometimes we'll plant and it will be someone else who waters. Other times we will water what someone else has already planted. Just be obedient, and as Elisabeth Elliot says, the result of our obedience is up to God.

Open-Ended Witnessing

When I say most of my evangelism has been open-ended, what I mean is this: while my ultimate hope in witnessing is to see God conclude things by giving the growth, let's be honest, that's not the case most of the time, at least as far as we can know at that moment. In fact, planting seeds or watering is as far as it goes in the greater part of our evangelizing. With that in mind, my goal is simply to get people to think about eternal things. Therefore, knowing that in the majority of cases, there won't be a conclusion to our conversation—things may remain open-ended. Ultimately, we plant some seeds that others down the line will hopefully water. In the meantime, our conversation is left open-ended with the hope that one day God will give the growth.

○ ○ ○

17 SHARING THE GOSPEL WITH FAMILY MEMBERS

"To refuse to share the gospel with a family member because you are afraid it might cost you the relationship is to love yourself more than you love them. In so doing, you are making your relationships of greater importance than their relationship with Jesus Christ." – Matt Slick[125]

It was 8:30 pm on Thanksgiving Eve, 2014. I was preparing to head into work for my overnight news anchor shift at Salem Radio in Irving, Texas. Just as I was about to say goodbye to my wife Kim, the phone rang. It was my older sister calling from Vidalia, Georgia.

---

[125] Matt Slick, How To witness to friends and family, https://carm.org/evangelism/how-to-witness-to-friends-and-family/

She told me that the doctors informed her that Dad would probably not survive the weekend. I knew that my 84-year-old father had recently been placed in hospice care but was surprised to find out that the end was this near.

I immediately called up my boss and he told me to go to be with my father. He said that he would have someone cover my shifts through the next several days or as long as I needed. I threw some items in a suitcase that I dragged down from the attic, and my wife packed me a lunch for my long drive to Georgia. She told me she would fly in early next week. As I stepped into my car, Kim and I prayed together one of many prayers I would make over the coming week.

The 17-hour drive was one my wife and I had made many times to visit my parents. Being familiar with the route and driving at a time I was normally awake made things easier. One might think working the overnight shift for the past twenty-five years would wreak havoc on my circadian rhythm. However, just the opposite has happened with me since I have always thrived as a night owl. As I drove off into the night on my long journey, tears welled up in my eyes while I thought about the love I had for my father.

Driving across Texas and through Louisiana and Mississippi, the star lit sky helped me collect my thoughts as I replayed my life experiences with my dad in my mind. I had prayed for years for God to give me more opportunities to witness the gospel to my father. Up to this point my witnessing efforts with him had not gone well. What would I say to him this time? Could he even hear me?

Highway of Tears

Fourteen years earlier, I had made the same nighttime drive under somewhat similar circumstances. It was Sunday, May 21, 2000 when I woke from an afternoon nap to a message on my answering machine. It was my mom crying in the message telling me that my 46-year-old, older brother Bob had died of a heart attack. I was in shock. I stood there frozen in my living room for several minutes before I played the message again. Did I hear that right?

I packed up and tossed my suitcase in my black Ford pickup. I brought along over a dozen gospel teaching cassettes and listened to all of them on the long overnight drive. When I arrived the next afternoon, the first person to greet me was Bob's wife, who gave me a big hug as tears welled up in her eyes. Was the brother who "allowed" me to push him on his skateboard for 2-cents an hour back in the early sixties really dead?

Wake Reflections

As I carried my Bible with me to my brother's wake, I clung to it for strength as I stood in front of Bob's open casket. One of my sisters walked up next to me and asked if I had "something appropriate" to read. This seemed an ironic request. Just the previous year in a phone conversation, my sister questioned the authority of the Bible by saying, "I watched a Discovery Channel documentary, and did you know that the Bible was written by men under a deadline." Despite being taken aback by the irony, I shared several resurrection verses with her and mentioned again, like I did in our phone conversation the year before, that it is Christ's righteousness, not ours, that allows us into heaven. Later at the wake, I walked up to my other older sister and said, "Christ gives us hope if we trust in Him and Him alone." She stared straight ahead and said, "I'm glad that works for you."

Funeral Testimony

The day of Bob's funeral, his 27-year-old son approached me. I said, "It must be tough to bury a father." As both our eyes started to water, he responded, "It must be tough to bury a brother." We hugged and then I started to go through the gospel with him, not knowing where he was. He acknowledged all my points and affirmed that it is not his righteousness but Christ's alone. As he told me how in his youth he had been "deceived" by his religion concerning the gospel, he mentioned that his wife had shared the good news of God's unmerited grace with him years ago.

Bob's funeral was originally scheduled to be officiated by a Baptist minister his wife had chosen. At the last moment, however, my dad stepped in and insisted that a Catholic priest co-officiate. Bob's second wife, who he married in 1982, had grown up Baptist and Bob Catholic. I talked to Bob on the phone a few months before his death, trying to get into a gospel conversation with him. Bob was not very openly religious, so when he cut off that part of our conversation with, "I have my own thing going on with Jesus", I was not surprised.

The Baptist minister, in a strong southern drawl, proceeded to read off several verses in an almost monotone way. To the untrained ear it might have seemed as if he was just Bible thumping. However, as he read off the Romans Road (see chapter 9), I bowed my head and silently thanked God for this pastor's loyal gospel testimony at my brother's funeral. In contrast, the Catholic priest spoke in a more conversational tone, but failed to quote a single scripture. When the priest said, "God showed his goodness through Bob", I shook my head in my seat and said to myself, "No, no, no! God showed His goodness through His Son!" Indeed, Jesus declared, "No one is good except God alone" (Mark 10:18). Paul also stated that same truth: "be found in him, not having a righteousness of my own that comes from the law, but that which comes through faith in Christ, the righteousness from God that depends on faith" (Philip. 3:9; cf., Rom. 3:11).

That day, I drove my mom and dad to the funeral and back. After the funeral, as my dad got into the front passenger seat, and my mom sat in the back, my dad proclaimed, "Boy, the Father really stole the show." I was not humble in my response as I blurted out, "How do you figure that?" After a few more words between Dad and I, Mom, the perpetual peacemaker, told us to stop. Both of us went silent on the drive back home.

Bible Stories

The night after the funeral, it was about 10:30 pm when Mom went to bed leaving my dad and I alone in the living room. I prayed that God would give me an opportunity to discuss the gospel with him. Such efforts over the phone years earlier did not go well. During those calls I asked him how familiar he was with the Bible and he said, "Not much and I don't plan on reading it." He wanted me to know two things in particular. He told me, "I'm a good person" and "I will never leave the Catholic Church."

I had sat with my dad late at night, after everyone had gone to bed, many times before. We both love football, and during my childhood my dad and I would be up near midnight many times watching the end of a Monday Night Football game or the News Year's Night bowl game. This time it was different. We had just buried a son and a brother and the mood was somber. After some small talk, I slowly worked the conversation into how I was saved in 1993. I have to admit that it surprised me that he allowed the conversation to continue this time. He responded by openly and honestly discussing the differences between our faiths.

Years earlier I had given my dad and mom an engraved study Bible. I had noticed upon my arrival earlier in the week that it had not been moved from its position on the bookshelf. As I flipped through it, the pages stuck together as new as the day I had given it to them. Dad never talked to me about God or the Bible growing up and he had already told me for years in our phone calls that he had no interest in the scriptures. So, what he told me next should not have surprised me. He said, "You believe in stories out of the Bible." I asked him what he meant by "stories." He told me he didn't put much stock in the Bible being true.

The Spiral Notebook [126]

Something my mom gave me many years after I had that witnessing encounter with my dad in 2000 put a different perspective on things. In 2018 as I was preparing to head back home after a visit with my mom, she handed me an old spiral notebook. She told me, "Your dad wrote this when he was thirteen years old, and I thought you would find it interesting reading." After I got home, I read very carefully what he wrote. It was a journal about his belief in having to keep God's law to be saved and his devotion to the Catholic Church. As I read his notebook, several things jumped out at me. First, I marveled that a thirteen-year-old boy would write so passionately about spiritual things. Second, he quoted the Bible numerous times throughout. It was clear that as a young boy he never gave a hint of questioning the authority of the Bible nor the stories in it,

---

[126] This is a picture of my father's actual notebook.

as he wrote in his journal about miracles in the scripture that he would later tell me were just stories written by men.[127]

Father and Son at a Crossroads

So, as my dad sat in his chair across from me on the couch, his arms were crossed and he had a defensive look on his face. After I laid out evidence for the Bible being authoritative and true, I reminded him of his own church's catechism that states that the Catholic Church welcomes the Bible "not as a human word, but as what it really is, the word of God" (Catechism 104), and that "Ignorance of the Scriptures is ignorance of Christ" (Catechism 133). Despite that, every time I quoted a scripture, he would say, "that's silly."

When I told him that one must be "born again", he skeptically asked, "Where does it say that?" As I got up from the couch and took a couple of steps to the bookshelf, I pulled out the Bible that I had sent to him and mom a few years earlier and started to turn to John chapter three. As I held God's word out in front of him, I said "Dad, Jesus commanded us to be 'born again' right here in John chapter three, verses one through eight." However, before I could read it, he told me to put the Bible back and made me sit down. At one point he said, "Pat, you're like a funnel and it's like you poured the Bible down your mouth." I said, "Amen!"

Dad slumped back in his chair and let out a sigh. He told me he was sad that I had fallen away from the Catholic Church where he had raised me. I responded that you can't fall away from something you never really had. Yes, I spent time in Catholic grade school, went through catechism classes, First Communion, Confirmation, and even spent many Saturday nights in the confession box. However, it was all an obligatory and meaningless routine to me. I assured him that it was not his fault and not to feel guilty about that.

He sat back up and told me that "from birth" he had never lost his faith. He then explained how he lived out his faith by helping to build four churches, and by doing charity work, good deeds and "being a good person." I asked him if all those things he mentioned would be the things that would allow him into heaven. He responded, "You bet it will."

---

[127] In the notebook, my father also wrote about being devoted to Mary and the saints. He wrote that Mary was "his most powerful friend in heaven." He wrote that he not only needed to pray for Mary and the saints to intercede for him, but that he also had to imitate their virtues. He mentioned the importance of indulgences, and his loyalty to the Pope and to the Catholic Church.

Years later, as I read through his spiral notebook, this sentence he wrote jumped out at me, "If I keep the commandments, I will please God and gain heaven."[128] While his early veneration of the Bible later changed, his belief that a person must follow God's commands for salvation had not. Sadly, even if he had maintained the esteem of scripture he had as a child, his understanding of the Bible was then, and later as an adult, missing the mark on the gospel. If one is using obedience to God's law to determine their entrance into heaven, they have missed the critical point that the law's main power is to reveal sin (Rom. 3:20). It has no ability to save us (Gal. 2:16; Rom. 3:28), only to point us to the Savior who kept the law perfectly in our place (Gal. 3:24; Acts 13:39; Matt. 5:17; 2 Cor. 5:21; 1 Pet. 3:18).

Honor Your Father

In looking back on that discussion with my father in 2000, I have come to realize what a lot of other Christians likely experience in a situation similar to mine. They might be in their late twenties, thirties, or forties, but their father or mother still sees them as the person they were when they were 16 years old. Most of the people I share the gospel with know nothing about me, and I will probably never see them again. On the other hand, our families often know us best. They are familiar with all our failures and have seen us at our worst. They have known us for years before we came to faith in Christ, and despite our Christian growth, they've seen some of our stumbles afterward. They often tell themselves, "I know what they are really like."

After listing off his good works, Dad said, "I do all these things at the church that I know you don't do!" Pointing out that we live over a thousand miles apart, I asked him, "Dad, how do you know I don't do this?" He said, as if he were lecturing his 16-year-old son, "Because I know you." At some point in our conversation, my dad went into defensive mode and did not see me as an adult trying to reason with him and challenge his beliefs about the Bible and salvation. Instead, he started

---

[128] That one must keep the commandments to please God and gain heaven is a common belief among Catholics. We can see why when the Catholic Catechism says things like, "We can merit for ourselves and for others all the graces needed to attain eternal life" (2027), "The work of redemption is carried on" (1405), and "The sinner must make satisfaction for or expiate his sins" (1459). The Council of Trent (1545-1563) has also issued the following binding decree on justification: "If anyone says that the sinner is justified by faith alone, meaning that nothing else is required to cooperate in order to obtain the grace of justification...let him be anathema" (Council of Trent Canon 9—note that anathema means to be cursed, damned, ex-communicated).

looking at me as the unsaved teenager who cared only about himself. I'm sure he thought, "What does he know!"

I told my father, "No, Dad, you really don't know me." He responded, "Maybe I don't. Okay, I wasn't right on that." Dad told me I was causing friction within the family with my witnessing. I responded, "Do you think I would put myself in this position with the father I dearly love if I wasn't convinced of the truth of my position?" He nodded his head in agreement. Dad then told me he did not want to talk about this anymore. I said, "The Bible tells us to honor your father, so I will submit to your wishes." As we both got up from our chairs to go to bed, I said, "Dad, I just want you to know I love and respect you. You have been a great father to me." We hugged each other tightly and he said, "I love you more than you know."

Foot on the Gas

By the time I crossed the Alabama state line, the sun was up. I still had a way to go and half of the sandwich that Kim made for me. I finished that off with the help of a Diet Pepsi. As I was driving along the highway, my mind raced with thoughts of my dad dying before I got there. Surely, God would not let my dad die before I had a chance to see him one last time. I had specifically prayed to God for years, if my dad was on his deathbed, to give me one last opportunity to speak to him. I called my sister later that morning for an update and she said he was not doing well.

Since our living room encounter in 2000, Dad all but shut down any more conversations about faith. During a phone call in 2004, I could tell he was still upset about those earlier discussions. When I told him I was heading to Africa on the first of what turned out to be over a dozen mission trips, he asked me about my reason for going by saying, "What religion are you again?"

Over the next decade, I looked for ways to rebuild our relationship. In December of 2011, Kim and I once again made the long drive from Texas to Georgia to see my parents for Christmas. I brought my video camera and tripod along with me and told them that I wanted to do an interview for a family video on which I was working. I set the camera up in front of the same couch I had sat on 14 years earlier while witnessing to my dad and had my mom and him go over details of our family history, including their parents, how they met and started our family, and special memories of us growing up in the 50s all the way to the present day.

After I worked on the video for almost a year, I sent a copy to my dad and he loved it. My mom told me that they sat together and watched in amazement. The next time I saw him, in the summer of 2012, he said, "You told the story of our lives." I told him I couldn't have done it without him and mom giving me my best interview ever on camera the previous Christmas. I saw my relationship with my dad change after that.

As I pulled into the hospice care center just after 1 pm, I said a prayer that dad would still be alive and be able to hear me. My sister greeted me by saying, "You'll be shocked, he's still alive." As I entered the room alone and closed the door, Dad could not speak or hardly move, but I was encouraged when he slowly turned his head and looked at me.

One Mediator

For the next 15 minutes, I sat beside my father's bed and went through the law and gospel with him. I told him that God's grace is free and that he could only enter God's kingdom by placing his faith alone in the only intercessor that secured that grace for us—Jesus Christ. At that point, a friend from his Catholic church entered the room while I was praying. This turned out to be quite an irony considering what I had just told my dad about there being one mediator. Without asking if she was interrupting, she took a seat on the other side of the bed. I was inclined to ask her to please allow me this private time with my father, but I decided against that for that moment. She then asked if we could pray together. Despite being dubious about her request, I agreed after she suggested we start with the Lord's Prayer. When that was over, she announced that she wanted "The blessed Mother's intercession." As soon as she started into the Hail Mary, I stopped her. Waving my hands, I said, "No! First Timothy 2:5, There is one God, and one mediator between God and men, the man Christ Jesus." After an uncomfortable silence, I was hoping she would leave, but she just sat there holding her rosary. I finally got up and left, saying goodbye to my father and hoping that I could see him again later.

Meeting Bob's Son Again

The next day, I met up with my nephew, who I had not seen since his father's funeral in 2000. He was now 41 years old and a father himself of two boys. We had a great talk in the hospice lobby, and he updated me on his growth in Christ. I told him that I had been praying and asked him to pray for his grandfather, with whom he lived for several years as a young boy, as well. He said we needed to pray and hope the Holy Spirit would do His work. When I told him my talk with him was the highlight of my week, he said, "So far."

Goodbye to Dad

Saturday morning, I relieved my mom and sister at Dad's bed. They had stayed up all night with him and thanked me for the chair cushions I had bought for them the night before. My younger sister came into the room at noon and we had a great talk about our childhood. I especially cherished my time with her since we had never made much of a connection growing up, due to her being five years younger than me. My younger brother entered the room about 1 pm. Typical for us, we talked football with the Georgia, Georgia Tech rivalry game being on the TV in the corner of the room. At 2:10 pm, we noticed a significant change in Dad's breathing. His breaths were very slow and about every nine to ten seconds. We called in the nurse and she noticed that his fingertips and toenails were turning blue. We asked what that meant, and she said he is losing oxygen and he has a half an hour at best. Ten minutes later, he would take his last breath.

> *"Faith comes by hearing, and hearing by the word of God"*
> (Rom. 10:17, NKJV).

Five minutes before Dad died, I opened my Bible to Romans chapter three. This was the moment for which I had prayed for decades, for God to give me one last opportunity to speak to my dad, even if that would be in his final moments on his deathbed. I took a deep breath and started with verse 10, "as it is written: 'None is righteous, no, not one.'" Why start there, one might ask? Maybe even a more pertinent question: with five minutes to his death and his mind in a comatose state, could my dad even hear or comprehend what I was reading? Let me address the latter question first. Hearing is widely thought to be the last sense to go in the dying process. A 2020 University of British Columbia study states, "Our data shows that a dying brain can respond to sound, even in an unconscious state, up to the last hours of life."[129] Medically speaking, I have little doubt that it is possible my father could have heard me.

To the former question, as we have seen, the issue of who is righteous and who isn't is at the core of the gospel message (see chapters 7-9). Simply put—there is only One who is righteous and that's Jesus Christ (1 Pet. 3:18; Philip. 3:9). For the rest of us, "None is righ-

---
[129] Hearing persists at end of life, July 8, 2020, University of British Columbia, https://www.sciencedaily.com/releases/2020/07/200708105935.htm

teous, no, not one" (Rom. 3:10). In the first two chapters of Romans, Paul searches for anyone who is righteous. It's not the ungodly and idolatrous pagans in chapter one, who by their unrighteousness suppress God's truth and refuse to acknowledge their Creator (1:18, 25, 29-32). It's not the self-righteous Jews of chapter two, who are hypocrites in not even keeping their own law (2:21-24). Finally, it's not even the Gentiles of the world, who Paul says will also perish (2:12), because even though they didn't have the law, it was still "written on their hearts" (2:15) and they didn't even respond correctly to their own consciences.

Paul wraps up his argument in chapter three, when he refers back to all the people in chapters one and two that he called unrighteous. He concludes, "for we have before proved both Jews and Gentiles, that they are all under sin; As it is written, There is none righteous, no, not one" (Rom. 3:9-10, KJV). This is pretty bleak news, it would seem. Paul just took all the groups of men and said that none are righteous. However, he then finishes chapter three by pointing out that if we place our faith, not in any alleged righteousness we have, but in the only One who is righteous—Christ Jesus, we are then "justified by his grace as a gift" (3:24). To sum up Paul's point in chapters one through three, none of us are righteous, but we can have God's righteousness imputed or credited to us[130] by placing our faith alone in God's Son, whom He "put forward as a propitiation by his blood, to be received by faith. This was to show God's righteousness" (3:25).

As I started reading in verse 10 and went to the end of the chapter, I asked God that He not only would open my dad's ears (John 10:27), but his heart as well (Acts 16:14). Some skeptics might say that the text in chapter three is difficult enough for a fully conscious person to comprehend, much less a comatose man taking his final breaths. To those skeptics I say, "For the word of the cross is folly to those who are perishing, but to us who are being saved it is the power of God" (1 Cor. 1:18).

I testify to you that I relied fully on the power of God as I shared the bad (there is no one righteous) and the good news (the righteousness of God that comes through faith in Jesus Christ for all who believe) to my father in his final moments. Dad, here's my

---

[130] Paul, continuing his argument that Abraham, like the New Testament saints, was justified by faith apart from works, said of Abraham's faith, "therefore it was imputed to him for righteousness" (Rom. 4:22, KJV).

message to you as you pass from this earth: true saving faith comes by hearing and hearing by the word of God, which tells us there is no one who is righteous. Not you, not me, not anyone. From your youngest years, you wrongly believed that if you kept the commandments, you would somehow please God and gain entrance into heaven. But listen to what God's word says, Dad: "For by works of the law no human being will be justified in his sight, since through the law comes knowledge of sin" (Rom. 3:20). God didn't give us the law so we could be saved by it, because nobody keeps it, not the Jews nor the Gentiles. He gave us the law to show us that "all have sinned and fall short of the glory of God" (3:23) and that only "through the redemption that is in Christ Jesus" (3:24) can we take on "the righteousness of God [which] has been manifested apart from the law" (3:21). Just as I finished reading, my younger sister said, "He's not breathing!"

I'm sure many at this point are asking, "So, what about the fate of your dad? What say you?" I say, with a humble awareness of the limits of my knowledge, I don't know. I do know this though, as I discussed in Chapter Thirteen, if the Father has drawn a person to come to His Son (John 6:44), and the Holy Spirit is working ahead of us in regeneration (John 16:8-11), God can and will use many things we say to bring a person into His kingdom, including my reading of scripture to my dad in his final moments. I have no doubt if this divine drawing was present, my dad's physical and cognitive state would not have been an issue to a sovereign God. In fact, when this drawing is present, we can be assured as Jesus tells us, "All that the Father gives me *will* come to me" (John 6:37). However, if this work by God was absent, I can only take solace in the fact that I honored God by faithfully presenting the gospel. Since that day in 2014, I have resolved to trust that God's will be done, for, "Shall not the Judge of all the earth do what is just?" (Gen. 18:25).

Eulogy to Dad

The following Wednesday, Dad's funeral was held in a small Catholic church in Vidalia, Georgia. In the previous days leading up to his funeral, I spent hours back in the woods close to my parents' house. I took along a pen and notepad and sitting on a tree stump laid out the foundation for the eulogy I would be giving. The night before the funeral, a family member informed me that the priest told me to keep my message short. I told them to tell the priest it was my dad's funeral, and I would speak as long as I wish.[131]

Before I got up to speak, the Catholic priest mentioned a few stories about my dad at the church. The one he focused on was quite embarrassing. He joked about my dad regularly falling asleep during the service. I'm sure he was trying to be funny, but considering the setting, I took great offense at it. I have never known a harder working man than my dad, but that's not the impression the priest gave. To make the focus of his brief comments a poor attempt at humor at my dad's expense was totally inappropriate, but there was more to come.

After the priest reminded everyone that this was a special Mass held for our late dad,[132] I was not surprised, but disgusted, when the priest, during his Eucharist preparation, said that he "hoped" this sacrifice would "wash away" dad's sins. He also said that we need to pray that such a sacrifice "may be acceptable to God." This is something that I had already prepared to address in my talk, but his comments only confirmed to me that God had placed me in this situation for a reason.

As the time came for me to get up and speak, Kim squeezed my hand. She whispered that she would be praying for me. I also remembered how so many of my fellow believers back home told me they would be praying for me. In particular, my longtime friend Tom Brown encouraged me "not to fear man." There was also a Georgia State Representative at the memorial that day. I had met him when I attended the First Baptist Church in Vidalia the previous Sunday. He came up to me and introduced himself, noticing that I was a visitor. He said he knew my dad (as so many people in Vidalia did) and was a friend of my sister and her husband. He greeted me Wednesday as I entered the memorial, telling me that he was praying for me to have strength during my eulogy.

---

[131] I later found out that, in 1989, the Vatican published the revised Order of Christian Funerals (OCF) for the United States. The long-standing prohibition of eulogies at Catholic funerals was again upheld and restated, "A brief homily based on the readings should always be given at the funeral liturgy, but never any kind of eulogy." In 2000, John Paul II restated this prohibition of eulogies, "At the Funeral Mass there should, as a rule, be a short homily, but never a eulogy of any kind." The fact that I was allowed to give a eulogy and share the gospel was due to God's grace and providence.

[132] If the body of the person who died is present, the Church refers to the ceremony as a Funeral Mass. If the body of the person who died was cremated, the Church refers to the ceremony as a Memorial Mass. My family elected to cremate my father's body. This was not my wish, as I believe the biblical pattern is clearly burial (1 Cor. 15:3-4; Rom. 6:4; cf., Col. 2:12).

I spoke for fifteen minutes, separating my talk into two parts. First, I thanked my dad for the service he gave to his country as a Korean War veteran, the service he gave to his community, and the loving care he gave to his family. I shared several stories of how my dad showed grace and love to me growing up despite my out-of-control temper that at times caused conflict in the family. I told the crowd of about five dozen people that Richard Foss was a great father to me, and that I would miss him dearly.

Then, using an anecdote to begin my gospel presentation, I related a story of how when I was 8 years old, I asked my dad if he would bring me home the new 12-inch-tall American cowboy action figure called Johnny West. "We'll see," Dad said. A few days later, my dad took off work early and had to go to several stores before he found the toy I requested. I was so excited when he brought it home and he was just as excited to give it to me. Looking around at the crowd, I asked them if it would have been appropriate for me to offer Dad my allowance, or money I expected to make from collecting empty coke bottles, for the toy. This was a rhetorical question of course, as this was a gift given to me freely and to be received freely. In fact, my father would have been rightly offended if I had offered to work for his gift.

Wouldn't our heavenly Father also be rightly offended if we tried to pay Him for the eternal gift of His Son, I asked? Of course, because this is a gift given freely and to be received freely. Paul, writing about salvation in Romans 11:6, said, "if it is by grace, it is no longer on the basis of works; otherwise grace would no longer be grace." I quoted Ephesians 2:8-9, "For by grace you have been saved through faith. And this is not your own doing; it is the gift of God, not a result of works, so that no one may boast." Biblical grace is free! It has to be, otherwise it is no longer grace. Grace is also not acquired by our works so that there can be no boasting before God.

After talking about our unrighteous standing and Jesus being our perfectly righteous substitute before the Father, I brought up Christ's one-time and fully sufficient sacrifice. I quoted the book of Hebrews about Christ being our High Priest in heaven (4:14-16) who "always lives to make intercession" (7:25) for us based on His *once for all* sacrifice (7:27), a sacrifice which was not only designed but prophesied[133] to bring an end to the Old Covenant priest's daily sacrifices. Now that Jesus, our High Priest "in the presence of God on our behalf" (9:24), has come "*once* to bear the sins of many" (9:28), He did not come "to offer

---

[133] Daniel 9:24.

himself repeatedly" (9:25). Because of Christ's finished work, believers are "sanctified through the offering of the body of Jesus Christ *once* for all" (10:10). A biblical Eucharist would be to take the Lord's Supper, as Jesus clearly said, "in remembrance of me" (Luke 22:19), that is, a remembrance of His once for all sacrifice, not a Catholic re-sacrifice that is never-ending and never brings assurance, but only a "hoped" for salvation as the priest earlier said.

After I stated that the biblical gospel is a once for all finished sacrifice with no more earthly priests,[134] I could feel and see the tension in the room rise, including among some family members. I also caught a glimpse of the church's priest a few feet away. The same man, who like other Catholic priests, had falsely taken on the title of "another Christ",[135] was sitting with his head up and his eyes closed as if he were tuning me out.

I told the gathering that instead of "hoping" that our sins can be washed away through one of the Catholic Church's continued and perpetual Eucharist offerings, and that we need to pray that such a sacrifice "*may* be acceptable to God," they should place their faith and trust in the once for all biblical offering of the true High Priest—Jesus Christ. That way, I said, we can be assured that God has accepted His Son's sacrifice (2 Cor. 5:18-19; Col. 1:21-23), and you can, as the book of First John tells us, "know that you have eternal life" (1 John 5:13) because "the blood of Jesus his Son cleanses us from all sin" (1:7).

I finished by thanking my earthly father for showing me patience and acts of love and grace. I said that was an act of common grace through God. However, most of all, I added, I want to thank my heavenly Father for the act of special saving grace He showed me through the sinless life, once for all sacrifice, and resurrection of His Son to secure my eternal life. I then scanned the crowd, which included looking back at the priest, saying, "May the Holy Spirit enlighten all of our minds."

Next Stop—Purgatory

I found it interesting that the funeral program for my dad stated that "He has been greeted in heaven." That of course would be my prayer, even though, as I stated earlier, my dad's final destiny is not known by me at this time. For the sake of argument, *if* Catholic doctrine were true, the statement in the program that Dad has been greeted in heaven was

---

[134] Nowhere in the New Testament will you find the office of priest among New Covenant believers, much less a sacramental or sacerdotal priesthood.
[135] "The priest, as is said with good reason, is indeed another Christ", Papal Encyclical 'Ad Catholici Sacerdotii' on the priesthood, Pope Pius XI, December 20, 1935.

not correct. According to their religion, deceased Catholics who depart this life in God's grace go to Purgatory, where they must suffer temporal punishment for their venial sins which they did not pay for on earth with penance (Catechism 1030-31). This Catholic retribution in Purgatory includes "fire and torments or purifying punishments" (Indulgentiarum Doctrina, chapter 1, paragraph 2). This cannot be denied by any Catholic unless they want to risk being under an "anathema" by their own church (Council of Trent, Canon 30).

It should be noted that the Catholic doctrine clearly states that Purgatory is not the final destination for those who die in God's grace. Those who go to Purgatory are eventually headed for heaven once their temporal punishments are over and they "achieve the holiness necessary to enter the joy of heaven" (Catechism 1030). One might ask, how long does a departed soul have to remain in Purgatory? I remember during my discussion with my dad in 2000, he told me, "If you want to know what Catholics really believe, you need to read the Baltimore Catechism."[136] Okay, the Baltimore Catechism 1384 tells us, "We do not know what souls are in Purgatory nor how long they have to remain there."

There is some apparent good news for those who believe in the Catholic doctrine of Purgatory. Family and friends on earth can perform indulgences to shorten a loved one's time in Purgatory (Baltimore Catechism 1385). This is "so that the temporal punishments due for their sins may be remitted" (Catholic Catechism 1479). You can even apply an indulgence to your own time in Purgatory (1498).

Just what is an indulgence you might ask? According to Baltimore Catechism 861, "Indulgences are: The saying of certain prayers, fasting, and the use of certain articles of devotion [rosary]; visits to Churches or altars [to light candles],[137] and the giving of alms…to go to confession and Holy Communion and pray for the intention of the Pope." Indulgences are granted by the Pope, or bishops in your diocese, from a "spiritual treasury" or a "treasure chest" of excess merit waiting to be dispensed to those who wish to work for indulgences. This treasure

---

[136] The Baltimore Catechism was the standard Catholic school text used from the late 19th century through the late 1960s. My dad, having gone to Catholic school in the 1930s and 40s, would have exclusively used this catechism. He told me that he would send me his 1933 Baltimore catechism. He never did.

[137] In front of the church where my dad's funeral was held were the traditional candles Catholics light. There was a sign listing a price of three dollars to light the candles. That three dollars is credited as a purchased indulgence.

chest of merit consists of "the merits of Jesus Christ, and the superabundant satisfactions of the Blessed Virgin Mary and of the saints" (853).

After my brother died in 2000, one of my siblings told me that they attended a special Mass for Bob, held at their Catholic church. That didn't surprise me as Catholic Masses for the dead are commonplace. In fact, family of the souls in Purgatory perform indulgences "by having Masses said for them" (Baltimore Catechism 1385). Catholics are told that they can purchase a Mass Card and the priest will lay this card on the altar during such a Mass. This purchased indulgence will shorten time in Purgatory[138] in the name of the deceased. However, no priest can tell you how much time was taken off or how many Masses must be purchased before the soul in Purgatory can be released.

The Futility of the Mass and Purgatory

As we have documented previously from the book of Hebrews, the repeated offering of the Catholic Mass demonstrates its insufficiency, whether it be during a traditional Sunday service, a funeral Mass, or a Mass for the dead. The fact that Rome tells their parishioners that they must partake repeatedly in this re-sacrificing of Christ[139] shows that the Catholic Mass has more in common with the Old Testament sacrifices that God said were insufficient (Heb. 9-10), than with the one-time sacrifice of Jesus on Calvary. The Bible says of Christ's once for all sacrifice, "Nor did he enter heaven to offer himself *again and again*, the way the [Old Testament] high priest enters the Most Holy Place every year with blood that is not his own" (Heb. 9:25, NIV).

---

[138] The book of Maccabees, part of the Catholic canon of scripture, alludes to this when it describes how sacrifices were offered in the Temple for the dead: "Therefore he made atonement for the dead, that they might be delivered from their sin" (2 Maccabees 12:40-45). 2 Maccabees, of course, is not scripture from a Protestant perspective. It is also not part of the Jewish Old Testament canon.

[139] Many Catholic apologists try and mitigate criticisms of this sacrament by claiming the Mass is *not* a re-sacrifice. They will claim that Christ's sacrifice is not continued or perpetuated in the Mass, instead it is *re-presented*. However, I would say they are just equivocating or playing semantical games at this point because the truth comes from official Catholic sources, including Vatican II pronouncements: "God Himself wishes that there should be a continuation of this sacrifice" (Mediator Dei 2nd Vatican council, Instruction on the manner of distributing the Holy communion no. 55). "The Mass, the Lord's Supper, is at the same time and inseparably: A sacrifice in which the Sacrifice of the Cross is perpetuated" (Vatican II, Eucharisticum Mysterium, 3). Also, why declare that one commits a mortal sin by missing an inoffensive "unbloody" (Catechism 1367) re-presentation? Baltimore Catechism 1329 states: "It is a mortal sin not to hear Mass on a Sunday or a holyday of obligation, unless we are excused for a serious reason."

If the Catholic Eucharist is truly the same sacrifice as that of Calvary (which Catholics want us to believe), then participating in *one* Mass should purify the attendee's sins "once for all!" However, a Catholic, who may attend thousands of Masses in their lifetime, has to ask themselves this question: "Which one of those Masses saves me? The one I attended decades ago, last year, last month, last week, or this coming Sunday?" If they say all of them, they defy the words of the Bible that clearly state that Jesus won't do this "again and again", because He has already done it perfectly once! If they say the next one in which I participate, then they should stop attending Mass after that to avoid the blasphemy of re-sacrificing Christ into a superfluous loop.

The perpetual Catholic Mass reminds me of something the late Dallas Cowboy's running back Duane Thomas once said. When asked about playing Sunday in the "ultimate game" before his team's 1972 Super Bowl win over Miami, he responded, "If it's the ultimate game, how come they're playing it again next year?" To paraphrase Duane Thomas, "If this Sunday's Eucharist is the ultimate Catholic sacrament that saves you, then how come they're offering it again next week?"

Let's face it, the Catholic Mass is anything but good news. If you did the math, all the Masses my 84-year-old dad attended in his lifetime could have surpassed well over 3000. Sadly, all those Masses did not add up to the ultimate salvific experience—being justified by Christ's once for all sacrifice. When Dad died, his own priest said at his Funeral Mass that he "hoped" that this *most recent* Catholic Eucharist sacrifice would "wash away" my father's sins and that those in attendance needed to pray that this *latest* sacrifice "*may* be acceptable to God." One can only wonder if attempts are still being made today for further Eucharistic sacrifices for Dad to shorten his time in so-called Purgatory. One has to ask: "When does it end? When is it finished?"

Purgatory is not only nowhere to be found in the Bible, it is an offense to the finished work of Christ. If "the blood of Jesus his Son cleanses us from *all* sin" (1 John 1:7), what sin is left to be paid for or purged in Purgatory? All the "purification for sins" (Heb. 1:3), suffering (1 Pet. 3:18), and temporal punishment (Isa. 53:10; John 19:30) have already been accomplished by Christ Himself. Wait! Don't we have to suffer in Purgatory to "achieve the holiness necessary to enter the joy of heaven" (Catechism 1030)? Again, that holiness is imputed to us by faith (Rom. 4:22), as it has already been achieved "through the offering of the body of Jesus Christ once for all" (Heb. 10:10). For we know that "by a single offering he has perfected for all time" (Heb. 10:14) those God "has now reconciled in his body of flesh by his death, in order to present you holy and blameless and above reproach before him" (Col. 1:22; cf., Eph. 1:4; Col. 1:28). Simply put—all the things Roman Catholicism claims Purgatory will do for their departed parishioners have already been done by Christ!

Nowhere in the Bible do we read about some "spiritual treasury" or a "treasure chest" of excess merit waiting to be dispensed to those who wish to work for indulgences. We are not involved in salvation from the punishment of sin, for the Bible testifies that salvation cannot be bought, sold, transferred or earned by anyone, for "No one can redeem the life of another or give to God a ransom for them—the ransom for a life is costly, no payment is ever enough" (Psalm 49:7-8, NIV).

For those witnessing to family members caught up in the unbiblical traditions of Catholicism, let us pray together, that just like God did for us, when our "minds were hardened" (2 Cor. 3:14), that He will take the veil off their eyes and hearts (3:15), knowing that "when one turns to the Lord, the veil is removed" (3:16). Having that "unveiled face, beholding the glory of the Lord" (3:18), one can then see clearly our Savior's once for all finished sacrifice, being assured that, "When you were dead in your sins and in the uncircumcision of your flesh, God made you alive with Christ. He forgave us *all* our sins" (Col. 2:13, NIV).

Sunday School to Atheist

My mother recently turned 90 years old. Unlike some other family members, who once called me "fanatical" and "mentally ill" for simply sharing the gospel, Mom has always allowed me to discuss salvation issues with her. This despite the fact that our conversations have almost always ended with her saying that I am not going to convert her. Soon after she turned 89, Mom reconfirmed to me over the phone something I already knew, "I am a devout atheist."

Barbara Jean Brown was born January 2, 1932 in Whitewater, Wisconsin. Her mother was an Episcopalian, but they did visit other Protestant churches on occasion. When Mom was in the sixth grade, she said because several of her friends went to the Lutheran Church, she decided to go with them to Lutheran Sunday School. In 1953, Mom agreed to attend catechism classes to join Catholicism so she and Dad could be married by the Catholic Church.

By the time Mom's sixth child arrived in 1962, she had started to disconnect from the Catholic religion. She didn't appreciate how the over-zealous disciplinarian nuns treated us in Catholic grade school. I can testify that the ear pulling and punitive use of the wooden ruler seemed to be something the nuns rather enjoyed. Mom said she was also tiring of the priest mentioning the evils of birth control in his sermons and how the church spent money. Several years later, she told her husband she was not interested in attending Mass anymore. She rarely stepped foot inside a Catholic Church during the next 50 years until Dad's funeral in 2014.

No One Can Know for Sure

One phrase Mom has used a lot is "No one can know for sure what will happen." One time when I was sharing with her how the Bible tells us that we can know we have eternal life right now (1 John 5:13; John 3:36, 5:24, 6:40, 10:28), she responded, "No one can know the truth." I asked her if that statement, that no one can know the truth, was true. Mom, always one to see the irony in things, laughed.

The fact is that we can know the truth about many things. Mom would not deny that, but when it comes to spiritual matters, she says that truth is subjective. I would agree with Nancy Pearcey when she wrote, "As Christians we must make it clear that we are not offering a subjective, private faith that is immune to rational scrutiny. We are making cognitive claims about objective knowledge that can be defended in the public arena."[140] As I argued for in Chapter Three (What is Pre-Evangelism?), we can present logical arguments for God, including His existence being necessary for the foundation of reason, logic, morality, the universe's design and first cause. There are also archeological finds and many evidences to prove the truth of Christianity.

In 2010, while on a visit to Georgia, I stayed up with Mom discussing spiritual things until 3 am in the morning. She told me she was a good person and had tried to live life the best she could. I asked her what she meant by the best, and she responded that no one is perfect. I said, "Except One—Jesus Christ, who lived a sinless life in our place, died on the cross for our sins and rose from the dead to perfectly fulfill all of God's requirements for us." After I told her that we can only stand before God by placing our trust in that fulfilled righteousness, she said, "If that's true, I'm in trouble."

Saying "I know one thing for sure", Mom stated that she would lay down her life for any of her children. I immediately thought how interesting

---

[140] Nancy Pearcey, *Total Truth*, p. 222.

her choice of words was—lay down her life. I told her that's exactly what Jesus said, "I lay down my life for the sheep" (John 10:15). She paused and then said, "I also know that I could never extend forgiveness to the man who sexually molested you when you were twelve." In one respect, I appreciated what she said as I have never doubted her loyalty to me, but I told her that, while I have never forgotten, I forgave him a long time ago and so should she. In fact, I said Jesus told us, "For if you forgive others their trespasses, your heavenly Father will also forgive you, but if you do not forgive others their trespasses, neither will your Father forgive your trespasses" (Matt. 6:14-15). She shrugged her shoulders and said, "So be it."

Well-Read Except...

My mom is one of the most well-read people I have ever known. When it comes to history, wars, cultures and philosophies, she is a fountain of knowledge. However, she has neglected to seriously consider the most widely read and influential book in the history of mankind—the Bible. Through the many years Mom and I have discussed religion, she would say things like, "Quit reading your Bible and go with your feelings." Another time she told me, "I've been around the block and know the ways of the world. I don't need the Bible to teach me." In 2017, when Kim and I stopped by to see Mom on our way to the Creation Museum in Kentucky, she had a skeptical expression on her face when I told her how excited I was to see the Genesis story laid out in the museum.

When Mom would criticize parts of the Bible she considered unbelievable, like the account in the Garden, the Flood, and Sodom and Gomorrah, she would always take the text out of context, or add something to the narrative that was not there. I asked her if I started to add things to the historical account of Custer's Last Stand (with which she has always been enamored) that were not part of the record, what her reaction would be. Her eyes got big as she sat forward in her chair saying, "Well, buster, I would correct you and tell you to go and familiarize yourself with the actual written account." I said, "Exactly! Will you do the same with the Bible?" We both laughed and she said, "I suppose so."

God Delusion

Mom told me that she has read The God Delusion by Richard Dawkins. Attempting to make a negative statement about religion, she said she believed that "Humans have always had a desire to believe in God or gods because that is part of our human nature." I said, "Actually, I agree because

Romans one and two tell us that God has placed the knowledge of Him in creation and in our hearts (Rom. 1:19-20, 2:15)." Because of that knowledge, some seek after the one true God and others after false gods.

Mom mentioned to me that she sees two possibilities when she dies. One, quoting her exactly, "Poof", as in going out of existence. Two, "Being rewarded." Personally, I don't think the atheist label Mom has given herself quite fits. Despite that label, in almost all the talks I have had with her, she has left open the possibility of some kind of life after death. On what that might be she hasn't really speculated, but she has said to me many times that there is likely something awaiting all of us and we will just have to wait and see. Mom once told me her grandmother spoke to her from the grave, while she was pregnant with me, saying, "Everything is going to be alright." Mom said, because of that experience, she knows that "There is something beyond the grave."

I Believed It

I was curious after Mom relayed her religious experiences growing up in Protestant churches. I recently asked her if she was just playing church to appease her mother. Did she go to the Lutheran Sunday School only because her friends went? She told me, "No, I believed it!" I asked her "Believed what?" She said, "You know, the doctrines of the Bible and Christianity." Knowing that Lutheran Sunday School would almost certainly be teaching sola fide, justification by faith alone, I asked her what she was taught in Sunday School about salvation and how one gets to heaven. Mom responded, "You know, behave yourself, be a good person, ask for forgiveness and you go to heaven."

Like my dad, who wrote in his spiral notebook as a boy about having to keep the commandments to please God to gain heaven, Mom may have been involved early on in church and Sunday School attendance, but she didn't then, and is not able today, to discern the majesty of the gospel. The simple truth is that this is not about one being capable or incapable of intellectually grasping the basics of the gospel, this is about one having a closed heart to it and calling it foolishness (1 Cor. 1:18, 2:14).

Pray with Me

I not only pray for my unsaved family members daily, I also seek out people to pray with me. I often remind some of my pastor friends in Africa of my request. Sometimes they will dedicate themselves to pray for my mom over several days and then e-mail me the next week asking, "Is Mum saved yet?" I have learned through decades of praying for my family that God's timeline is seldom ours. I have come to realize that my prayers in this area are not a sprint, but a marathon.

During that marathon, I have to admit there are times when my prayers for family members seem futile. They have been opposed to the gospel for so long, I start to wonder if God will ever change their hearts. I say to myself, "It will take a miracle." Wait! When people prayed for me to be saved years before I repented and yielded my life to Christ, such a miracle did happen! Sometimes we have to remind ourselves of the miracle of our own conversion to help us press on for the supernatural conversion of others.

Daydream Believer

Someone once asked me the outcome of my witnessing to family members. I paused for a moment, took a deep breath, and then told them there has been a scenario where some in my family have yielded their lives to Christ after I shared the gospel with them. Their objections and roadblocks were smoothly and adroitly answered by me and I said all the right things at just the right time. I then told them that this scenario, unfortunately, has only happened while I was daydreaming on solitary walks or alone in my hot tub.

Our family witnessing opportunities seldom if ever go the way we daydream them. Most of the time things aren't so smooth. We fail to say the right things at just the right time. In fact, sometimes we say the wrong things! Let's be honest, there's something about a family dynamic that changes things. We can normally have fun talking about family memories or how the kids or grandkids are doing. However, tell them they need a rescue plan, and the response is likely to be, "From *you*! What makes *you* so sure?" That's when we have to rely on the power of the word of God to change minds and hearts. I'm not the rescuer, God is, for, "Salvation is from the LORD" (Jonah 2:9, NASB). What makes me so sure? It's because I'm just like you, I need a rescue plan too, and God has already laid that plan out for us in the Bible.

Our job is to evangelize our unsaved family members, not to convert them—only God can do that. When I witness the gospel to strangers, I always remember that the power of my message is not with me but with God who opens the heart (Acts 16:14) and gives the growth (1 Cor.

3:6). Shouldn't I have that same confidence when witnessing to family members? The obvious answer is—yes, of course! When I share the salvation message with non-family members, I share with them their need to "repent and believe in the gospel" (Mark 1:15). That's the exact same message I need to share with lost family members. In the end, the only dynamic we have to be concerned with is the dynamic of "the gospel, for it is the power of God for salvation to everyone who believes" (Rom. 1:16).

○ ○ ○

18) ALL ABOARD

"You may conclude that evangelism is not your gift, but it is still your duty. Not having the gift of mercy in no way excuses us from being merciful." -
Mark Dever[141]

When it comes to evangelism, the call to Christians is "All aboard." Let's all get on the evangelism train, ship or bus and not miss our responsibility to preach the gospel. If you have missed this call, don't panic, there are always other evangelism trains that will come your way. Next time be ready to hop on board. The only thing you need to pack is your Bible, which will either be in your hand or in your mind.

---
[141] Mark Dever, *The Gospel and Personal Evangelism*, p. 25.

Types of Evangelists

The word evangelist is used only three times in the Bible. While the Bible gives one person the title of an evangelist, "Philip the evangelist" (Acts 21:8), Paul uses the term "evangelists" in Ephesians as he speaks about the leadership gifts in the church (Eph. 4:11). Paul also instructs Timothy to "do the work of an evangelist" (2 Tim. 4:5), but he was never called an evangelist. Here, Paul seems to be speaking of evangelism as one aspect of Timothy's total ministry.

While many have endeavored to define the distinctions between the three references where the word evangelist is used (Acts 21:8; Eph. 4:11; 2 Tim. 4:5), I don't believe there is enough clarification given for us to be dogmatic about it. I would say two things we know for sure—the evangelist shares the good news of the gospel, and all Christians are called to do the work of an evangelist.

In Ephesians chapter 4, we read when Christ ascended, "He gave the apostles, the prophets, the evangelists, the shepherds and teachers, to equip the saints for the work of ministry, for building up the body of Christ" (4:11-12). The context of this passage is gifts, "Christ's gift" (4:7), as "he gave gifts to men" (4:8). Thus, the list in verse 11, including evangelists, appears to be a list of spiritual gifts. My position is that this passage teaches that evangelism *is* a spiritual gift.[142] So, who has this gift? Well, we know the Holy Spirit gives gifts according to His will, not ours (1 Cor. 12:11; Heb. 2:4). Paul also stresses in 1 Corinthians 12 that God has appointed all members of the body to have at least one gift (12:7). In verses 27 through 31, Paul makes it clear that while members of the church have different gifts from one another, no one has all the gifts.

If evangelism is a spiritual gift, we know that not everyone has this gift. However, for those that do, it was given to them by the Holy Spirit, as gifts are "empowered by one and the same Spirit, who apportions to each one individually as he wills" (1 Cor. 12:11; cf., Heb. 2:4). If the Holy Spirit gives a person the gift of evangelism, He will also empower them to use this specific gift (Acts 1:8, 4:33, 6:5, 6:8; Rom. 15:19; 1 Cor. 2:4-5;

---

[142] The late Dr. Harold Hoehner, biblical scholar and professor of New Testament studies at Dallas Theological Seminary, once mentored me on the mention of "evangelists" in Ephesians chapter 4. While attending the same church in Dallas with Dr. Hoehner, he pointed me to his 1000 page tome— Ephesians: An Exegetical Commentary. On pages 538-540 he laid out his case that the list mentioned in Ephesians 4:11, in context, are gifts. Therefore, Dr. Hoehner's conclusion was that there is a spiritual gift of evangelism. That is the positon I also take, even though I know others view this differently.

2 Cor. 6:7, 10:4; 1 Thess. 1:5; 2 Tim. 1:7-8).

What are some of the convictions a person with the spiritual gift of evangelism might have?

- They submit to the church to be "equipped" for this ministry (Eph. 4:11-16), as they realize they are here for a "partnership in the gospel" (Philip. 1:5), working "side by side in the gospel together" (Philip. 4:3). For we are "God's fellow workers" (1 Cor. 3:9).
- They understand their gift is "for building up the body of Christ" (Eph. 4:12).
- They have sanctified Christ as Lord in their hearts (1 Pet. 3:15, NASB).
- They have a burden for the lost (Rom. 9:1-3, 10:1).
- They don't boast about the number of people they "converted", knowing all they do is plant and water—God gives the growth (1 Cor. 3:6).
- They proclaim not themselves, "but Jesus Christ as Lord" (2 Cor. 4:5). They always point away from themselves and to Christ crucified (1 Cor. 2:2), knowing that the gospel's power comes through the message, not the messenger.
- While understanding the cross can bring an offense (1 Pet. 2:7-8; 1 Cor. 1:18) and the preaching of Christ crucified is called "folly" (1 Cor. 1:23), they know it pleases God through the folly of what they preach to save those who believe (1 Cor. 1:21).
- They preach the gospel to bring glory to God (Acts 21:20; 1 Cor. 10:31).
- They understand the root (1 Cor. 15:3-4; 2 Cor. 5:21) and the fruit (Rom. 6:22) of the gospel and are able to clearly explain the distinction.
- They focus on a call to repentance and faith when presenting the gospel (Mark 1:15; Acts 2:36-41).
- In witnessing, they never shy away from quoting the Bible, "the sword of the Spirit, which is the word of God" (Eph. 6:17). They know God's word will pierce right to the thoughts and intentions of the hearer's heart (Heb. 4:12) and will never fail to accomplish its purpose (Isa. 55:11).

- They have a competent knowledge of the scriptures (Acts 8:31-35; 2 Tim. 2:15) and devote themselves to sound doctrine (Titus 1:9, 2:1, 7; 1 Tim. 4:16).
- They teach "the whole counsel of God" (Acts 20:27).
- They are "put here for the defense of the gospel" (Philip. 1:16), to "guard" the truth of the gospel (1 Tim. 6:20; 2 Tim. 1:14) and are ready to rebuke the strange fire of a false gospel (Gal. 1:6-9; 2 Cor. 11:4).
- They are ready to play both offense and defense on "God's field" (1 Cor. 3:9).
- They are ready to contend for the faith (Jude 1:3). This can include arguing (Acts 25:8), disputing (Acts 9:29), refuting (Acts 18:28) and debating (Acts 15:2) in defense of the gospel. They will "reprove, rebuke, and exhort with complete patience and teaching" (2 Tim. 4:2).
- They are always prepared to answer objections or questions (1 Pet. 3:15; Col. 4:6).
- They maintain a balance of truth in love (Eph. 4:15) and grace and truth (John 1:14).
- They are a humble student, never saying, "I'm really good at this", or "I got this down", but always willing to learn from other evangelists (Acts 18:24-27).
- They are "ready in season and out of season" to preach the good news (2 Tim. 4:2), for "Woe to me if I do not preach the gospel!" (1 Cor. 9:16).
- They are willing to "become all things to all people" using a hearer's own beliefs and culture to show them the truth of the gospel (1 Cor. 9:19-23; Acts 17:22-32).
- They have a keen sense of timing of knowing when to share the gospel (Acts 16:14) as they go about "making the best use of the time" (Eph. 5:16; Col. 4:5; cf., Acts 5:42).
- They understand that most of the time there will not be a conclusion to a dialogue with a person to whom they are witnessing, "We will hear you again about this" (Acts 17:32). Things may remain open-ended.
- They know when the time is right to walk away (Luke 10:10-11;

Acts 13:44-46, 51, 18:6) and when to call for decisions (Acts 16:31, 17:30; Mark 1:15; 2 Cor. 5:20).

- They have the discernment to spot worldly grief that produces death, or godly grief that produces a repentance that leads to salvation (2 Cor. 7:10).

- They obey God rather than the authorities who try to stop their witness (Acts 5:29).

- They will travel wherever necessary to reach the lost (Acts 1:8, 8:5, 40; Mark 16:15).

- They know that sharing the gospel can bring suffering and persecution (2 Tim. 1:8; 2 Tim. 3:12). However, they also know that any insult for the name of Christ brings a blessing (1 Pet. 4:14).

- Knowing the fear of the Lord, they seek to persuade men (2 Cor. 5:11).

- While a certain boldness comes with the preaching of the gospel (Acts 4:31; Eph. 6:19-20; 1 Thess. 2:2), during times of "fear and trembling," they trust that the scripture they present will display a demonstration of the Spirit and of power and that God's wisdom will prevail over the wisdom of men (1 Cor. 2:1-5).

- By their life and conduct, they "put no obstacle in anyone's way" (2 Cor. 6:3). At the same time, they realize their life is not the gospel; preaching the good news is (Romans 10:14-17).

- They are not so caught up with what they are saying that they forget to listen to the person to whom they are witnessing (James 1:19; Proverbs 18:13).

- They are always praying (1 Thess. 5:17) that God may open to them a door "to declare the mystery of Christ" (Col. 4:3; cf., 2 Thess. 3:1).

- They have a desire to see and encourage continuous growth in each convert (Matt. 28:19-20; Luke 14:27; 1 Tim. 4:6, 11, 16). This continuous growth includes themselves (2 Pet. 3:18).

A person who has not been given the spiritual gift of evangelism can still apply many of the points in this list above to themselves when doing the work of an evangelist.

DNA Evangelism

What if you conclude you don't have the spiritual gift of evangelism? Does that mean you, as a follower of Christ, don't need to share the good news? Not at all. Think about this, some people have the spiritual gift of abundant giving (Rom. 12:8; 2 Cor. 8:2; 2 Cor. 9:11, 13), but we are all called to give (1 Cor. 16:2; 2 Cor. 9:7). Others have a special gift of mercy (Rom. 12:8), yet we are all called to show grace and compassion (2 Cor. 1:3-4; Matt. 5:7; Luke 6:36; 1 Pet. 4:10; Rom. 12:18). The same principle applies to evangelism: while some have the gift of evangelism (Eph. 4:11), we are all called to share the gospel. Those with the special gift of evangelism, in most cases, may simply be more fruitful than others who don't have this gift.

There are many people who do not have the spiritual gift of evangelism who still faithfully plant and water. God can and does use their efforts to bring about the salvation of many souls (1 Cor. 3:6). God uses these loyal differently gifted Christians just as much as He uses believers that He has gifted as evangelists. I, for one, am glad that several of these loyal Christians shared the gospel with me. They didn't do it because they had that specific spiritual gift, but because they understood evangelism is not just something other people do, it's something all Christians do, as it is in all of our DNA (2 Cor. 5:17-20).

Be Imitators of Me

Paul was gospel-driven like no other (Rom. 1:1, 15:20). He said, "I have become all things to all people, that by all means I might save some. I do it all for the sake of the gospel" (1 Cor. 9:22-23). He also told the Corinthians, "I became your father in Christ Jesus through the gospel. I urge you, then, be imitators of me" (1 Cor. 4:15-16). Paul then used Timothy as an example of one who follows his ways, "I sent you Timothy, my beloved and faithful child in the Lord, to remind you of my ways in Christ" (4:17). This is the same Timothy who was told by Paul to "do the work of an evangelist" (2 Tim. 4:5). There is an important connection here. Paul instructed the Corinthian church to be imitators of him in his work for the gospel, the same way Timothy imitates him in doing the work of an evangelist. In essence, Paul is telling all of us, if you want to imitate me—do the work of an evangelist.

Also notice that Paul said, "Be imitators of me, as I am of Christ" (1 Cor. 11:1). Christians are imitators of Jesus (Matt. 10:38; John 14:21) and thus "fishers of men" (Matt. 4:19). Jesus told us to "Go into all the world and proclaim the gospel to the whole creation" (Mark 16:15). This command was not just for the apostles but to all followers of Jesus "to the end of the age" (Matt. 28:19-20; cf., Acts 1:8). Imitators of Jesus will also take note that He said, "Everyone to whom much was given, of him much will be required" (Luke 12:48). Since Christ followers have been given no greater gift than the gospel, to do the work of an evangelist would be the ultimate form of imitating of our Savior. To be Christ-like is to share the gospel. Jesse Johnson, Professor of Evangelism at The Master's Seminary, writes, "Evangelism is not one thing that Christians are called to do; it is the primary task. All other tasks are intermediate."[143]

Below is a list of other reasons why the Bible teaches all Christians should evangelize:

- Right after Paul told the Corinthian Church that he does everything for the sake of the gospel, he said, "Do you not know that in a race *all* the runners run" (1 Cor. 9:24). Christians don't stand on the sidelines and watch the "super" evangelists run the race, Paul said we *all* run the race. When Paul told Timothy to fulfill his ministry by doing "the work of an evangelist" (2 Tim. 4:5), he then said, "I have fought the good fight, I have finished the race, I have kept the faith" (4:7). Sharing the gospel is the race—in which *all* the runners run.

- Paul doesn't seem to restrict sharing the good news to those with the special gift of evangelism. He talked about how some "women" and "the rest of my fellow workers" had "labored side by side with me in the gospel" (Philip. 4:3).

- Paul wrote, "To *all* the saints in Christ Jesus who are at Philippi" (1:1), make sure "you are standing firm in one spirit, with one mind striving side by side for the faith of the gospel" (1:27). Robert P. Lightner, in his commentary on The Book of Philippians, writes, "Paul was burdened that they [all the saints at Philippi] stand firm in one spirit and contend as one man (lt., "in one soul") for the faith of the gospel, the body of truth (cf. "faith," Jude 3)." All the saints at Philippi were involved in evangelism.

- Since all Christians are a part of the priesthood of all believers

---
[143] Jesse Johnson, John MacArthur, *Evangelism*, p. 20.

(1 Pet. 2:5-9; Rev. 1:6, 5:10), like Paul, we are called to a "priestly service of the gospel of God" (Rom. 15:16; cf., 1:1). Peter told us that we are "a chosen race, a royal priesthood, a holy nation, a people for his own possession, that you may proclaim the excellencies of him" (1 Pet. 2:9).

- In speaking to the church at Corinth, Paul said, "*we* persuade others" (2 Cor. 5:11) that Christ "died and was raised" (5:15). He said this persuasion should be made by all in the church, because "if anyone is in Christ, he is a new creation" (5:17), and God has entrusted to all "in Christ" (5:19) this "message of reconciliation" (5:19). Every follower of Jesus at Corinth was called to be "ambassadors for Christ, God making his appeal through *us*" (2 Cor. 5:20). Notice the plural pronouns we and us.

- We see an example of these plural pronouns in the letter to the church of the Thessalonians. Paul told the whole church that God "has chosen *you*, because our gospel came to you not only in word, but also in power and in the Holy Spirit and with full conviction" (1 Thess. 1:4-5). He then said "*you* became an example to all the believers in Macedonia and in Achaia. For not only has the word of the Lord sounded forth from *you* in Macedonia and Achaia, but *your* faith in God has gone forth everywhere" (1:7-8). The whole church at Thessalonica was praised for evangelizing, as their faith in God had gone forth everywhere!

- After the stoning death of Stephen, we read, "And there arose on that day a great persecution against the church in Jerusalem, and they were all scattered throughout the regions of Judea and Samaria, except the apostles" (Acts 8:1). Notice that the apostles stayed in Jerusalem, but other believers were scattered throughout the regions. What did these other believers do? "Now those who were scattered went about preaching the word" (Acts 8:4). Other believers in the church, not just those with the spiritual gift of evangelism, also need to go about preaching the word.

- All believers are called "in your hearts [to] honor Christ the Lord as holy" (1 Pet. 3:15a). Because of that lordship, we all should be prepared to give "a reason for the hope that is in you" (1 Pet. 3:15b). Lordship and evangelism go together.

When scripture says, "How beautiful are the *feet* of those who preach the good news!" (Rom. 10:15), "feet" is not limited to those with the spiritual gift of evangelism. Let each of us do our part in evangelizing, because "The harvest is plentiful, but the laborers are few" (Matt. 9:37).

Be Faithful in a Little

Jesus told us, "One who is faithful in a very little is also faithful in much" (Luke 16:10). When some evangelists think about preaching the gospel, they have grand visions of God using them to have hundreds or maybe even thousands come to Christ. While God certainly has prepared beforehand mighty works for some (Gal. 1:15; Acts 9:15; Rom. 1:1; Gen. 15:5, 22:18; Jer. 1:5; Heb. 11:4-39), most of us are called to just be faithful in the little things. If God sees fit to call us to much more, all glory to Him.

Sowing and Reaping

Some on The Evangelism Circle will plant while others will water (1 Cor. 3:6). We also see that while some sow, others reap. Jesus told His disciples, "Do you not say, 'There are yet four months, then comes the harvest'? Look, I tell you, lift up your eyes, and see that the fields are white for harvest. Already the one who reaps is receiving wages and gathering fruit for eternal life, so that sower and reaper may rejoice together. For here the saying holds true, 'One sows and another reaps.' I sent you to reap that for which you did not labor. Others have labored, and you have entered into their labor" (John 4:35-38).

While Paul tells us some plant and some water, Jesus says those actions in evangelism can be a labor separate from those who reap. In other words, while some evangelists have planted the seeds of the gospel message in a person's heart and others have followed that effort by reconfirming or watering that message, other evangelists come along at the appointed time (Acts 13:48) to be involved in a conversion. They reap what their fellow evangelists who came before them had sowed and watered. They entered into their labor.

Both Paul and Jesus tie these three groups of evangelists together as one. Paul says, "He who plants and he who waters are one, and each will receive his wages according to his labor. For we are God's fellow workers" (1 Cor. 3:8-9). Jesus told us that the final evangelist who reaps also receives his wages for gathering fruit for eternal life. In the end, all of God's fellow workers "rejoice together" (John 4:36).

For the sower and the waterer, their labor may have resulted in them saying, "We have only done what was our duty" (Luke 17:10; cf. 2 Tim.

4:2, 5). They were faithful in the little things. For the reaper, God allowed them to be "faithful in much" (Luke 16:10)—"receiving wages and gathering fruit for eternal life" (John 4:36). Yet, those same reapers were no doubt, at other times, fulfilling the roles of the sowers and the waterers. God knew they were faithful in the little things and thus He entrusted that they would also be faithful in much! If you want God to allow you to gather fruit for eternal life, first prove faithful as a planter or a waterer. Be faithful in the little things and then watch for God to entrust you to be faithful in much.

Recap

As we close part two on evangelism, here are some points to keep in mind:

- The gospel is an unchanging message in changing times. While God has allowed different methods to be used in delivering the gospel—the message never changes.

- The root of the gospel is the good news of salvation through the life, death, burial and resurrection of Jesus Christ.

- The fruit of the gospel is its sanctifying work in changing our lives and positively changing the lives of others.

- When sinners receive the gospel by repentance and faith, they are united together with Christ in the gospel. They die with and are buried and raised with Christ.

- The gospel was revealed in stages. All the prophets testified to it, Jesus lived it out, the Holy Spirit guided the disciples into all the truth of it, and Paul and his fellow disciples fully proclaimed it and made it the center of their lives and witness.

- Evangelists proclaim the gospel in different ways (Law and Gospel, Good Person Test, Romans Road, etc.), but always include a call for a person to repent of their sin and unrighteousness and to place their faith in Christ alone.

- Pastors need to present the gospel in every sermon.

- Confrontational Evangelism involves challenging unbelievers with the law and how their sin (law-breaking) separates them from God. This bad news approach is always followed by the good news of the gospel.

- The Type A and Type B approaches the disciples used worked together in perfect synergy to deliver the gospel.

- The disciple's balance of making sure they shared the truth in love mirrored their Lord, for "grace and truth came through Jesus Christ" (John 1:17).

- Christians, in a spirit of grace, need to love unbelievers enough to tell them the truth about their sin and unrighteousness before God.

- Jesus didn't call us to be serpents *or* doves but to be serpents *and* doves. We are called to be wise *and* graceful, not just one or the other.

- Instead of being "wise in your own sight" (Rom. 12:16), let us be "wise in Christ" (1 Cor. 4:10).

- The disciples argued, disputed, refuted, rebuked and debated when the truth of the gospel was at stake. They did it by speaking the truth in love and by grace and truth. We need to find this balance as well.

- When the Father draws someone to Jesus and the Holy Spirit is working ahead of us in regeneration (John 16:8-11), God can and does use our "spirited" arguments to lead people to Christ.

- We need to be loyal to the scriptures and not adopt approaches that fail to flip the pancake. If we present the whole counsel of God (Acts 20:24-27), we will have a fully baked gospel.

- A good evangelist is prepared to go on offense or defense depending on the situation.

- As defenders of the gospel and guardians of the truth, we must have wisdom and discernment to recognize the strange fire of false gospels and extinguish them.

- When we understand that the gospel has "enemies" (Rom. 11:28), that people will preach "a different gospel" (2 Cor. 11:4; cf., Gal. 1:6-9) and that Satan has a power over "unbelievers, to keep them from seeing the light of the gospel" (2 Cor. 4:4), we will take our "partnership in the gospel" (Philip. 1:5) more seriously.

- There are some self-proclaimed "Christians" who are ashamed of the gospel. They are ashamed of its exclusivity, ashamed that it is not politically correct, and some are ashamed because they don't really believe the message is true.

- Developing a proper fear of God, even if this brings about moments of fear and trembling in our witnessing, is a critical key to produce bold, healthy evangelism.

- The real boldness in evangelism isn't about starting a conversation, it's about turning that conversation towards the gospel.

- Let us be truthful and humble about our missed opportunities and missteps. Let us learn from these mistakes so we can be better used by God.

- Be careful not to count false converts. True converts will always count the cost and will never mind being measured before they are counted.

- A person who has shared the gospel for a good amount of time knows that in the majority of cases, there will not be a conclusion to our conversations—things may remain open-ended.

- Pray for unsaved family members and seek out others to pray with you. Realize that our prayers in this area are not a sprint, but a marathon.

- Instead of worrying about how a family dynamic may impede our gospel presentation, let us trust that the dynamic of the gospel will do the work it is called to do.

- The time to get on board the evangelism train is now, as all Christians are called to share the good news.

- Some plant and some water; some sow and another reaps. However, all of God's fellow workers rejoice together.

- Sharing the gospel is in the DNA of all Christians.

- To be Christ-like is to share the gospel.

Faithful in the Message

Mike Gendron, of Proclaiming the Gospel, talks about three Rs that are often left out of many gospel presentations. The first R is repentance. Our gospel conversations should always mention repentance, the change of mind that accompanies belief (Luke 3:8; Acts 3:19). Remember that Jesus said, "I have not come to call the righteous but sinners to repentance" (Luke 5:32). Jesus started His ministry by putting the gospel and repentance together when He said, "repent and believe in the gospel" (Mark 1:15). He concluded His ministry by saying "that repentance for the forgiveness of sins should be proclaimed in his name to all nations" (Luke 24:47). Jesus tied repentance together with salvation as did His disciples (Mark 6:12) and John the Baptist (Matt. 3:2).

The second R is resurrection. When Paul defined the gospel "by which you are being saved" (1 Cor. 15:2), he said that Christ "was raised on the third day in accordance with the Scriptures" (15:4). He added, "if Christ has not been raised, your faith is futile and you are still in your sins" (15:17). Paul also wrote that Jesus "was delivered up for our trespasses and raised for our justification" (Rom. 4:25). The resurrection is integral to the gospel message.

The third R is righteousness. The people to whom we witness need to hear that their "unrighteousness serves to show the righteousness of God" (Rom. 3:5). In contrasting Adam's unrighteousness with Christ's righteousness, Paul wrote, "as one trespass led to condemnation for all men, so one act of righteousness leads to justification and life for all men" (Rom. 5:18). We need to explain The Great Exchange—that the righteousness of Christ is substituted for our unrighteousness. Paul stated this clearly when he wrote, "For our sake he made him to be sin who knew no sin, so that in him we might become the righteousness of God" (2 Cor. 5:21).

As we have seen, the gospel message includes repentance, Christ's resurrection and Christ's righteousness imputed on our behalf. Let us not talk about faith but ignore repentance, focus on the crucifixion but overlook the resurrection, or neglect to contrast our unrighteousness with the righteousness of Christ. All three are necessary for us to be faithful in the message of the gospel.

Faithful in the Method

The Sinner's Prayer is a prayer a person is often prompted to recite in order to acknowledge that they are a sinner and in need of a Savior. Such a prayer is frequently found at the end of religious tracts or in books, urging unbelievers to "repeat these words from the bottom of your heart." Often times the evangelist will pray and ask their hearer to repeat something like this: "God, I know that I am a sinner. I believe that Jesus Christ died on the cross for my sins. I now accept Jesus as my personal Savior. Please save me. In Jesus' name, Amen."

In modern evangelism, many people assume that the Bible teaches a "Sinner's Prayer" for salvation. However, we should ask ourselves if this method of evangelism has a foundation in scripture. When we look at the New Testament, nowhere do we find such a prayer being used. The closest one might come is Luke 18, where the tax collector prayed, "God, be merciful to me, a sinner!" (Luke 18:13). We should note, though, that this man did not have to be led in such a prayer; it came from his own recognition of his utter sinfulness before God.

The Book of Acts should give us an indication as to whether the Sinner's Prayer is biblical. We see dozens of conversions in Acts without a single instance where the lost sinner is instructed or encouraged to "pray" for his or her salvation. Instead, their heart was opened by God (Acts 16:14) and they were told to "Believe in the Lord Jesus, and you will be saved" (16:31). When Nicodemus asked how one is born again, instead of giving him a prayer to pray, Jesus told him that salvation is a work of the Holy Spirit who comes and goes as He wills, for, "The wind blows where it wishes, and you hear its sound, but you do not know where it comes from or where it goes. So it is with everyone who is born of the Spirit" (John 3:8).

While many evangelists today accept and use the Sinner's Prayer as a way for an unbeliever to become a Christian, I believe it is not biblical and thus can lead to many false conversions. It is important to note that such a prayer often casts God as the passive Savior watching and waiting for the sinner to respond before He can move and bestow upon them His free gift of salvation. However, the only ones being gifted salvation have already been drawn by the Father (John 6:44, 65), received the gifts of faith (Eph. 2:8-9) and repentance (2 Tim. 2:25), and have had their hearts changed by God (Ezekiel 36:26). Any prayer or confession will reflect the reality of that initiation by God.

Could an evangelist lead someone, who has already experienced the above drawing, gifting and initiation by God, in the Sinner's Prayer and witness a true conversion? Of course! That will happen every time, with or without the Sinner's Prayer. However, since we have already seen that there is no legitimate example of such a prayer in the New Testament, we have to ask if such a prayer is helpful. God can and will use some of our unbiblical approaches to convert a person He has drawn to Himself, but that doesn't give us a license to use such approaches.

I have to admit that in my early years of evangelism, I did use the Sinner's Prayer and have asked people to repeat such a prayer after me. However, after growing in my knowledge of God's sovereignty in salvation, I have discontinued this practice. Then what do I do if a person shows a true understanding of the gospel message and expresses an intense desire to be saved? I simply open my Bible to Mark 1:15 and repeat the words of Jesus, who said, "Repent and believe in the gospel." If we are loyal to the biblical message, we would have already laid out the gospel clearly, including discussing the three Rs listed above. I would then show the person the response Paul and Silas gave to the Philippian jailer: "Believe in the Lord Jesus, and you will be saved" (Acts 16:31).

For some people, trusting in Christ begins with a simple prayer like "Jesus save me." The prayer did not save them but was just a confirmation of what the Holy Spirit had already been doing in their life (John 16:8). For others, the decision to trust in Jesus takes place gradually, as God draws them to Himself. They may have no recollection of a single moment when salvation came into their life.

If you tell someone that by simply praying the Sinner's Prayer, they are guaranteed to be saved, you are giving them a false assurance. A biblical assurance comes when "The Spirit himself bears witness with our spirit that we are children of God" (Rom. 8:16). If one's spirit has truly been changed by the Holy Spirit, repentance, belief in the gospel, justification and sanctification will follow in their life. Such a transformation will be publicly testified, not by repeating a prayer offered by an evangelist, but at baptism, and as they take up their cross and follow Christ.

Rather than using the Sinner's Prayer, we should let the Holy Spirit do His work, and be faithful in the method in which we reach the lost.

We remind everyone once again what God says about those sharing the gospel, "How beautiful are the feet of those who preach the good news!" (Rom. 10:15). 19th century Presbyterian theologian Charles Hodge tells us that a Christian who doesn't do any gospel walking has soft, pedicured feet. However, the feet of those doing the work of an evangelist are worn and scarred. Pastor Hodge asked, "if God were to look upon your feet, would He say they were beautiful?"

So far, we have seen that being on The Evangelism Circle includes pre-evangelism and evangelism. In our next section, we will complete the circle as we see how God sanctifies us in the post-evangelism stage.

O O O

PART THREE—POST-EVANGELISM

(19) FROM MILK TO MEAT

"Everyone who lives on milk is unskilled in the word of righteousness, since he is a child. But solid food is for the mature" (Heb. 5:13-14).

One year after the best-selling book *The Da Vinci Code* by Dan Brown came out, I was just getting on a stationary bicycle at the gym when I noticed a man on a bike next to me reading that book. I prayed that God would give me an opening to start a conversation. On the TV screen on the wall in front of us, the Atlanta Braves were playing the Houston Astros in the 2004 National League Division Series. Rafael Furcal – aware that once the Braves were eliminated, he was going to jail – hit the game-winning two-run home run in the 11th inning to tie the series at one game apiece. The man on the other bike looked at me and pointed to the TV saying, "Furcal shouldn't have even been in the game because of his DWI conviction." There was my opening.

I asked him his name and he said Mason. I asked Mason if he was enjoying the book, and he said he had just started it. I informed him that book was fiction, yet the author told ABC he is so confident in the validity of his claims that he could write the Da Vinci Code as a nonfictional book and not change a thing. I then went through all the historical inaccuracies and Mason was stunned. Mason became more concerned when I told him that Brown wrote in the book that Jesus married Mary Magdalene and intended her to be the head of the church; that the Bible is a product of man, not of God; that the New Testament is false testimony; that religion is a fairy tale; and that Christianity is rooted in paganism.[144]

Mason almost fell off his bike. As his peddling slowed down, he shut the book and asked me if I was a Bible scholar. I chuckled and said, "No, not at all. I'm just a Christian who knows what he believes." Mason humbly responded, "I guess I'm a Christian who doesn't know what he believes." We spent the rest of our time on the bike talking about his church and family. I checked to make sure he knew the gospel and he absolutely did. I told him I would pray for him and his family, and he asked if he could pray for me.

The previous discussion was between two Christians in the post-evangelism stage. I have experienced post-evangelism by both mentoring and by being mentored by other Christians. We should always be open to both, as "Iron sharpens iron, and one man sharpens another" (Proverbs 27:17). As we enter into the final phase in our three-fold evangelism formula, let's remember Peter's call for all Christians to "grow in the grace and knowledge of our Lord and Savior Jesus Christ. To him be the glory both now and to the day of eternity. Amen" (2 Pet. 3:18).

Defining Post-Evangelism

Post-evangelism involves teaching Christians how to live their lives with a clear understanding, experience and joy of living out the hope that the gospel brings, both now and in the future (1 Tim. 4:7-8). Paul, address-

---

[144] I have given similar warnings to Christians for heretical books like *Jesus Calling* by Sarah Young and *The Shack* by William P. Young. How great it would be to see Christians have more discernment about these types of books and remove them from their libraries (Acts 19:18-19).

ing "the saints and faithful brothers in Christ at Colossae" (Col 1:2), said we should "continue in the faith, stable and steadfast, not shifting from the hope of the gospel that you heard" (Col. 1:23). If we as Christians do not fully understand the hope of the gospel, we can be unstable in our faith and end up shifting from that hope to focusing on the things of the world. Paul also told the Colossians, "If then you have been raised with Christ, seek the things that are above, where Christ is, seated at the right hand of God. Set your minds on things that are above, not on things that are on earth. For you have died, and your life is hidden with Christ in God. When Christ who is your life appears, then you also will appear with him in glory. Put to death therefore what is earthly in you: sexual immorality, impurity, passion, evil desire, and covetousness, which is idolatry." (Col. 3:1-5).

Post-evangelism is reserved for genuine Christians, who have been justified by the root of the gospel; it is only for those who have already entered into a saving relationship with Christ but need to have their faith reinforced, or to grow in their faith. Post-evangelism can also be a time where we prepare ourselves for the other two aspects of The Evangelism Circle. We can learn how live out our faith with the goal of getting a hearing for the gospel (Col. 4:3-6). We can study to show ourselves approved (2 Tim. 2:15) to be able to not only become more proficient at answering questions (1 Pet. 3:15), but to be ready to share the gospel at any moment (2 Tim. 4:2). Post-evangelism can be our classroom for pre-evangelism and evangelism.

Maturing in Our Common Salvation

Christians can be on different levels of growth in our "common faith" (Titus 1:4), or "our common salvation" (Jude 1:3), in the post-evangelism stage. Paul told the Corinthians that wisdom comes from the Holy Spirit "so that your faith might not rest in the wisdom of men but in the power of God" (1 Cor. 2:5). In the next verse he says, "Yet among the mature we do impart wisdom" (2:6). This wisdom is so "that we might understand the things freely given us by God" (2:12). Paul then says, "to those who are spiritual" (2:13), "we have the mind of Christ" (2:16; cf., 1 John 5:20).

What about those who are not spiritually "mature"? Paul addresses those next, "But I, brothers, could not address you as spiritual people, but as people of the flesh, as infants in Christ. I fed you with milk, not solid food, for you were not ready for it. And even now you are not yet ready, for you are still of the flesh. For while there is jealousy and strife among you, are you not of the flesh and behaving only in a human way?" (1 Cor. 3:1-3). The writer of Hebrews said, "everyone who partakes only of milk is unskilled in the word of righteousness, for he is a babe" (Heb. 5:13, NKJV). The verses immediately following this passage tell the infant to move on to maturity, "But solid food is for the mature, for those who have their powers of discernment trained by constant practice to distinguish good from evil. Therefore let us leave the elementary doctrine of Christ and go on to maturity, not laying again a foundation of repentance from dead works, and of faith toward God, and of instruction about washings, the laying on of hands, the resurrection of the dead, and eternal judgment. And this we will do if God permits" (Heb. 5:14-6:3; cf., Titus 2:12-14; 1 Pet. 1:14).

New converts can learn the simplicity of the gospel and then allow that teaching to become stale in their lives. For some, time has minimized the true miracle of their salvation. Instead of sparking the fire within them by searching out the depths of their salvation, going on to maturity and stretching themselves, they convince themselves that it is safer to be an infant in Christ. They retreat to the comfort foods of the world in which they are so used to indulging. However, for a mature Christian, this retreat will never satisfy. Richard Owen Roberts writes, "Suppose one turns to Christ because of Christ's excellencies. How far toward Christ will that person turn? Because the motivation is God Himself, he will never cease turning. Those who are Christians for Christ's sake are never content with half measures. They simply cannot get close enough to Christ to be fully satisfied, and so they keep pressing closer and closer."[145]

The Bible tells infant Christians to "grow up in every way into him who is the head, into Christ" (Eph. 4:15; cf., Col. 2:19). A Christian growing up into Him will eventually confess that they want to "know Him and the power of his resurrection and the fellowship of His sufferings, being conformed to His death" (Philip. 3:10, NASB; cf., Gal. 6:14). An infant Christian, moving from milk on to maturity, is one who will "make every effort to add to your faith goodness; and to goodness, knowledge" (2 Pet. 1:5, NIV; cf., 2 Tim. 2:22). These new believers should, "Like newborn infants, long for the pure spiritual milk, that by it you may grow up into salvation" (1 Peter 2:2). All believers should go about "building yourselves up in your most holy faith" (Jude 1:20), "Be

---

[145] Richard Owen Roberts, *Repentance: The First Word of the Gospel*, p. 120.

sound in the faith" (Titus 1:13) and have "a sincere faith" (1 Tim. 1:5; 2 Tim. 1:5). Therefore, "Let those of us who are mature think this way" (Philip. 3:15).

Easier to be an Infant

It was midnight when 30-year-old Belinda from New York City clicked on the chat line: "Hello Patrick, I don't know exactly what I believe and feel stuck." After I went through the gospel with her, she said, "I believe this." Belinda then said, "I've kind of been cold, like not hot in my faith." When I asked her if she was attending a church and involved, studying God's word daily, involved in a daily prayer routine, or using the gifts God has given her in the body, she replied, "No, no, no and no."

When I told Belinda, "Okay, there's your problem," she agreed, but then went on to tell me about how she was sexually abused in foster homes and how this led to her falling into lesbian encounters. She later told me she now has a boyfriend but can't seem to get past her homosexual feelings. She also said she did not trust the church, because her pastor was fired for sexual immorality. I spent the next two hours talking to Belinda about passages like 1 Corinthians 6:9-11 and how mature Christians can say about the trap of homosexuality, "And such were some of you. But you were washed, you were sanctified, you were justified in the name of the Lord Jesus Christ and by the Spirit of our God" (1 Cor. 6:11). When I told her that she could truly find freedom in Christ, Belinda responded, "I want that more than anything, peace and freedom."

I again pointed her to all the verses about Christians training themselves for godliness, standing mature and growing up in the faith. Belinda responded, "It's easier to be an infant. It's hard to grow up and face stuff." I told Belinda it was time to take up her cross, or question whether she was really in the faith (2 Cor. 13:5). Belinda admitted, "I'm a lazy believer." When she said she could not muster up the strength to get back to Christ, I told her that making Christ the center of our life means that our Christian life is empowered by God: "work out your own salvation with fear and trembling, for it is God who works in you, both to will and to work for his good pleasure" (Philip. 2:12-13).

At the almost two-hour mark, Belinda surprised me when she said, "I love you Patrick, I've been on here a few times and you by far have had the most patience and most effective feedback. Thank you, it really meant a lot that you talked me through where I was. This will all make sense one day, God and his big divine puzzle." I told Belinda I would be praying for her that she in all things would grow up in Christ. God permitting, she will do so, as such godliness "holds promise for the present life and also for the life to come" (1 Tim. 4:8).

Supplement Your Faith

In his second letter, Peter said as a consequence of growing in knowledge of God, there will be qualities that we acquire—things that pertain to life and godliness, "For this very reason, make every effort to supplement your faith with virtue, and virtue with knowledge, and knowledge with self-control, and self-control with steadfastness, and steadfastness with godliness, and godliness with brotherly affection, and brotherly affection with love. For if these qualities are yours and are increasing, they keep you from being ineffective or unfruitful in the knowledge of our Lord Jesus Christ. For whoever lacks these qualities is so nearsighted that he is blind, having forgotten that he was cleansed from his former sins. Therefore, brothers, be all the more diligent to confirm your calling and election, for if you practice these qualities you will never fall. For in this way there will be richly provided for you an entrance into the eternal kingdom of our Lord and Savior Jesus Christ" (2 Pet. 1:5-11).

Peter added, "I will make every effort so that after my departure you may be able at any time to recall these things" (2 Pet. 1:15). We can recall these things thanks to the scripture that was not "produced by the will of man, but men spoke from God as they were carried along by the Holy Spirit" (2 Pet. 1:21). Praise God that in our post-evangelism, we have the "Scriptures" (2 Pet. 3:16) as our reminder so that we can "grow in the grace and knowledge of our Lord and Savior Jesus Christ" (3:18).

Age Defying Christians

One's chronological age does not necessarily determine whether a person is an infant in the faith. A person can be 80 and be an infant in Christ. Conversely, another person can be in their teens, or a young adult, and be mature in the faith. In 1 Corinthians 4:17, Timothy was called by Paul his "faithful child in the Lord." About a dozen years later, Paul told Timothy, "from childhood you have been acquainted with the sacred writings" (2 Tim. 3:15). He also said, "Let no one despise you for your youth" (1 Tim 4:12; cf., 5:1). While we can't be sure how old Timothy was at either of these times,[146] we know from the time he was called a "faithful child in the Lord" (1 Cor. 4:17), Paul referred to him as "A disciple" (Acts 16:1), "my fellow worker" (Rom. 16:21), "our brother" (2 Cor. 1:1) and "God's coworker in the gospel of Christ" (1 Thess. 3:2).

While a person can be chronologically young in age, they can be making progress in the faith and not be considered an infant. In Timothy's case, he was told to "set the believers an example in speech, in conduct, in love, in faith, in purity…so that all may see your progress" (1 Tim. 4:11-15). The Bible calls us to make progress in our faith whether we are a child in the Lord (2 Tim. 2:22) or are older men and women (Titus 2:2-3). For "you yourselves like living stones are being built up as a spiritual house, to be a holy priesthood, to offer spiritual sacrifices acceptable to God through Jesus Christ" (1 Pet. 2:5; cf., 1 Pet. 9-10; Rev. 1:6; Heb. 4:16).

At the same time, Paul told Timothy to treat the elder men as fathers, elder women as mothers, younger men as brothers, and younger women as sisters (1 Tim. 5:1-2). If you are young, show a deference to those who are aged (1 Pet. 5:5; Eph. 6:1; Lev. 19:32; Proverbs 16:31), obey your leaders (Heb. 13:7, 17; 1 Thess. 5:12-13; Titus 3:1) and be "be self-controlled" (Titus 2:6). If you are old, don't discourage those who are younger by always seeking out fault in them (Col. 3:21; Eph. 6:4).

Paul talked about how "Older men are to be sober-minded, dignified, self-controlled, sound in faith" (Titus 2:2). "Older women likewise are to be reverent in behavior" (Titus 2:3). Older women also "are to teach what is good, and so train the young women to love their husbands and children" (2:3-4). Paul mentioned a "sincere faith" that dwells in our grandparents and parents (if they are Christians) and in us (2 Tim. 1:5-6). "So then, as we have opportunity, let us do good to everyone, and especially to those who are of the household of faith" (Gal. 6:10). Peter said to "Clothe yourselves, all of you, with humility toward one another" (1 Pet. 5:5).

We should also ask fellow believers to pray that we "may stand mature" (Col. 4:12). That is why Paul said about those seeking leadership roles in the church, "He must not be a recent convert, or he may become puffed up with conceit" (1 Tim. 3:6). When we add to our faith godly knowledge, this will "keep you from being ineffective and unproductive in your knowledge of our Lord Jesus Christ" (2 Pet. 1:8; cf., Heb. 5:12).

---

[146] Commentators vary quite a bit on Timothy's age. Some say he was as young as 16 at this time, others suggest 30 or even 40.

Spiritual Development

The Apostle John seems to address the spiritual development, or the various stages of the Christian life, when he says, "I am writing to you, little children, because your sins are forgiven for his name's sake. I am writing to you, fathers, because you know him who is from the beginning. I am writing to you, young men, because you have overcome the evil one" (1 John 2:12-13).

Most commentators interpret "little children" as a reference to all believers as John uses this phrase elsewhere similarly, "Little children, you are from God" (1 John 4:4; cf., 1 John 2:1, 12, 13, 18, 28; 3:1-2, 7, 10, 18; 5:2, 21; 2 John 1:1, 4, 13; 3 John 1:4). When John mentioned "fathers", this is seen as a reference to mature Christians. For example, Paul told the Corinthians, "For I became your father in Christ Jesus through the gospel" (1 Cor. 4:15). Elsewhere Paul said, "Fathers, do not provoke your children to anger, but bring them up in the discipline and instruction of the Lord" (Eph. 6:4; cf., Heb. 12:9). The "young men" (Strong's Concordance, neaniskos, 3495) generally describes men between 20-40 years of age. The Rich Young Ruler who was challenged by Jesus to sell all his possessions was called a "young man" (Matt. 19:20). Before his Damascus Road conversion, Saul was referred to as "a young man" (Acts 7:58). The "young man" (Mark 14:51) who followed Jesus after His arrest is believed to be the author of the Gospel of Mark. Therefore, the breakdown in 1 John 2:12-13 is all believers (little children), mature believers (fathers) and new Christians to adult believers (young men).

While John, by now an older man, refers to all Christians, whether on milk or into solid food, as little children, every child of God needs to mature in the confidence that our sins are forgiven. We also need to know about our eternal God and that we can win the battle against the evil one. This way, whether one is a new Christian on milk, or a more established believer on solid food, they can move onto the goal of becoming a spiritual father, like John himself.

New Christians have an intense desire to learn more about God. New believers can be anyone from an adolescent to an adult to a senior. Whatever stage you start at, the goal moving forward is to never lose that desire. As we learn more about God, we move out of the infancy stage (1 Cor. 3:1; 1 Pet. 2:2) into a seasoned and well-versed (pun intended) Christian. Our ultimate goal on The Evangelism Circle is to become a spiritual father like Paul so we can say to the people we have discipled, "For I became your father in Christ Jesus through the gospel" (1 Cor. 4:15).

Adolescent to Senior

Whether one is an adolescent, adult, or a senior, there are many examples where God has used all three of these groups in His service. Joseph was 17 (Gen. 37:2) when God allowed him to be sold into Egypt, a move that would later see him take charge of all Egypt's affairs and preserve Jacob's family who were to become the nation of Israel. David was around 15 when he slew Goliath (1 Sam. 17). Josiah, one of Israel's most upright and humble leaders (2 Kings 22:2, 19, 23:25), became King of Israel at only 8 years old (2 Chron. 34:1). At sixteen, "In the eighth year of his reign, while he was still young, he began to seek the God of his father David" (2 Chron. 34:3, NKJV). Mary was in her teens when God called her to be the bearer of the Savior of the world (Luke 1:26-33). Paul told Timothy, "Let no one despise you for your youth, but set the believers an example in speech, in conduct, in love, in faith, in purity" (1 Tim. 4:12).

The twelve apostles Jesus called were likely either in their late teens or early twenties. Daniel was brought into King Nebuchadnezzar's court at about age 15 (Daniel 1) and over the next seventy years became an amazing testament to God and His coming Messiah (Daniel 9:24-26). Jeremiah was about 17 when God called him. He said, "Ah, Lord God! Behold, I do not know how to speak, for I am only a youth" (Jer. 1:6). However, over the next 40 years he preached to the nation of Judah about their lack of faith and trust in God.

Deborah, called "a mother in Israel" (Judges 5:7), judged and led Israel for 60 years. Anna lost her husband at a very early age and lived as a widow for approximately 60 years after that, worshiping and prophesying night and day about the Messiah to come. She was there when Mary and Joseph brought baby Jesus to the temple and at 84 years old gave witness of her Savior "to all who were waiting for the redemption of Jerusalem" (Luke 2:36-38). Timothy's grandmother Lois and mother Eunice had a huge impact on his faith (2 Tim. 1:5), teaching Timothy the scriptures "from childhood" (2 Tim. 3:15). Yes, senior citizens, you are still in the race. Joshua was a servant of the Lord (Judges 2:8) all the way up until his death at the age of 110 (Joshua 24:29). Noah, "a preacher of righteousness" (2 Pet. 2:5, NASB), lived to the ripe old age of 950 (Gen. 9:29)!

Augustine (A.D. 354-430) did not become a Christian until his early 30s and then went on to become a theological genius. Martin Luther (1483-1546) was thirty-four when he nailed his famous Ninety-five Theses to the door of the Wittenberg church, protesting the Catholic religion's trafficking in indulgences. John Bunyan (1628-1688) was thirty-two when he was jailed in his native England for preaching without the permission of the Church of England. Near the end of his 12-year prison term, he wrote The Pilgrim's Progress, one of the most widely read books by a Christian author. William Wilberforce (1759-1833) was 27 when he started a campaign to abolish slavery in his native England. His battle would last 47 years and culminate with victory right before his death at the age of 74. Baptist missionary William Carey (1761-1834), called the father of modern Protestant missions, was still in his teens when he could read the Bible in six languages. When he died at 73, he had translated and printed the Bible into forty languages.

Jonathan Edwards (1703-1758) entered Yale at 13 and was licensed to preach at 20. One of America's most accomplished theologians, his preaching helped spark the First Great Awakening. His final years were spent as a missionary pastor to Native Americans in Stockbridge, Massachusetts. William Booth (1829-1912) was thirty-six when he founded the Salvation Army. He and his wife were also itinerant evangelists into their senior years. At the age of 18, Dwight L. Moody (1837-1899), a shoe salesman from Chicago, became a Christian. For the remainder of his life, he traveled across the American continent, through Great Britain, and to other parts of the world in some of the greatest and most successful evangelistic revival meetings communities have ever known.

> *"The one indispensable requirement for producing godly, mature Christians is godly, mature Christians."* - Kevin DeYoung[147]

Godly mature Christians teach us and help us to store up the word of God in our hearts (Psalm 119:11). They "teach what accords with sound doctrine" (Titus 2:1). They show us how God will work in our lives as "we live by the Spirit" (Gal. 5:22-25). Those who take post-evangelism seriously will make it a point to seek out these godly teachers. This way, they will move from milk to solid food and may one day become teachers themselves (Heb. 5:12). This will result in a lifetime of learning, growing, and then equipping others.

---

[147] Kevin DeYoung, https://www.thegospelcoalition.org/blogs/kevin-deyoung/reaching-the-next-generation-hold-them-with-holiness/

Grounded in the Word

It is understandable that a new convert could get caught up in false doctrine, for there are a lot of false teachers in the world (Matt. 7:15; 2 Pet. 2:1, 3:16-17; Gal. 2:4; 2 Cor. 11:13; 1 Tim. 1:3; Heb. 13:9; Jude 1:4; Acts 20:30; 2 John 1:7-11). That is why we need to grow up and ground ourselves in the word, so we can test false teachers (1 John 4:1, 6; 2 John 1:7; Rev. 2:20; 1 Thess. 5:21; 1 Cor. 12:10) and determine which teachers are speaking the truth (Acts 17:11). When we face Jesus "before the judgment seat of Christ" (2 Cor. 5:10), we won't be able to say our maturity in the faith was halted because false teachers we sat under led us astray. No! Instead, Jesus may remind us what He said about false teachers like the Pharisees, "They are blind guides. And if the blind lead the blind, both will fall into a pit" (Matt. 15:14). Those who become Bereans and examine the scriptures (Acts 17:11) to see if what these blind teachers are saying is so will not be blind themselves and thus will avoid the pitfalls of stunted growth in their Christian life.

Be sure to be in a church where the word of God is being properly taught from the pulpit. Again, if you ground yourself in scripture, you will know where those pulpits are and where they are not. Paul, in taking on the false teachers in Corinth, said, "For we are not, like so many, peddlers of God's word, but as men of sincerity, as commissioned by God" (2 Cor. 2:17). He added, "We refuse to practice cunning or to tamper with God's word, but by the open statement of the truth we would commend ourselves to everyone's conscience in the sight of God" (2 Cor. 4:2). By grounding ourselves in scripture and "rightly handling the word of truth" (2 Tim. 2:15), we will know those who are commissioned by God and those who are not.

Our conscience in the sight of God will also be able to say, we will not "be children, tossed to and fro by the waves and carried about by every wind of doctrine, by human cunning, by craftiness in deceitful schemes" (Eph. 4:14). Commenting on this passage, Ray Stedman writes, "The Scriptures often exhort us to be child*like*, but never to be child*ish*. These are two very different things! Childlikeness is that refreshing simplicity of faith which believes God and acts without questioning. But childishness is described here by the apostle as instability and naivete."[148]

Those who sink themselves into the word of God (2 Tim. 2:15) will not be fooled by health and prosperity teachers who can "entice unsteady

---
[148] Ray Stedman, *Body Life*, p. 176.

souls. They have hearts trained in greed" (2 Pet. 2:14; cf., 2 Cor. 2:17). Infants who desire "to be rich fall into temptation, into a snare…. For the love of money is a root of all kinds of evils. It is through this craving that some have wandered away from the faith" (1 Tim. 6:9-10). Paul admonishes us to grow up in the faith and don't fall for those who are "lovers of money, proud, arrogant, abusive…having the appearance of godliness, but denying its power. Avoid such people" (2 Tim. 3:2, 5). Paul added, "these men also oppose the truth, men corrupted in mind and disqualified regarding the faith" (3:8-9). Even though such teachers are disqualified regarding the faith, many infants still follow them! However, those trained in godliness and mature in the faith avoid such people.

Grow Up in the Body

Paul exhorts Christians that "we are to grow up in every way into him who is the head, into Christ, from whom the whole body, joined and held together by every joint with which it is equipped, when each part is working properly, makes the body grow so that it builds itself up in love" (Eph. 4:15-16). Jesus is head over "the church, which is his body" (Eph. 1:22-23; cf., Col. 1:18). In His body, "you are fellow citizens with the saints and members of the household of God" (Eph. 2:19). In this household we are "being joined together…built together into a dwelling place for God by the Spirit" (2:21-22). This household is being built "until we all attain to the unity of the faith and of the knowledge of the Son of God, to mature manhood, to the measure of the stature of the fullness of Christ" (Eph. 4:13).

Gospel Teachers

Paul spoke about how the "truth of the gospel might be preserved for you" (Gal. 2:5, 14; cf., 2 Thess. 2:10; 2 Tim. 2:18, 25, 3:8). He said he was "a teacher… in faith and truth" (1 Tim. 2:7). In regard to the gospel, Paul said he "was appointed a preacher and apostle and teacher" (2 Tim 1:11). As we preserve the truth of the gospel, we need "to equip the saints for the work of ministry" (Eph. 4:12) so these saints "will also be qualified to teach others" (2 Timothy 2:2, NIV).

Jesus said "to go and learn" about what He taught us (Matt. 9:13). Those mentoring people in post-evangelism will help others grow in Christlikeness as we are called to imitate others who are following Christ (1 Cor. 4:16, 11:1; 1 Thess. 1:6; 2 Thess. 3:7, 9; Philip. 3:17; 2 Tim. 3:10; Heb. 13:7). As disciples of Christ, let us encourage each other as our mutual "faith is growing abundantly" (2 Thess. 1:3). Let us go on to maturity in our post-evangelism, preparing ourselves to preach and teach the gospel. We need to get off milk and into the meat, heeding this warning from Hebrews, "For though by this time you ought to be teachers, you need someone to teach you again the basic principles of the oracles of God. You need milk, not solid food, for everyone who lives on milk is unskilled in the word of righteousness, since he is a child. But solid food is for the mature" (Heb. 5:12-14).

○ ○ ○

20) A TEACHABLE DISCIPLE

"Wisdom is with those who receive counsel"
(Proverbs 13:10, NASB).

In our post-evangelism, we need to have a teachable spirit. If we are going to grow from milk into solid food, we should have the mindset of a lifelong learner. Keep in mind that Jesus called us to be disciples. The word disciple literally means a learner or student. Since we are a disciple of Christ, we learn from Him. Jesus "called his disciples and chose" (Luke 6:13) them. Christ's "disciples followed him" (Matt. 8:23; cf., Mark 6:1). He went about "instructing" (Matt. 11:1), "teaching" (Mark 9:31), and even at times rebuking (Mark 8:33) His disciples. "The disciples did as Jesus had directed them" (Matt. 26:19). He said, "Whoever does not bear his own cross and come after me cannot be my disciple" (Luke 14:27) and "If you abide in my word, you are truly my disciples" (John 8:31). He added, "By this all people will know that you are my disciples, if you have love for one another" (John 13:35). Jesus said His followers would bring glory to the Father, "By this my Father is glorified, that you bear much fruit and so prove to be my disciples" (John 15:8).

After the Lord's resurrection, "in Antioch the disciples were first called Christians" (Acts 11:26). Jesus' "disciples were filled with joy and with the Holy Spirit" (Acts 13:52). They followed His orders to "make disciples" (Matt. 28:19) and "strengthen" (Luke 22:32) each other: "When they had preached the gospel to that city and had made many disciples, they returned to Lystra and to Iconium and to Antioch, strengthening the souls of the disciples, encouraging them to continue in the faith, and saying that through many tribulations we must enter the kingdom of God" (Acts 14:21-22; cf., 18:23, 20:1).

Disciple Parable

Jesus gave us one of the best explanations of being a disciple in Luke chapter 6, "He also told them a parable: 'Can a blind man lead a blind man? Will they not both fall into a pit?' A disciple is not above his teacher, but everyone when he is fully trained will be like his teacher. Why do you see the speck that is in your brother's eye, but do not notice the log that is in your own eye? How can you say to your brother, 'Brother, let me take out the speck that is in your eye,' when you yourself do not see the log that is in your own eye? You hypocrite, first take the log out of your own eye, and then you will see clearly to take out the speck that is in your brother's eye" (Luke 6:39-42). When the parable, the blind leading the blind, is quoted in Matthew 15, the Pharisees are the "blind guides" (Matt. 15:14). In Luke's context, the blindness is related to judging hypocritically (6:41-42). In both instances, Jesus is warning His disciples against following blind/false teachers.

Jesus did not want His disciples to end up like the Pharisees, as a Pharisee will just reproduce another Pharisee (the blind leading the blind, see Matt. 23:15). He also did not want us to end up following a teacher so blind to their own sinfulness that they hypocritically judge others for violating the same law they themselves are breaking (Luke 6:41-42). In the end, we will become like those we follow. Sit under a blind/false teacher, and as their disciple, you will only reproduce their error and end up falling into the same pit as them.

One Teacher

What did Jesus mean when He said, "A disciple is not above his teacher" (Luke 6:40)? Jesus told His disciples elsewhere, "you have one teacher" (Matt. 23:8). When we make Jesus the one teacher to whom we are accountable, we will never fall into a pit, because "No one ever spoke like this man!" (John 7:46; cf., Luke 4:32). A student will be restricted by the limitations of their teacher, but Jesus had "the Spirit without measure" (John 3:34). That's why "the crowds were astonished at his teaching, for he was teaching them as one who had authority, and not as their scribes" (Matt. 7:28-29).

The one teacher to follow is Jesus, including through those who authentically imitate Him. Paul encouraged his disciples to follow his example only to the extent that he was following Christ, "Be imitators of me, as I am of Christ" (1 Cor 11:1). In writing to the church of the Thessalonians about the spreading of the gospel, Paul said, "you became imitators of us and of the Lord" (1 Thess. 1:6). When urging the Philippians to move on to maturity, Paul said, "Brothers, join in imitating me, and keep your eyes on those who walk according to the example you have in us" (Philip. 3:17; cf., 1 Cor. 4:16, 2 Thess. 3:7, 9; 2 Tim. 3:10).

A New Testament to Imitate

Matthew was an apostle of Jesus, as were John and Peter. These disciples of Christ gave us two gospels, five epistles and The Book of Revelation. Paul, "called to be an apostle" (Rom. 1:1), wrote thirteen epistles. Just one degree of separation away from these men was Mark, a disciple of Peter who wrote The Gospel of Mark. We also have Luke, a disciple of Paul, who wrote the Gospel of Luke and The Book of Acts. Additionally, just a degree of separation away were James and Jude, both believed to be half-brothers of Christ (Jude 1:1). They both became believers, and thus disciples, after the resurrection (John 7:5; Acts 1:14). Finally, the author of Hebrews says he was taught by eyewitnesses of the Lord (Heb. 2:3) and was a "brother" of Timothy (13:23).[149] The twenty-seven

---

[149] The writer of Hebrews states that the message of our salvation "was declared at first by the Lord, and it was attested to us by those who heard" (Heb. 2:3). Since "us" included the author, it appears he was not an eyewitness of Jesus, but received information from those who heard Jesus.

New Testament scriptures make us disciples of Jesus through these men who imitated Christ in their life, penned those very writings under the inspiration of the Holy Spirit (2 Pet. 1:21), and were loyal to their Lord's teaching.

As the list of disciples and faithful teachers of Christ grew, the early church was told to "Remember your leaders, those who spoke to you the word of God. Consider the outcome of their way of life, and imitate their faith" (Heb. 13:7; cf., 13:17; 1 Thess. 5:12). There have been many disciples of Christ down through the millennia that have spoken the word of God faithfully. As long as we discern that their way of life is a truthful reflection of Christ and that they are "rightly handling the word of truth" (2 Tim. 2:15), we are called to imitate their faith.

Duplicating Teachers

Finally, Jesus said, "everyone when he is fully trained will be like his teacher" (Luke 6:40). When we sit under a teacher who is imitating Christ in both their life and teaching, we will have secured a faith that has been fully trained—a faith which endures to the end. Such teachers create disciples who are on the same path as they are, so that in the end, the disciples will be like their teachers. Being involved in this duplication process, we can say with Paul, "For I became your father in Christ Jesus through the gospel" (1 Cor. 4:15).

Self-Evaluating Teachers

In 2017, I was preparing a class called "Servant Leadership" that I would teach at a Christian seminar in Uganda. As I put together the booklet, a disturbing thought crossed my mind—am *I* a servant leader? Have I done the very things about which I am going to be teaching? I had to be honest with myself and wonder if I would get a passing grade on the very thing I was about to tell my African brothers and sisters to do.

As I started the seminar in Masaka, Uganda, in a room packed with 100 African Christians, I admitted to them I had come up short at much of what I was about to teach them. As a demonstration of my Christian path, I walked in front of them in an erratic pattern confessing that too much of my own Christian walk was like this. I then asked them if despite that, God could make my crooked line straight. I told them God is perfect, people are not. He is the straight path; we are the crooked road. The comforting thing to know is that God will achieve his perfect plan through the imperfect actions of people. As God told King Cyrus, "I will go before thee, and make the crooked places straight" (Isa. 45:2, KJV; cf., Psalm 5:8).

Do leaders stop self-evaluating or learning when they become teachers? If we are a follower of Christ, we are His eternal students and Jesus is our infinite teacher. Jesus' disciples will always be students, even when we become teachers with our own students. Christ's students do not graduate and think—I am the expert at this, I have no more to learn. Just as we teach our students how to become servants, we should be constantly re-evaluating our own status as servants.

Teachers should think of themselves as perpetual students and seek out mentors of their own. One is never too old or wise for a mentor. Teachers, "Let the wise hear and increase in learning" (Proverbs 1:5). "In an abundance of counselors there is safety" (Proverbs 11:14), and "Iron sharpens iron, and one man sharpens another" (Proverbs 27:17). Teachers will remind their students that Paul had an unquenchable desire to grow in the knowledge of Christ, "that I may know him and the power of his resurrection" (Philip. 3:10). Teachers should always want that for their students and for themselves. When Paul told Timothy to devote himself to the public reading of scripture and to teaching, he said to use your gift "so that all may see your progress. Keep a close watch on yourself and on the teaching. Persist in this, for by so doing you will save both yourself and your hearers" (1 Tim. 4:15-16).

Apollos, a Teachable Disciple

Apollos was an Alexandrian from Egypt and an important figure with Paul at Corinth (1 Cor. 3:6, 4:6). However, Apollos knew only the baptism of John. John had preached the coming of the Messiah, baptized Christ, identified Him as the Son of God, and had proclaimed the baptism of the Holy Spirit; nonetheless, John had not seen the cross, the resurrection of Jesus, nor the great Day of Pentecost before he died. If we assume Apollos had been baptized by John or one of his disciples, it makes sense that he may have not yet learned about the new light which the outpouring of the Spirit at Pentecost had thrown upon Christ's death and resurrection—as indicated from Acts 19:2-3.

Apollos was competent in the Scriptures, yet he did not have complete knowledge. When Aquila and Priscilla, both close associates of Paul and approved by him (1 Cor. 16:19; 2 Tim. 4:19; Rom. 16:3-4; Acts

18:1-4), heard Apollos speak, they took him aside and explained to him the way of God more accurately: "Now a Jew named Apollos, a native of Alexandria, came to Ephesus. He was an eloquent man, competent in the Scriptures. He had been instructed in the way of the Lord. And being fervent in spirit, he spoke and taught accurately the things concerning Jesus, though he knew only the baptism of John. He began to speak boldly in the synagogue, but when Priscilla and Aquila heard him, they took him aside and explained to him the way of God more accurately. And when he wished to cross to Achaia, the brothers encouraged him and wrote to the disciples to welcome him. When he arrived, he greatly helped those who through grace had believed" (Acts 18:24-27).

Apollos, after being taught the ways of God more accurately, was now better equipped. With the encouragement of fellow believers, he went about "powerfully refuting the Jews in public, showing by the Scriptures that the Christ was Jesus" (18:28). Paul used himself and Apollos as examples of those who plant and water in evangelism, "I planted, Apollos watered, but God gave the growth" (1 Cor. 3:6).

Some post-evangelism points here: those who do believe through grace still need help to grow in their knowledge of the ways of God more accurately. Apollos humbled himself and showed himself approachable and teachable before more learned Christians—so should we. Christians, who need to grow in their knowledge of scripture, can add to their faith by listening to more mature believers. When explaining the way of God more accurately to Apollos, Aquila and Priscilla "took him aside." They showed grace by not correcting him publicly.

Areas of Uncertainties

"Everyone's faith has a central core of firm conviction surrounded by an area of uncertainties." - George E. Sweazey[150]

While our goal is to grow into a foundational core of firm convictions, at the same time there are going to be uncertainties or doubts all of us have about the faith. Part of our post-evangelism training is addressing those uncertainties. While many of our uncertainties can be answered with further study, sometimes we have to admit like Job, "I have uttered what I did not understand, things too wonderful for me, which I did not know" (Job 42:3). Moreover, as Isaiah reminds us of God, "For as the heavens are higher than the earth, so are my ways higher than your ways and my thoughts than your thoughts" (Isa. 55:9). Paul adds, "Oh, the

---

[150] George E. Sweazey, *Effective Evangelism*, p. 51.

depth of the riches and wisdom and knowledge of God! How unsearchable are his judgments and how inscrutable his ways!" (Rom. 11:33). Who of us knows the decretive will of God, where the Lord sovereignly brings to pass whatsoever He wills, "The secret things belong to the Lord our God" (Deut. 29:29). Many people chase after knowledge that God has not chosen to reveal. Sometimes we have to admit to ourselves that God has allowed us to go only so far and no farther.

While acknowledging that there are some unsearchable things about God, we also know that we have been given the God-breathed scriptures that are "profitable for teaching, for reproof, for correction, and for training in righteousness, that the man of God may be complete, equipped for every good work" (2 Tim. 3:16-17). To be properly equipped for every good work, there are certain truths about the faith in which mature Christians must train themselves. Paul told Timothy that overseers and deacons "must keep hold of the deep truths of the faith" (1 Timothy 3:9, NIV). When defining the gospel, Paul said, "For I delivered to you as of first importance what I also received" (1 Corinthians 15:3). Jude tells us "to contend for the faith that was once for all delivered to the saints" (Jude 1:3). The word "faith" in this passage is the Greek word *pistis,* which means a belief in or conviction of the truth.

A Deeper Dive

Many Christians today want to stay in the shallow end of the pool. They will just go from one devotional to another while neglecting to ever read the Bible. Some will object, "The devotionals I read quote the Bible extensively." This may be true, but most rarely quote the Bible in its proper context, and even those that do should never be a substitute for reading God's word. Others have a checklist of the latest Christian best-sellers they must read, while they neglect to read the best-selling book of all time—the Bible. Ray Stedman writes, "There are fads and fashions in the religious life, and immature Christians are forever riding the crest of some new fad. They are always running after the newest book or teacher, extolling them as the ultimate answer to spiritual need. This instability and 'short spiritual attention span' are marks of immaturity. They do not seem to understand that the oldest book, the oldest teacher, is the most exciting of all: the Bible!"[151]

I am not saying that Christians should never read Bible-centered books. My library at home is full of them. I am saying that the *center* of our reading should be the Bible. It is perfectly appropriate to supplement

---

[151] Ray Stedman, *Body Life*, p. 177.

our Bible reading with books that are faithful to God's word. However, if your reading wanders off into popular books like *Jesus Calling*,[152] *The Shack*[153] or *Heaven is for Real*,[154] all of which include disturbing unbiblical writings, get yourself out of the wading pool and take a deeper dive.

To be a teachable disciple, we need to be trained and equipped by God-gifted "pastors and teachers" (Eph. 4:11, NASB) who are in the deep end of God's word, "rightly handling the word of truth" (2 Tim. 2:15). Such teachers help us to "be sound in the faith" (Titus 1:13), to have "a sincere faith" (1 Tim. 1:5; 2 Tim. 1:5) and to "stand mature" (Col. 4:12; cf., 1:28; 1 Cor. 14:20) in the faith. This way you can go about "building yourselves up in your most holy faith" (Jude 1:20) so as not to be "ineffective or unfruitful in the knowledge of our Lord Jesus Christ" (2 Pet. 1:8).

In our post-evangelism, God wants to take us from the shallow to the deep end so that we can "be a good servant of Christ Jesus, being trained in the words of the faith and of the good doctrine" (1 Tim. 4:6). This is "so that the truth of the gospel might be preserved for you" (Gal. 2:5). Few ever mine the truths of the gospel in the shallow end. The real nuggets of the good news are found in the deep end. The deeper we understand the gospel, the more we will "advance the gospel" (Philip. 1:12).

Acknowledging and Taking on Doubts

A Barna Group survey in 2017 showed that of American adults who self-identify as Christian, 25% said they experienced spiritual doubt. 40% admitted having experienced doubt in the past but had worked through it. 35% actually claimed to have never experienced doubt at all. I found the most interesting response from "devout practicing Christians": 19% said they still experience doubt. 42% of this same group said they had worked through their doubts due to support systems and resources

---

[152] See Warren B. Smith and his book *Another Jesus Calling*. Young has said that "God Calling", a book that practices medium channeling, was her inspiration and the method used for "Jesus Calling." Since medium channeling is something God specifically forbids (Deut. 18:10-12), why would any Christian give validity to Young's book? Young claims in her book that Jesus channelled things to her like, we are co-creators with Jesus. About our Savior's birth, Young's Jesus said, "it was a dark night for Me." The original 2004 edition of Jesus Calling has seen many of these so-called chanelled quotes changed in future editions after critics complained of there heresy. Did Young "hear" her Jesus figure wrong the first time? If Young and her publisher can change Jesus' alleged words to her, how can any Christian trust the rest of what Young's Jesus said?

[153] See Albert Mohler, The Shack — The Missing Art of Evangelical Discernment, https://albertmohler.com/2017/03/06/shack-missing-art-evangelical-discernment

[154] See Tim Challies, *Heaven Is For Real*, https://www.challies.com/book-reviews/heaven-is-for-real/

of a church community. Believers should acknowledge and wrestle with their doubts. By working with apologetic resources and attending Bible study groups in a church community, they become better prepared to answer not only their doubts and uncertainties, but their family, friends and neighbors' doubts as well.[155]

One of Satan's main goals in the Bible is to stir up doubt. He did it with Adam and Eve in the Garden (Gen. 3:1-7) and tried to do it with Jesus in the wilderness (Matt. 4:1-11). In fact, the Bible contains many examples of believers who doubted (Abraham, Gen. 17:17; Sarah, Gen. 18:12; Elijah, 1 Kings 19:1-18; Peter, Matt. 14:31, 26:74; Zechariah, Luke 1:20; John the Baptist, Luke 7:20; the Apostles seeing the resurrected Christ, Luke 24:38; Thomas, John 20:24-25). That is why it is important to "Put on the whole armor of God, that you may be able to stand against the schemes of the devil" (Eph. 6:11). The most important part of that armor is "the sword of the Spirit, which is the word of God" (6:17).

Sometimes the key to a more solid faith is to confess our doubts before God. The father of a demonic possessed son came to Jesus and pleaded, "if you can do anything, have compassion on us and help us" (Mark 9:22). Jesus said to him, "'If you can'! All things are possible for one who believes" (9:23). The father's response was to again ask for help for his son, but this time also for himself, "Immediately the father of the child cried out and said, 'I believe; help my unbelief!'" (9:24). After the father cast his doubts before Jesus, his Lord then cast the demon out of his son. If doubt is present in our lives, that does not mean faith is absent. We should teach ourselves to question our doubts not our faith!

Nobody who goes into evangelism goes in without some uncertainties. Some have fewer questions than others, but we all have some. A believer does not have to possess an exhaustive knowledge of the Christian faith to be used by God in evangelism, but we should be grounded in "matters of first importance" (1 Cor. 15:3-4). Mark Dever writes, "None of us ever has a complete understanding of the gospel, but we must have a clear idea of the basics of our message, and we must be clear in our expression of them."[156] Will Metzger writes, "We all have blind spots."[157] He adds, "No one can claim to have the perfect gospel outline or the right approach for each situation. We are all humbled by the sovereign and compassionate God who works as he wills to bring someone

---

[155] https://www.barna.com/research/two-thirds-christians-face-doubt/
[156] Mark Dever, *The Gospel and Personal Evangelism*, p. 63.
[157] Will Metzger, *Tell The Truth*, p. 32.

to himself. The amount of truth God will use to regenerate a person is something we cannot dictate."[158]

Have uncertainties or doubts? Cast them before God like the father with the demon possessed son did. Do like the apostles who said to the Lord, "Increase our faith!" (Luke 17:5). Also remember, when skeptics or even so-called believers try to place uncertainty or doubt in our hearts, "We destroy arguments and every lofty opinion raised against the knowledge of God, and take every thought captive to obey Christ" (2 Cor. 10:5).

We need a faith that doesn't use a rope-a-dope strategy[159] where we cover up on the ropes and take punches hoping that our opponent just becomes exhausted. We need to get in the center of the ring and counter our opponent's best shots and trust that the Holy Spirit will take them captive to obey Christ.

---

[158] Ibid., p. 99.
[159] Former world heavyweight champion boxer Muhammad Ali used the rope-a-dope strategy in defeating George Foreman in 1974.

21) YOUR BEST LIFE NOW VERSUS SUFFERING FOR CHRIST

"If anyone suffers as a Christian, let him not be ashamed, but let him glorify God" (1 Pet. 4:16).

Megachurch prosperity teacher Joel Osteen is a popular speaker and author. He has a large following, which includes many infant Christians. The title of his best-selling book, "Your Best Life Now", sums up his weekly messages. For Osteen, your speech controls your life. At the moment you speak something out, you give birth to it—positive or negative. He tells us that we need to know that God wants to pour out favor upon us through our positive speech. Stop the negative thoughts and speech, Osteen says, because you are cancelling out God's plans for your favor in the here and now. Any suffering in our lives just comes from our negative attitudes.

Osteen slips in a brief, perfunctory statement at the end of his self-help prosperity sermons to tell people to turn to Christ.[160] However, Osteen followers will turn to Jesus only as far as they think they must, and no farther, in order to get what they want. When suffering and persecution interrupt or derail Osteen's promises, they fall away. Osteen's model is to get the most favor out of God and live a glorious life now. To contrast, the biblical model is suffering now, glory at the end.

Those who are drawn to Christianity with the hope that it will bring them prosperity respond by "trying" Christianity to see if it will work for them. However, because they have no root of the true gospel in themselves, they may endure for a while; then, when tribulation or persecution arises on account of the word, or the deceitfulness of riches overtake them, they inevitably fall away. That is because "Your Best Life Now" is theology derived from bad soil (Mark 4:13-19). Bad soil cannot produce good fruit, and those who have been taught to till away on rocky ground will soon become exhausted.

The Good Soil of Post-Evangelism

Christians who are "sown on the good soil are the ones who hear the word and accept it and bear fruit, thirtyfold and sixtyfold and a hundredfold" (Mark 4:20). Also note, for those "in the good soil, they are those who, hearing the word, hold it fast in an honest and good heart, and bear fruit with patience" (Luke 8:15). This good soil, that God has prepared, makes them hear, receive, and respond to the seed planted within them. These new converts hold fast to scripture, allowing God's word to grow in them. Their honest and good heart means they are interested in the truth and keep false teachings far from them (Proverbs 30:8; 2 Pet. 1:12). Because of all this, they bear fruit with patience.

What does it mean that we bear fruit with patience? If we are patient and faithful through trials, we will bear much fruit. When Paul addressed the faithful brothers in Christ at Colossae, he reminded them that "the word of the truth, the gospel, which has come to you" (Col. 1:5-6) was bearing fruit and increasing. Paul also taught the Colossians (and all churches) that persecutions and trials will follow our acceptance and

---

[160] At the end of his sermon, Osteen will give a short "gospel" message inviting people to accept Christ. The problem is that call doesn't have any connection with the pep talk he just gave.

subsequent proclamation of the gospel. Indeed, Paul himself was "suffering" (Col. 1:24) in jail for his spreading and defense of the gospel when he wrote to the Colossians. Persecutions, trials, sufferings and afflictions are a reality for all true Christians. "All who desire to live a godly life in Christ Jesus will be persecuted" (2 Tim. 3:12). Because of such persecution, trials and sufferings, *patience* is required for us to bear fruit. We persevere through such trials and persecution, patiently waiting on the Lord to make our fruit ripen (Philip. 2:13).

Those who don't have much fruit in their lives are often impatient, many times because they are sitting under false teachers who are telling them to just speak something into existence that their heart desires. What they are missing out on is what the heart of mature Christians already knows: "Count it all joy, my brothers, when you meet trials of various kinds, for you know that the testing of your faith produces steadfastness. And let steadfastness have its full effect, that you may be perfect and complete, lacking in nothing" (James 1:1-4).

Those standing on the good soil are called to hold fast to the word of God with an honest and good heart. When that happens, the gospel will bear fruit and increase. In our post-evangelism, we will learn that despite the many persecutions, sufferings and afflictions that are sure to come, by being patient, we will bear fruit as we are tested with trials of various kinds. The afflictions we suffer can bear fruit, for we know the "God of all comfort, who comforts us in all our affliction, so that we may be able to comfort those who are in any affliction, with the comfort with which we ourselves are comforted by God" (2 Cor. 1:3-4).[161]

Rejoice in Sufferings

Christianity teaches that there is redemptive value in suffering. For example, scripture says, "we rejoice in our sufferings, knowing that suffering produces endurance, and endurance produces character, and character produces hope" (Rom. 5:3-4). How does suffering produce endurance? Many new converts, and even some older Christians, panic when persecutions, trials, sufferings or afflictions arise. They cry out and ask God, "Why is this happening to me? What have I done?" I would like to suggest that Christians who dedicate their walk to holding fast to scripture have

---

[161] Persecutions, trials, sufferings, and afflictions can and do come in different forms for Christians. While such trials are to the extreme for Christians in concentration camps in North Korea or the persecuted churches in China, India and Pakistan, Christians in the West can suffer persecution to a less severe extent by having our speech curtailed. One thing is for sure, no Christian is exempt from trials, sufferings and afflictions.

developed a patient and honest heart when it comes to trials of various kinds. They have learned what it means to endure through these trials.

God used a chronic pain condition in my neck as one of the ways to draw me to Himself. In the first few years after my conversion, I, too, cried out to the Lord, "Why me?" I even told God that if He wanted to use me as a tool to advance His kingdom, He would have to heal me. How naïve I was about God's grace and His power. I can tell you that almost 30 years later I still have chronic neck pain, and yet our great God has used me over and over again.

God has shown me that suffering produces endurance. Yes, at first, I panicked. However, I then became a student of the Bible and held fast to God's word. I developed a patient and honest heart about my chronic pain and God gave me endurance to press on. God specifically taught me about endurance when I read where Paul had prayed for a thorn in his flesh to be removed: "a thorn was given me in the flesh, a messenger of Satan to harass me, to keep me from becoming conceited. Three times I pleaded with the Lord about this, that it should leave me. But he said to me, 'My grace is sufficient for you, for my power is made perfect in weakness.' Therefore I will boast all the more gladly of my weaknesses, so that the power of Christ may rest upon me. For the sake of Christ, then, I am content with weaknesses, insults, hardships, persecutions, and calamities. For when I am weak, then I am strong" (2 Cor. 12:7-10).[162]

Paul prayed three times for the Lord to remove this fleshly ailment.[163] I can promise you that I prayed a lot more than three times! Yet, the apostle's words have become such an encouragement to me over the decades. I discovered that God's grace is truly sufficient for me and that His power and strength are displayed in and through my weaknesses (2 Cor. 4:7-12). So, how can suffering produce endurance? At first you may panic, but then you experience God calming the storm. A short while later, that panic starts to rise again, but then you remember how you endured when God brought you through the first time, and the panic does not overtake you as much. Over time, your endurance grows. You learn to release all your anxiety "with thanksgiving" (Philip. 4:6) to the Lord.

---

[162] There are many interpretations of what Paul's thorn in the flesh was. We do know that elsewhere he said, "it was because of a bodily ailment that I preached the gospel" (Gal. 4:13). He also talked about his bad eyes (Gal. 6:11). Paul said the affliction was given to him by a "messenger of Satan" (2 Cor. 12:7). When God allowed Satan to torment Job, "Satan went out from the presence of the Lord and struck Job with loathsome sores from the sole of his foot to the crown of his head" (Job 2:7; cf., 1 Cor. 5:5).

[163] Notice that Paul specifically said his thorn was "in the flesh" (2 Cor. 12:7), countering many who try to interpret Paul's thorn as a spiritual ailment.

When you do that, "the peace of God, which surpasses all understanding, will guard your hearts and your minds in Christ Jesus" (4:7).

Ray Stedman, one of the 20th century's foremost pastors, commenting on the passage in Romans 5, writes, "You learn something about the Lord – you learn how gracious he is. You learn that he can handle events in ways that you couldn't dream of or anticipate. You see him work things out in ways that you could never have guessed. So, the third and fourth times a trial comes up, you are steadier. You don't panic, you don't bail out. You stay under and let it work itself out. That is what Paul is saying here. Suffering produces steadiness [endurance]. If you didn't suffer you would never have that quality."[164]

You become even more aware of how the Lord endures us when you start to read and absorb God's word, which becomes the remedy to all our distress. Listen to what Paul, the "apostle to the Gentiles" (Rom. 11:13), said about how God gave him endurance through his many afflictions, "For we do not want you to be unaware, brothers, of the affliction we experienced in Asia. For we were so utterly burdened beyond our strength that we despaired of life itself. Indeed, we felt that we had received the sentence of death. But that was to make us rely not on ourselves but on God who raises the dead. He delivered us from such a deadly peril, and he will deliver us. On him we have set our hope that he will deliver us again" (2 Cor. 1:8-10).

We come to learn that God will indeed deliver us again and again. God will always "provide the way of escape, that you may be able to endure it" (1 Cor. 10:13). Paul says, "If we are afflicted, it is for your comfort and salvation; and if we are comforted, it is for your comfort, which you experience when you patiently endure the same sufferings that we suffer" (2 Cor. 1:6). Of course, our evangelism is centered around enduring trials that will push back against us, "As for you, always be sober-minded, endure suffering, do the work of an evangelist, fulfill your ministry" (2 Tim. 4:5). Finally, remember, "If we endure, we will also reign with him" (2 Tim. 2:12).

Character and Suffering

How does suffering produce character? Endurance through suffering is what develops our character. Biblical character is an unattainable achievement for those who do not embrace suffering or understand the endurance that comes from it. However, for those that do, our character

---

[164] Ray Stedman, https://www.raystedman.org/new-testament/romans/rejoicing-in-suffering. I credit Pastor Stedman, who went to be with the Lord in 1992, for the insights I wrote about on this passage.

grows when we experience God's repeated faithfulness in growing our endurance through trials of many kinds. In the end, the suffering that produced endurance, and the endurance that produces our character, ultimately produces our hope. This hope is based on the fact that "since we have been justified by faith, we have peace with God through our Lord Jesus Christ" (Rom. 5:1). Furthermore, we know that this "hope does not put us to shame, because God's love has been poured into our hearts through the Holy Spirit who has been given to us" (5:5).

God has delivered me again and again through physical pain and various trials in my life because of my "living hope through the resurrection of Jesus Christ from the dead" (1 Pet. 1:3). Let all of us on The Evangelism Circle understand that "now for a little while you may have had to suffer grief in all kinds of trials. These have come so that the proven genuineness of your faith—of greater worth than gold, which perishes even though refined by fire—may result in praise, glory and honor when Jesus Christ is revealed" (1 Pet. 1:6-7, NIV).

Suffering for Christ's Sake

Paul wanted to know Christ so intimately that he said it was of paramount importance "that I may know him and the power of his resurrection, and may share his sufferings" (Philip. 3:10). Earlier, he told the Philippians, "For it has been granted to you that for the sake of Christ you should not only believe in him but also suffer for his sake" (Philip. 1:29). In regeneration, we are raised from the dead. In sanctification, we experience the power of Christ's resurrection and share in His sufferings. As Paul said, "Now if we have died with Christ, we believe that we will also live with him" (Rom. 6:8; cf., Gal. 2:20).

Jesus, the God-man, "learned obedience through what he suffered" (Heb. 5:8). Why would the Father exempt us from what He allowed His Son to experience? Indeed, we read, "Since therefore Christ suffered in the flesh, arm yourselves with the same way of thinking" (1 Pet. 4:1). We should "Share in suffering as a good soldier of Christ Jesus" (2 Tim. 2:3; cf., 2 Cor. 4:8-11). Jesus' suffering applies in our lives, "because he himself has suffered when tempted, [and] he is able to help those who are being tempted" (Heb. 2:18). Let us remember that we are "fellow heirs with Christ, provided we suffer with him in order that we may also be glorified with him. For I consider that the sufferings of this present time are not worth comparing with the glory that is to be revealed to us" (Rom. 8:17-18; cf., 2 Cor. 4:17; Acts 5:41; 1 Pet. 4:14).

Paul told us to "Share in suffering for the gospel" (2 Tim. 1:8). Peter said, "If anyone suffers as a Christian, let him not be ashamed, but let him glorify God" (1 Pet. 4:16). Peter added several other insights: "If when you do good and suffer for it you endure, this is a gracious thing in the sight of God" (1 Pet. 2:20); "But even if you should suffer for righteousness' sake, you will be blessed" (1 Pet. 3:14); "Therefore let those who suffer according to God's will entrust their souls to a faithful Creator while doing good" (1 Pet. 4:19); "And after you have suffered a little while, the God of all grace, who has called you to his eternal glory in Christ, will himself restore, confirm, strengthen, and establish you" (1 Pet. 5:10). Too many false preachers today tell Christians to expect only good things from God, but Peter tells us just the opposite, "Beloved, do not be surprised at the fiery trial when it comes upon you to test you, as though something strange were happening to you" (1 Pet. 4:12; cf., Acts 14:22; 1 Pet. 1:6).

God will deliver us again and again despite the persecution and suffering we will experience. Jesus promised us, "In the world you will have tribulation. But take heart; I have overcome the world" (John 16:33). He also said, "Come to me, all who labor and are heavy laden, and I will give you rest" (Matt. 11:28). We should also remember, "Blessed is the man who remains steadfast under trial, for when he has stood the test he will receive the crown of life, which God has promised to those who love him" (James 1:12).

Finally, Jesus told His disciples, "Remember the word that I said to you: 'A servant is not greater than his master.' If they persecuted me, they will also persecute you" (John 15:20). If we could ask the long roll of Christian martyrs about their best life on earth, I am pretty sure they would say it was the suffering and persecution they endured for the sake of Christ and His gospel. For the same suffering and persecution, they will be awarded the crown of life from their Lord.

22) PREACHING THE GOSPEL TO OURSELVES

"Preach the gospel to yourself every day."
Jerry Bridges[165]

Part of our post-evangelism is allowing the good news of the gospel to become more and more the center of our lives every day. Paul told the Colossians to "continue in the faith, stable and steadfast, not shifting from the hope of the gospel that you heard" (Col. 1:23). We are also told, "We have come to share in Christ, if indeed we hold our original confidence firm to the end" (Heb. 3:14). If we preach the hope

---

[165] Jerry Bridges, *Respectable Sins*, p. 36.

of the gospel to ourselves every day, we know that Christ, who is our original confidence (2 Cor. 3:4-5; Eph. 3:12; Col. 1:27; Acts 4:12), will hold us firm to the end (Philip. 1:6).

Standing on the Foundation of the Gospel

The success of our evangelism, before anything else, is dependent upon *our* right standing in the gospel. Our right standing in the gospel is based solely on Christ's right standing with the Father (Rom. 5:8-9). If we are "in Christ" (Rom. 3:24), we are in a right standing in the gospel and in a right relationship to God, because Christ completed the work the Father sent Him to do (John 17:4) on our behalf (2 Cor. 5:21). Therefore, our right standing in the gospel is a matter of trusting what the Father has done in Christ. That way, we know that "All this is from God, who through Christ reconciled us to himself and gave us the ministry of reconciliation; that is, in Christ God was reconciling the world to himself, not counting their trespasses against them" (2 Cor. 5:18-19). We cannot evangelize correctly and have the ministry of reconciliation unless we first understand and trust in this good news ourselves.

Preaching to the Choir

If we preach to the choir, we are preaching biblical truths to people who are already converted. Often, we will hear a Christian respond, "Hey brother, you're preaching to the choir. I agree with all you are saying." How about when we preach to ourselves? Do we say, "I'm not shifting from the hope of the gospel that I've heard; my confidence will be firm to the end?" A person in post-evangelism needs to learn not only how to preach the gospel to others, but also how to preach the good news to ourselves!

Our Daily Bread

Years ago, when I was reading Jerry Bridges book, "Respectable Sins", he talked about how Christians need to "Preach the gospel to yourself every day."[166] That was an important message for me as I began to realize that while the gospel is the foundation of our right standing with God, the gospel is also our daily bread. Our daily nourishment comes from preaching the gospel to ourselves every day. I would soon learn that this is a discipline that would help me stay grounded in the good news.

---

[166] Jerry Bridges says he first heard this phrase from his friend Dr. Jack Miller, a professor at Westminster Theological Seminary.

Diamond in the Rough

The gospel is all about God's holiness in contrast to our sin. One of the things that happens when we preach the gospel to ourselves every day is that we will see more of God's holiness and more of our sin. Paul writes, "our unrighteousness serves to show the righteousness of God" (Rom. 3:5). Pastor John MacArthur gives an illustration of a jeweler wanting to display a diamond in all its splendor. In order to accomplish this, they show the diamond on a black velvet background. The glorious diamond (God's righteousness) on black (our sin) provides a contrast that illuminates the diamond's purity. This contrast of God's righteousness and our sin is a good thing, because we become more and more aware of how the holiness and righteousness of God have been manifested through Christ. His perfectly righteous life on our behalf, substitutionary death on the cross and resurrection from the grave were all necessary to show God's righteousness, overcome our sin and to defeat death.

The Just and the Justifier

Preaching the gospel to ourselves will also grow us into an understanding of His justice, as God becomes both the "just and the justifier of the one who has faith in Jesus" (Rom. 3:26). If the justifier of our salvation is God plus our "works of the law" (Rom. 3:28), that combination could never bring about the righteousness that makes God just. It, in fact, would nullify God's righteousness, as we read, "I do not nullify the grace of God, for if righteousness were through the law, then Christ died for no purpose" (Gal. 2:21). Righteousness never comes through the law (Gal. 2:16), but by faith in Christ alone (Rom. 3:21-22). The only way God can be both just and the justifier is for Him to be the *only* justifier (Rom. 8:33). Because His Son was pierced for our transgressions (Isa. 53:5), God is just in canceling the debt of sin that stood against us by nailing it to the cross (Col. 2:13-15). He is the justifier because He is the One who offers up His Son (John 3:16).

As I preach the gospel to myself, God's word speaks truth and comfort into my life:

- Being in the first Adam (Rom. 5:19), I was by nature a child of wrath, like the rest of mankind (Eph. 2:3). However, in Christ, "The last Adam" (1 Cor. 15:45), I was "made alive" (1 Cor. 15:22) into "a new creation" (2 Cor. 5:17), a child of God (John 1:12).

- When God drew me to Himself (John 6:44) and gave me the gifts of faith (Eph. 2:8) and repentance (2 Tim. 2:25), I repented and believed in the gospel (Mark 1:15). I then became a vessel of God's mercy (Rom. 9:23; 2 Tim 2:21).

- "I received mercy because I had acted ignorantly in unbelief" (1 Tim. 1:13). I now know "that Christ Jesus came into the world to save sinners, of whom I am the foremost" (1 Tim. 1:15). Christ did "not come to call the righteous but sinners to repentance" (Luke 5:32), as "Christ died for the ungodly" (Rom. 5:6).

- My many sins are forgiven, just like the woman who washed the feet of Jesus: "I tell you, her sins, which are many, are forgiven" (Luke 7:47). I can't count up my many sins, but I know that Christ "offered for all time a single sacrifice for sins" (Heb. 10:12).

- The gospel tells me I am the man that God has cleansed from his former sins (Titus 3:5; Acts 15:9), the man whose "lawless deeds are forgiven, and whose sins are covered" (Rom. 4:7). The Lord "freed us from our sins by his blood" (Rev. 1:5), for "the blood of Jesus his Son cleanses us from all sin" (1 John 1:7).

- Since we have been "justified by faith" (Rom. 3:28) in Christ's shed blood on the cross (Rom. 5:9) and by His resurrection (Rom 4:24-25), "we have peace with God through our Lord Jesus Christ" (Rom. 5:1). "There is therefore now no condemnation for those who are in Christ Jesus" (Rom. 8:1).

- God has delivered me from the domain of darkness and transferred me to the kingdom of his beloved Son (Col. 1:13-14). He has called me "out of darkness into his marvelous light" (1 Pet. 2:9).

- The good news tells me that Jesus has "abolished death and brought life and immortality to light through the gospel" (2 Tim. 1:10). He has given life to my mortal body through His Spirit who dwells in me (Rom. 8:11), for "It is the Spirit who gives life" (John 6:63).

- When I "heard the word of truth, the gospel" and believed, I was "sealed with the promised Holy Spirit, who is the guarantee of our inheritance" (Eph. 1:13-14). For "The Spirit himself bears witness with our spirit that we are children of God, and if children, then heirs—heirs of God and fellow heirs with Christ" (Rom. 8:16-17).

- While the gospel moves me from being a slave of sin (Rom. 6:17) to a slave of righteousness (Rom. 6:18), I ask God to search me "And see if there be any grievous way in me" (Psalm 139:23-24). "If anyone does sin, we have an advocate with the Father, Jesus Christ the Righteous One" (1 John 2:1, NET Bible).

- An honest recognition of the battle we have with our flesh (Rom. 7:15-25; Gal. 5:16-17) requires daily repentance in our life (Rom. 6:6, 18; Eph. 4:22-24; Col. 3:9-10). As we grow in our understanding of the gospel, our daily repentance will draw us nearer to the cross, knowing when we "confess our sins, he is faithful and just to forgive us our sins and to cleanse us from all unrighteousness" (1 John 1:9).

- "I have been crucified with Christ. It is no longer I who live, but Christ who lives in me" (Gal. 2:20). Having been "raised with him through faith" (Col. 2:12), I now "walk in newness of life" (Rom. 6:4).

- In this new life, "My aim is to know him, to experience the power of his resurrection" (Philip. 3:10, NET Bible).

- Giving me "a new heart, and a new spirit" (Ez. 36:26) to honor Christ as Lord (1 Pet. 3:15), God has chosen me "to be saved, through sanctification by the Spirit and belief in the truth" (2 Thess. 2:13). "The truth of the gospel" (Gal. 2:5) is a sanctifying work in changing my life (Col. 1:5) and me positively changing the lives of others (Phil. 1:27).

- The gospel came to me "not only in word, but also in power and in the Holy Spirit" (1 Thess. 1:5). This power is so I may walk in the good works that God prepared for me beforehand (Eph. 2:10).

- The gospel has trained me to renounce ungodliness and worldly passions, and to live a self-controlled, upright, and godly life. I am redeemed and purified by Christ to be "zealous for good works" (Titus 2:11-14).

- In the gospel, I am "set apart as holy, useful to the master of the house, ready for every good work" (2 Tim. 2:21). Therefore, I must take up my cross daily (Luke 9:23) and let my "life be worthy of the gospel of Christ" (Philip. 1:27).

- Because of the hope laid up for me in heaven, the truth of the gospel (Col. 1:5-6), I strive to bear much fruit and so prove to be one of Christ's disciples (John 15:8).

- When I preach the good news to myself every day, I will not be "shifting from the hope of the gospel" (Col. 1:22-23). I will have faith to the end and will not "shrink back" (Heb. 10:39), knowing that "He who began a good work in me will bring it to completion at the day of Jesus Christ" (Philip. 1:6).
- Because Jesus has delivered me from the wrath to come (1 Thess. 1:10; 1 Thess. 5:9), I am an "ambassador for Christ" (2 Cor. 5:20). "I am eager to preach the gospel" (Rom. 1:15; cf., Eph. 6:19-20) in order to "save others by snatching them out of the fire" (Jude 1:23).
- In the end, knowing that God "saved us, not because of works done by us in righteousness, but according to his own mercy" (Titus 3:5), I will join other believers in saying, "We are unworthy servants; we have only done what was our duty" (Luke 17:10).
- Since I have "been raised with Christ" (Col. 3:1), I "draw near to God through him, since he always lives to make intercession for me" (Heb. 7:25).
- Because Jesus is "bringing many sons to glory" (Heb. 2:10), "all the saints" (Rom. 16:15) trust that "He called you through our gospel, so that you may obtain the glory of our Lord Jesus Christ" (2 Thess. 2:14).
- Because "our citizenship is in heaven" (Philip. 3:20), "When Christ who is your life appears, then you also will appear with him in glory" (Col. 3:4). Moreover, "when the chief Shepherd appears, you will receive the unfading crown of glory" (1 Pet. 5:4).
- Because of the gospel, "I am sure that neither death nor life, nor angels nor rulers, nor things present nor things to come, nor powers, nor height nor depth, nor anything else in all creation, will be able to separate us from the love of God in Christ Jesus our Lord" (Rom. 8:38-39).

Can I Get a Witness?

When we witness the good news to ourselves every day, we won't get gospel amnesia. A daily dose of gospel truth exposes our sin and continues to point us toward our Savior. As Martyn Lloyd-Jones once said, "The Christian life starts with grace, it must continue with grace, it ends with grace."[167] The gospel is not just for unbelievers but for believers as well. The gospel is not only a message that delivers us into God's kingdom, it's a message that empowers us to live within and sustains us in His kingdom. When we are saved, we don't depart from the message that saved us. Instead, we grow into a deeper understanding of that message. Preaching the gospel to ourselves every day is one of the ways God makes sure that we are "conformed to the image of his Son" (Rom. 8:29).

Reflecting on how the gospel has brought me "from death to life" (John 5:24; cf., Col. 1:13-14; 1 Pet. 2:9) reminds me of where God brought me from (Col. 2:13) and where I am now (Eph. 2:5-6). Living in the joy of such a great awakening spurs me on to continue my pursuit of holiness (Eph. 4:24; 2 Pet. 3:11-14), something that was impossible when I was dead in my trespasses, in which I once walked, following the course of this world (Eph. 2:1-2). Recalling my former position makes me resist the deceitful part of my heart that can be so susceptible to wander from God (Jeremiah 17:9).

Go Away, Devil

Preaching the gospel to ourselves helps us fend off the attacks of the evil one—to defeat the condemning lies of Satan. We know we can "be outwitted by Satan" (2 Cor. 2:11). There are also moments when, like Paul, we can say that "Satan hindered us" (1 Thess. 2:18). Bitter jealousy and selfish ambition can at times make us "be false to the truth" (James 3:14). However, "This is not the wisdom that comes down from above, but is earthly, unspiritual, demonic" (3:15). Satan can even tempt some in the church into "sexual immorality" (Rev. 2:20-24). Yet, when we center ourselves on the gospel, it reminds us to put on the whole armor of God "to stand against the schemes of the devil" (Eph. 6:10-18a). We resist the devil to make him flee (James 4:7). We are always watchful of this "roaring lion" (1 Peter 5:8) so as to "give no opportunity to the devil" (Eph. 4:27), because God "who is in you is greater than he who is in the world" (1 John 4:4). A daily review of the gospel helps us remember that "The reason the Son of God appeared was to destroy the works of the devil" (1 John 3:8).

If we stay gospel-centered, death will have no hold on us, as the good news reminds us that Christ came to "destroy the one who has the power of death, that is, the devil, and deliver all those who through fear of death were

---

[167] Martyn Lloyd-Jones, quoted from https://www.monergism.com/d-martyn-lloyd-jones

subject to lifelong slavery" (Heb. 2:14-15). Having had that fear of death put to rest in us, "We know that we are from God" (1 John 5:19). When we stay established in the gospel and go about sharing the good news, we look to deliver those who, just like we used to be, are afraid of death and are currently subject to the slavery of Satan. Just as Satan once blinded our eyes, hardened our hearts (John 12:40; 2 Cor. 4:4) and made us "the sons of disobedience" (Eph. 2:2), the gospel the Holy Spirit entrusted us to guard in our hearts (2 Tim. 1:14) can now help unbelievers "turn from darkness to light and from the power of Satan to God" (Acts 26:18).

Gospel Booster

The unmerited grace the gospel brings to mind mounts a powerful assault against my pride. It strips me of any self-righteousness. At the same time, it addresses the guilt for past, present and future sins. As Dr. Jerry Bridges wrote, "Preaching the gospel to ourselves every day addresses both the self-righteous Pharisee and the guilt-laden sinner that dwell in our hearts."[168] I don't know about you, but I need a daily booster shot of the justifying power of the root of the gospel.

The Old Rugged Cross

One of the problems with the world is that they "spend their time in nothing except telling or hearing something new" (Acts 17:21). For some Christians, this is also the case. They want a new "prophecy" or new "revelation" from their favorite prosperity "gospel" teacher. They get excited about a new teaching like the so-called "Gospel in the Stars."[169] They devour books that reinterpret the gospel, stripping it of its redemptive and transformative power. They fall for the new tolerance or new acceptance that the world demands. They have "itching ears" (2 Tim. 4:3) and seek out teachers who wander off into myths. However, when it comes to the truth of the gospel, Christians don't need something new, but something old—the old story of Christ crucified and resurrected, the One "who was delivered up for our trespasses and raised for our justification" (Rom. 4:25). A recital of "The Old Rugged Cross"[170] will bring a newness to our hearts every day.

---

[168] Jerry Bridges, *The Discipline of Grace*, p. 182.
[169] Gospel in the Stars theology teaches that the constellations depict the twelve zodiac signs, visibly displaying the gospel message for everyone to see. Each of the signs is said to depict a specific phase in God's plan of salvation. See refutation here: https://creation.com/images/pdfs/tj/j12_2/j12_2_169-173.pdf
[170] The Old Rugged Cross, a popular Christian hymn written in 1912 by evangelist and song-leader George Bennard.

Note to Self

Put a Post-it Note out as a reminder to daily preach the gospel to yourself. This way we can "reassure our heart before him" (1 John 3:19). The gospel keeps us anchored in "the promise that he made to us—eternal life" (1 John 2:25). The more I see the eternal value of the gospel, the more it develops within me a yearning for heaven (Col. 1:5; Philip. 3:20). It also spurs me on to sharing the gospel with others, so that they, too, may have the white garments of true believers (Rev. 3:5, 19:8; Isa. 61:10).

23) FINISHING THE RACE

"I have fought the good fight, I have finished the race, I have kept the faith" (2 Tim. 4:7).

When Olympic long-distance runners start a race, they have several things in mind. First, they remember all the training, sweat and hard work it took them just to qualify for the race. Second, they know the race is not a sprint but a marathon; endurance is the key. Third, they must follow the rules of the race, otherwise they can be disqualified. Fourth, their goal is to cross the finish line. Fifth, only one receives the gold medal, so they run in such a way as to obtain it.

For the Christian's race, there are many comparisons to the above five points, except for the first one. It is not us, but God Himself who qualifies us for His race by justifying us by grace alone through faith alone in Christ alone. Only those who come through the root of gospel qualify for His race.

If you are not a Christian, you are not even in this race. 18th century Baptist pastor J. C. Philpot wrote, "None can run this race but the saints of God, for the ground itself is holy ground, of which we read that 'no unclean beast is to be found therein.'"[171] Christians are not running the race to be justified before God; they are in the race because they have *already* been justified by God (Rom. 8:33). Our conversion is not the end of the race, it is the start. This race is about our sanctification—the fruit of the gospel.

---

[171] J. C. Philpot's Daily Words For Zion's Wayfarers, January 30, gospelweb.net.

Another way to look at this is when God brings us into His kingdom, He qualifies us for His race. You have an automatic entry to the starting line. Your training is a lifelong process that goes on during the race and doesn't finish until the end. Your uniform will be the "white garments" of Christ (Rev. 3:18; cf., Isa. 61:10). Therefore, Christians, suit up! Put on your track "shoes for your feet, having put on the readiness given by the gospel of peace" (Eph. 6:15). Don't forget, followers of Christ, "in a race all the runners run" (1 Cor. 9:24).

Not a Sprint but a Marathon

In a sprint, you exhaust all your efforts into a short distance, but in a marathon, the kind of race about which the Bible is talking, endurance is the key. You also do not want to be weighted down in the race that is set before us. The writer of Hebrews, in talking about our race, said, "Therefore, since we are surrounded by so great a cloud of witnesses, let us also lay aside every weight, and sin which clings so closely, and let us run with endurance the race that is set before us" (Heb. 12:1). The great cloud of witnesses, highlighted in Hebrews 11, are all part of the Hebrews Faith Hall of Fame. God listed many heroes in the faith who ran the race before us, including Abraham, Joseph and David, all of whom endured through trials and persecution to show their faith to God. God's former work through them should inspire us to endure as well and to shed any sin and every weight in our lives that will slow us down in the race.

As we are running the race, what is the extra weight? The writer of Hebrews was addressing Jews who were being tempted to go back to the legalism and rituals of Judaism rather than pledge to run the race exclusively for Christ. As we run the race, does Christ have our undivided attention? Are we distracted by pursuits other than Christ? As Paul told Timothy "No soldier gets entangled in civilian pursuits, since his aim is to please the one who enlisted him" (2 Tim. 2:4).

The race also requires that we lay aside the sin which clings so closely to us. Again, the writer of Hebrews rebuked the Jews who were going back and forth between "the offering of the body of Jesus Christ once for all" (Heb. 10:10) and the ongoing animal sacrifices of the temple (Heb. 10:4, 26). Some could not decide one over the other, and others wanted them both. As you run the race, are you vacillating between a trust in Christ's one time sacrifice for sins and the sway of other religions? Is this sin of unbelief (Acts 4:12; John 14:6; 2 Cor. 6:14-16) something that clings so closely to you? As you run, be warned! If you have signed a sponsorship deal with religions outside of Christianity, it will not only weight you down, it will put you in danger of being judged by the Lord, for "It is a fearful thing to fall into the hands of the living God" (Heb. 10:31).

A Race of Suffering and Endurance

Abraham and the great cloud of witnesses endured plenty of suffering. However, we've already learned "that suffering produces endurance, and endurance produces character" (Rom. 5:3-4). Paul also tells us, "through endurance and through the encouragement of the Scriptures we might have hope" (Rom. 15:4). Elsewhere, our endurance can signify our faith, service and works (Rev. 2:19). The Jews suffered persecution for their newfound faith in Jesus. Some considered returning to the safety of Judaism, but were warned, "For you have need of endurance, so that when you have done the will of God you may receive what is promised" (Heb. 10:36). Notice what God said of Abraham, "After he had patiently endured, he obtained the promise" (Heb. 6:15, KJV).

We can get a glimpse of what our race should look like by reading about the great cloud of witnesses that ran before us. When they ran, they "pleased God" (Heb. 11:5); they had "reverent fear" (11:7); they "obeyed" God (11:8); they were "looking forward" (11:10), "looking to the reward" (11:26); they "received power" (11:11); they were "tested" (11:17); they chose "to be mistreated with the people of God than to enjoy the fleeting pleasures of sin" (11:25); and they were not "afraid" (11:27). It was these saints "who through faith conquered kingdoms, enforced justice, obtained promises" (11:33). They "escaped the edge of the sword, were made strong out of weakness" (11:34). "Some were tortured, refusing to accept release, so that they might rise again to a better life. Others suffered mocking and flogging, and even chains and imprisonment. They were stoned, they were sawn in two, they were killed with the sword" (11:35-37).

Run Your Appointed Race

The Bible tells us to run the race that God has chosen for us. Notice that the course of the race that we are to run has already been "set before us" (Heb. 12:1). This "race" is the Christian life that God has called each of His children to run—a faith race that is specifically designed for you. There have been many who have tried to run a race *not* set before them. For example, a Christian may have been given "the ability to distinguish between spirits" (1 Cor. 12:10), but instead self-appoints themselves to the role of "pastor" (Eph. 4:11, NASB), a race that was not set before them (James 3:1; 1 Tim. 2:12). God may place some in the role of "service" (Rom. 12:7) or "mercy" (12:8), but when they venture off course into "administration" (1 Cor. 12:28, NASB), they are trying to run a race God did not design them to run.

Every Christian has a different race—a different course. God has a work for every believer for which no other brother or sister in Christ has been specifically gifted or will be granted success. It is our responsibility to discover our gifts and use them in the race that God has set before us. We should run the race God has ordained for us, not another person's race. Unfortunately, too many try to run in someone else's race, and they end up being a hindrance to everyone around them.

Stay in Your Lane

To make sure we stay in our lane, we should understand how God has distributed spiritual gifts in the body. Paul says there are varieties of gifts and varieties of service (1 Cor. 12:4). He goes on to say every Christian has been empowered with a spiritual gift(s), "it is the same God who empowers them all in everyone. To each is given the manifestation of the Spirit for the common good" (12:6-7). He then goes on to list the spiritual gifts concluding with "All these are empowered by one and the same Spirit, who apportions to each one individually as he wills" (12:11). God bestows upon each of us "gifts of the Holy Spirit distributed according to his will" (Heb. 2:4), not ours.

Notice that our gifts differ from one another, "Having gifts that differ according to the grace given to us, let us use them" (Rom. 12:6). That is because "God arranged the members in the body, each one of them, as he chose" (1 Cor. 12:18). So, since "each has received a gift, use it to serve one another, as good stewards of God's varied grace" (1 Pet. 4:10; cf. Rom. 1:11-12), because "grace was given to each one of us according to the measure of Christ's gift" (Eph. 4:7). Notice the diversity of gifts when scripture says "He gave the apostles, the prophets, the evangelists, the shepherds and teachers, to equip the saints for the work of ministry, for building up the body of Christ" (Eph. 4:11-12; cf. 1 Cor. 12:28).

Part of our post-evangelism training is to know the race God has set before us. We do this by discovering the gifts God has appointed to us. Part of growing up in the faith is making ourselves available to serve in any area that might bring our spiritual gifts to light. If God has gifted you in a certain area, He will also likely give you a desire to exercise that gift. Mature Christians not only know about the race—they run it. They run it to the end, knowing that God has set their course with works He has already prepared specifically for them, "For we are his workmanship, created in Christ Jesus for good works, which God prepared beforehand, that we should walk in them" (Eph. 2:10; cf., Col. 2:6; 1 Thess. 2:12, 4:1; 2 Thess. 3:13; 1 Tim. 6:18; Titus 3:8).

Too many infant Christians want to set their own course. While they choose a potato sack or egg relay race, the mature Christian is running the race God has set before them. The great cloud of witnesses accepted the course God set before them; we should also run the race that is set before us. Don't demand of God that He hand out participation trophies just for showing up. No, Paul said, don't you know that "only one receives the prize? Run in such a way that you may win" (1 Cor. 9:24, NASB). While no one gets to choose the race they run, we do get to choose how we run it.

Paul's Race

Paul understood the race God had set before him. He said God "had set me apart before I was born, and… was pleased to reveal his Son to me, in order that I might preach him among the Gentiles" (Gal. 1:15-16). When Paul, then known as Saul, met the risen Jesus on the road to Damascus, he asked, "'What shall I do, Lord?' And the Lord said to me, 'Rise, and go into Damascus, and there you will be told all that is appointed for you to do'" (Acts 22:10). He was later told, "The God of our fathers appointed you to know his will, to see the Righteous One and to hear a voice from his mouth; for you will be a witness for him to everyone of what you have seen and heard" (22:14-15). Paul was "appointed" by Jesus to preach the gospel, as the Lord said, "he is a chosen instrument of mine to carry my name before the Gentiles and kings and the children of Israel" (Acts 9:15; cf., 20:24) so "that they may receive forgiveness of sins and a place among those who are sanctified by faith in me" (26:18). Paul later said, "I was appointed a preacher and an apostle" (1 Tim. 2:7; cf., 2 Tim. 1:11).

Paul knew that God had appointed him "to be an apostle of Christ Jesus" (1 Cor. 1:1). He told the church in Corinth, "we were the first to come all the way to you with the gospel of Christ" (2 Cor. 10:14). However, Paul warned the church about some who he sarcastically called "super-apostles" (2 Cor. 11:5), those who were trying to supersede his authority. Paul said these teachers were so man-centered that they "are commending themselves... they measure themselves by one another and compare themselves with one another, they are without understanding" (2 Cor. 10:12). Paul did not commend himself or try to measure himself by other men. He also did not try to take over a territory that God had assigned to others. He said, "we will not boast beyond limits, but will boast only with regard to the area of influence God assigned to us, to reach even to you" (10:13).

The Free Bible Commentary, in discussing the previous verse, states, "The picture Paul has in mind may be that of an athletic contest in which lanes are marked out for the different runners.... In intruding themselves into Corinth, the false apostles [super-apostles] had crossed into Paul's lane, which was the lane that God had marked out and that had brought him to the Corinthians as their genuine apostle. He has no intention of invading the territory marked out for others and claiming their work as his own, as these false teachers were doing."[172]

Looking to Jesus

When we run our race, on whom are we focused? Ourselves, other runners, the world? If the goal is to race to the end, the finish line is Jesus Himself. Christian runners run their race always "Looking unto Jesus the author and finisher of our faith; who for the joy that was set before him endured the cross" (Heb. 12:2, KJV). The main message of Hebrews to the Jews was—Don't take your eyes off of Jesus! He is superior to the prophets (Heb. 1:1-2); the angels (chapters 1-2); Moses (chapter 3); the Old Testament priesthood (chapters 4-7); the Old Covenant (chapter 8); the temple (9:1-5); and the Old Testament sacrifices (9:6-10:22). Jesus is also the Messiah to whom the great cloud of witnesses looked

---

[172]http://www.freebiblecommentary.org/new_testament_studies/VOL06/VOL06B_10.html

forward, as Abraham (John 8:56; Gal. 3:8), Moses (John 5:46); Job (Job 19:25-27) and David (Psalm 16:10, 110:1-4) all did. In our race, we have the examples of the great cloud of witnesses to follow, but our unequaled standard is Jesus Himself, the One who will be waiting for us at the finish line to say "Well done, good and faithful servant… Enter into the joy of your master" (Matt. 25:23).

Follow the Rules of the Race

As we have seen, God sets the course. If you are running a marathon, you can't make up your own course. If you stray from the course, you will be disqualified. As Paul said, "An athlete is not crowned unless he competes according to the rules" (2 Tim. 2:5). All athletes running a marathon learn the rules as part of their training. Christians running God's race learn the rules from the Bible, which fully prepares them "for training in righteousness" (2 Tim. 3:16). For the grace of God that has brought us salvation is "training us to renounce ungodliness and worldly passions, and to live self-controlled, upright, and godly lives in the present age" (Titus 2:11-12). At the starting line, the Christian running in God's race will say to their fellow brothers and sisters in Christ—be ready to "train yourself for godliness" (1 Tim. 4:7).

Those who are guided by the Lord's will (Eph. 5:17; Col. 1:9) and who have trained themselves for godliness will not be in doubt as to what the rules of God's race are. These rules, revealed in the Bible (John 17:17; 1 Thess. 2:13), will fully equip us (2 Tim. 3:16) and teach us how we ought to believe and live. We first get wisdom by fearing the Lord (Proverbs 1:7). Then, we delve into the deep things of the root (Rom. 4:22-24, 5:9; 1 Cor. 15:1-4) and the fruit of the gospel (Rom. 6:22). We humble ourselves (Philip. 2:3-5); are open to instruction (Proverbs 9:9); follow Christ's commands (John 14:21); become slaves to righteousness (Rom. 6:18); learn how to forgive (Eph. 4:32; Col. 3:13; Matt. 18:21-22); become merciful (Luke 6:36); and are obedient in preaching the word (2 Tim. 4:2) and defending the gospel (Philip. 1:16; Jude 1:3). We teach others (2 Tim. 2:2) and walk in Christ (Col. 2:6).

Those who run in God's race compete according to the rules because they have the training manual—God's word. During the race, they "Pursue righteousness, godliness, faith, love, steadfastness, gentleness" (1 Tim. 6:11). They "walk by the Spirit", not gratifying "the desires of the flesh" (Gal. 5:16). They have the fruit of the Spirit, which "is love, joy, peace, patience, kindness, goodness, faithfulness, gentleness, self-control"

(5:22-23). As we run, we know "His divine power has granted to us all things that pertain to life and godliness, through the knowledge of him who called us to his own glory and excellence" (2 Pet. 1:3).

The faithful runners have "exalted above all things" God's name and His word (Psalm 138:2). Because they believe "The sum of your word is truth" (Psalm 119:160; cf., 1 Thess. 2:13), they do not "go beyond what is written" (1 Cor. 4:6), and they test all claims by the Bible (Acts 17:11; 1 Thess. 5:21; Rev. 2:2). Because they "have stored up your word" in their heart (Psalm 119:11), they won't stumble on the track over "sin which clings so closely" (Heb. 12:1). The God-fearing runners know that "Your word is a lamp to my feet and a light to my path" (Psalm 119:105). Therefore, they ask God to "Keep steady my steps" (Psalm 119:133) so they can "keep in step with the Spirit" (Gal. 5:25).

Since the race lasts our entire Christian life, we should confess to God, "I will run in the way of your commandments" (Psalm 119:32) and "turn my feet to your testimonies" (119:59). We say with the Psalmist, "I know, O Lord, that your rules are righteous" (119:75); "Let your rules help me" (119:175). When we believe that "Your law is my delight" (119:77), we "meditate on it day and night" (Joshua 1:8). During God's race, "Let your eyes look directly forward, and your gaze be straight before you. Ponder the path of your feet; then all your ways will be sure. Do not swerve to the right or to the left; turn your foot away from evil" (Proverbs 4:25-27). As we are running a steady race in step with the Spirit, we can say, "He made my feet like the feet of a deer" (Psalm 18:33). For those who "turn aside from your rules" (Psalm 119:102) or take just a cursory look at God's training manual, their race will be disjointed and inconsistent, as they will have a hard time maneuvering the potholes of the course. Without studied and measured time in God's training manual, the runner's "joints and ligaments" (Col. 2:19; cf., Heb. 4:12) will get stiff, slowing them down.

Race Distractions

People who reject the rules of God's race, and have made up their own, will be yelling at you from the sidelines. Such people, "disguising themselves as apostles of Christ" (2 Cor. 11:13), "who come to you in sheep's clothing but inwardly are ravenous wolves" (Matt. 7:15), will try to toss you "to and fro" (Eph. 4:14). Their goal will be to have you "turn away from listening to the truth and wander off into myths" (2 Tim. 4:4). These "ungodly people, who pervert the grace of our God" (Jude 1:4), will try to lure runners in the race to "a different gospel" (Gal. 1:6). Remember, let your gaze be straight before you and do not get off your path.

Even though the race believers are running is only for Christians, the weeds (false teachers) will always be intruding themselves among the wheat (believers). While the wheat is running their race, the weeds will try to run alongside and draw them off course. The weeds will say things like "I have a much wider lane…we are more inclusive…we are more tolerant…we have new teachings to show you…God has given us new revelation…God has more rules for us to follow than in the Bible…our lane is the true lane… Jesus is not really the finish line…our race requires an unknown number of extra laps and suffering in Purgatory." Beware, as "The weeds are the sons of the evil one, and the enemy who sowed them is the devil" (Matt. 13:38-39). Instead of kicking the weeds off the race course, Jesus said, "Let both grow together until the harvest, and at harvest time I will tell the reapers, 'Gather the weeds first and bind them in bundles to be burned, but gather the wheat into my barn'" (Matt. 13:30). The wheat will finish the race for God's glory; the weeds will only find an eternal fire at the finish line.

The Faith Lane

Knowing that the enemy would "distort the gospel of Christ" (Gal. 1:7) in order to distract runners, Paul told those in the race to "be imitators of me" (1 Cor. 4:16, 11:1) and to imitate other runners who are faithfully following Christ (1 Thess. 1:6; 2 Thess. 3:7, 9; Philip. 3:17; Heb. 6:12, 13:7). The call for runners to emulate those setting the pace in the race is one way to demonstrate that all runners share a specific common faith. That's why when Paul said, "I have finished the race, I have kept *the faith*" (2 Tim. 4:7), he was referencing a "common salvation" (Jude 1:3) all Christians have called "*the faith.*" The New Testament speaks of Christians as involved in "*the faith*" (Acts 6:7, 13:8, 14:22, 16:5). Paul told Christians to "stand firm in *the faith*" (1 Cor. 16:13; cf., 2 Cor. 13:5; Col. 1:23, 2:6-7; Eph. 4:13; Philip. 1:25; 1 Tim. 1:2, 3:9, 4:1, 6; 5:8, 6:10, 21; 2 Tim. 3:8; Titus 1:13, 3:15; Jude 1:3).

The faith, of which all the runners in God's race are a part, holds to the essential belief in Jesus as the Messiah (Acts 5:42) who came to die on the cross for our sins (Col. 2:13-14). The faith teaches that Jesus "suffered once for sins, the righteous for the unrighteous, that he might bring us to God" (1 Pet. 3:18; cf., 2 Cor. 5:21). These believers in a common salvation held firm to the eyewitness testimony (1 Cor. 15:5-8; Acts 2:32, 3:15; 1 John 1:1) that Christ "was raised on the third day in accordance with the Scriptures" (1 Cor. 15:4). The faith acknowledged Jesus as God coming in the flesh, for "God was manifest in the flesh" (1 Tim. 3:16, KJV; cf., John 1:1, 14).

Runners in God's race, who hold to the essential doctrines of the faith, will stay on the specified narrow road and not be tempted to divert off course to the wide road "that leads to destruction" (Matt. 7:13-14). Many who are behind the race barricades will tempt those of the faith to join them on the wide road in following another Jesus, a different spirit, a different gospel (2 Cor. 11:4) and a different god (Exodus 20:3). Others, who sneak their way onto the course illegally, will tempt those of the faith into bondage by telling them they have to keep the law and perform works of righteousness as a way to salvation. Paul called that "a yoke of slavery" (Gal. 5:1). He said if you want to join those on the wide road, you will be "obligated to keep the whole law" (Gal. 5:3) in order to "be justified by the law" (5:4). He said of anyone who seeks to gain a righteousness outside of the completed work of Christ, "You are severed from Christ…you have fallen away from grace" (5:4). Paul then asked the Galatians, "You were running well. Who hindered you from obeying the truth?" (5:7).

Paul told us, "do not run aimlessly" (1 Cor. 9:26). If we follow "the faith" and compete according to God's rulebook, no one can hinder us from obeying the truth. We will not run aimlessly, be tempted by weeds around us, or be hindered from saying like Paul, "I have fought the good fight, I have finished the race, I have kept the faith" (2 Tim. 4:7).

Get to the Finish Line

Whether one has a short time or a long time left to run, we should all have this in common—keep your eyes on Jesus (Heb. 12:2). This means we know the Father has put us in the race, because we were "justified freely by his grace through the redemption that is in Christ Jesus" (Rom. 3:24, KJV). We endure during the race to "receive what is promised" (Heb. 10:36). In our race, we honor the Son and honor the Father (John

5:23) as we "keep in step with the Spirit" (Gal. 5:25). If we honor the triune God throughout the race, we will finish well. We will finish in such a way that our race glorifies God (1 Cor. 10:31; Rom. 11:36, 15:6-7; 2 Thess. 1:12; 2 Cor. 8:19).

Some Christians sprint from the starting line and then soon grow weary. Others start slowly but pick up momentum as the race goes along, only to get distracted later down the line. Some find their comfort zone and then go into cruise control, never getting past second gear. Certain people are more interested in who is watching them run, rather than obedience to the race itself. Still others, after running well, suffer a setback in their faith. They lose perspective, but then get a second wind and return to their earlier pace. One thing is for sure, all of us running the race will experience ups and downs as we move towards the finish line. It is those who learn to shed the weight of sin, get rid of worldly distractions, endure through suffering, trials and persecutions, follow the rules, run the race God has set before them, stay in their lane, and always look to Jesus, who will finish well.

Forgetting What Lies Behind

Some Christians have a hard time focusing on the finish line because they can't get over their past. Even though they know that "the blood of Jesus his Son cleanses us from all sin" (1 John 1:7), they experience flashbacks of certain grievous sins. This can slow them down during the race. The Apostle Paul addressed this in one of his letters. He gave the Philippians a testimony of his life before and after Christ. Before meeting Christ on the Damascus Road, Paul talked about how he was among the elite of the Hebrews. He had the right lineage. He was a Pharisee.

In fact, Paul said he was "as to righteousness under the law, blameless" (Philip. 3:4-6).

After meeting Christ, Paul said he counted all that "as loss because of the surpassing worth of knowing Christ Jesus my Lord" (Philip. 3:8). Paul realized that the righteousness that he thought he had attained through the law was "rubbish" (3:8) compared to Christ. He now realized that any righteousness he, or anyone else, can ever hope for only "comes through faith in Christ" (3:9). Paul looked at his life before and after Christ, and he discovered that what he thought was a blameless righteousness he had possessed before Christ was nothing but spiritual bankruptcy in light of the perfect righteousness of his Savior.

Having come to this realization, Paul wanted the Philippians to know that his sanctification was far from over. He said he desperately wanted to know the power of Christ's resurrection and to share in His sufferings for the sake of righteousness (Philip. 3:10, 1:29). Paul said of this sanctification, "I press on to make it my own, because Christ Jesus has made me his own" (3:12). Paul then said something very interesting: "forgetting what lies behind and straining forward to what lies ahead, I press on toward the goal for the prize of the upward call of God in Christ Jesus" (3:13-14).

Paul had just told us of his life before Christ, a life he realized was "rubbish" (Philip. 3:8). Part of that previous life was being a zealous "persecutor of the church" (3:6). He referred to himself elsewhere as being "a blasphemer, persecutor, and insolent opponent" (1 Tim. 1:13). However, Paul said he was forgetting what was behind him. Paul said thoughts of those grievous sins he committed in his past were not going slow him down. He pressed on towards the goal—to finish the race and obtain his prize.

Keep Your Eyes on the Prize

Paul talked about some runners receiving a "prize" at the end of the race. He told the Corinthians, "Do you not know that in a race all the runners run, but only one receives the prize? So run that you may obtain it" (1 Cor. 9:24). Greek athletic games were well known to Paul's audience. He was using these games as a metaphor for a Christian's faith journey. With that in mind, the Christian race is not about the fastest time; it's not about who comes in first. This is a spiritual race to see who endures and finishes faithfully.

Paul's illustration does not limit the Christian race to one winner. While only one will win in an earthly race, all have an opportunity to win in our race of faith. In the earthly race, opponents compete against one another. In the Christian race, we compete with ourselves. Many believers can win the prize, and many can fail to obtain it. Since we already know that we run "the race that is set before *us*" (Heb. 12:1), not the race set before others, God has given each of us our own "lane" in which to run. Our lane is set off and distinct from our fellow runners. If we stay in the lane in which God placed us, we are not competing with the other runners. Therefore, each lane offers the possibility of receiving a reward from God. In other words, "the prize" is within the grasp of every Christian runner.

What is the prize? The ultimate prize is the joy of hearing Jesus say, "Well done, good and faithful servant. You have been faithful over a little; I will set you over much. Enter into the joy of your master" (Matt. 25:21). Those who run the race faithfully will also be given crowns. Paul reminded us, "An athlete is not crowned unless he competes according to the rules" (2 Tim. 2:5). The main rule is for us to keep our eyes on Jesus, who Himself was "crowned with glory and honor because of the suffering of death" (Heb. 2:9; cf., Rev. 6:2). Jesus, who will award us on that day, said, "I am coming soon. Hold fast what you have, so that no one may seize your crown" (Rev. 3:11).

Race Crowns

The New Testament describes five crowns that believers may receive:

1. The Crown of Life: "Blessed is the man who remains steadfast under trial, for when he has stood the test he will receive the crown of life, which God has promised to those who love him" (James 1:12; cf., Rev. 2:10).

2. The Unfading Crown of Glory: Peter told his fellow elders to "shepherd the flock of God that is among you, exercis-

ing oversight, not under compulsion, but willingly, as God would have you; not for shameful gain, but eagerly; not domineering over those in your charge, but being examples to the flock. And when the chief Shepherd appears, you will receive the unfading crown of glory" (1 Pet. 5:2-4).

3. The Imperishable Crown: "Everyone who competes for the prize…they do it to obtain a perishable crown, but we for an imperishable crown" (1 Cor. 9:25, NKJV).

4. The Crown of Rejoicing: "For what is our hope, or joy, or crown of rejoicing?" (1 Thess. 2:19, KJV).

5. The Crown of Righteousness: "There is laid up for me the crown of righteousness, which the Lord, the righteous judge, will award to me on that day, and not only to me but also to all who have loved his appearing" (2 Tim. 4:8).

Paul ran his race for crowns; so should we. One of his most cherished crowns was discipling fellow believers. Paul wrote to the saints at Philippi, "Therefore, my brothers, whom I love and long for, my joy and crown, stand firm thus in the Lord" (Philip. 4:1; cf., 2:17-18). The Philippians' spiritual success was one of Paul's crowning achievements. He also told the Thessalonians, "what is our hope or joy or crown of boasting before our Lord Jesus at his coming? Is it not you? For you are our glory and joy" (1 Thess. 2:19-20).

Imperishable Wreaths

Notice that Paul said that the Greek athletes run "to receive a perishable wreath, but we an imperishable" (1 Cor. 9:25). A wreath woven from the evergreen branches of a wild olive tree would be placed like a crown on the head of the winner in the Greek athletic games. Yet, their prize would not last, as such a wreath would soon wilt and perish. However, Christians receive a crown that is imperishable. The crowns faithful runners receive will last forever, as they are a part of "our heavenly dwelling" (2 Cor. 5:2).

Casting Crowns

Any crowns or rewards we may receive ultimately are for bringing glory to God. Since "it is God who works in you, both to will and to work for his good pleasure" (Philip. 2:13), these crowns will likely be laid back before Him. In Revelation 4, we see a scene in heaven with twenty-four elders "clothed in white garments, with golden crowns on their heads" (Rev. 4:4). We then read where "the twenty-four elders fall down before him who is seated on the throne and worship him who lives forever and ever. They cast their crowns before the throne, saying, 'Worthy are you, our Lord and God, to receive glory and honor and power, for you created all things, and by your will they existed and were created'" (Rev. 4:10-11). Just like the elders cast their crowns before the throne, our response will most likely be the same, as we make sure it is God who receives all the glory and honor.

Other Runner Rewards

Faithful runners can also expect rewards for seeking God diligently (Heb. 11:6); preaching the gospel (1 Cor. 9:16-17; 1 Cor. 3:8); giving money for God's work (Matt. 6:4; cf., 19:21; 2 Cor. 9:6-7; 1 Tim. 6:17-19); being faithful leaders (Heb. 13:17); treating God's people with honor (Matt. 10:41); rejecting the fleeting pleasures of sin for obedience to Christ (Heb. 11:25-26); enduring for the will of God (Heb. 10:36); a life of holiness and godliness (2 Pet. 3:11-14); keeping an eternal perspective in trials (2 Cor. 4:16-18); faithfulness through trials (1 Pet. 1:6-7); enduring suffering (Rom. 8:18); being falsely accused of evil on Christ's account (Matt. 5:11-12; Luke 6:22-23); loving your enemies (Luke 6:35); guarding yourself against false teachers (2 John 1:7-8); working heartily and sincerely for your employer (Col. 3:22-24); praying in private (Matt. 6:6); humility in fasting (Matt. 6:17-18); denying yourself and taking up your cross (Matt. 16:24-27); abounding in the work of the Lord (1 Cor. 15:58); ministering to people's basic needs (Matt. 10:42); being generous to the poor (Proverbs 19:17); not putting hopes on the uncertainty of riches, but on God (1 Tim. 6:17-19); humbling yourself like a child (Matt. 18:4); and basing all of your work on the foundation of Christ (1 Cor. 3:14).

Lost Rewards

Please note that while rewards can be obtained, they can also be lost. John tells us, "Watch yourselves, so that you may not lose what we have worked for, but may win a full reward" (2 John 1:8). John also says some will have nothing much to show when they cross the finish line of their race, "And now, little children, abide in him, so that when he appears we may have confidence and not shrink from him in shame at his coming"

(1 John 2:28). Jesus said people lose rewards by practicing their righteousness before other people (Matt. 6:1) and sounding a trumpet when giving to the needy (Matt. 6:2). Jesus told the church in Philadelphia, "I am coming soon. Hold fast what you have, so that no one may seize your crown" (Rev. 3:11).

Disqualified for the Prize

> *"But I discipline my body and keep it under control, lest after preaching to others I myself should be disqualified"* (1 Cor. 9:27).

Many are confused about what Paul meant when he said, "lest after preaching to others I myself should be disqualified." Does Paul mean we can be disqualified from salvation? I would like to make three points here. First, Paul did not teach disqualification from salvation. He taught that "since we have been justified by faith, we have peace with God through our Lord Jesus Christ" (Rom. 5:1). Furthermore, since "It is God who justifies", Paul rhetorically asks, "Who shall bring any charge against God's elect?" (8:33). He proclaimed, "There is therefore now no condemnation for those who are in Christ Jesus" (Rom. 8:1). Paul said God has "put his Spirit in our hearts as a deposit, guaranteeing what is to come" (2 Cor. 1:22, NIV; cf. Eph. 1:13). "And I am sure of this, that he who began a good work in you will bring it to completion at the day of Jesus Christ" (Philip. 1:6; cf., 2 Cor. 1:9-10; 2 Tim. 1:12, 2:19; Col. 3:3).

Second, Paul wrote just six chapters previously about losing rewards but still being saved. In 1 Corinthians chapter three he wrote, "For no one can lay a foundation other than that which is laid, which is Jesus Christ. Now if anyone builds on the foundation with gold, silver, precious stones, wood, hay, straw— each one's work will become manifest, for the Day will disclose it, because it will be revealed by fire, and the fire will test what sort of work each one has done. If the work that anyone has built on the foundation survives, he will receive a reward. If anyone's work is burned up, he will suffer loss, though he himself will be saved, but only as through fire" (1 Cor. 3:11-15). Rewards or crowns we receive for running our race faithfully will have been built on the foundation of the root of the gospel— the person and redemptive work of Jesus Christ. If anyone builds on this foundation using gold, silver, or precious stones, they will receive their reward. Gold, silver, and precious stones are symbolic of work that is born out of an abiding relationship with Jesus Christ (John 15:1-11). Wood, hay, and straw are symbolic of work done in the flesh (Heb. 6:1, 9:14; Rev. 3:1-2, 3:15; Rom. 8:8)—work that is not led by the Spirit but is merely human prideful effort.

Notice also that Paul talks about how our works will become manifest on "the Day" (1 Cor. 3:13). Elsewhere when Paul references "the Day", he is speaking of a future day of blessing and reward (see 1 Cor. 1:8; Eph. 4:30; Philip. 1:6, 10; 2 Tim. 1:18). Paul told the Philippians that the work he did in them will bear fruit: "you shine as lights in the world, holding fast to the word of life, so that in *the day* of Christ I may be proud that I did not run in vain or labor in vain" (Philip. 2:15-16). He told the Corinthians, "on *the day* of our Lord Jesus you will boast of us as we will boast of you" (2 Cor. 1:14). Finally, he also told Timothy, "there is laid up for me the crown of righteousness, which the Lord, the righteous judge, will award to me on *that day*, and not only to me but also to all who have loved his appearing" (2 Tim. 4:8).

Paul concludes by saying, "If the work that anyone has built on the foundation survives, he will receive a reward. If anyone's work is burned up, he will suffer loss, though he himself *will be saved*, but only as through fire" (1 Cor. 3:14-15). If our works are built on the foundation of Christ, rewards and crowns will be awaiting us on "the Day." If our works are done in the flesh, outside of Christ, they will be burned up. We will fail to obtain rewards and crowns, but we *will be saved*. The only disqualification will be for "the prize", not for our salvation.[173]

The third and final point on the disqualification question is to understand that the context of verse 27 and all of 1 Corinthians 9 is preaching the gospel. He starts out the chapter by stating that the conversion of the Corinthians through his preaching of the gospel is proof of his apostleship (9:1-2). In verses 3 through 18, he acknowledges "that those who proclaim the gospel should get their living by the gospel" (9:14), but then says he is willing to give up his right to financial support for his

---

[173] Christians enter heaven on one condition only—grace through faith (Ephesians 2:8-9). However, our obedience in our faith for deeds done while on earth will be judged to determine our heavenly rewards. The Bible speaks of believers appearing before a judgment seat, "For we must all appear before the judgment seat of Christ, so that each one may receive what is due for what he has done in the body, whether good or evil" (2 Cor. 5:10). "We will all stand before the judgment seat of God… each of us will give an account of himself to God" (Rom. 14:10, 12). In both of these passages, where this judgment is mentioned, Paul is addressing Christians. This is a judgment seat for service for an already justified Christian—not a judgment seat for salvation.

ministry in order that "I may present the gospel free of charge" (9:18).[174] In verses 19 through 23, the gospel continues to be the theme. Paul says, "I have become all things to all people, that by all means I might save some" (9:22). All of chapter 9 is about Paul setting aside his own rights to make sure the gospel gets a hearing. He had forsaken his right to be married (9:5) and refused his right of requesting material support from the church (9:6-15). He was also free from Jewish laws (Gal. 5:1) but waived that freedom to win an audience with the goal of showing the Jews that "Christ is the end of the law for righteousness to everyone who believes" (Rom. 10:4).

Chapter nine of 1 Corinthians is about Paul's motivation for presenting the gospel. Does he receive financial support for doing so, or should he present the good news free of charge? If he chooses the former, he's just doing his duty, thus, no reward. However, since he chose the latter, he gets a reward (1 Cor. 9:17), or a prize (9:24). How is Paul just doing his duty? God had appointed Paul to preach the gospel (Acts 9:15, 22:10, 14-15, 26:16; Gal. 1:15-16; 1 Tim. 2:7; cf., 2 Tim. 1:11). Because he was commanded by God to preach the gospel, he was only fulfilling a duty. As Jesus said, "when you have done all that you were commanded, say, 'We are unworthy servants; we have only done what was our duty'" (Luke 17:10). Paul looked upon his call to spread the gospel as an obligatory act. When he followed this order, he considered himself an unworthy servant, only doing the duty he was called to and not expecting a reward. Paul explains this duty here, "For if I preach the gospel, that gives me no ground for boasting. For necessity is laid upon me. Woe to me if I do not preach the gospel!" (1 Cor. 9:16).

On the other hand, if he were to raise his mission above the level of mere obedience and preach the gospel without using his right to financial support, doing so of his own will—a reward would be expected. Indeed, Paul said, "For if I do this of my own will, I have a reward" (1 Cor. 9:17). Rewards come when we act above and beyond the call of

---

[174] We see this type of approach when Paul told the Thessalonians, "For you remember, brothers, our labor and toil: we worked night and day, that we might not be a burden to any of you, while we proclaimed to you the gospel of God" (1 Thess. 2:9; cf. 1 Cor. 4:12; Acts 18:3, 20:34-35). He added, "nor did we eat anyone's bread without paying for it, but with toil and labor we worked night and day, that we might not be a burden to any of you" (2 Thess. 3:8). Paul, who had often provided for his own necessities, did not enter Corinth with a plan to rely on material support to sustain his ministry, even though he had that right (1 Cor. 9:14). He entered Corinth with a plan "that by working hard in this way we must help the weak and remember the words of the Lord Jesus, how he himself said, 'It is more blessed to give than to receive'" (Acts 20:35).

duty. Charles Hodge writes, "A physician may attend the sick from the highest motives, though he receives a remuneration for his services. But when he attends the poor gratuitously, though the motives may be no higher, the evidence of their purity is placed beyond question." Hodges added, for Paul, "Mere preaching, therefore, was not a ground of boasting, but preaching gratuitously was."[175]

Paul didn't ask the Corinthians to spend anything on him, but he freely spent all of himself on them. When he said, "I discipline my body and keep it under control" (1 Cor. 9:27), that discipline included forsaking material support for proclaiming the gospel, working night and day for his own provisions as not to be a burden to others, and making himself a servant to all, that he might win more (9:19). Paul freely gave and accepted nothing in return. His passion for delivering the gospel transcended any duty he had to fulfill. Much like Jeremiah, nothing could hold Paul back from sharing the truth of God's word, "His word was in my heart like a burning fire Shut up in my bones; I was weary of holding it back, And I could not" (Jer. 20:9, NKJV).

In reviewing the three points made above, disqualification does not mean being disqualified from salvation, for Paul taught God's perseverance of the saints all the way to "the day" (Philip. 1:6). He also taught that if the works in our race are built upon an abiding relationship with Christ, we will receive a reward; if not, there will be no reward, but either way, we will be saved. Finally, Paul said when he preached the gospel free of charge and of his own will, he would receive a reward (1 Cor. 9:17), or a prize (9:24). The only way he would be disqualified for that reward would be if he failed to discipline his body and took material support instead of working night and day for his own provisions as not to be a burden to others.

Citizenship Assurance

As we have seen, chapter nine of 1 Corinthians is not about being disqualified for salvation but about the possibility of being disqualified for a reward or future crown. Runners in the Greek athletic games had to be citizens, as no outsiders were permitted to compete. When disqualified, these runners did not lose their citizenship. In the Christian race, though some runners may be disqualified for the prize, all runners have the assurance that "our citizenship is in heaven" (Philip. 3:20), a citizenship

---

[175] Charles Hodge's Commentary on First Corinthians 9:17. https://truthaccordingtoscripture.com/commentaries/hdg/1-corinthians-9.php#.XwgXLihKiUk.

from which all true believers will not be disqualified (Rom. 8:33; Rev. 3:5). We are not running *for* assurance of salvation, but *from* assurance as already secured citizens of heaven.

A Crown of Righteousness

Years later, Paul told Timothy that he had finished his race and kept the faith, "Henceforth there is laid up for me the crown of righteousness, which the Lord, the righteous judge, will award to me on that day" (2 Tim. 4:8; cf., Col. 1:5). Because Paul said that he did not have "a righteousness of my own" and that his only righteousness "comes through faith in Christ" (Philip. 3:9), the crown of righteousness does not determine whether we gain or lose salvation. It is, in fact, a crown our King, the only righteous One, will award us on that day for having faithfully run the race from the foundation of His righteousness (1 Cor. 1:30-31; Philip. 1:11).

"The sower sows the word" (Mark 4:14).

Running for the Gospel

I find it interesting that in the approximately dozen passages where Paul discusses running the race, sharing and defending the gospel is always the main context. We have just seen where 1 Corinthians chapter nine is about the sacrifices he made in running the race to preach the gospel. Elsewhere, Paul said, "*I press on toward the goal for the prize* of the upward call of God in Christ Jesus" (Philip. 3:14). His call was to preach the gospel (Acts 9:15, 22:10, 14-15, 26:16; Gal. 1:15-16). In Acts 20:24 Paul stated, "I do not account my life of any value nor as precious to myself, if only I may *finish my course* and the ministry that I received from the Lord Jesus, to testify to the gospel of the grace of God." When Paul met with leaders of the Jerusalem church, he wanted to make sure they were not being influenced by the Judaizers and insisting on circumcision and other requirements of the law for Gentile converts to be saved. If that were the case (it wasn't), Paul said the truth of the gospel he was presenting to the Gentiles would have been compromised, meaning he would have "*run in vain*" (Gal. 2:2). Later, Paul warned the Galatians that if you insist upon adding circumcision to the gospel, you have been "severed from Christ" and "you have fallen away from grace" (Gal. 5:2-4). He then adds, "*You were running well.* Who hindered you from obeying the truth?" (5:7).

In instructing Timothy to "preach the word; be ready in season and out of season" (2 Tim. 4:2) and to "do the work of an evangelist" (4:5), Paul said he had done that very thing, "I have fought the good fight, I have *finished the race*, I have kept the faith" (4:7). As Paul neared the end of his life, he encouraged Timothy to pass the gospel on to "faithful men, who will be able to teach others also" (2 Tim. 2:2). He then told Timothy that such a passing on of the gospel would involve suffering and obedience to God's truth. Paul then used his familiar metaphor of an athlete to tell Timothy, "*An athlete is not crowned unless he competes according to the rules*" (2 Tim. 2:5).

In other references Paul makes to the race, they all have a connection to advancing or defending the gospel. One example is: "How beautiful are the *feet* of those who preach the good news!" (Rom. 10:15). Another is how believers should take up the whole armor of God, including "*shoes for your feet*, having put on the readiness given by the gospel of peace" (Eph. 6:15). Warning Timothy to defend against those exchanging gospel doctrine for myths, Paul told his protégé, "*Train* yourself for godliness" (1 Tim. 4:7). Paul told the Philippians, who had served with him "side by side for the faith of the gospel" (Philip. 1:27), to "shine as lights in the world" (Philip. 2:15) as fellow sharers in the good news as they continue "holding fast to the word of life" (2:16a). Paul encouraged them to continue offering this word of life (the gospel), so that he may be able to boast about them "in the day of Christ" and "be proud that I did not *run in vain*" (2:16b).

A Gospel Race

What does this mean for your race? If you are not sharing and defending the gospel as you advance along the course, you are missing out on the main point of the race. This is not to say that other parts of The Evangelism Circle are not part of the race—of course they are. In our pre-evangelism, we let our light shine before others (Matt. 5:16) and pray for the Lord to open a person's heart to respond to the gospel message (Col. 4:3-4; 2 Thess. 3:1). In our post-evangelism, we mature in the faith (Heb. 5:14; Philip. 3:15) so that we are "not shifting from the hope of the gospel" (Col. 1:23). We study to show ourselves "to God as one approved" (2 Tim. 2:15). Making all of the above principles a part of our race is all a means to an end. If you are not using those means to accomplish the end goal of sharing the gospel, then you are not running the race Paul describes. Are you running to obtain the prize? Are you on The Evangelism Circle?

Recap

Here are some points to keep in mind about post-evangelism:

- Post-evangelism is about Christians growing and maturing in the faith (1 Peter 2:2; Jude 1:20), with the goal of sharing the gospel with others and making disciples. In order to make disciples we have to become a disciple.

- Post-evangelism is reserved for Christians, who have been justified by the root of the gospel; it involves those who have already entered into a saving relationship with Christ but need to have their faith reinforced, or to grow in their faith, in order to have "a sincere faith" (1 Tim. 1:5; 2 Tim. 1:5).

- Christians train themselves for godliness in post-evangelism, learning how to live their lives with a clear understanding, experience and joy that the gospel brings, both now and in the future (1 Tim. 4:7-8).

- We produce the fruit of the gospel (Col. 1:5-6).

- Believers learn how to "continue in the faith, stable and steadfast, not shifting from the hope of the gospel that you heard" (Col. 1:23) so that "we hold our original confidence firm to the end" (Heb. 3:14).

- We put to death what is earthly in us and set our minds on things that are above, not on things that are on earth (Col. 3:1-5).

- We are in a church where the word of God is being properly taught from the pulpit.

- The one teacher to follow is Jesus, as well as those who authentically imitate Him (1 Cor. 4:16, 11:1; 1 Thess. 1:6; 2 Thess. 3:7, 9; Philip. 3:17; 2 Tim. 3:10; Heb. 13:7).

- We need to have a teachable spirit (Proverbs 1:5) and be able to teach each other (Proverbs 27:17).

- If we are going to grow from milk into solid food, we should have the mindset of a lifelong learner.

- We should be approachable and teachable before more learned Christians (Acts 18:24-27).

- We learn how to contend for (Jude 1:3), defend, confirm (Philip. 1:7) and guard the truth of the gospel (Acts 20:28; 1 Tim. 6:20; 2 Tim. 1:14).

- We learn that we "must keep hold of the deep truths of the faith" (1 Timothy 3:9, NIV). A believer does not have to possess an exhaustive knowledge of the Christian faith to be used by God in evangelism, but we should be grounded in matters "of first importance" (1 Cor. 15:3-4).

- In order not to get gospel amnesia, we preach the gospel to ourselves everyday (1 Tim. 1:15). The deeper we understand the gospel, the more we will "advance the gospel" (Philip. 1:12) to ourselves and to others.

- When we preach the gospel to ourselves, we will see more of God's holiness and more of our sin. Paul writes, "our unrighteousness serves to show the righteousness of God" (Rom. 3:5).

- As we grow in our understanding of the gospel, our daily repentance will draw us nearer to the cross, where we confess our sins daily (1 John 1:9).

- We study to show ourselves approved (2 Tim. 2:15) to be able to become more proficient at answering questions or objections to the faith (Col. 4:3-6; 1 Pet. 3:15) and to be ready to share the gospel at any moment (2 Tim. 4:2).

- We test false teachers (1 John 4:1, 6; 2 John 1:7; Rev. 2:20; 1 Thess. 5:21; 1 Cor. 12:10) and determine which ones are teaching the truth (Acts 17:11).

- We do not follow blind/false teachers lest we become blind ourselves.

- The Bible does not teach retirement from the faith. Spiritually mature older men, be prepared to disciple younger men; and likewise, mature older women will disciple younger women.

- Young and old should strive to "set the believers an example in speech, in conduct, in love, in faith, in purity…so that all may see your progress" (1 Tim. 4:12-15).

- Whether one is an adolescent, adult, or a senior, there are many examples where God has used all three of these groups in His service.

- Our goal is, like Paul, to be able to say to the people we have discipled, "I became your father in Christ Jesus through the gospel" (1 Cor. 4:15).

- Christianity teaches that there is redemptive value in suffering (Rom. 5:3-4). Paul told us to "Share in suffering for the gospel" (2 Tim. 1:8). Peter said, "If anyone suffers as a Christian, let him not be ashamed, but let him glorify God" (1 Pet. 4:16; cf., 2 Tim. 3:12).

- Take heart because Jesus will deliver us again and again despite the persecution and suffering we will experience (John 16:33).

- We should confess our doubts before God (Mark 9:24) and teach ourselves to question our doubts, not our faith!

- When it comes to the gifts God gives us (1 Cor. 12:18), "let us use them" (Rom. 12:6). Part of our post-evangelism is to know the race God has set before us. We do this by discovering the gifts God has appointed to us (1 Cor. 12:11).

- God alone qualifies us for His race by justifying us through the root of gospel. For a Christian, the motto should be, "all the runners run" (1 Cor. 9:24). Your uniform will be the "white garments" of Christ (Rev. 3:18; cf., Isa. 61:10). If you are not a Christian, you are not in this race.

- This race is about our sanctification—the fruit of the gospel. It is not a sprint, but a marathon. Your training in godliness is a lifelong process and doesn't end until the finish line.

- While we take encouragement from the great cloud of witnesses that ran before us (Heb. 11), we run the race always "Looking unto Jesus the author and finisher of our faith" (Heb. 12:2, KJV). The finish line is Jesus Himself.

- Those who run in the race compete according to the rules (2 Tim. 2:5) because they have the training manual—God's word.

- Runners in God's race will stay on the specified narrow road and not be tempted to divert off course to the wide road "that leads to destruction" (Matt. 7:13-14). Don't let the weeds tempt you to sway out of your lane.

- The Christian race is not about the fastest time or about who comes in first. This is a spiritual race to see who endures and finishes faithfully.

- When Paul discusses running the race, sharing and defending the gospel is always the context.

- Paul ran his race for rewards and crowns; so should we.

- Any crowns or rewards we may receive ultimately are for bringing glory to God (Acts 21:20; 1 Cor. 10:31; Rom. 11:36, 15:6-7; 2 Thess. 1:12; 2 Cor. 8:19).

- Run in such a way that you may obtain "the prize", which is within the grasp of every Christian runner. Many believers can win the prize, and many can fail to obtain it (2 John 1:8; 1 John 2:28; Matt. 6:1-2; Rev. 3:11).

- Disqualification from "the prize" (1 Cor. 9:24) does not mean being disqualified from salvation, which is secured for all those "who are in Christ Jesus" (Rom. 8:1; cf., 5:1, 8:33; 2 Cor. 1:22; Eph. 1:13; Philip. 1:6). Disqualification is missing out on an opportunity for a reward or crown when you fail to remove obstacles that are in the way of preaching the gospel.

- The prize is not only crowns and rewards, but the joy of hearing Jesus say, "Well done, good and faithful servant. You have been faithful over a little; I will set you over much. Enter into the joy of your master" (Matt. 25:21).

- Post-evangelism can be our classroom for pre-evangelism and evangelism.

Post-evangelism is all about growing us in the knowledge of the gospel. This stage will strengthen our faith and show us how to bring others into the faith. It will help us disciple ourselves and others. Remember, Christianity is not a spectator sport. We do not count ourselves exempt from the race, as "all the runners run" (1 Cor. 9:24) with the ultimate goal of bringing glory to God (Acts 21:20; 1 Cor. 10:31).

Always be mindful that it is God who placed you in the race and God who sustains you, otherwise you might become impressed with your own abilities and fist bump your chest when you cross the finish line. Such is not a time to wrap yourself in an earthly flag and do a victory lap. Rather, this will be an occasion, as a citizen of another kingdom (Philip. 3:20), to point to heaven in recognition of the One who is the author and finisher of our faith race (Heb. 12:2)—Jesus, who said on "the third day I finish my course" (Luke 13:32).

CONCLUSION

It was Thursday night, December 12, 2002, and 34-year-old Leslie was staying late following another long day as a teacher for her fifth grade class in Minnesota. As she deliberated again about calling a Christian salvation line she had heard about, anxious thoughts of getting off the treadmill life had placed her on raced through her mind. For the past 16 years, she kept looking for a way out of a life that had beaten her down. During that time, thoughts of suicide would often enter her mind. On that fateful night, as she was wrapping up her work, she reached for the note on her desk with the salvation number. As I answered the phone, a thousand miles away, a life-long friendship was about to begin.

Leslie told me she was searching for a relationship with God. She had often cried out for such intimacy with her Creator through the religion she grew up with but told me repeated attempts at a relationship with God in Catholicism had failed. She had come to realize that the repetitive religious vows in her religion would never bring the true union she yearned for with God. Right away, I knew we had a connection. I told her about my life of searching for salvation as a Catholic and the legalism that resulted from it. After I first spoke of the bad news of the works-righteousness we both grew up with in Catholicism, I then pivoted into the good news of the gospel.

One year later, Leslie wrote me an email. Referring to our conversation that night she said, "I'm not sure if you will remember me. The reason I am writing is to tell you how my life has changed since I accepted Jesus' free and freeing gift of salvation. As I was praying to receive the Lord, I heard Him clearly: "Behold, I make all things new." I prayed that my commitment to Him be for longer than one day. Ever since that night, I have had the most amazing, steadfast sense of peace."

As I recently reflected on what Leslie wrote next, it occurred to me that she had entered The Evangelism Circle: "I am sharing His saving gift with others. Never before would I have talked about who He is, or what He has done for us. He does make all things new. I have started to read the Bible, I look forward to it. The Holy Spirit is really opening my eyes and ears to the truth of the word. That night when you talked to me, each time you shared a scripture, it was so powerful. I have even found a church that feels like the right place. For the first time I am truly worshiping Him for His great love. I feel put back together."

In 2004, I met Leslie when she made a trip to Dallas. My wife Kim and I heard more of her testimony and were able to see the excitement she had about her growing relationship with Christ. I consider it a great privilege to have seen Leslie grow through the years since her conversion. While most of the time you never hear again from people to whom you have witnessed, Leslie has kept in contact with me over the years through cards and e-mails. Recently we spent two hours on the phone reminiscing about that night on December 12, 2002.

As we discussed in Chapter Twenty-One, part of being on The Evangelism Circle is to learn how to deal with suffering. This precious sister in Christ has experienced much of that in her life. When I met Leslie, she had both of her legs. Since that point, she has had both legs amputated and is a cancer survivor. How has she responded? By questioning God, or maybe getting angry with God? Not at all! Leslie has matured on The Evangelism Circle to the point where she can say, "Having lost both legs and having gone through cancer, there has never been a moment that I doubted that He loved me. He has taken what my enemy meant for ill and turned it for His glory."

Today Leslie works for a prosthetic company helping fellow amputees adjust to their new lives. She is an inspiring testimony of how God can transform and sustain a person through His amazing grace. Leslie walked into The Evangelism Circle on that cold Minnesota night in 2002 after hearing the gospel preached to her. One of the first things she did was to start reading and studying her Bible for the first time. She found a church where she could grow in the grace and knowledge of our Lord and Savior Jesus Christ. She began to speak to others about Jesus' free and freeing gift of salvation. She witnessed to and prayed for years for her unsaved mother before seeing her mom repent and believe the gospel before she died. Today, when people try to credit her for having the character to persevere as a double amputee, she immediately points away from herself and to the God who saved her and has sustained her through it all.

I wanted to share this last story to hopefully inspire people to get on The Evangelism Circle just like my friend Leslie has for the past twenty years. Leslie cannot physically run these days due to her handicap, but she is definitely running the spiritual race in which God has placed her, and she is running it all the way to the finish line.

We enter The Evangelism Circle after hearing and being justified by the gospel. As we grow in our understanding of justification, the root of the gospel, God will then sanctify us by allowing us to participate in the fruit of the gospel. That fruit takes many forms, including our pre-evangelism of shining our light before others and being prepared to answer objections and questions about our faith. In evangelism, we are always prepared to preach the gospel day and night. In post-evangelism, we are growing and maturing in our faith as we sanctify Christ as Lord in our hearts. God justifies us, places us on the circle and then sanctifies us through the circle, allowing us to be His ambassadors to save others, bringing them into the circle. There is no better place to be than on The Evangelism Circle because it is the reason for which God saved us.

As I mentioned earlier, while a believer should be grounded in matters "of first importance" (1 Cor. 15:3-4) and sound doctrine (1 Tim. 4:6), one does not have to possess an exhaustive knowledge of the Christian faith to be used by God in evangelism. God uses all kinds of people, not just pastors, seminary graduates or Christian apologists with doctorate degrees. In fact, I am living proof of that. Despite having no formal seminary or Bible College training, God has allowed me to fully participate in The Evangelism Circle. If you rightly prepare to present the gospel, your participation is not only welcome, but expected (2 Tim. 4:1-5).

Finally, Dave Harvey, president of Great Commission Collective, sums up The Evangelism Circle when he says, "Everything in Scripture is either preparation for the Gospel, presentation of the Gospel, or participation in the Gospel."[176] May your participation in The Evangelism Circle prepare you to present the gospel in a way that is honoring to God and allow you to "continue in the faith, stable and steadfast, not shifting from the hope of the gospel that you heard" (Col. 1:23).

Patrick Foss

You can contact the author at:

patrickfoss@yahoo.com

Or visit his website at:

TEVC.org

---

[176] Dave Harvey, *When Sinners Say "I Do"*, p. 24.

Made in the USA
Columbia, SC
30 March 2022